Praise for *We Were There*

An *Observer*, *GQ Magazine* and *Esquire* best book of the year 2025

'Lanre Bakare's first book is not just a work of history – it is a necessary and urgent recalibration of the way we think about Black Britain ... An expansive, deeply researched work that insists on a broader, richer understanding of Black life'
Guardian

'Lanre Bakare's *We Were There*, a bracingly readable social history, celebrates the UK as a bastion of Black culture, Black music and food ... Vivid, well written ... Bakare's excellent book captures the life and glory of a culture that changed the face of Britain for good'
Spectator

'[Bakare writes] with quiet enthusiasm and sharp intelligence about Black communities, including those in Bradford, Wolverhampton, Manchester, Liverpool, Cardiff and Edinburgh ... *We Were There* bridges the gaps to missing links and admirably achieves what it sets out to provide: further evidence of Black people's influence on the UK'
Observer

'Like much of how we view and discuss history in the UK, the story of Black Britain often has a London bias. But as [*We Were There*] explores, there is a rich story to be told outside the capital too ... A joyous and fascinating corrective'
GQ Magazine

'The premise of this non-fiction book is a deceptively simple one: to consider the influence of Black culture in modern Britain, and, critically, beyond London ... It's a part of Britain's collective heritage that has been woefully under-reported and makes for a book that is fact-packed and fascinating'
Esquire

'A meaty social history study [with] interesting things to say about race and class ... Packed with revealing content'
Independent

'A tender yet determined, century-defining record of what Black resistance, grief and celebration looked like in the testing era of Thatcher's turbulent Britain'
Dazed

'Bakare shines a light on largely uncovered stories ... These hidden Black histories show how close one can be to the truth about Black British contributions without ever realising it'
Tribune

'*We Were There* tells a remarkable story with flair and passion. In shining a light on a new cast of characters the length and breadth of the country, the book is an important contribution to our understanding of the making of Black Britain'
Times Literary Supplement

'*We Were There* is a vital corrective that enhances our understanding of Black British history in the twentieth century by moving the narrative outside of London'
Steve McQueen

'Bakare takes us on a rare journey, rearranging
our understanding of Britain's racial geography
with an open mind, perceptive eye and
an accessible style'
Gary Younge, author of *Dispatches from the Diaspora*

'An essential, unique and joyful contribution to the
full understanding of Black Britain. It broadens
our story and ensures that the scale of our
influence across the UK is fully recognised
and appreciated. Utterly brilliant'
Dipo Faloyin, author of *Africa Is Not a Country*

'A chronicling of Black British life told with such love
and tender, evocative prose that it immediately
colourises the present. In tracing this history,
Bakare offers not just a homage to Black British
identity, but a reinforcement of it'
Nesrine Malik, author of *We Need New Stories*

'Fascinating. Bakare's story is told with pace, wit,
scholarship, and nuance. It taught me so much'
Ed Caesar, author of *The Moth and the Mountain*

'An urgent conversation about Britishness
and the breadth of Black British experience ...
Affecting and insightful'
Arifa Akbar, author of *Consumed*

'Told with urgency, empathy and a skilled journalist's
ability to connect the dots across race, power and
national identity, this is essential reading'
Ekow Eshun, author of *The Strangers*

'This is an important and ambitious book, and Bakare has found the right stories and language to do it justice'
Andy Beckett, author of *Promised You a Miracle*

'Lanre Bakare's writing captivated me from the first page ... It will help you see Britain with completely fresh new eyes'
Pragya Agarwal, author of *Sway*

'An exquisitely cathartic and powerful journey though some of the most important, but untold chapters of our recent history'
Gus Casely-Hayford, Director of the Victoria and Albert Museum East

'Uplifting and empowering. By looking outside of London, *We Were There* – with its stories of survival and overcoming, strength and resilience – gives us a fuller picture of who we have been in the UK and who we are'
Marvin Rees, former mayor of Bristol

LANRE BAKARE

Lanre Bakare is the arts and culture correspondent for the *Guardian*, where his writing focuses on the intersection of art, race and culture across multiple disciplines. He was senior correspondent on the Cotton Capital project – an exposé on the *Guardian*'s founders' links to transatlantic slavery and was recognised at the Press Awards as a 'breathtakingly honest *mea culpa*'. He was born and grew up in Bradford, West Yorkshire.

LANRE BAKARE

We Were There

How Black Culture and Community
Shaped Modern Britain

VINTAGE

1 3 5 7 9 10 8 6 4 2

Vintage is part of the Penguin Random House group of companies

Vintage, Penguin Random House UK, One Embassy Gardens,
8 Viaduct Gardens, London SW11 7BW

penguin.co.uk/vintage
global.penguinrandomhouse.com

First published in Vintage in 2026
First published in hardback by The Bodley Head in 2025

Copyright © Lanre Bakare 2025

The moral right of the author has been asserted

Penguin Random House values and supports copyright. Copyright fuels
creativity, encourages diverse voices, promotes freedom of expression and
supports a vibrant culture. Thank you for purchasing an authorised edition of
this book and for respecting intellectual property laws by not reproducing,
scanning or distributing any part of it by any means without permission.
You are supporting authors and enabling Penguin Random House to
continue to publish books for everyone. No part of this book may be used or
reproduced in any manner for the purpose of training artificial intelligence
technologies or systems. In accordance with Article 4(3) of the DSM Directive
2019/790, Penguin Random House expressly reserves this work from
the text and data mining exception.

Printed and bound in Great Britain by Clays Ltd, Elcograf S.p.A.

The authorised representative in the EEA is Penguin Random House Ireland,
Morrison Chambers, 32 Nassau Street, Dublin D02 YH68

A CIP catalogue record for this book is available from the British Library

ISBN 9781529931334

Penguin Random House is committed to a sustainable future
for our business, our readers and our planet. This book is made
from Forest Stewardship Council® certified paper.

For my parents, Debra and Adewale Sefiu Bakare.
Thank you for showing me the way

Contents

	Introduction	1
1.	Northern Souls – 1977	11
2.	Free George Lindo – Bradford, 1978	34
3.	Jah Warriors – Birmingham, 1979	63
4.	The Ghost of William Huskisson – Liverpool, 1981	89
5.	Black Art an'done – Wolverhampton, 1982	118
6.	The Black Door – Manchester, 1986	145
7.	The Last Fort – 1987	174
8.	The Myth and The Bay, Cardiff – 1988	201
9.	The English Disease, Edinburgh – 1989	230
10.	People of the Future – 1990	256
	We Were There: Coda	284
	End Notes	287
	Acknowledgements	335
	Credits	341
	Index	345
	About the Author	369

Margaret Thatcher quoting St Francis of Assisi on the steps of 10 Downing Street after her first election victory:

'Where there is discord, may we bring harmony. Where there is error, may we bring truth. Where there is doubt, may we bring faith. And where there is despair, may we bring hope.'

Bobby Nyahoe, activist and poet from Liverpool 8, speaking to The New York Times *after widespread unrest during the autumn of 1985:*

'At the moment, there are no politicians to appeal to who have any sway over anything. It is all just a mess . . . the normal channels are reduced to chaos.'

Introduction

The DVD slips into the loading tray, and I wait, then watch in hope rather than expectation. I've been told Tony Palmer's *Wigan Casino* is the greatest-ever depiction of a Northern Soul all-nighter, and I want to see it for myself. The film is a window onto the underground scene that emerged in the 1970s, powered by soul records that'd flopped years earlier. But I'm not interested in the music or the dancing – it's the crowd I've got an eye on. I'm on the lookout for something rare. I've heard rumours, but I'm not holding my breath; a sighting would challenge everything I've been told so far.

Then I spot what I'm after. A young man, glistening under the spotlight as he spins balletically in a yellow vest. Then another person catches my eye with his perfectly picked-out Afro. It's a blink-and-you'll-miss-it moment, so I rewind to check, and yes, it's true. A few minutes later, two girls clamber onto a coach, and one waves goodbye down the camera lens. Another boy squeezes through the crush at the front door. These young people are there for the same reason as everyone else: hard-to-find soul music that's perfectly crafted for dancing. But all of them stand out. They're different from the majority of the 1,200 dancers crammed into Wigan Casino. They're Black and British.

We Were There started as a cultural expedition. I wanted to find something that wasn't supposed to exist: Black Northern Soul fans from the 1970s and 80s. Seeing those Black faces contradicted what I'd heard about the scene. Northern Soul was about white working class audiences falling in love with and coveting forgotten Black American music. When I tracked them down, I found their stories changed the way I thought, not just about Northern Soul but about Britain at the start of the Thatcher era. The scene's dancers and DJs were on the frontline of racial politics in the UK during a time of immense change. Old industry was dying, the power of unions was about to be challenged, racial tensions were simmering and a new world – driven by the political tenets of Thatcherism – was on the horizon. The Black Northern Soul fans came from Africa and the Caribbean, were wealthy and working-class. And all were drawn to a scene that wasn't supposed to have involved them. I wanted to know why. I began to wonder what other stories I might have been mistold or had never explored at all – and what those stories could reveal to me, and others, about Britain then and now.

No European country has been changed by Black culture more than the UK. British music, fashion, sport, literature, TV and film have had their DNA altered by the influence of millions of people who have come to this small island from across the African diaspora. Our sounds, food, languages, intellect and sartorial choices have meshed with what was already here to create modern British culture. Our biggest Hollywood stars (Daniel Kaluuya, Naomie Harris, David Oyelowo, Letitia Wright, John Boyega, Steve McQueen) are Black; designers like Nicholas Daley and Grace Wales Bonner transmit our styles globally; artists such as Sonia Boyce and John Akomfrah represent Britain on the biggest stages; most of England's men's football team is of Black heritage. Black British culture is an inseparable part of British culture.

Modern Black Britishness, which has spread and organically morphed into myriad forms, was forged in the late 1970s and the 80s. *We Were There* covers a time of huge ruptures and tumult – social, economic and political. Everywhere you looked, a battle was taking place; and every single gain had to be fought for.

In Bradford, a small Black community campaigned against a miscarriage of justice as a documentary team who captured their story faced censorship. Birmingham was home to academics and Rastafarians who took on racism in the media, while in Liverpool, the oldest Black community in the country used the widespread unrest of 1981 as a platform to tell Britain about the way they'd been treated. There were young artists in Wolverhampton who confronted racism within the art establishment; a nightclub in Manchester became a hub that connected Pan-Africanism to acid house; and Black Britons took to the countryside to claim their own place in the UK's rural idyll. Cardiff's Butetown – one of the most diverse places in Europe – came under attack; Scotland's small Black community organised to fight complacency and denial after a racist murder; and, as the 1980s ended, music producers and Rugby League players from the north of England expressed a new Black British confidence.

This was a time of artistic and cultural creation unrivalled in the twentieth century. A period when Black British culture flourished and contemporary British culture began to form. But our understanding of that influence is limited, and for many, it starts and ends in one place: London.

I was born in the middle of the Thatcher era: 1984. My memories are fuzzy, softened by time; half-remembered fragments. Images of the poll tax riots, milk breaks at primary school, Ian Wright's gold tooth, Norman Lamont's eyebrows and red box. But when I think of my hometown of Bradford, there are details that come into focus. I can still run through the surnames like a Rolodex in my head: the Taylors, the Sarrs, the Davids, the Ibegbunas, the Ekongs, the Fehintolas, the Cookes, the Oakleys and the Braithwaites. The families you knew and the families you knew of – either by reputation or connection. I can still plot a chart that links the Black families in my area of Bradford: the faces, the cars, the haircuts, the living room furniture and the intellects.

I left Bradford at the age of eighteen and lived all over the UK – Liverpool, Newcastle, Sheffield, Bristol – in my early twenties before settling in London fourteen years ago. In the capital, I've often been met by other Black people who express amazement at the fact Black life existed beyond the M25. Their responses weren't hostile – there was an anthropological desire to understand this otherness. My time away didn't make me reassess the Black culture I grew up in around Bradford – but it did make me question why it was so rarely acknowledged and little understood by everyone from the average person on the street to the institutions and centres of power in London.

I think of *We Were There* as a road trip around Black Britain in the Thatcher era – one that attempts to fill those cultural gaps. Too often on these excursions, London is in the driving seat. Someone from the capital is controlling the music and managing the navigation. But this time, London is in the back seat and Bradford's our driver. Liverpool's choosing the music. Edinburgh's navigating. None of the stories here are based in London. Not because events in the capital aren't important – they are, and there are plenty of Londoners in the book. But their stories are in the background, while others take their place in the foreground.

If you want to understand the unrest that spread around the country in 1981, you'll most likely be pointed towards events in Brixton. While the South London neighbourhood was a centre of Black culture and resistance, it wasn't the only one – there were dozens around the UK, like in Liverpool, which had a different, older connection to the unrest. If you want to understand the far right and resistance to groups like the National Front (NF), you'll find documentary makers, journalists and writers referring to the Battle of Lewisham in 1977 as a moment, *the* moment, when communities came together to fight back against the provocative marches. The Rock Against Racism concert in Victoria Park one year later, where 100,000 people turned out to see The Clash, X-Ray Spex and Steel Pulse perform and call for 'Black and White [to] Unite and Fight', has become legendary – and is held up as the exemplar of when culture was used to counter rising fascism. If you want to understand the hostile relationship between the police and Black communities, you'll find accounts of the unrest at Notting Hill Carnival in 1976 as the totemic battle when Black Britain fought back.

All those events were crucial, but all feed into a simplistic narrative about Black Britishness, which suggests that a group of people, most of whom arrived in the UK after the Second World War, took to the streets to rebel – with anger and with violence.

Introduction

This consensus view allows little room for nuance, and obscures myriad threads of a bigger, more complex tapestry of life in Britain during the Thatcher years. There are people in this book whose families go back five or six generations in the UK – long before the *Windrush* arrived; there are artists and authors; legal campaigners, feminists, ravers, rudeboys, and Rugby League superstars. *We Were There* shines a light on those hidden strands to illuminate a broader, richer view of what it meant to be Black and British then and, by extension, what it means to be British now.

It's no coincidence that the figures I write about in *We Were There* emerged during the Thatcher era, arguably the most restive period in post-war British history and a key period when the country fundamentally realigned, both politically and economically. When Margaret Thatcher – the first female leader of the Conservative Party – defeated Labour's James 'Jim' Callaghan and took up residence at 10 Downing Street in 1979, she would stay in place for over a decade, winning three consecutive elections, and transforming Britain in the process.

The children of the Windrush Generation – those who migrated from across the Commonwealth in the post-war period – were coming of age in a country on the cusp of transition. The 1970s had been a time of strikes and multiple, often inconclusive, general elections, as politicians seemed unable to get a grip on the economy.

Thatcher's economic policies – steered largely by Milton Friedman's theory of monetarism, which focused on limiting inflation by controlling the money supply and dismantling all but 'essential' elements of the welfare state – caused widespread damage. Manufacturing, once the lifeblood of many cities in the north, Midlands, Wales and Scotland, went into a steep decline. By 1981, unemployment was at 14 per cent with around two and a half million people jobless, while Thatcher's approval rating slumped to the lowest of any post-war leader.[1] In Black communities, those statistics were often much starker, particularly for young people, with some areas experiencing more than 40 per cent youth unemployment.[2]

In the lead-up to Thatcher's tumultuous first term, Black British people had already been confronted by a country that was increasingly hostile to their presence. During the 1970s, far-right groups marched through immigrant areas and made gains at the ballot box. Mainstream politicians, including Thatcher, used the Black presence as a wedge issue, weaponising race in a way no other prominent politician had done before.

In August 1980, the economics writer John Kenneth Galbraith said that Britain was now a 'guinea pig' for Thatcher's Friedman-inspired economic policy. 'There could be no better choice,' he wrote. 'Britain's political and social institutions are solid and neither Englishmen, Scots nor even the Welsh take readily to the streets.'[3] But in 1981, thousands did head out, causing unrest that spread around the country, from Birmingham to Bradford, as a whole generation rejected what little they were being offered in Britain. Cities such as Liverpool and Manchester smouldered after summer nights of clashes between police forces and the communities that rejected their presence.

Law enforcement around the country used the arcane Sus laws to stop young Black men on mere suspicion of a crime at fifteen times the rate they did for white men. The education system saw a disproportionate number of Black Britons placed in approved schools or so-called schools for the educationally subnormal. This was a time of conflict, not just in the Falklands, the small islands off the coast of Argentina where Britain fought its first war in decades, but here, on the home front, in cities and towns up and down the country, wherever Black Britons were found.

In many – but by no means all – cases, the protagonists in these stories are the children of Windrush. Their parents – or in some cases, grandparents – came to Britain in that great wave of immigration that reshaped Britain in the post-war era. Their parents might have felt they were British because of their new citizenship, but once they got to the UK, they found they were 'West Indian', a catch-all term that no one from the Caribbean would use. Their children were in a different position – yes, they were born in Britain but the question that hung over them was: did that make them British?

Introduction

Other Black Britons have a different origin story. Their parents weren't from the Caribbean or Africa. Neither were their grandparents nor, in many cases, great-grandparents. In Liverpool and Cardiff, we find communities with roots dating back to before slavery was abolished across the British Empire in the 1830s. These communities were the original multicultural Britain, and they often faced hostility which saw them segregated and attacked. Their stories, at present, are hiding in plain sight.

For many years, London was where the majority of Black British people lived – hardly surprising given its economic power and the opportunities it offered. Notting Hill, Ladbroke Grove, Hackney, Peckham and Brent: all over the capital you'd find Black communities, growing and adjusting to life in Britain. But that is changing. The last census showed that for the first time since ethnicity was included in 1991, the majority of Black British people live outside of the capital.

As these communities develop, it's becoming increasingly unlikely they'll see themselves represented in popular culture. After the watershed moment of the global Black Lives Matter (BLM) movement in 2020, a difficult and stilted conversation about race was forced in the UK. The creative industries tried – often cynically – to address long-standing absences in their collections or portfolios where Black British art should have been. Books, TV shows, films were commissioned and became part of a cultural wave that broke in the wake of BLM.

Series about frustrated creatives (*Dreaming Whilst Black*), opulent family sagas (*Riches*), Black kids in public schools (*Boarders*), sci-fi films set on dystopian housing estates (*The Kitchen*), award-winning gang tales (*Top Boy*), mould-breaking urban drama (*Blue Story*), unique accounts of trauma and creativity (*I May Destroy You*), Black women navigating love and life (*Queenie*) – there's been so much, yet every single one of those shows or films is set in London or is about Londoners. Every. Single. One. These weren't Black British stories; they were part of an ever-increasing Black London canon. For commissioners and editors, London *is* the Black story. But for me and thousands of others, it isn't – and never could be.

*

In 2018, a photographer called Karis Beaumont started an Instagram account called the Bumpkin Files, an ironic reference to an uncultured country dweller. Growing up, I'd often hear Nigerians from Lagos call those from smaller cities or rural villages 'Bushman', an insult that poked fun at their parochial background. The Bumpkin Files was an attempt to flip that dynamic: Beaumont made the regional Black communities the centre of her focus.

On the account, she posted family photographs and video clips from communities around the UK: Chapeltown in Leeds, family BBQs in Herefordshire, carnivals in Luton. 'I've always liked watching documentaries about Black British history but there was almost . . . not quite a void but something was missing,' Beaumont said when asked why she started the site. 'I couldn't put my finger on it.' Reading those words, I knew exactly what she meant. 'After listening to my parents' stories about their upbringing in different parts of Hertfordshire,' she went on, 'the coin dropped. The thing that's missing from Black British storytelling is stories beyond London.'

Sometimes, that otherness is barely there at all, with shared culture and similar experiences meaning the only tangible difference will be an accent or slang used. Other times it's profound and shows how the environment you grow up in shapes your entire approach to life. The Black London experience doesn't map neatly onto every Black British experience. There are similarities and staples – food, language, music, hair products – but what makes the experiences different is history.

Looking through the videos and images on the Bumpkin Files, I saw the Black Britain I grew up in; the part that was missing and that needs to be seen. I've found that as soon as you widen the parameters of Black British culture beyond the capital, there's an untapped reserve to draw from. There are stories that make us reassess cultural movements and moments in our recent history; by examining them, we can understand ourselves and our impact on culture and life in the country as a whole. That reassessment is necessary.

Just as I was finishing this book, a new piece of research was released showing that 50 per cent of Britons couldn't name one Black

Introduction

British historical figure. The UK, the authors said, knew 'shockingly little' about its own Black history.[4] We've had an important wave of corrective histories from David Olusoga, Jason Okundaye, Jim Pines, June Givanni, Ferdinand Dennis, Stella Dadzie, Paterson Joseph, Hakim Adi, Marika Sherwood and Stephen Bourne, but clearly, we need more. Perhaps one way of addressing this lack of cut-through is to make these stories *truly* Black and British – rooting these new histories in locations that have been overlooked, in areas that people think of as not Black. Maybe then more British people will pay attention to the history of this small but important island and think of Black history as having taken place in their own towns, cities or parishes, as well as in London.

Watching Tony Palmer's film about Wigan Casino set me off on an expedition, one that took me to places I never thought I'd go. The journey sent me into well-kept archives and on internet trawls searching for names that had been scrawled down on yellowed paper. I spoke to people at the centre of extraordinary events who've never been asked about them. I managed to get hold of some interviewees a few months before they died and discovered many others I wanted to speak to had already passed on. This history might have been staring us in the face, but it's fragile.

We Were There contains a fraction of the stories from this era. There are so many more waiting to be unearthed. In cities like Nottingham and Belfast, and towns, including Luton and Plymouth – Black history is everywhere on these islands. Without Black people in places like Wigan, Bradford, Ambleside and Wolverhampton, the country we live in and the culture it has produced would look completely different. What I've discovered made me reconsider what I thought Black Britain was and is, what it can encompass and where it might go next.

I.
Northern Souls – 1977

Vernon Pryce and friend at the last night of Wigan Casino in 1981

Steve Caesar stepped out onto the stage at Wigan Casino and took a deep breath. The teenager had arrived in the UK from the tiny Caribbean island of St Kitts just five years earlier, and now he was preparing to compete in the first-ever Wigan Casino dance contest. As the DJ cued up the next song, the ballroom fell silent. Caesar did his best to keep his heart rate down, replaying in his mind the hours spent practising moves in his bedroom in Chapeltown, Leeds. The needle dropped on the seven-inch single and the room was filled with the pumping sounds of 1960s soul music.

In another life, the Casino was known as the Empress Ballroom, or The Emp. It opened in 1916 and for the first sixty years of its life, it offered residents of Wigan, the northern town just outside Manchester, a typical British night out. Couples would dance to the in-house Empress Band or one of the visiting acts – like Tom Jones or Ronnie Carr and the Beat Boys – on the sprung maplewood dance floors surrounded by ornate balconies. When Caesar took the stage, he was following in the footsteps of thousands before him, but the moves he was making were from a rebellious new sub-culture, one that would reshape British nightlife over the next quarter of a century: Northern Soul.

A decade after their careers had peaked in the United States, musicians like Otis Brown, Gloria Jones and Dobie Gray were being given unlikely second acts, as thousands of kids from Blackburn, Widnes and all over the north sought out their recordings like Holy Sacrament. One of Britain's most important youth movements, Northern Soul offers a prism through which to see the racial politics of 1970s Britain in all its complexity. For one of the first times in the country's history, Black music was being danced to by large majority-white audiences. Dancers, like Caesar, bounced to the driving four-to-the-floor stompers the DJs played, creating their own athletic arsenal of moves at the all-night venues where fans congregated. There were the Catacombs in Wolverhampton, the Torch in Stoke-on-Trent, Va-Va's in Bolton, the Ambassador in Bradford, Samantha's in Sheffield, Up The Junction in Crewe and Blackpool's Mecca. But Wigan Casino was the biggest of them all.

Black figures like Caesar are too often relegated to the edge of the dance floor in the substantial body of literature and film about Northern Soul. If this book has a thematic motif, it's the desire to push Black Britons and their stories into the centre, under the spotlight, where they belong.

The Black Soul fans were often recent arrivals, part of the wave of immigration that reshaped Britain in the post-war era, the generation that would become associated with the name of the HMT *Empire Windrush*.[1] These new Britons were crossing boundaries, entering into mostly white spaces in a way few could during the 1970s, when colour bars still imposed segregation in clubs and pubs. That racist environment made many Black Britons suspicious of Northern Soul, whose powerbrokers – the DJs, promoters, club owners – were white.

It was the start of the Thatcher era, and all-nighters took place in towns and cities where tensions were inflamed by far-right groups – including the National Front, which had used anti-immigrant campaigning, provocative marches through Black areas and outright racism to become the fourth biggest political party (in terms of party membership) in Britain by 1974 – the same year Caesar stepped out on the floor at Wigan. With the music blaring from the speakers, and his heart rate back under control, Caesar started to move. Tall and elegant, he glided along the floor, bouncing to the music rather than deploying the eye-catching drops and spins favoured by some dancers. Caesar was different, and was on his way to winning the first-ever dance contest at Wigan Casino. When he picked up his prize – £50, a hefty sum in the mid-1970s, equal to almost £400 today – he made history. Caesar wasn't just the first winner of a dance contest, he was a pioneer, one who staked a claim for Black Britain in the most unlikely of places.

Three years after Caesar won the inaugural dance competition at the Casino, a filmmaker called Tony Palmer arrived in the north-west of England and made a documentary called *The Wigan Casino* that offered a glimpse inside the counter-cultural movement.

Palmer visited the Casino and took in the sights and smells: the talcum powder on the dance floors and the sartorial choices of the punters who valued freedom of movement over the most en-vogue fashion. He decided to shoot his film over a weekend, bringing in full lighting rigs and a team of camera people – the results were spectacular.

Filming for two nights in the winter of 1977, Palmer shot some of the most iconic footage ever captured of a Northern Soul all-nighter in full swing. There's the crush at the front door as dancers attempt to get in and a lone doorman tries in vain to instil some sense of order; the gravity-defying spins and splits that light up the dance floor; the interviews with fans referencing obscure soul records in thick Lancastrian accents – all punctuated by the thousand-yard stares from spaced-out punters – you can almost smell the Brut aftershave and sweat. The scene was powered by amphetamines, often purloined from unsuspecting pharmacists in the north of England, who would have their windows put through by dealers or dancers on the hunt for pills to give them pep for a night of high-energy moves.

Weaving together a story about the working class, the power of dancing and African American soul, Palmer's camera subtly highlights another aspect of the scene as it lingers throughout the documentary on the faces of several Black teenagers. They are blink-and-you'll-miss-them moments, but they offer an alternative to the prevailing narrative – then and now – that casts Northern Soul as an exclusively white movement.

'The whole Northern Soul scene was white,' said the Black Scouse DJ and actor Craig Charles in 2015.[2] 'Some Black people who went to those events suffered racism. I suppose young Black people are always looking to be ahead of the curve – in the 1970s, rather than Northern Soul, Black people were into P-Funk and Earth, Wind and Fire, and so on, not the 60s soul.' I heard that theory many times when talking to other journalists and writers about Northern Soul: Black kids were on the cutting edge – they had no time for this atavistic white-led sub-culture. But by tracking down and talking to the dozens of Black Northern Soul fans who went to all-nighters, I found a more complicated version of the story.

Ian Obeng was at the Wigan Casino when Caesar danced his way to victory. He remembers seeing him dance, gliding along the stage. But Obeng, like many regulars, stayed off the dance floor when Palmer turned up with his camera. The lights Palmer's film crew had brought ruined the atmosphere. It wasn't Wigan, but a circus where they were the performers. Four years after the first all-nighter, Wigan Casino was known all over the world: Northern Soul records had featured on *Top of the Pops* and there was even a *Billboard* magazine article which claimed the Casino was the 'greatest disco in the world', even better than the New York disco mecca, Studio 54.[3]

All the publicity had brought rubberneckers and diluted the purity of the experience for people like Obeng. 'We didn't want the dickheads, the boozers and the fighters to come and mess the scene up,' says Obeng. 'So we refused to be in the documentary.' The defensiveness in Obeng's voice even now, fifty years later, is revealing – for some Black Britons, Northern Soul wasn't just a fun sub-culture, it was a haven and they wanted to protect it.

Obeng's family had moved to Manchester from Ghana in 1960, part of a wave of arrivals to the country at the beginning of the new decade. Obeng, like many in British-controlled states, had a rose-tinted view of the mother country. British newspapers were sold in Accra and portrayed the UK as a flourishing bastion of democracy with work for all, an obsession with fair play and cherished – if slightly odd – traditions. But on the journey from Accra to Liverpool, the reality of Britain began to sink in for Obeng. 'We stopped at the Canary Islands, Lisbon and lots of places before we actually hit Liverpool,' he said. 'Then, as soon as we got to England, the skies went grey. The sea was grey. I'd never seen anything like it.' That year, Obeng was one of 58,300 immigrants from the Commonwealth, compared to only 21,550 the previous year, as many rushed to enter the country before the 1962 Commonwealth Immigrants Act came into force.[4]

The controversial legislation imposed limits on British subjects migrating to the UK for the first time since 1948, when Clement Attlee's post-war administration had introduced the British Nationality Act. In need of workers to help rebuild the country after the Second World War – and, in particular, to power the newly formed National Health Service (NHS) – Attlee's Labour government had allowed Commonwealth immigrants to come to the UK and have all the same rights as British citizens. Recruitment offices for nurses, porters and doctors were set up in Nigeria, Trinidad and Tobago, Guyana and all over the Commonwealth.[5] But the arrival of this new workforce wasn't welcomed by all in the government: just two days after the *Windrush* docked, eleven of Attlee's own MPs wrote to him, asking him to stop the 'influx of coloured people', while the Colonial Secretary Arthur Creech Jones called Black Britons a 'problem' who could trigger a 'public scandal'.[6]

Between 1948 and 1962, people like Obeng were considered British by law and had the right to move to the UK, but ever since the first arrival of these new Black Britons, successive governments had been searching for ways to reduce their numbers. Only two years after the British Nationality Act was ratified, a cabinet committee was established that sought to find 'ways which might be adopted to check the immigration into this country of coloured people from British colonial territories'.[7]

This work was mostly covert. Labour and Conservative prime ministers didn't want to appear to be discriminating against arrivals on account of their race – this was, after all, the generation that had fought the Nazis and their fascist ideology. The political establishment's true views on Black immigration were uttered in private or whispered along the corridors of Whitehall. In a memo, the Conservative Home Secretary Rab Butler admitted that although the 1962 act appeared not to discriminate on the grounds of race 'its restrictive effect is intended to, and would in fact, operate on coloured people almost exclusively.'[8] It was people like Obeng who the Home Office wanted to keep out of Britain.

As the debate about the new wave of immigrants raged, the Obeng family made their way from the docks of Liverpool to a leafy suburban street in Sale, on the outskirts of Manchester. Obeng found himself attracted to two things: football and mod culture. Mods (taken from 'modernist') bought sharp clothes, rode scooters and were obsessed with US soul records. Obeng wore drainpipe trousers and polo shirts and became hooked on Manchester United after visiting Old Trafford with his father. 'Everyone had rattles, and they made this unbelievable noise,' he told me. 'There was a togetherness. It was just magical.' As Britain was attempting to close its doors to people like Obeng, young Black people were finding a place within it.

In Northern Soul, Obeng found a scene that married the collectivism of the Stretford End swaying in unison and the American records he coveted as a mod. The name of the scene originated in London in the Soul City record shop. Its owner was Black music obsessive David Godin, who recognised that northern football fans who came to the capital weren't interested in contemporary releases but rather older soul singles that had flopped on their first release. The tracks dubbed 'Northern Soul' by Godin were bombastic cuts like the MVP's 'Turnin' My Heartbeat Up', Martha Reeves & The Vandellas' 'Nowhere To Run', The Vel-Vets' 'I Got To Find Me Somebody', Don Ray's 'Born a Loser' or The Epitome of Sound's 'You Don't Love Me'. They had a danceable four-to-the-floor beat and carried a message of lost love, defiant resolve in the face of defeat or hedonistic escape. Sheffield, Blackpool, Bradford, Bolton, Crewe, Stafford and Stoke-on-Trent all had their own clubs, but none was bigger than Wigan Casino.

'It was basic, atmospheric and had the biggest and best-kept dance floor anyone had seen to that point,' wrote one regular.[9] 'The only lighting was provided by two fluorescent lights over the oblong-shaped sprung maplewood dance floor, ensuring that anyone with bright colours glowed brilliantly as they danced.' The scene was counter-cultural and transgressive: Black music had always had an underground following in Britain, whether it was the blues of Memphis, skinhead reggae or the jazz of New Orleans, but never before had it captured the hearts and minds of young white Britons on this scale. At its peak, Wigan Casino boasted a membership of 100,000.

Many of the Black Northern Soul fans were part of the Windrush Generation. That influx of new dark-skinned immigrants, who technically had the same rights as white Britons was anathema to some. Fascist groups, including Oswald Mosley's Union Movement, called for repatriation of Black Britons; while graffiti that read 'KBW' (Keep

Britain White) appeared on the doors of new arrivals. Violent racist attacks, such as the murder of Kelso Cochrane in West London in 1959, showed the human cost of the racist rhetoric, while the riots that preceded it in the capital and Nottingham a year earlier had already exposed the tensions that were simmering beneath the surface.

The north wasn't immune from this charged environment. In the same towns and cities that Northern Soul drew its devotees from, there was another political force on the rise: the far-right National Front. Made up of ultra-conservatives, 'empire loyalists' and neo-Nazis[10] – they pledged to repatriate non-white Britons, celebrated Nazi ideology and spouted debunked race science – with members often believing that whites were 'intellectually superior' to Black people based on IQ scores.[11]

But the group wasn't just a force at the ballot box, its leaders, just like Mosley's Union Movement, demanded shows of force on Britain's streets. In the late 1970s, there was another burgeoning youth sub-culture that it would co-opt. Skinhead culture had started in

The National Front marching through Blackburn, Lancashire, 20 January 1973

Jamaica with the rudeboy – street-smart young men who dressed in suits and fought in dance halls – before travelling over the Atlantic to Britain. Dressed in rebellious, working-class attire – Doc Martens, skinny jeans, Fred Perry polo shirts and a buzz cut – it was initially a non-racist movement, with some groups including Black members.[12] But by the late 1970s, the NF – now under the leadership of a younger generation led by Martin Webster, who favoured thuggish street tactics – saw an opportunity to influence skinheads. The Young National Front launched a youth magazine, *Bulldog*, which helped promote racist punk bands, such as Skrewdriver. *Bulldog* was sold outside Elland Road, the stadium of Leeds United – a club with a large skinhead following and a reputation for violence.[13]

Two young Black players – Leroy Rosenior and Paul Parker – recalled what it was like to play at Elland Road. During a game for Fulham against Leeds, Rosenior went to take a corner in front of the Kop End. 'Paul and I were greeted with 5,000 or more Leeds fans with their right hands, erect to the sky, shouting *"Sieg Heil"* as if not attending a Second Division football match on a rainy Yorkshire afternoon but a 1930s Nuremberg rally,' wrote Rosenior in his memoirs.[14]

The scene inspired literature, most notably Richard Allen's *Skinhead* series, which followed the exploits of a group of skinheads from the east end of London. Joe Hawkins, the series' sixteen-year-old protagonist, maps out the group's philosophy on race during a scene in a pub: 'He hated "spades" – wished they'd wash more often or get the hell back where they came from . . . they were impositions on the face of a London that should always be white. Cockney, true-British . . . no so-called British because they claimed a passport and insisted on rights their own independent nations did not grant the inhabitants of the British isles.' For many skinheads Black Britons were an aberration; an oxymoron to be booted out of existence.[15]

Despite the dangers, other Black Britons were drawn to the glow of the Casino lights. Rhonda Finlayson was born in Jamaica but moved to Manchester with her family as a three-year-old and started going to all-nighters after attending the Twisted Wheel as a teenager.[16] Escapism and excitement drew Finlayson into the scene. As the second oldest of seven children, Rhonda was expected to set an example, but she'd fallen in love with soul music.[17] 'I didn't exactly have permission to go – I just used to go missing,' says Finlayson. She'd meet friends and catch trains around the north of England, or sometimes hitch-hike – even by herself – to nights at clubs like the Torch in Stoke, Up The Junction in Crewe, Samantha's in Sheffield and Va-Va's in Bolton.[18] Finlayson worked as a silver service waitress in Wales, and previously at a dry cleaners in Manchester, but her focus was on the weekend's Northern Soul adventure. The music's energy, its raw yet defiant lyrics, worked as a salve on her feelings of detachment as she tried to find her place in Britain. 'I've got a song that I loved so much, Smokey Robinson and the Miracles – "I Gotta Dance To Keep from Crying". At that time, I was very mixed up as a kid, and dancing was massive for me – it kept me sane,' she told me.

The Black Northern Soul fans crisscrossing the country on the hunt for all-nighters would sometimes be exposed to the racial toxicity of 1970s Britain. Dean Anderson, a Black soul DJ from Newark, stopped at a service station on his way to a party with a racially mixed group of friends and was confronted by a dozen skinheads. The racists shouted '*Sieg Heil!*' in unison and threatened to kill them, telling the group they shouldn't be seen together. 'It was the worst moment of my life,' Anderson said.[19] 'I went to the all-nighter and I was just numb.'[20] Those tensions had not dissipated by the time Palmer arrived in Wigan with his film crew. On the contrary, with an election on the horizon and immigration being such a divisive issue, they were about to ramp up.

Just over a year after Palmer's *Wigan Casino* aired, in January 1978, Margaret Thatcher went on the current affairs programme *World in Action* on Granada Television, the same broadcaster that had aired Palmer's film. 'People are really rather afraid that this country might be swamped by people with a different culture,'[21] she said, at the start of an interview that would become infamous. 'We do have to hold out the prospect of an end to immigration, except, of course, for compassionate cases.' Thatcher's comments were chillingly effective.[22] Four weeks later, her party won an ill-tempered by-election in North Ilford (5,000 police were deployed with Scotland Yard fearing violence)[23] which the National Front had been expected to win.[24] Thatcher's comments caused serious concern among some politicians, who were worried about the rise of support for far-right ideology. One-nation Conservative MP, Peter Walker, told an interfaith rally in London a couple of months after Thatcher's interview that if racism wasn't tackled, it could become 'the greatest threat to world peace,'[25] while the chairman of the recently formed Commission for Racial Equality said Britain was in a state of 'national neurosis verging on hysteria' on the issues of race.[26] Black Northern Soul fans were about to find themselves in the eye of the storm as Britain's politicians began to use their presence as a wedge issue.

Steve Caesar was one of the new Black Britons who'd grown up in the racial 'hysteria' taking hold of the UK and he was also one of Wigan Casino's early icons. He moved to Leeds as a thirteen-year-old from St Kitts, where he'd been brought up by his aunt, while his older brothers had arrived in England years earlier, with his parents. Caesar moved to Chapeltown in 1968, which by then had become a multiracial district of Leeds. He remembers the area's cosmopolitan mix: Caesar had Pakistani friends, walked past the Serbian Club on the way home, shopped at the Polish delicatessen and was a fan of the Italian cured meat he could get from the deli. But the city's politicians saw Chapeltown's multicultural population as something that was weighing them down.

Three years before his arrival, the Leeds City Labour Party warned that Chapeltown's high 'concentration of Commonwealth immigrants' made some members fear that 'an education problem . . . at certain schools will soon have to be faced.'[27] The new Britons such as Caesar were seen as a burden the education system had to bear. To appease complaints, a radical solution was introduced in Leeds: bussing. No school would be allowed to have more than 30 per cent immigrant children in its classrooms. Those who lived in areas with schools that had reached that capacity were sent – by bus – to other areas. As a result, Steve and his older brother, Donald, were sent to school in Gipton, a white working-class neighbourhood in Leeds. 'It was a very white school,' says Caesar. 'My brother and I were the first two Black kids.'

After several legal challenges, bussing would be phased out entirely in West Yorkshire almost twenty years later, in 1980, but education and immigration continued to be at the forefront of conversations about race. In 1971, the Grenadian writer Bernard Coard published the landmark pamphlet *How the West Indian Child is Made Educationally Subnormal in the British School System*, which argued that Black children were being targeted and sent to schools for the educationally subnormal, which stigmatised them for life.

According to Coard, who was a teacher, the entire school system was making Black children feel inferior to their white peers. The Grenadian observed Jamaican children pretending they'd never heard of their home country, Indian children denying they were Indian (despite wearing a sari to school) and encountered white children who refused to believe that Coard was 'coloured' because he didn't fit the negative stereotype. 'In addition to being told he is dirty and ugly and "sexually unreliable", he is told by a variety of means that he is intellectually inferior,'[28] wrote Coard. 'Through the belittling, ignoring, or denial of a person's identity, one can destroy perhaps the most important aspect of a person's personality – his sense of identity, of who he is. Without this, he will get nowhere.'

For Caesar, Northern Soul was a pillar of that new sense of identity. He was instantly hooked. Caesar loved the fashion of the mod scene and asked his mum – who had been a well-known seamstress in St Kitts – to make him a Harrington jacket. When I met him in central London for our interview, his style still harked back to mod-style staples – trilby hat, drainpipe jeans, bomber jacket and fitted polo shirt. Culturally, the scene and its sartorial choices were a world away from the modest, God-fearing home life he was used to in St Kitts, and it was intoxicating. 'Northern Soul helped me find a sort of way of belonging; especially as a young sixteen-year-old,' he told me. Caesar was still a relatively new arrival from St Kitts, and here he was at the epicentre of the most exciting underground movement in the UK, being championed. 'Everybody referred to me by my surname "Caesar" or they'd say, "that's Caesar from Leeds,"

Margaret Thatcher meets voters while campaigning during the 1978 by-election in High Wycombe

and your reputation grows as the winner of the dance competition. It brought me recognition on the scene.' Acceptance, belonging, respect: Northern Soul gave those things to Caesar, it offered it to Obeng and Finlayson too – young immigrants to the UK who were seeking belonging in a country that by the late 1970s had a government that openly rejected them.

Not all Black British people embraced Northern Soul or felt a personal connection to it – many hated it. All the dominant Northern Soul DJs – Russ Winstanley, Colin Curtis, Richard Searling and Ian Levine – were white. So were the promoters, venue owners and most of its fanbase.[29] The DJs and promoters decided which songs made by working-class Black Americans would be dug out of obscurity and celebrated. They were, in effect, the custodians of Black culture.

Norman Jay was one of the millions who had seen Tony Palmer's film on Granada in December 1977. The north London DJ and soul boy was an avid Tottenham Hotspur supporter and decided that, after an away game in the north-west, he'd go to an all-nighter. When he arrived at the Casino he was stunned by how white the scene was. 'I was always going out listening to music that I loved, but attendant on that was a vague sense of disillusion with the scene I was in. I think a lot of Black kids, consciously or otherwise, felt that same thing. All these white people were supposedly championing our culture,' he said, 'while we stood on the sidelines, without a face or a voice. I remember thinking: I don't really need this.' [30] [31]

The racial fissures provoked by Northern Soul were nowhere more fiercely debated than on the letters page of a magazine. *Black Music* had launched in 1974 and was – along with *Blues & Soul* and *Echoes* magazine – one of the most respected publications covering music from across the Black diaspora and developed a loyal readership. No issue it covered seemed to generate the same level of feeling as Northern Soul. 'I'm sick to the back teeth reading in *BM* every month about a bunch of ignorant white kids and DJs who are supposed to represent the Northern Soul Scene,' started one letter.

'I'm sure there are hundreds of Black people like myself, who are not interested in what white kids and DJs like in the North.'[32] (The issue of race became so divisive in the magazine that it eventually ran an article calling for mutual 'respect and love'. 'Let's take the bitterness and prejudice out of it and respect each other's differences, whether racial, geographical or musical,' it pleaded.)

The whiteness of the scene clashed with the new defiant Black British identity that was emerging in the 1970s, powered by sounds emanating from Jamaica. The Northern Soul scene had come to prominence just as reggae sound system culture was emerging from Black British communities. Crews of young people would build speakers, buy records and 'toast' on microphones over records as they sought to beat rivals in sound clashes where the crowd's response would signal the winner. In the UK, sound clashes between the biggest sounds, like Sir Coxsone or Jah Shaka, drew dedicated reggae fans wherever they were hosted. In *Bass Culture*, Lloyd Bradley's exhaustive history of reggae and sound systems, he compares followers of Jamaica's crews to football fans of the UK, with aficionados following their sounds wherever they played – home and away. 'You were standing up for your area, your friends, your good name,' he argues.[33]

In towns like Huddersfield in West Yorkshire, sound systems created their own micro-economy with groups – such as the Earth Rocker sound system – turning to local electricians to provide them with amps to power the speakers they'd made themselves.[34] Shortly after Caesar had won the first dance contest at Wigan Casino, reggae had established itself as the forward-thinking political sound of young Black Britain. It was a scene built (literally by hand) by hundreds of young Black people. In this world of Black empowerment and self-determination, Northern Soul – with its white power brokers – was seen by some as an affront.

Black people who chose Northern Soul over reggae or more cutting-edge soul could pay a price – particularly Black women. Idell Kamili had grown up in north London but moved to Northampton as a teenager, where she first heard about Northern Soul.

Her decision to attend Northern Soul nights turned heads in the close-knit Black community she came from. 'By the time I'd got into Northern Soul, the Rasta scene was in full swing. I did go to a few [sound system] nights, but I just found it too constrictive. I wanted a bit more freedom,' she says. 'You can imagine the names I got called, because it was a predominately white scene, but for me, it was about the music.' Others were similarly committed.

'I didn't stick to the West Indian community,' Caesar tells me. 'I was happily moving beyond the surroundings of Chapeltown. It didn't hold me, but I don't know why. I can't tell you why. I was not on any sort of crusade, but I just didn't feel the same as a lot of kids who didn't go beyond the confines of Chapeltown. I went to town; I went to Leeds Central [soul club], I got on buses and went to Wigan, and I did it without any fear.' Caesar was also a huge Leeds United fan and was often found on the terraces at Elland Road. He remembers his first-ever trip to Blackpool Mecca, where Ian Levine hosted the biggest rival of Wigan Casino. He drove via Hebden Bridge, and on the winding roads of the Calder Valley he recalled seeing the sun setting as he made his way into Lancashire. It's a scene that could have been plucked out of Jack Kerouac's *On The Road* – Caesar, the young man with insatiable wanderlust, travelling between towns on the hunt for his soul fix.

But the soul sound was shifting, too. By the early 1970s, American soul was developing a harder edge, inspired by the militant Black Power Movement that had emerged in the wake of the civil rights era. Unlike civil rights leaders such as Martin Luther King who preached pacificism and non-violent protest, Black Power saw groups including the Black Panthers take up arms and encourage African Americans to, as Malcolm X said, defend themselves 'by any means necessary'. When Black Power leader Stokely Carmichael delivered a speech about the movement at the Roundhouse in Camden,[35] he spelled out the new direction, simply and directly: 'We are not talking anymore. We have talked for 400 years; it has gotten us nowhere.'[36]

A new breed of soul acts combined instrumentals with lyrics that took their inspiration from Black Power messages. The Rance Allen Group and S.O.U.L. implored politicians to 'Tell It Like It Is' and stop 'Lying On The Truth' in the wake of the Watergate scandal in 1974, when the corruption of Richard Nixon's administration was laid bare. DJ turned artist Gary Byrd asked listeners 'Are You Really Ready For Black Power?', while the Watts Prophets warned that 'Dem Niggers Aint Playing' in reference to the Watts riots in Los Angeles during the summer of 1965, where thirty-four people died and $40 million worth of damage was done.

Mainstream soul acts like Stevie Wonder, who'd had a string of inoffensive pop hits, started to embrace the new Black Power-infused sound, eventually inviting the Watts Prophets to perform on his 1976 album, *Songs in the Key of Life*. No transformation was as dramatic as that of the Isley Brothers. In the 1960s, the act had been part of Motown's huge commercial success with tracks like 'This Old Heart Of Mine' and 'Twist and Shout'. But by the mid-1970s they'd embraced a harder form of soul and their track 'Fight The Power (Parts 1&2)'[37] projected an angry, disillusioned perspective a world away from the bubble-gum pop of a decade earlier.

In contrast to the tougher soul sound, Northern Soul is often cast as being softer – detached from the racially charged world that had forged the tracks that were being coveted. But all-nighters were situated on the frontline of 1970s racial politics. The parties were taking place in towns and cities where the NF and other far-right groups were a force: Blackburn was a huge soul town, but it was also where the National Party had been established. Wigan Casino's main rival, the Blackpool Mecca, was the hometown of Skrewdriver, the most notorious of fascist punk bands. Leeds Central was a key soul club and operated in a city where the far right had not only infiltrated the football terraces but the British National Party had been founded there. Northern Soul and fascism were often cheek by jowl.

Contemporary Northern Soul message boards are full of people dismissing the idea that racism existed in places like the Casino, but the reality was more complicated. Ian Obeng says he never witnessed racism directly ('Overtly? No. Covertly? Probably.') but knew there wasn't a magic forcefield preventing the racism of 1970s Britain from coming through the doors of the all-nighters. 'They'd always say, "Oh no, we can't be racist because we like Black music", but there were a number of them that were,' Obeng told me. 'It's difficult because they weren't like the racist football fans, who were just racist, and didn't like anything about Black people or Black culture. They liked Black music, but I guess they wouldn't like a Black guy going out with their daughter.'[38]

Even though Northern Soul all-nighters weren't immune from prejudice, they were still a world away from the racism of mainstream British clubbing in the mid-1970s. Colour bars operated in Britain from before the arrival of the *Windrush* in 1948, with campaigns being fought against them in London, Manchester and all over the country.[39] Pubs would have separate rooms for Black and Asian patrons, while white customers who came in with Black friends were often barred.[40] Many of the Black Northern Soul fans would have been turned away from mainstream venues where they grew up, with soul venues offering a sanctuary where their race wasn't a barrier.

'It felt like you'd died and gone to heaven,' said Idell Kamili of her first visit to Wigan Casino. 'I know it sounds really over-dramatic, but that's how I felt when I went in there. I just felt accepted, and that was the thing – everybody seemed to be equal. [The first time] I walked through the door, they were playing "Do I Love You" by Frank Wilson. Then I went up on to the balcony and that's when they played Cecil Washington, "I Don't Like to Lose", and it was like time just stopped. Even now when I hear it, the tingles go up and down my spine.'

In the twelve months after Tony Palmer's film aired, London was starting to be seen as the centre of a new Black British identity, one that was beginning to – in places – meld with the white working-class culture around it, while fiercely opposing the daily racism of 1970s Britain. In 1976 there were pitched battles between Black revellers and police at the Notting Hill Carnival.[41] Around one hundred officers were injured. Following the disorder, seventy-nine people were charged with criminal violence and damage, as Junior Murvin's reggae anthem 'Police and Thieves' blasted out of sound systems in West London.[42] That year, at carnival, the more militant brand of Black Britishness was on show, but as well as resistance there were displays of reconciliation.

Two years later the Rock Against Racism concert in Victoria Park – when 100,000 people came together to see The Clash play alongside X-Ray Spex, Steel Pulse and Matumbi – helped neutralise the far-right threat by putting Sham 69 (a group with a large skinhead following) on stage with Black bands and those who were overtly anti-racist.[43] Despite Rock and Racism being a nationwide phenomena that started in 1976 and went to cities like Bradford, Bolton and Manchester, the 1978 gig in Victoria Park is often presented as the singular moment from the movement that is picked out in popular retellings, and elevated above other regional concerts. A year before Rock Against Racism, the DJ Don Letts had introduced reggae to the Roxy Club – London's first punk venue – via his sets. 'What was interesting was white working-class youth really dug the sound. They dug the anti-establishment vibe of the whole thing,' said Letts.[44]

I've lost count of the times I've heard interviewers ask Letts about that anecdote, as the night of punk and reggae is given huge symbolic status, just like Rock Against Racism and the 1976 Notting Hill Carnival. They are stories that filmmakers, journalists and writers reach for because they help us understand 1970s Britain, a fractious place with seemingly unbreachable racial and social divides. At its core, the story of reggae and punk tells us to look at these two contrasting sounds and groups; they could come together, put aside their differences and unite in a love of Black music. Put simply, this is culture acting as anti-racist balm.

Northern Soul, with its hedonistic lyrics about love, lust and loss, isn't included in that conversation: it's often framed as apolitical, or even socially conservative. Writers often focus on the inherent nostalgia of the music and the white power brokers who decided which rare African American records were worthy of selection.

One theory goes that Northern Soul is melancholic and wistful because the young white kids dancing to it were angry that the hope and progress of Britain in the 1960s, when society became more open and less constrained, had faded into a grim, grey reality where opportunities were hard to come by.[45] 'You live in a nondescript town somewhere in the north of England. Row upon row of factories fill the horizon with chimneys, scarring the sky with belches of dark grey smoke. During the week, in one of those factories, you work the nine-to-five drudge: manning a production line, sweeping the yard, shovelling shit,' is how Bill Brewster and Frank Broughton described the life of a typical Northern Soul fan in the 1970s. They assumed those fans, 'almost all white', were drawn to the 'fast, escapist style' of the music because it 'somehow resonated with their mechanised existence'. In this world, it was class, rather than race, that mattered.

Another, more optimistic, reading is that Northern Soul is the start of a transatlantic relationship where working-class white kids from the industrial north of England covet and rekindle love for working-class Black music from the industrial north of America. A pattern that continues to this day via Britain's embrace of all forms of African American dance music and hip-hop. Neither of those positions considers the significant Black British presence at all-nighters or the political elements at play within Northern Soul.

When looked at alongside Rock Against Racism or punks listening to reggae at the Roxy, the scene measures up well. An estimated 100,000 people were in Victoria Park that day to symbolically say 'no' to the far right, but the same number of people were signed up to a club that played subversive Black music in the north-west of England every weekend. The whiteness of the scene – even though most of the music played was made by African Americans – means it's not put in the same anti-racist conversation as Rock Against Racism or Don Letts' DJing. But most of the people in Victoria Park on that day in 1978, and the punks at the Roxy were also white. That was why those moments were so important: a white majority was being set off on a path of anti-racism by Black culture.

White Northern Soul fans may not have been going to all-nighters for political motivations, but they were still listening to political anthems. 'Dancing In The Street' by Martha Reeves & The Vandellas was a call to action in the civil rights era, as was Aretha Franklin's 'Respect' – both of which were mainstays at Northern Soul clubs, while James Coit's 1968 track 'Black Power' directly referenced the new Black political consciousness. At the Blackpool Mecca, Colin Curtis played Gil Scott-Heron's 'The Bottle' and The Last Poets' 'It's a Trip'. The latter came out in 1977 and commented on the plight of inner-city populations in the US, representing the avant-garde of Black soul music.

But there's an even more obvious link to anti-racism that is often overlooked: the Northern Soul scene's iconic emblem – embroidered on thousands of badges and bags – is a raised Black fist. It was inspired by the 1968 Olympic protest by Tommie Smith and John Carlos, who both silently raised a fist covered in a Black glove while the American anthem played during the medal ceremony for the 200-metre final. The symbol was accompanied by the scene's slogan 'Keep the Faith', three words that suggest dedication and religious fervour but also served as a reminder of the music's Black origin. 'There was a camaraderie about the whole thing – people really believed in "Keep the Faith",' says Caesar. 'I remember going to Leeds Central and seeing white kids wearing one Black glove.'

White soul fans who crossed the threshold of Wigan Casino, the Mecca or the Torch plunged themselves into a world of Black music, only to emerge a few hours later into towns and cities that were being targeted by the far right. Not everyone who went to all-nighters became anti-racist, but some did, while others would at the very least develop a love of Black music which lasted entire lifetimes. That makes Northern Soul dance floors political spaces, ones that have a place in the wider narrative of anti-racist cultural movements that emerged in the 1970s. It wasn't just on the streets of Notting Hill where a new understanding of Black consciousness could be forged among both Black and white; it could – incredibly – happen in a small mill town.

*

In 1981, the Wigan Casino was demolished. What once was the most talked-about dance floor in the world made way for a car park. But the scene continued, and still does to this day, with newspaper articles marvelling at the revival of Northern Soul coming along at least once a decade – ignoring the fact it never really went away. Obeng, Caesar and Finlayson slowly drifted into different scenes from post-punk to acid house, while other Black British dancers kept the faith. What Palmer captured in his documentary was an ephemeral moment that has passed into myth and legend: a snapshot of the original scene that future fans and those who were there could cling to.

Caesar still has photographs from the night he won the inaugural dance competition at Wigan Casino on his phone. He shows them to me as we talk. In the photos, his face looks focused and composed as he dances, concentrating on the movement of his body. When he's presented with his prize, his expression has morphed into disbelief. Rhonda Finlayson, too, was well known for her moves, coming joint first in a competition at the Torch in Stoke-on-Trent in the early 1970s. It was the main reason she chose soul over reggae. '[With soul] it was always because of the music and the dancing,' she told me. Rhonda loved how it felt to dance in the glow of the lights at the Casino. 'It was like being in another world,' she said.

After watching Palmer's documentary, I turned to the internet to find out more about the Black fans and discovered pictures of a young man from Bradford called Vernon Pryce competing in the final dance contest at Wigan Casino in 1981. Taken by the Italian photographer Francesco Mellina, the images show Pryce athletically pulling off moves that look impossible.[46] Pryce's braided hair flares outwards as he jumps, spins and drops to the floor during his competition-winning routine. Pryce's victory in the club's final contest provides a neat, Black British bookend to the club's history. But I believe it's much more important than that.

The presence of people like Pryce and Caesar doesn't fit into the neat stories we like to tell ourselves about the era, or about Black British people. Within Northern Soul there are complexities.

Northern Souls – 1977

When you hear the stories of Ian Obeng, Rhonda Finlayson and Steve Caesar, you see that Northern Soul is directly linked to 1970s immigration policy, bias in the education system and the huge anti-racism push the era witnessed.

The Black British generation who came of age during the Thatcher era were anything but monolithic – some embraced the music and culture that grew from their own, often isolated, communities. Others, like Steve Caesar, looked beyond those parameters for an outsider scene that accepted him. Whether Northern Soul or reggae, cultural sanctuaries provided an escape in a country that was increasingly hostile to their presence.

Northern Soul, the outsider scene with its own strange rules and rituals, I'd argue, is the perfect prism through which to see the racial politics of 1970s Britain, in all its complexity. White fans who went could be racist, despite loving Black music. Black dancers like Caesar and Finlayson could be heralded and celebrated, despite wider society rejecting them. The towns and cities where the scene flourished were also breeding grounds for far-right groups. All this happened in a country with a political leadership that publicly welcomed the Black dancers but privately schemed to reduce their numbers.

A year after Palmer's film was shown, another documentary offered a glimpse of where Britain was heading next on the question of immigration and race. As Margaret Thatcher edged closer to Downing Street, her 'swamped' comments had legitimised a worldview that said the Black populations of the UK were alien and dangerous. In Bradford, a court case would show the cost of that hostility – and the campaign to overturn an unjust verdict would reveal how even the smallest of Black communities could fight back. The whole thing would be captured by another filmmaking team – this time from America – who wanted to show the world what they saw as the truth about life in Britain for its growing Black population.

2.

Free George Lindo – Bradford, 1978

In September 1977, the director David Koff and his co-producer and wife Msindo Mwinyipembe sent a proposal for a film project to the offices of the North American public broadcaster WGBH Boston. Their pitch was for a landmark production: a half-hour documentary project about the Black population of the United Kingdom. Koff was a tall, long-haired Jewish Californian and a socialist who staged sit-ins in the American South during the civil rights era, where he met Jesse Jackson and Martin Luther King. Mwinyipembe was, on the surface, his polar opposite – a five-foot-one broadcaster from Tanzania who'd travelled to Britain as a six-year-old to be treated for polio, stayed on to be educated in a convent school in Sussex, and returned to Africa for her undergraduate studies.

The pair met in Kenya. Koff had studied in Nairobi before making a trilogy of films about the push for independence and the Mau Mau rebellion. Mwinyipembe had become a news presenter on Tanzanian television. The pair were already together when Koff was nominated for an Oscar in 1976 as part of the team behind the documentary *People of the Wind* about a Nomadic tribe in Iran.[1] *People of the Wind* was an elegiac portrait, while the Kenyan films were also beautiful, featuring footage of the verdant African Serengeti shot via helicopter. The films weren't just aesthetically pleasing; they had a sharp, political edge and gave a platform to those who'd been previously ignored, especially those from the margins. Throughout the Kenyan trilogy, Koff portrayed Britain as the aggressor during the conflict that started in 1952, lasted eight years and saw British forces send approximately one and a half million Kenyans to detention camps. Mwinyipembe provided the voice-over for the films, which featured rare interviews with Mau Mau operatives who'd survived and shared their stories of British colonial rule. According to his son, Kimera, Koff's films were often asking the same two questions: 'Will power yield to people who don't – individually – have any leverage at all? And can people organise to force change?'

After they moved to the US to continue making films, Koff and Mwinyipembe wanted to challenge the consensus view of race in the UK: namely, that Britain was a welcoming, liberal democracy without a race problem. In the words of Mwinyipembe, she wanted to make British people 'spit out their tea' in surprise and disgust at the image of the country before them.

WGBH had put out a call for stories from outside the US. Their executives wanted viewers to 'take off their "special American glasses" and look at the world through the eyes of others.'[2] The filmmakers knew a project about Black Britons, an oxymoron in the eyes of many Americans, had a good chance of success. Their instincts were right: they won the commission for a thirty-minute documentary that would air in 1978.

Koff's and Mwinyipembe's pitch was for *Blacks Britannica*, a polemic documentary arguing that, far from being welcomed to their new home, Black Britons were – thirty years after the *Windrush* docked – being attacked by the state.

By the late 1970s, Black Britons and South Asians numbered around 1.7 million or 3 per cent of the population. But Mwinyipembe noticed that she rarely heard from these new arrivals on TV or in print. 'It was as if nobody else (but whites) existed on the island,' she told the *Washington Post*.[3] She wanted to make a film from the point of view of the people who had, up to that point, been 'objects of discussion'.[4]

Giving Black people a platform to speak about their experiences would prove to be a hugely controversial undertaking. The film's release was hampered at every turn, and would ignite a heated debate among diplomats, journalists and politicians. Some tried to defend or – in most cases – kill it. *Blacks Britannica* was censored in the US and banned in the UK, but it nevertheless achieved Mwinyi-pembe's goal of letting Britain's increasingly disillusioned Black population tell their own story. One thing that makes it remarkable is the fact so much of it takes place outside of the capital. It's easy to find documentaries that talk about this period from a London perspective, detailing the problems faced in Tottenham and Brixton. But films about Bradford, Wolverhampton or Sheffield's Black communities are rare and precious.

A sizeable portion of the film was shot in Bradford, the West Yorkshire city whose once towering textile industry had attracted around 2,000 Black migrants by the end of the 1970s. The dominant narrative about Bradford and race is one of distrust between the white population of the city and the Pakistani Bradfordians. Today, people of South Asian origin make up 32.1 per cent of Bradford's population, the vast majority from Pakistan.

The influence from the Asian subcontinent is everywhere in the city, from the architecture of the many mosques to the sound of Bhangra and bassline house rattling car stereos. After racial unrest in 2001, sparked by rumours of a police-protected far-right march, a government report declared Bradfordians of different races were living 'a series of parallel lives'.[5] It earned the tag 'segregation city', a moniker it's never truly shaken off. A newspaper columnist pondered if it was the 'next Detroit' because of its high unemployment and racial unrest that mirrored the US city;[6] TV programme-makers tried to *Make Bradford British*;[7] and fifteen years on, the author of the 2001 report despaired that things had only got worse.[8] It's a simple, potent narrative: racist disenfranchised whites and regressive, insular South Asian immigrants who just can't get along. Black Bradfordians rarely feature in this narrative and make up around 2 per cent of the population.

Like Tony Palmer's film about Northern Soul fans at Wigan Casino, *Blacks Britannica* shed light on a largely hidden Black community. At present, the story that the filmmakers worked so hard to unearth and bring to popular awareness has once again become obscured by a simplified, one-dimensional tale of Bradford, a city that in the late 1970s – along with much of Britain – seemed to be unravelling.

When the *Blacks Britannica* team arrived in Bradford in 1978, it was in the middle of a deep freeze. The UK was experiencing its coldest weather for decades, with an average temperature of just 1.17°C.[9] The country was a few months away from entering the famous 'Winter of Discontent', punctuated by strikes, piles of rubbish, union battles and the continued rise in popularity of Margaret Thatcher's opposition. As unemployment crept up above 6 per cent, the Conservative Party launched its 'Labour's Not Working' campaign featuring images of a snaking, seemingly endless, line of jobseekers.

Prime Minister Jim Callaghan had taken over the leadership of the Labour Party in 1976. 'Uncle Jim', who had cut his teeth as a union leader at the Inland Revenue, came to power in the middle of one of the most restive periods in Britain's post-war history. Edward Heath's government had been hobbled by a miners' walkout in 1974, which created a national energy shortage and reduced the country to a three-day working week. But Callaghan boasted strong union connections and had held the most senior positions in the British government – Home Secretary, Foreign Secretary and Chancellor of the Exchequer. 'At a time of insecurity and turmoil he represented stability,'[10] asserted one newspaper profile. Three years into his time in office, however, the country was once again being hit by strike action.

Callaghan and his Chancellor Denis Healey had put an advised limit on wage rises to keep inflation down. When workers began to demand more than the mandated 5 per cent limit, the prime minister lost the support of the unions, resulting in the images his tenure is remembered for. Bin men left mounds of rubbish twelve-foot high outside of Berwick Street market in central London, and Leicester Square became an impromptu dumping ground. Petrol pumps ran dry. Operation Drumstick – a proposal to have military personnel ferry in petrol and work the pumps – was planned for but never initiated. The country's hospitals were so depleted by strikes

Rubbish piles up on the streets of Soho during industrial action by refuse collectors during the Winter of Discontent

that half were reduced to dealing only with emergencies, while rail strikes put still more pressure on the beleaguered Callaghan administration. When gravediggers in Merseyside downed their shovels, macabre images of piled-up coffins with bodies awaiting burial appeared in newspapers.

Bradford was not immune from the unrest spreading around the country. At the turn of the twentieth century, its wool traders had made the city rich, attracting businessmen from all over the world to West Yorkshire. T. S. Eliot's classic poem 'The Waste Land' refers to Bradford millionaires and their 'silk hats', which was a dig at the crop of rich wool traders who were suddenly able to buy Rolls-Royces, grand homes and silk top hats, to the bemusement of the south's gentry and London's literary circles. Italian street performers brought dancing bears to the city centre, Jewish traders built beautiful warehouses in the neighbourhood dubbed 'Little Germany', and the wealth generated by a robust transatlantic trade paid for a towering gothic Wool Exchange with roof parapets and corbelled turrets. The city specialised in high-quality wool yarn known as 'worsted', which earned it the nickname the Worstedopolis.

In the early 1950s, Bradford's wool trade still boasted more than 130 weaving plants and 110 spinning mills, while 45,000 people were employed in wool-textile processing. But by the second half of the 1960s, the industry was crumbling. Mills were closing at a frightening rate as Bradford's companies were undercut by cheaper foreign imports and consumer choices shifted, with shoppers opting for synthetic materials over wool.

Strikes became commonplace as workers attempted to cling onto what only a few years earlier had looked like jobs for life. Mill owners' cars were stoned, and a series of suspicious fires at mills across the district caused millions of pounds worth of damage, making the situation even more desperate. Slowly, job titles such as ligger, tatler, burler, hoodturner, and capsteamer became obsolete. In 1969, a report into the decline recommended a radical overhaul: the industry would need to shrink by 40 per cent in order for the city to cling onto at least some of the mills that had made it.[11]

The malaise and decline that was gripping Bradford was being mirrored across the UK. Bradford had flourished while Britain still had an empire, one that stretched across the globe and made it a genuine superpower. But those days, like the dominance of Bradford's wool merchants were over.

In *Blacks Britannica*, the academic Colin Prescod delivers a cutting critique of the UK's international status. 'The truth is that Great Britain is not so great any more,' he says. 'Its Empire has been taken away and the economy is technically bankrupt.' He was right. By the early 1960s, most former British colonies had gained independence. In 1976, the Callaghan government was forced to borrow money from the International Monetary Fund, a nadir known as the Sterling crisis, when the currency depreciated while inflation rose to 25 per cent.[12] But the Winter of Discontent wasn't Britain's first moment of unwelcome humility on the international stage. The Second World War signalled the beginning of the end for Britain as an imperial power. The Suez Crisis of 1956, in which Britain, along with Israel, attempted to overthrow President Gamal Abdel Nasser of Egypt, resulted in a humiliating defeat that alienated many of the UK's allies. By the turn of the 1960s, the United States and Soviet Union had taken Britain's position as true superpowers.

Prescod wasn't alone in his assessment of Britain as a country in decline. At the climax of the BBC's 1979 adaptation of John le Carré's spy thriller *Tinker, Tailor, Soldier, Spy*, the treacherous British agent explains their motivations for switching allegiance to Russia: 'Britain? Oh dear,' says the turncoat. 'No viability whatsoever in world affairs. I suppose that's when it began: turning my eyes to the East. When I saw how trivial we'd become as a nation.' In his view, Britain had lost its lofty international position and become 'America's streetwalker'.[13] Norman Tebbit, who would become a mainstay in Margaret Thatcher's government, said, looking back at the 1970s, that Britain didn't have 'the power, the bite or the prestige' and that it was 'a terrible feeling'.[14] Bradford's decline was a key example of that as the textile boom turned into a seemingly unstoppable bust.[15]

In her very first speech as leader in 1975, Thatcher rallied against those who would depict the UK as 'a poor nation whose only greatness lies in the past.'[16] Four years later, at the Conservative conference in Blackpool, she returned to the idea: 'It is said that Britain's time is up, that we have had our finest hour,' she told members,[17] referencing one of the most famous speeches from the Second World War, made by her political hero, Churchill. But Britain, Thatcher argued, was a sleeping giant that should be shaken out of its slumber with radical right-wing policies. The UK needed to become a 'wealth-creating society', where free market principles, a new radical economic programme in the form of monetarism, and an adversarial approach to dealing with the unions were embraced. She was rejecting the post-war consensus that allowed for collectivist policies and a large welfare state. Her vision for a bold, neo-liberal Britain was a key selling point of the Conservative leader – but Thatcher would also use immigration as a wedge issue to set her apart from Callaghan as she geared up for a charge toward 10 Downing Street.

The Conservative leader had set out her stall as anti-immigration with her explosive 'swamped' interview on *World in Action* in January 1978. A year on, charged with having changed her position on immigration, she stated, defiantly, 'I never modified it. I stood by it 100 per cent.'[18] She continued, 'Some people have felt swamped by immigrants. They've seen the whole character of their neighbourhood change.' It was cities like Bradford that she was referring to.

Before the First and Second World Wars, immigration into the city was mostly Irish, with a smaller proportion coming from southern and central Europe – including a substantial German population. But post-war Bradford became a destination for refugees from Poland, Ukraine and others fleeing the Soviet regimes of Eastern Europe, while citizens of Commonwealth nations, including Caribbean islands, but primarily Pakistanis, moved to Bradford to work in its wool industry. Over the course of a couple of decades in the post-war period, the city went from a largely white, Northern European city to a cosmopolitan centre with a population drawn from all over the former British Empire.

Thatcher's approach to Britain's new Black population wasn't original, although she was the first prime ministerial candidate to openly appeal to a racist voter base since the Second World War. She was echoing the sentiments of the far-right National Front, which, as we've seen, had become one of the most important political forces of the 1970s.

In 1976, the National Front leadership was buoyant – they'd just had a breakthrough set of election results in Bradford. The group won 9,399 votes in the district council elections, up from 1,364 the year before. The group's leaders John Tyndall and Martin Webster pronounced that they were keen to use the result to 'build their most powerful regional organisation outside of London'.[19]

They'd been targeting the city for years. When the anti-fascist play *Do You Remember Cable Street?*, which told the story of pitched battles in 1936 between Jews and fascists in Bethnal Green, was put on at Bradford Central Library in 1975, National Front members attempted to storm the building. Anti-Semitic abuse and threats were made to the owners of the left-wing Fourth Idea bookshop, which would go on to have its windows smashed. NF supporters even attacked the local Labour Party Christmas fayre.

In April 1975, the NF marched through Bradford for a meeting at St George's Hall in the city centre. *Searchlight*, the anti-fascist magazine, reported that around 1,000 people attended, and that once inside St George's Hall, NF leader Martin Webster led the crowd in a call and response. When he shouted, 'If they're Black', the crowd responded, 'Send them back'.[20]

The NF's attention shifted between northern cities like Bradford and the capital. In August 1977, there was a huge confrontation between the National Front and anti-fascists on the streets of Lewisham in South London, a location picked – like Bradford – because of its large immigrant population and because the group had substantial support in the area.[21] 'The Battle of Lewisham' was a day when the NF were physically and mentally battered: a community stood up and collectively said no to their presence.[22] But a year earlier, an equally significant clash had already taken place in Bradford; one which showed the city's Black population was beginning to organise against the threats it faced.

The NF came to Bradford in the spring of 1976 and were allowed to hold a meeting in a school in Manningham – a suburb just outside of the city centre that once housed wool merchants but was a multicultural area by the mid-1970s – 85 per cent of the children came from immigrant homes. The NF members were met by violent opposition on one of Manningham's main thoroughfares: Lumb Lane. The street, which still housed mills and other remnants of the textile industry, was known as the centre of Manningham's Asian community and would become the city's red-light district.[23] It still was when I grew up in the 1990s, and was the site of unrest in 1995 and 2001 when rioting swept through Asian communities in the north of England. But it was also the frontline for Bradford's Black population during the late 1970s.

A frontline could be found in every town and city with a Black presence – it was a physical space occupied by Black Britons, one where outsiders, especially the police, had to tread carefully. On the frontline, pubs didn't operate a colour bar, the record shops sold reggae, and the cafes were Black-owned and had names like Young Lion, a nod to the growing influence of Rastafarianism.[24]

It could be an intimidating space for outsiders. The filmmaker Pratibha Parmar was at Bradford University and remembers the palpable racial tension in the neighbourhood. 'There I was this South Asian chick from London, with my long black hair and the Afghan coat, platform shoes. There would be a lot of staring: a combination of what are you doing here that were really hateful, to just pure curiosity as to who I was,' she told me. 'Because no South Asian girls went into a pub in Lumb Lane at that time, particularly with white boys – I was a bit of an anomaly.'

The frontline was also a boundary which some Black Bradfordians stayed within. When Mwinyipembe came to the city and spoke to young people, she'd find many of them 'had not travelled more than maybe a square mile where they live from home, maybe to school and back, and home to the shops, and that you don't go into that broader world – that was not open to you. Or you might go for a bit to get into trouble if you did.'

On hot summer days, groups of older West Indians would hang out by the Super Discount clothing shop, while youngsters played pool or the one-armed bandit.[25] Black Bradfordians might have to be on alert in the city centre where their presence could lead to arrest under Sus laws, which gave police the ability to stop and search people and arrest them on the mere suspicion of a crime. But on Lumb Lane, they felt safe. The street was a centre of Blackness, just like Lewisham was in south-east London, and the NF knew that the mere act of walking through it was a provocation.

Photographs from the NF march in 1976 show police cowering as bricks rain down, and people recall seeing older West Indians, in some cases likely parents or relatives of the young people throwing missiles and breaking paving stones to create more projectiles.

Around 600 NF supporters were met by a counter-protest that grew to 3,000, made up of anti-fascists, the anti-racist Asian Youth Movement and Black Bradfordians.[26] The confrontation would become known as the 'Battle of Bradford'.

In the aftermath of the confrontation, a journalist captured a conversation between a West Indian man and his teenage nephew that hints at the new, more militant attitude that was emerging in Bradford's Black population. In a cafe on Lumb Lane, the older man chastises his nephew. He warns him about alienating local white people who would otherwise reject the NF's racism by retaliating violently against them. 'There's no way they will understand that things are changing fast around here, and the time's come when either the police stop them or we try to,' says the teenager. 'Some whites have protested for us, but they are not enough. There are enough of us round here, though. What else can we do?' The young man wasn't the only person searching for an answer to that question. Though a relatively small population, a core of activists in the city formed Bradford Black: a pressure group that mounted campaigns against poor housing conditions, racist employment practices and police harassment. An editorial in the first issue of the *Bradford Black* community magazine declared: 'There is a rebellion taking place in Britain today and the source of that rebellion is the Black community.' Word of this small but combative Black community was spreading far beyond the Worstedopolis of West Yorkshire.

When *Blacks Britannica* was greenlit, Koff and Mwinyipembe had travelled to London to speak to people connected to Black communities across the country. One of those people was Colin Prescod, a young academic who had grown up in the Black activist milieu of 1960s West London. His mother was Pearl Prescod, the actor and activist from Trinidad. Marcus Garvey's first wife, Amy Ashwood Garvey, was a regular visitor to the house and – as a key organiser of the fifth Pan-African Congress in Manchester, where anti-colonial leaders met to discuss the future of the continent – she'd instilled

Free George Lindo – Bradford, 1978

in him a sense that Black Britain was far bigger than the confines of the capital.

Once on board, Prescod was a hands-on rather than a back-seat consultant. He would venture out with Koff on shooting trips. The academic describes the team as 'storm chasers', loading up Koff's car with cameras and equipment and then heading out of London to cities and towns including Wolverhampton, Sheffield, Manchester and Bradford to film groups who, like the young man on Lumb Lane, were questioning their position in Britain. Everywhere they looked, it seemed another Black community was fighting a battle, whether against the far right, a deportation case against the Home Office or, increasingly, against police harassment.

'Somebody would say, "Well, actually, this action is happening, or this meeting is happening, right now or next week",' says Prescod, and the car would be loaded up. The team's approach was simple: 'We deliberately and very clearly go to the people who have authority in those spaces and we say, "What's happening?"' When the team got to Bradford, there was only one name on everyone's lips: George Lindo.

Born in Kingston, Jamaica on 12 December 1951, George Lindo moved to the UK in 1968, settling with his family in Bradford. After stints working in a warehouse and as a bus conductor, he became one of the thousands of new immigrants working in the city's fading textile industry, taking up a position at Tyersal Combing Company as a wool spreader – a physically taxing job that brought Lindo a weekly wage of £50. Lindo had a wife and two daughters and lived close to his parents and the majority of his eleven brothers and sisters.

The family home was busy as the siblings came and went, while the Lindos were known to help out Black Bradfordians who were struggling – offering food and sometimes a place to stay while people settled in the city. It wasn't unusual for people to stop by just to spend the day at the bustling house by St Luke's Hospital where George's mother Caroline Lindo worked (his father had a job in a foundry). Caroline's son rarely missed a day of work; he'd never been in trouble with the police, until one summer evening.

A keen amateur boxer and an occasional gambler, on 3 August 1977, Lindo went to a branch of William Hill's after work, at around 5 p.m. He placed his bet, then travelled to his parents' house, where he stayed for the rest of the evening. After Lindo had left the William Hill branch, it was robbed. A 'coloured' man wielding a knife and wearing a hooded top got away with £67 in a plastic bag after threatening the manager. Two witnesses who worked at the bookies named 'George Linda' as a suspect. On the same day that the *Telegraph and Argus* ran a photo-fit of the suspect, two police officers – including Police Constable David Brierley – went to Lindo's address and asked him why he'd robbed the William Hill's. Lindo said he hadn't, he'd been at his parents' house. The officers then took him to Laisterdyke Police Station before transferring him to Bradford Central Station, the Tyrls.

He was refused a phone call to his family or solicitor. As he sat in a cell in only a T-shirt, he felt as if cold air was being piped into the room.[27] The officers then began a series of interrogations where they put pressure on Lindo to confess. He refused. Lindo asked for a phone call – he was denied again. He later reported that he was denied even a glass of water. After twenty hours in custody, and more pressure applied by the commanding officer, who allegedly threatened to put Lindo in handcuffs and parade him in front of his neighbours, he agreed to confess, with an officer writing down his dictated statement. On 8 August, Lindo was charged and released on bail. Tired, worn out and traumatised, Lindo's life had just changed forever. 'My brother was the last person you'd expect to do something like that,' John Lindo, George's younger brother, told me. 'It was so completely out of character that it seemed like it must be some sort of terrible joke.'

On 15 February 1978, an all-white jury at Bradford Crown Court found George Lindo guilty. Two weeks later, on 2 March, Lindo was sentenced by Judge Bennett of Leeds Crown Court to two years in prison, despite the judge saying in his summing up that there was no evidence except for the police officers' account. When the sentence was passed, Lindo went into a state of shock, and as he was taken down to the cell, he started to cry and pull his hair. Lindo's barrister and a supporter came down to console him and tell him that it hadn't finished yet: they were going to fight this case to the end.[28] He was twenty-six years old.

What had happened to Lindo wasn't uncommon in 1970s Britain. Young Black men being framed or 'fitted up' by the police happened at an alarming rate. In 1972, four men were arrested and charged with assaulting an officer and attempted theft at the underground stop in Oval, London. Known as the 'Oval Four', Winston Trew, Sterling Christie, George Griffiths and Constantine 'Omar' Boucher would be convicted after signing confessions written by Derek Ridgewell, who was British but had trained as a police officer in white-minority-ruled Rhodesia (now Zimbabwe) before returning to the UK and joining the British Transport Police.[29] He first came to people's attention after he fled the African country claiming the force he'd joined was 'a military organisation designed to suppress the Africans'. Despite his apparent concerns about prejudice, Ridgewell was in fact one of the most notorious racist officers in British history. His usual tactic was to confront young Black men at Tube stations, accuse them of theft, and then arrest them for assaulting police officers. He was involved in several cases that were acquitted, including the Waterloo Four and the Tottenham Court Road Two. An appeals court freed the Oval Four in 1973 but it took forty-seven years for the convictions to be quashed.[30] Five of the Stockwell Six were convicted in 1972 and it took until 2021 to have their convictions overturned.[31] But he was by no means alone: other officers in the capital would boast about being able to fit up young Black men for ridiculous crimes, knowing that a judge would side with the police.

It wasn't just in London where police racism was rife. The police in West Yorkshire already had a reputation among Black Britons following the death of David Oluwale in Leeds. Oluwale came to the UK from Nigeria in the 1940s with hopes of becoming an engineer;

when he was not able to secure a place as a student, Oluwale worked as a tailor, foundry worker and slaughterhouse labourer before being sectioned and institutionalised for eight years. After his release, Oluwale became destitute and homeless on the streets of Leeds. Here, he became the target of persistent harassment by two West Yorkshire Police officers, Inspector Geoffrey Ellerker and Sergeant Kenneth Kitching. They'd search for him in shop doorways, beat him up, and sometimes drive him miles out of town – dumping him in a remote location without any means of returning to the city. Eventually, the thirty-eight-year-old's body was found in the River Aire in 1969.[32]

In 1976, twelve Black teenagers from Leeds were arrested and charged after disturbances during Bonfire Night in Chapeltown. Just like with Lindo, forced confessions were the basis of the police case, but inconsistencies in the case meant the jury acquitted the young men on twenty-one out of the twenty-five charges.[33] By the mid-1970s, concerns over police tactics – especially the safety of confessions – were becoming harder to ignore. What had happened to Lindo wasn't an improvised ruse; it was a well-rehearsed routine taken from a playbook used by officers across the UK to secure swift convictions, especially in cases involving young Black men.[34]

The community couldn't believe what had happened. Della George, a young fashion student in a relationship with one of Lindo's cousins, remembers the news spreading through the Caribbean community. People would talk about it in the cafes on Lumb Lane: how did the police think they'd get away with doing this to Lindo? He was a family man. 'It was unbelievable that something like that could happen in our community,' George told me. 'We would hear about things going on in London, but for it to be on our own doorstep was shocking.'

The guilty verdict might have surprised Black Bradfordians, but the last decade of National Front provocation and harassment by the police had prepared them to respond. Once in Bradford, the *Blacks Britannica* filmmakers' main contact was a man called Courtney Hay. On-screen, he wears a black, gold and green beanie, a bomber jacket, a turtle-neck jumper and dark sunglasses – the picture of Black British radical chic.

Born in Jamaica, before settling in Coventry and studying in Hull, Hay moved to Bradford in 1976 and brought with him a new, militant approach to community activism that was imbued with the energy of Black Power and the defiance of his mother. In the film he says, 'I learned my politics in my mother's kitchen,' before drawing a line between his mother's activism – she burned sugar cane fields in Jamaica – and his own in 1970s Bradford. 'The point that I was making was that I didn't come to the beliefs that I have, and the view that I have, by necessarily reading books,' Hay tells me. He listened to his parents talking about the Moyne Commission,[35] set up by the British after a series of violent rebellions in Jamaica during the 1930s that paved the way for independence. Defiance was something Hay had grown up with and now he and the rest of Bradford's Black population were going to have to react.

On the night of Lindo's conviction, Hay, other supporters and the Lindo family met in a flat off Manchester Road just north of the city centre. The mood was one of disbelief among the forty or so people who had gathered. George had an alibi and no criminal record, and his case was supported by evidence that undermined the flimsy police account but, still, an innocent man was going to prison. People tried to lift the mood; George's legal team offered potential appeal tactics. That night, the George Lindo Action Committee was formed. Made up of local activists, including Gus John (who was studying at the university), Ali Hussein, Sister B (who was Hay's wife Beryl) and Hay, they would lead a campaign to free Lindo.

There were dozens of action or defence committees around the UK in the 1970s, as Black communities fought back against what they saw as unjust verdicts. Made up of activists and volunteers, they would raise awareness of an issue through protests and media campaigns. Lindo's defence committee would be run from Textile Hall, a remnant of the old industry that had been turned into a community hub. Hay and the rest of the committee, which included

Pratibha Parmar, would also start a new publication: *Bradford Black*, a community magazine that would be their mouthpiece.

The case had made waves in the capital, too: many Black Bradfordians drove down the M1 to party in London at the weekends, and news of the case had travelled with them, as well as through the networks that Hay and other committee members were plugged into. Joining the committee would be London-based activists, primarily from the Race Today Collective, made up of Darcus Howe, Leila Hassan Howe, John La Rose, Roxy Harris and Linton Kwesi Johnson. The group were the best allies the Lindo campaign could have had.

Hay had met Howe while he was studying in Hull and knew of him as part of the Mangrove Nine, a group of activists from London who'd won a landmark case in 1971. They took part in a fifty-five-day trial at the Old Bailey, accused of incitement to riot, affray and – in some instances – attacking police officers. Assisted by defence barrister Ian MacDonald, who would be part of Lindo's legal team, they sought to expose racial bias. The strategy worked: all nine defendants were acquitted of the main charges of incitement to riot. But what really moved the needle was Judge Edward Clarke's closing comments. 'What this trial has shown is that there is clearly evidence of racial hatred on both sides,' he told the courtroom.[36] It was the first judicial acknowledgment of racism in the Met, nearly three decades before the Macpherson Inquiry that would follow the murder of Stephen Lawrence in 1993.

Hay was impressed by Howe's ideas and oration, and he knew Race Today supported grass-roots campaigns, which chimed with its three core aims: supporting anti-colonialist movements, women's liberation and advancing the Black Power struggle.[37] The group was battle-hardened and experienced. They'd used inventive methods to outwit the state and had a network of press connections who, while they wouldn't necessarily give them the most favourable coverage, would provide them with a platform.

The battle lines were drawn: the police had targeted Lindo, a perfect everyman figure for a campaign about corrupt and racist policing. He was innocent, had no prior record and came from one of the most respected Black families in Bradford. The police could have hardly picked a worse person to target. Moreover, the city's Black population was used to fighting back, be it against the far right or police harassment. The defence committee that had assembled, helped by Race Today who brought with them a national profile, would ensure this wasn't just another case of a young Black man being fitted up. It was an attack on Black Bradford itself, and one that would mobilise thousands of supporters.

One of the very first scenes in *Blacks Britannica* is of the defence committee outside of Armley Prison in Leeds on a miserable rainy day, as dozens of Black Bradfordians scream George's name. Lindo could hear the chanting from inside of Armley; other prisoners would comment on the support he was getting, while prison guards would taunt with sarcastic pronouncements of 'Free George Lindo' when he picked up his breakfast.

Bradford textile mills dominated the city's skyline but by the late 1970s were beginning to close

Outside the prison, the George Lindo Action Committee was busy. Protests were happening on a regular basis as the Lindo family and their supporters continued to make noise about George's conviction, seeing an opportunity to reframe the event in a wider context of institutional racism that went to the top of government.

In February 1978, Howe travelled to Bradford to deliver a speech titled 'Enter Mrs Thatcher'. It was a month after Thatcher's 'swamped' comments and Howe told the crowd in Bradford who'd gathered to celebrate the first anniversary of Bradford Black how he saw her as another British leader Black people would have to fight against. 'Maggie Thatcher, I knew her before,' said Howe. 'She was [Stanley] Baldwin, she was Churchill, she was Ramsay MacDonald, she was Ernest Bevin, she was all those in the history of our constant struggles against them. Sometimes we won a bit, other times we lost, but it is a struggle which has been going on for a very long historical period. This is only another stage.'[38] In April, there was another 300-person strong rally that ended with a young man reciting a powerful poem about Lindo over a megaphone. The man was the British-Jamaican musician and activist Linton Kwesi Johnson, who'd arrived in London with his family aged eleven. The poem would eventually become a song, 'It Dread Inna Inglan', appearing on his 1978 album *Dread Beat An' Blood* – a record that mixed dub-reggae and poetry, while capturing the disaffection of a generation of Black youth in Britain. 'Linton was quick to remind his audience that Britain's first generation of Black workers had been offered unskilled, exploitative jobs,' wrote the Black British author and academic Caryl Phillips. 'While their children, the second generation, were being marginalised by the school system, harassed by the police and faced the seemingly lifelong prospect of unemployment.'[39]

What Howe, Kwesi Johnson and the other activists knew was the Lindo case was symbolic of the wider struggle they were engaged in with the British state. They wanted to raise people's awareness, not only in the Black community but also wider white society, of what racist policies were doing to new Britons who had moved to cities like Bradford. *Blacks Britannica*'s 'storm chasers' were on hand to witness what was happening to George Lindo. The film starts with a shot of individuals playing tennis, and exterior shots of grand, white-walled West London homes, before cutting to people outside Armley shouting for George's release. The flattened vowels of the accents placing the protestors firmly in Bradford. Shots of Bradford's mills, defunct, derelict – a reminder that the city's textile industry had collapsed at the same time racism against its Black population had spiked.

Blacks Britannica does something no other production had done up to that point: it gives Black Britons a platform and takes their arguments seriously. Their points aren't dismissed, as they might be in newspaper columns or television interviews, but instead they're allowed to resonate and linger. After Colin Prescod argues that the state 'manipulates' Black people by rehousing them and demolishing their homes in so-called 'slum clearance' programmes, there's an image of a policeman on a white horse riding through the rubble of Moss Side and Hulme. The activist Ron Phillips argues that the intention of these urban renewal programmes isn't to improve the lives of residents but to 'destroy the Black community', a line of thinking that few British people watching would have ever heard before.

Those calling for the repatriation of Black Britons also appear: Enoch Powell warns in a speech that Black people are increasingly 'occupying' key areas and functions in the 'heartland of the kingdom', while the National Party leader John Kingsley Read promises to 'fight you with every bone, every nerve, every feeling, every ounce of blood we've got,' before screaming 'we will have our country back'. Two young Black men talk about how police use the Sus laws (aka the Vagrancy Act of 1824, brought in after the Napoleonic wars to control the homeless population) against them when they head into the centre of London to see a friend and buy a coat. A plainclothes officer followed them down Oxford Street and arrested the pair for 'loitering with intent to commit an arrestable offence'. Ian Macdonald, the QC who defended several of the Mangrove Nine and later represented George Lindo, explains on camera that Sus is used to stop someone who the police believe is 'about' to commit a crime. The precise number of young Black people arrested using Sus is unknown, but in 1979 Home Office research showed that Black people were fifteen times more likely to be stopped by police using the law than whites.[40]

There's a rotating cast of voices, from the activists John La Rose and Darcus Howe to the founder of Notting Hill Carnival Claudia Jones and Manchester community figures Ron Phillips and Kath Locke. They spell out the issues being faced by Black Britons. British education 'sets out to remove any feature that might threaten society . . . and Blackness is a threatening feature', says Phillips. The left-wing intellectual Ambalavaner Sivanandan argues that 'what Enoch Powell says today, the Conservative Party says tomorrow and the Labour Party legislates on the day after', while John La Rose says if Black communities were to organise self-defence groups to protect themselves from fascists 'you can rest assured the police would be attacking us'.

It's not just a list of grievances – there's an implicit warning that the status quo can't continue. Courtney Hay argues that capitalism is failing Black Britons: 'if capitalism is not working then capitalism has to go'. Then there's a jump cut to a brick being thrown through a police car windscreen at the 1976 Notting Hill Carnival.

What's remarkable now is that the film doesn't condemn this violent act – it presents it as a natural reaction to the circumstances Black Britons found themselves in. 'When a policeman step on one of your foot, you step back,' says Hay. 'You won't stay in your place – that's why they're gunning for you.' Sivanandan reappears towards the end of the film and says that Black youth are refusing to occupy the place in society that the state wants them to. 'You want to make us do the shit work that our parents did,' he says. 'They're saying get stuffed, fuck you – we're not going to do that.' Even after only a few minutes, it's clear what the throughline is: Black Britain feels under attack, not just from far-right groups but from the state itself, and Black Britain is more than prepared to fight back.

*

Free George Lindo – Bradford, 1978

Lindo was moved from Armley to Strangeways Prison in Manchester, notorious for its NF-supporting prison guards, for a brief spell before eventually being transferred to Preston. After a few weeks, he was called into the governor's office. On the outside, the defence committee had had a breakthrough. News had reached them that Constable Brierley, one of the two men who'd extracted Lindo's 'confession', had been suspended – and gone on to resign – from the West Yorkshire Police several months earlier. Brierley had been working on the Yorkshire Ripper case, which was the biggest investigation ever mounted by police in the county and had been asked to re-interview a potential suspect who had been interviewed by another officer earlier in the investigation. When the two interviews were reviewed, even the most basic of facts didn't tally – senior officers were forced to face the fact Brierley had made up evidence in the most notorious serial murder investigation the UK had ever seen. He'd also been involved in the arrest of a man accused of rape who had allegedly confessed, only for another man to come forward and admit to the crime a few days later. Although Brierley had resigned on 25 September 1978, the police, the Director of Public Prosecutions and the Court of Appeal, didn't inform Lindo's defence team until late February 1979.[41]

On 8 March, a successful bail application was made and George Lindo walked out of Preston. He'd served just over a year of his sentence and would have been due for parole on 19 March. When George was finally cleared, and his conviction quashed in June 1979, Lord Justice Lawton, Mr Justice Wien and Mr Justice Eastham who oversaw the appeal said they found it 'the most disturbing case'. Lindo didn't say anything to the assembled journalists when he left the appeals court. Instead, his mother Caroline told reporters: 'I knew my boy hadn't done this because I was cooking a meal for him at the time he was supposed to have done the job. We're going straight back to Bradford and tonight we're going to have a big West Indian party.' An editorial in *Bradford Black* celebrated the outcome, declaring, 'George Lindo is back in town', while the *Daily Telegraph* ran with the headline 'INNOCENT MAN FRAMED BY DETECTIVE' and accompanied it with a picture of Lindo and his two daughters: Dawn and Rachel, who clung tightly to their father.

In April 1982, Lindo was awarded almost £25,000 in compensation – a quarter of the George Lindo Action Committee's demand for £100,000. Lindo needed the money. He'd struggled to find work after his release, eventually getting a job alongside his father at the foundry in Low Moor. 'When the money comes through, I will pay my debts,' he told reporters. 'Then take my family on holiday to try and relax for the first time in four years. I should have got more, but my needs are urgent.' Despite the disappointing compensation, the Lindo case had been – in comparison to almost every other similar campaign at the time – a resounding success. He'd been released, the conviction quashed, and the state had paid compensation after a locally run campaign that made him a household name. Bradford's Black community had, as Johnson said in 'It Dread Inna Inglan', rallied round and shown that fewer than 3,000 Black Bradfordians could bring change. It was a landmark result for everyday Black Britons, too. 'The Mangrove Nine were activists,' says Hay. 'George Lindo was a textile worker. That was the first successful campaign for a rank-and-file, working class, Black guy who'd been fitted up by police and it was won within fifteen months.'

Even though the campaign had been relatively swift, the impact of the case affected Lindo for the rest of his life. Time in prison had changed George. His brother John noticed how quiet he'd become, and how he threw himself into religion. He began attending Bible groups, reading scripture – searching for solace in the word of God. Others who'd been wrongly imprisoned also struggled to piece their lives back together. Winston Trew of the Oval Four said his experience of being arrested in 1972 destroyed his life. 'My marriage broke up,' he said in 2019.[42] 'I lost confidence, and I felt incredibly lonely.' Just as for Lindo, the trial and sentence caused great distress to his family. Trew said that the corrupt police officer Derek Ridgewell had thrown 'a hand grenade into my life and shattered it'; just as Brierley had done to Lindo. It took Trew decades to rebuild his confidence. Lindo wouldn't talk about the case or his time in

Free George Lindo – Bradford, 1978

George Lindo with his wife Carole and daughter Rachel after his release in 1979

prison, right up until his death from leukaemia a decade after his imprisonment, aged only thirty-seven years old.

Blacks Britannica was supposed to air in the US in July 1978. It didn't. When Koff played the original cut to WGBH-Boston director David Fanning, the network boss was so disturbed by the film and its polemic nature that it was pulled, and another version was recut without Koff's or Mwinyipembe's consent. 'What about the guy in the wheat field in Kansas?' Fanning reportedly asked Koff. 'He'll call us Communists.'[43] In Britain, the reaction was even stronger: *Blacks Britannica* was seen as so dangerous that diplomats scrambled to ban it outright.

In the UK, the film was shown at the Scala cinema in London's

King's Cross, then a hotbed for left-wing cinephiles. WGBH got an injunction against the film being shown, just as Margaret Henry – an American PhD student who worked as a researcher on the film and was briefly married to Koff – was coming to the end of hosting two daily screenings of the documentary at the Scala. 'They put an injunction forbidding us from showing it to anybody, so I just stole the print after one of the screenings,' said Henry. She had some help from sympathetic employees at the Scala who turned a blind eye as she made off with the only copy not in the possession of WGBH, and the subterfuge was important. The filmmakers had hoped that their documentary would have a second life in the UK after it aired in America. Henry continued to arrange private screenings, inviting TV executives and prominent critics. The idea was once America had had its assumptions about Britain and race challenged, the UK itself would be confronted by the arguments of Prescod and the Lindo protests.

WGBH was concerned about the film's Marxist perspective and, by extension, accusations of communist sympathies. The US had been deeply affected by the McCarthyite 'red scare' of the 1950s in the midst of the Cold War with the Soviet Union, when anyone with even a loose connection to far-left politics could be dragged before a committee or blacklisted. The station was also a bastion of liberal America, and saw its role as a race relations mediator: after the assassination of Dr Martin Luther King in 1968, the station had agreed to screen a live James Brown concert that was happening in Boston in an attempt to keep young Black people off the street.[44] The plan worked and the widespread violence that had engulfed many cities did not occur in Boston, a city with a long history of racial tension. *Blacks Britannica*, with its confrontational style and polemic arguments, grated against those softer liberal ideals. In Britain, the pushback was about preserving Britain's image as a country free from racial conflict. The film was hammered from the left and right of the political divide.

After Conservative MP Dudley Smith, who was vice-chairman of the Select Committee on Race Relations and Immigration,[45] complained about *Blacks Britannica* to the US ambassador, its UK premiere was cancelled by court order. Edinburgh Film Festival was pressured to pull a screening, while the Commission for Racial Equality prepared statements that countered the film's claims and would run on editorial pages if it was shown.

Back in the US, diplomats were also applying pressure. The Deputy Director of the British Information Service – an arm of the UK government that sought to promote the country's interest in America – called the film 'dangerous', and demanded that WGBH produce a programme showing race relations in Britain in a better light.[46] The reaction led to calls of censorship on both sides of the Atlantic. The film critic Peter Biskind said that the recut version, which aired in America on 10 August, was 'an object lesson in the anatomy of censorship', while adding that the decision was 'a serious setback not only for Britain's Blacks, who rarely get a chance to make themselves heard, but also for American independent filmmakers'. 'The mere thought that this upstanding and well-thought-of country could be somehow described as being something other than that was really, really hard for people to take,' Mwinyipembe told me. 'It's a bit like [someone saying] "racism, *moi*? No that happens over there in America". We don't do that.'

The response to *Blacks Britannica* became one in a series of examples of repressive British state intervention in films made about Black Britons. Horace Ové's 1977 landmark production *Pressure*, the first ever Black feature film, had its release delayed by three years because Ové refused to recut a scene depicting police brutality, which its funder – the British Film Institute – believed was too radical. Three years later Franco Rosso's *Babylon*, about the exploits of a young reggae sound system in South London, was given an 'X' certificate in the UK, meaning no one under the age of eighteen could watch it, while it was banned outright in the US because of its depiction of the sound system crew fighting back against the police and racists. One scene in particular, which depicted the lead character stabbing a far-right street thug, was seen as too controversial.

Even though *Blacks Britannica*'s British premiere had been pulled,

Margaret Henry had arranged successful press screenings at the Scala. *Time Out*'s Mike Phillips – whose brother Ron was in the film – called it 'a bold, thoughtful and penetrating [film]', *Variety* described it as 'an unsettling portrait of an England in transition', while the *Village Voice*'s critic, Alexander Cockburn, claimed it was a film 'that not only reveals, analyses and explores, but mobilised'. There were dissenting voices, too. The *Observer*'s Philip French dismissed it as 'a slick, simple-minded agitprop picture of the sort that unfairly brings serious Marxist thought into disrepute.'[47] BBC executives also hosted a screening but decided against airing it because it wasn't 'balanced'.

Koff, Mwinyipembe, Prescod and Margaret Henry fought, and ultimately won, a four-year legal battle to be able to show their version of the film in the US. That meant the film was able to have the second life they craved for it, although mostly outside the UK. Henry and Koff showed it to enthusiastic audiences at festivals around the world, including Melbourne, Leipzig, Florence and even Baghdad. Their victory came with a high price: they were labelled 'difficult'. Koff and Mwinyipembe made one more film, the 1981 documentary *Occupied Palestine*, which looked at life for Palestinians under Israeli occupation.[48] But, increasingly, television executives and film producers gave them a wide berth, the upward trajectory they'd enjoyed since the Oscar nomination in 1976 slowing to a grinding halt. 'The filmmaking dried up, they couldn't get funding for any more documentaries,' says the pair's son, Kimera. 'If you're going to make a film like *Blacks Britannica* and fight for it to be shown the way you made it, while everyone is saying no, it's going to make life very difficult for you. It was also politically very volatile to talk unapologetically about racism in England, or to look with an historical viewpoint about the displacement of Palestinians. They weren't welcomed messages.' Koff and Mwinyipembe had already sacrificed a lot to make *Blacks Britannica* – moving their two small children, Kimera and his sister Clea, first to London and then to rural Norfolk where they were cared for by a nanny so the pair could go storm chasing around Britain. Now they were essentially blacklisted – seen as troublemakers whose politics didn't fit with the America of neoconservatives like Ronald Reagan.[49]

Despite the legal victory in the US, *Blacks Britannica* was never shown on British TV. Perhaps if it had been, I'd have come across George Lindo's name as a child and young man growing up in Bradford. I am part of that story: my Nigerian father moved to the city in March 1978, after studying in Stuttgart, to work in the textile trade – where he met my mother. When, while writing this book, I mention the case with people of my generation, no one has any knowledge of it. Despite having made local and national headlines, the Lindo story and *Blacks Britannica* have since faded from view, known only to the generation of Bradfordians for whom Lumb Lane was a frontline.

The banning of *Blacks Britannica* was a wasted opportunity to listen to the complaints that were coming from frontlines up and down the UK, including Bradford. Despite the film's arguments being dismissed by some quarters of the liberal media, George Lindo was framed, unemployment among Black people was eye-wateringly high, Sus was being disproportionately used against young Black men. Communities were being denied access to good-quality housing, while immigration law was being tweaked to make it harder for more Black people to become British. These weren't paranoid delusions or a Marxist fantasy. They were problems that continued to be denied until the summer of 1981, when thousands of Black Britons made their anger known during months of unrest.

In 1978, *Blacks Britannica* offered the political establishment an opportunity to look at the treatment of Black Britons and change direction. The police could have been reformed, the criminal justice system investigated for racial bias, confessions could have been ruled out as key evidence unless there was certainty they weren't taken under duress.

Instead, when Margaret Thatcher became prime minister, one of the first things she did was give the police a 45 per cent pay increase – an endorsement for hardline policing that echoed Darcus Howe's prediction toward a more authoritarian politics coming from 10

Downing Street. She knew that her new vision of Britain wouldn't come into being without conflict, and having the police onside was vital to her success. As Martin Amis observed, the creation of the 'ten-grand-a-year policeman' was to create someone 'who could be trusted to keep a lid on the new underclass, once it started to boil'.[50]

The final scene of Koff and Mwinyipembe's original version of *Blacks Britannica* features the Birmingham reggae group Steel Pulse performing their song 'Handsworth Revolution'. In the same year as Lindo's conviction was quashed, Birmingham's Black population – especially in Handsworth, where Rastafarianism was taking hold – was thrust into the media spotlight. The streets of the West Midlands were becoming another frontline, one where artists and academics would take on Thatcherism, her growing Law and Order agenda and the media portrayal of Black Britain, creating their own landmark productions. An academic called Stuart Hall, like Bradford Black, would counter the negative press Black Birmingham was receiving with his own broadside. He'd use his experience in Birmingham to take on the biggest media organisation in Britain, the BBC, and show how the publicly funded broadcaster, known affectionately as 'aunty', was complicit in the racism Black Britons faced.

3.

Jah Warriors – Birmingham, 1979

In 1975, the photographer Vanley Burke received a commission to take a portrait. Since arriving in Birmingham ten years earlier from a farm in the foothills of Jamaica's Blue Mountains, Burke had used his lens to cover the everyday lives of the second largest Black population in the UK. In his archive, images of well-heeled Jamaicans gathering for funerals sit beside placard-holding protesters and dancers enthralled by reggae sound systems. Parishioners close their eyes in prayer at church services, while tears of joy fall down their faces during weddings. But the commission represented something different. Burke reflected on its significance as he made his way to the University of Birmingham, where he was to take a portrait of a man who would become, arguably, the most important public intellectual of his generation, one who would challenge the media's racist portrayal of Black life in Britain, especially in its second city.

Like Burke, Stuart Hall had made his way to Birmingham from Jamaica. He arrived in Oxford as a Rhodes Scholar in 1951 and became a member of Britain's New Left – a group influenced by the Italian political theorist Antonio Gramsci and the Frankfurt School of Marxist academics. By the late 1970s, he was in charge of the Centre for Contemporary Cultural Studies (CCCS) at the University of Birmingham, a department that would produce pioneering work in the new field of cultural studies.

Burke photographed Hall in his office with papers spread across his desk, filing cabinets lining the walls and a noticeboard full of impending engagements. Hall appears to be in mid-conversational flow, with one arm outstretched as if to emphasise an important point. His beard is grown out and his hair is long enough to show his curls. The academic looks established, comfortable, confident – perhaps for good reason. Under his leadership, the CCCS had become a groundbreaking centre of intellectual study, one that shone a light on the ways in which the media, popular culture and politics interconnected to shape people's perceptions of the world around them. Hall would often look to the media for material to critique, but when it came to producing one of his most important pieces of work – a searing TV programme about racism in the British media – he would find inspiration directly outside his front door.

In the mid-1970s, no Black community's reputation was as bad as Birmingham's. The tabloid press had sparked a moral panic over mugging in the city – portraying Black areas as no-go zones for whites. A report by the race equality think-tank the Runnymede Trust described a state of 'warfare' between the police and local Black populace,[1] while Birmingham Council's housing strategy was declared racist.[2] The growing Rastafarian movement, which had a large base in Handsworth, was demonised by the press, while the police saw dreadlocked youth as deviants who were part of a subversive alien culture. It wasn't just Hall and Burke who were inspired by that combustible mix. By 1979, other Black British artists mined their experiences in the city to create groundbreaking work. Guyanese writer Michael Abbensetts would create the Black British sitcom *Empire Road*, shot on location in the city. The reggae band Steel Pulse released music that gave the city's Rasta movement a voice and called for a Handsworth Revolution. 'There were problems of housing, racial discrimination, policing, the "sus" laws; a second generation feeling they neither belonged in England nor anywhere else; the influence of reggae and Rastafarianism,'[3] Hall said when asked about his time in the city. 'It was impossible to be active and alive in Birmingham without being drawn into all that.'

I'd arranged to meet Vanley Burke at the Midlands Arts Centre (MAC) in the south of the city. It was lunchtime and the gallery's cafe was packed with young families. Burke emerged from the other side of the cafe and made his way slowly towards me through the

Jah Warriors – Birmingham, 1979

Vanley Burke's portrait of Professor Stuart Hall in his office at the Centre for Contemporary Cultural Studies at the University of Birmingham

din and half-eaten pizza slices. Tall and slim, often photographed wearing sunglasses and a trilby, Burke is a distinct presence in any space. But in the 1970s, he was often trying to blend in, in order to go unnoticed. 'I was witnessing a group of people coming into the country,' he said. Burke saw an opportunity to record one of the modern era's 'great migrations', like the Israelites following Moses out of Egypt, or the millions of African Americans who swapped the southern states for life in the north during the first half of the twentieth century. 'Imagine what a unique position I was in,' he said. As Burke focused his lens, it was on a city that was changing rapidly.

During the 1950s, West Indian immigration to the city rocketed. At the start of the decade, there were around 500 people from the Caribbean in the city – by 1961, the number had grown to 17,000. They arrived to a thriving city: the statesman and philosopher Edmund Burke had once called Birmingham the 'toy shop of Europe' – a reference to the city's numerous small manufacturers – and, shortly after the Second World War, around 400,000 people, or two-thirds of the workforce, were employed in some form of manufacturing. The new arrivals found jobs in automobile factories and foundries with relative ease, even if workplaces were not always welcoming. Racism was common: there were accusations of colour bars at motor companies, while an informal quota system was said to operate at a bus company to ensure Caribbean worker numbers were kept down.[4] During the 1965 general election in Smethwick, a town to the north-west of Birmingham, its Conservative MP, Peter Griffiths, had been elected on the slogan: 'If you want a nigger for a neighbour, vote Labour.'[5] The campaign had worked by inflaming white resentment over a lack of council housing, with the Conservatives blaming Labour and recent immigrants.[6] Those tensions would only get worse as the economic picture began to darken.

Up until 1966, the unemployment rate in the city was at a steady 1 per cent or 2 per cent. But by the start of the Thatcher era, Birmingham was in the middle of a period of intense and rapid decline, as the industry that powered the city began to falter. Just as in Bradford, where the textile trade had lost out to cheaper competitors, so too did Birmingham, as European and Japanese cars began to dominate the market. The recession that started in 1979 caused manufacturing output in the city to slump by 20 per cent and dramatically alter Birmingham's prospects. Derek Bishton, a photographer who worked for the *Birmingham Post* in the early 1970s, remembers the sudden shift in the city's fortunes. 'You could just walk into jobs in a place like Birmingham and now suddenly factories are closing down, and everything is changing,' he said. 'The whole landscape changed, and it changed in a decade.' The Typhoo Tea Factory in Digbeth and motorcycle company BSA (Birmingham Small Arms Company) in Small Heath closed, while the car manufacturer British Leyland had to seek government help to stay afloat.[7]

Just as in Bradford, another urban area with growing immigrant communities and climbing unemployment, the far right targeted the city. The National Front showed up in numbers to support Robert Ralph,[8] a white resident of Winson Green, who had been imprisoned for refusing to sell his house to an immigrant. Burke was on the street with his camera, taking a shot of the police line that protected the far-right group, with officers using dustbin lids as makeshift shields. Burke was present again when the NF were allowed to hold a meeting in Boulton Road School in 1977, just down the road from Handsworth.

Once a rich suburb of Birmingham, Handsworth's glory had faded during the first half of the twentieth century. Huge Victorian properties lined its main throughfare, Soho Road, while the grand neo-Gothic architecture of King Edward VI Grammar School nodded to its affluent past. By the 1970s, the area had become a centre not just for new Britons but for a thriving voluntary sector that helped people with issues ranging from housing to immigration. Multi-faith NGOs attempted to create racial harmony, while progressive organisations supported sex workers who walked the streets of Handsworth and Balsall Heath. There were pubs like the Crompton Arms where Lionel Martin, the Jamaican saxophonist known as Saxa, would play ska, reggae and two-tone with The Beat.[9] Communes could be found in Handsworth. Burke remembers droves of white middle-class sociologists coming to the area to study its Black residents. Bishton set up a photography collective on Grove Road – the same street where Burke's family ran a shop, while Black community groups like the African Caribbean Self-Help Organisation and Harambee OBU (Organisation of Black Unity) based themselves in the heart of the neighbourhood. 'Someone once told me that Handsworth in those days was a bit like what they imagined Greenwich Village was like,' Bishton said.

Paul Gilroy, the academic who studied for his PhD in Birmingham under Stuart Hall, said that Handsworth became the cultural and political frontline of Black Britain, just as Bradford had become during the campaign to free George Lindo in 1978. 'The frontline was like a prism,' Gilroy said. 'You put the light through it and then all the other things that were happening, race problems, are suddenly visible to you. And I think there was a spell when Handsworth was [that centre].' The Handsworth frontline that Gilroy witnessed was starting to come under the influence of a new movement. Birmingham's Black population – especially in the suburb of Handsworth – was distinctly Jamaican, and by the late 1970s Rastafarianism, a new import from the island, was about to dramatically change Britain's second city.

Leonard Percival Howell had a front-row seat to the Harlem Renaissance. The young Jamaican seaman relocated to the New York City borough in the 1920s, when writers like Langston Hughes and musicians like Louis Armstrong were turning the neighbourhood into a cultural mecca for Black Americans. But it wasn't the radical new literature or jazz that would capture Howell's imagination. Instead, in 1930, the coronation of a new African monarch would alter Howell's life forever.

Ras Tafari Makonnen Woldemikae, a thirty-eight-year-old member of the Ethiopian royal family and part of a dynasty that claimed lineage from King Solomon of Israel, was crowned king in a ceremony broadcast around the world. In Jamaica, people watched as the Duke of Gloucester, son of King George V, bowed respectfully before the new Black king. The author Evelyn Waugh travelled to East Africa to witness for himself the event that stretched to six long days of celebration. Film cameras followed the Duke as he arrived at Addis Ababa train station where the British national anthem was played while the Ethiopian monarch and the Englishman saluted.[10]

Howell watched Harlem as Ras Tafari officially became Emperor Haile Selassie, his guard mixing with British troops as equals. As the British representatives made their way to the ceremony, Waugh wrote that the Ethiopians 'supposed, rightly enough, that this magnificent array was there with the unequivocal purpose of courtesy towards their emperor.'[11] Millions watched as a European Duke did that rarest of things: paid respect to an African – something unimaginable during the era of British Imperialism where African monarchs were forced to pledge allegiance to Queen Victoria or King George.

The symbolic importance of the event was huge. Ethiopia was the only African country never to have been colonised, and because of that occupied a special place in the imagination of Pan-Africanist and Black Nationalist figures like Marcus Garvey, who argued that formerly enslaved peoples should 'return to Africa'. This was a country whose very existence pushed back against the racist idea that Africans were essentially infants in need of nurture and, if necessary, control through brute force.

In Harlem, Howell saw the coronation of the new king as a prophetic moment. Inspired by what he'd seen in New York and what he'd heard from Ethiopia, he began to preach that Jamaicans should no longer pay taxes to a white English king from a small island that had colonised and enslaved Black people. His position was considered 'seditious, revolutionary and insane' in Jamaica, but it would go on to inspire a worldwide movement. Howell had credentials: he'd met Garvey in Harlem and joined his Universal Negro Improvement Association, which advocated for the rights of Black people around the globe and had branches in dozens of countries. Howell's membership eventually saw him deported to Jamaica, along with Garvey, after the US government cracked down on the UNIA's leadership. Once back in the Caribbean, Howell instilled an idea that would prove potent: Black Jamaicans didn't owe their former colonisers a thing. Just the opposite, in fact: they had a huge debt that needed to be repaid after years of subjugation. Shortly after his return to Jamaica, he established a new religion, which took its name from the Black king. Rastafarianism was born.

Pogus Caesar[12] still remembers the first time he saw a Rastafarian on the streets of Birmingham. His friend Donville Lorenzo had been living in London and when he came back to the West Midlands, he had a nest of dreadlocks – the coiled hairstyle that would become synonymous with the religion – on his head. 'I'm talking natty dreads,' says Caesar of his friend, who would go on to become a roadie for The Clash. 'One thin, one thick. One looking like a tree trunk, another running down his back.'

When Caesar, who had arrived in Birmingham as an eight-year-old from St Kitts, walked the streets of Handsworth in the mid-1970s, he noticed a new ideology and aesthetic emerging. Rasta-led community groups had sprung up, the music of Burning Spear, Abyssinians and Dennis Brown were dominating the city's sound systems and communes run by Rastas were dotted around the area, including the House of Dread. Made up of three houses that had been knocked into one, and with around thirty Rastas living in it at any one time, the House of Dread was similar to a hippy commune, but with regular Bible-reading sessions and chanting accompanied by nyabinghi drums. No one owned a car; residents used bicycles. It was egalitarian and counter cultural. 'Everything was owned collectively, duties were shared and, as much as possible, we tried not to use money,'[13] said the poet Benjamin Zephaniah, who lived there briefly as a teenager.[14]

The core tenets of Rastafarianism were a rejection of western capitalism, its apparatus and the society it created – collectively referred to as 'Babylon'. Some Rastafarians smoked marijuana, ate a vegan ('Ital') diet and meditated. Followers of the new religion rebelled against what they saw as a system that could only produce racial oppression and disharmony. Musicians such as Count Ossie and the Mystic Revelation of Rastafari,[15] Ras Michael & the Sons of Negus and Ashanti Roy made records that exalted the teachings of the religion, while Bob Marley – who moved to the UK in 1976 – took Rastafarianism and reggae music to a worldwide audience.[16]

For young British Jamaicans like Mykaell Riley of the Birmingham reggae group Steel Pulse, Rastafarianism provided a potent new ideology. Riley, who attended church on Sundays, recalls feeling increasingly disillusioned with Christianity and unconvinced it could provide answers for a generation of young people questioning the logic of their parents, who still – on the whole – respected the Commonwealth and the mother country. 'As young Black males in the UK, we started to discover a narrative that challenged having the queen on the mantelpiece, because that represents the state,' he says. 'We started to find a narrative that challenged the constant racism within school that said, "we don't expect better of you. It is in your DNA to be late; it's in your DNA to fail". And that challenge

Jah Warriors – Birmingham, 1979

Steel Pulse pose for a portrait (Mykaell Riley stands third from the right)

was coming out of the music, is how I put it. It was coming out the lyrics, it was coming out of a message in the music. It was also coming out of a new sense of it being embedded in Rastafarianism at that moment in time.'

In Birmingham, Black Christian churches were the dominant religious force. Anglican, Methodist, Seventh Day Adventists and Pentecostal congregations, such as The Church of the Morning Star that – like Rastafarianism – had its roots in Harlem, could all be found in Handsworth.[17] Many families continued practices that had been imported from Jamaica, which had been brought in by colonising forces initially. Now a new dogma that centred Black African ideas and a radical worldview had landed in the West Midlands and was causing generational divides. 'There was always tension; I think that was exciting,' the artist Barbara Walker, who grew up in Handsworth, said. 'At that time, Bob Marley was in the background or Burning Spear, and it was a thing about consciousness and those opposites: Christianity and the Rastafarian sub-culture ... it was a penetrating voice at the time. You felt drawn to it, in many ways.'

But feeling drawn to religion was one thing, growing your hair into dreadlocks was something else entirely. Paul Gilroy, the academic who was studying in the city in 1979, decided to 'locks' his hair after interviewing Steel Pulse's David Hinds and talking at length with the musician – a Rastafarian – about the movement. 'I don't know if it's possible to really communicate these days how completely unacceptable it was,' Gilroy said. 'The equivalent today would be to have your face tattooed. Walking around [with dreads] produced maybe some fear, but mostly hostility. And not just from white folks on the bus or whatever, but from Black people too.' (One white pastor of a Black congregation of an Anglican church in Aston said parishioners were regularly asking him to help 'save their children from the Rastafarians'.)[18]

By adopting dreadlocks, Gilroy, Zephaniah, Hinds and Donville Lorenzo were doing something radical, but in Handsworth there were those who went much further. Rastas would attempt to stick to a rigid vegan diet, which was not easy in 1970s Britain, where processed meat was a staple, and a varied selection of vegetables (especially from the Caribbean) was hard to come by. They'd adhere to a strict dress code, which sometimes meant wearing sandals even as snow fell during a frigid Birmingham winter.

The religion also started to impact people's relationship to the police and the courts. The writer Ferdinand Dennis spent time working as an educational researcher in Handsworth during the 1970s, and the following decade would write a report on young Black offenders in the city, spending time at Birmingham's Victoria Law Courts. What he saw there was a display of defiance. 'The first Rasta defendant was charged with burglary,' he wrote. 'He dismissed the magistrate as an "agent of Babylon" unfit to pass judgment on him, a child of Zion. Soon, he warned, Babylon would be destroyed by thunder and lightning, brimstone and fire, and "the down-pressers of Jah's children" would perish.' Zephaniah articulated the sense of freedom and empowerment that the movement brought. 'There was something about the attitude we had that said: "We are taking on Babylon; we are Jah warriors."'[19] The fact that hundreds of young Black people were turning to this new Black religion didn't go unnoticed by the press or the police. Rasta was about to come under attack.

By 1979, a moral panic about Rastafarianism had taken hold in Birmingham, spread by newspaper articles that some Rastafarians believed were planted, possibly by the state, in an attempt to undermine the movement.[20] Headlines, including 'STREETS OF FEAR', 'WAVE OF TERROR', 'TERROR GANGS SHOCK' and one report in the *Birmingham Evening Mail* about two police officers being sent to Jamaica to 'gain a better understanding between Blacks and police', conjured a 'Handsworth Panic'.

Birmingham police, especially those operating out of Thornhill Road Station in Handsworth, had a terrible reputation among Rastafarians. Gilroy remembers the Union Jack, which by the late 1970s had become synonymous with far-right nationalism, flying over the police station in Handsworth. 'They weren't flying their Union Jack over Balsall Heath police station and the smaller police station and in Sparkbrook,' he said. 'Handsworth was symbolic.' Zephaniah was once taken to the station for questioning and shown into a side room. As he entered, he saw there was a collection of hats with the Rasta colours of red, gold and green pinned to the wall. Next to these was a wall of dreadlocks. 'They were like scalps,' he said.

Rastafarians were being branded as criminals, either for selling drugs – which some did – or for committing petty crimes, the most common being muggings. The impact of the press coverage was such that by 1979, according to one academic, the stereotype of the Rasta man as a racist thug 'lurking in the ghettos of big cities and waging war with the rest of the community ... had become cemented in the public consciousness'.[21] Others saw Rastafarians as more benign; the latest youth culture movement, such as the mods and rockers – or even skinheads – to be demonised.[22]

The single biggest contributor to the moral panic around Rastafarianism in Handsworth was a report commissioned by the police and written by an academic called John Brown, who emerged in the late 1970s as an expert on Black youth and criminality.[23] A senior academic at the Cranfield Institute of Education (an institution located on a former RAF base in Bedfordshire and best known for its links to the aeronautics industry) Brown produced his 'Shades of Grey' report during the summer of 1977. The forty-five-page report left little doubt where Brown believed the problem lay. 'Many of the couple of hundred "hardcore" Dreadlocks who now form a criminalised sub-culture in the area live in squats. Almost all are unemployed. And apart from the specific crimes for which they are responsible, they constantly threaten the peace of individual citizens, Black, brown and white, whilst making the police task both difficult and dangerous, since every police contact with them involves the risk of confrontation or violence.'[24]

The report's impact was immediate: news reports claimed that *all* crime in Handsworth was being perpetrated by Rastas, who'd made it the centre of 'Black crime' in Britain,[25] even though the report made it clear the area had one of the lowest levels of illegal activity in the whole of the West Midlands. Police patrols in Handsworth were stepped up, although Chief Constable Philip Knights insisted to a reporter that it wasn't a 'panic situation'.[26] Not only did 'Shades of Grey' influence the police response to Rastafarianism but it helped paint the religion as merely a cover, a thin veneer that hid its followers' true intent: crime. This wasn't about pious devotion, or even Black empowerment, but an elaborate ruse designed to circumvent the norms of society and steal a living in the process. While there was certainly an element within the new religion that saw Babylon as 'owing them a living', the report painted all Rastafarians as dangerous foreign bodies within British life.

There was a swift local reaction to the 'Shades of Grey' report from the left-wing voluntary groups of Handsworth. Clare Short, the future Labour cabinet minister who ran the multi-faith NGO All Faiths For One Race (AFFOR) at the time, commissioned a report of her own called 'Talking Blues'.[27] She'd heard the stories of Thornhill from a Black pastor who said young Black men were having their heads put down the toilets by officers, and argued that Brown's report almost completely ignored these complaints. Short sent out an interviewer called Carlton Green with a tape recorder to capture the thoughts of Black people in Birmingham. He spoke to university graduates and nurses, church ministers and Rastafarians. The alternative picture that emerged was one of police harassment, unemployment and a whole section of society that felt marginalised and passed over. A young graduate talks about her boyfriend being beaten up by the police when he refused to say that presents she'd given him on his birthday were stolen; an unemployed lorry driver recalls having dogs set on him by police outside a concert; a vicar's daughter says the police still see Black people as 'slaves'; while several of the parents and the ministers see the young people themselves as being responsible for the problem. It's a messy picture, but one motif keeps recurring – the younger generation, emboldened by the teachings of Rastafarianism, will not continue to take police harassment. 'If dem keep on oppressing . . . I have to just fight back,' said one interviewee. 'And if it is blood, let it run.'

Stuart Hall was watching this play out from his offices at the CCCS.[28] At the core of his work in Birmingham were essays, articles and TV which examined the police behaviour that had traumatised Benjamin Zephaniah's generation, but also the media that had painted their image as deviant outsiders.

In 1978, Hall co-authored *Policing The Crisis*, an exploration of the fractious world of the city he lived in. The book considers white Britain's response to Birmingham's Black population, focusing on the moral panic surrounding mugging, and shows how the press constructed a narrative around race, youth and crime that turned Handsworth into a 'ghetto' where Black people and police were at war. Hall predicted that politicians would leverage the moral panic to justify a move toward an American-style Law and Order society, like the one President Richard Nixon had ushered in across the Atlantic.

In the build-up to the 1968 US election there was widespread rioting in more than a hundred US cities, fuelled by anger over the Vietnam War and the assassinations of Robert Kennedy and – especially – Martin Luther King. Nixon used the unrest to paint himself as a hardliner who would quell the unrest, violently if necessary. Nixon was on the side of the 'silent majority' (white America) – a majority at war with those trying to undermine their way of life (Black Americans and those on the left). The approach was a resounding success and saw him defeat Democratic candidate Hubert Humphrey, promising in his acceptance speech to represent 'forgotten Americans', the 'voice of the great majority – the non-shouters, the non-demonstrators'.[29]

Hall saw similarities in the way Thatcher's campaign was framing its approach to the rule of law. At the 1978 Conservative Conference in Brighton, Thatcher claimed that Callaghan's Labour had weakened respect for the criminal justice system. 'When a rule of law breaks down, fear takes over. There is no security in the streets, families feel unsafe even in their own homes, children are at risk, criminals prosper, men of violence flourish,' she said, suggesting that if Labour continued in power, the dystopian world of Stanley Kubrick's 1971 *A Clockwork Orange* – where violent gangs terrorise the UK – could 'become a reality'.[30] 'We are 100 per cent behind the police, the courts, the judges, and not least the law-abiding majority of citizens.' In opposition, she'd successfully tested out her hardline approach; first with immigration, neutralising the threat posed by the National Front by stealing their political idiom. Once she came to power, Thatcher would embrace the Law and Order doctrine (or 'authoritarian populism' as Hall put it) as wholeheartedly as any politician in the western world.

In May 1979, Thatcher led the Conservative Party to a stunning election victory which saw her party take 43.9 per cent of the vote, winning 335 seats to Labour's 269 seats. The Winter of Discontent, with its endless strikes and powerful images of a nation trapped in stasis by union disputes helped to unseat Callaghan – who hadn't accepted he was in trouble until it was too late. Once in office, Thatcher introduced the staggering 45 per cent pay rise for the police,[31] and called Law and Order a 'social service' designed to defeat the 'swaggering violent bully who achieves predatory control over the streets'.

If her 'swamped' comments were aimed at cities like Bradford, her Law and Order doctrine was justified by the nightmarish tales coming out of places like Handsworth, exaggerated and sensationalised by the media. Hall, meanwhile, saw the alarming changes around him and considered how to respond in a way that could have an impact beyond the university campus. He developed an ambitious plan – one that would use the same apparatus Thatcher had used to counter her vision of a new Britain: the media itself.

A few months after the election, Hall would have a chance to present his ideas on a far bigger stage, thanks to an initiative spearheaded by David Attenborough. In the early 1970s, the naturalist and presenter was an ambitious director of programmes at the BBC, where he conceived an idea that would become one of the most divisive projects the broadcaster ever commissioned.

In an internal memo from 1972, Attenborough argued that his new initiative would bring 'voices, attitudes and opinions that, for one reason or another, have been unheard or seriously neglected by mainstream programmes'.[32] Inspired by a similar concept at WGBH-Boston, the public service broadcaster that had commissioned *Blacks Britannica*, Attenborough decided to introduce a weekly thirty-minute slot where the corporation would cede editorial control to 'the people'. Outside organisations – with the assistance of the BBC studios – could make a film and have it shown on what would become known as *Open Door*.

Starting in 1973, the programme gave space to groups as diverse as Black teachers, trans organisations and the anti-immigration lobby. It was controversial but brave commissioning that pushed at the boundaries of free speech and undermined the elitist principles articulated in 1924 by the first director general of the BBC, Lord Reith, who said that 'only those who have a claim to be heard above their fellows' should get access to the microphone.[33] *Open Door* challenged that position and was referred to as 'cranks' corner' by many within the BBC, and dubbed 'ghetto telly' by *Time Out*.

Hall appeared on *Open Door* in 1979 with a collective called the

Campaign Against Racism in the Media (CARM) – a left-wing pressure group made up of media professionals.[34] Working with the Anti-Nazi League, they picketed broadcasters who gave softball interviews to the National Front.[35] CARM called their *Open-Door* project *It Ain't Half Racist, Mum*, a title that riffed on the colonial-era comedy *It Ain't Half Hot Mum*, and used it to turn the lens back onto the BBC and other broadcasters to show how popular TV reinforced racism.

Racism did not merely go unchallenged on British TV in the 1970s – some of the most popular shows on air were explicitly racist. *The Black and White Minstrel Show*, which featured 'Blacked up' performers, ran from 1958 to 1978, and claimed an audience of sixteen million at its peak. When a senior BBC producer who'd spent time in New York and been influenced by the civil rights movement complained about the show on behalf of Black Britons, the reply came that 'coloured people' should 'for Heaven's sake shut up'.[36]

Black performers would sometimes be booked onto the show, including the Birmingham comedian Lenny Henry. Aged sixteen when he made his TV debut, his impressions of Stevie Wonder, Muhammad Ali and Frank Spencer were good enough for him to win the talent competition *New Faces* and thrust him into the world of mid-1970s light entertainment. Black performers had few opportunities in British TV: although 40 per cent of the drama produced by the BBC had 'non-white actors' in the late 1970s, only 4 per cent of those actors had speaking parts.[37] Henry would go on to star in the first Black-led sitcom, *The Fosters*, and become the biggest Black British TV star of the 1980s. Some of his early characters, including a Rastafarian called Algernon Winston Spencer Churchill Gladstone Disraeli Palmerston Pitt the Younger Pitt the Elder Razzmatazz whose catchphrase was 'Ooookaaaay', didn't go down well in his hometown. But his appearance on the minstrel show would linger over his career. Some within the Black community treated him with suspicion, while he regretted the appearance. When I asked Henry about the minstrel show performance, he said: 'I do know this: if it's me, and I'm that person's parent or guardian, I'm not going to let them be in a minstrel show.' It was the kind of performance Black comedians and actors were forced to make if they wanted exposure – comedy that took aim at Black people for the amusement of a white audience.

There was one noticeable counter to the thin and often racist portrayal of Black Britons on television: *Empire Road*. *The Fosters* might have been the first Black British soap opera, but the Birmingham-based *Empire Road* would be the first to be written and directed by Black talent. While the show was in development, the Guyanese playwright and creative force behind the sitcom – Michael Abbensetts – would spend time in Handsworth talking to locals about their experiences. Unsurprisingly, the social issues that Birmingham was becoming notorious for also bled into *Empire Road*. Rastafarianism and the moral panic surrounding it was introduced via Desmond, a young Rasta who worked at the shop owned by the Jamaican patriarch Everton, played by Norman Beaton. Police harassment was part of a storyline, while the main love story featured an interracial relationship – between Everton's son and an Indian girl. Horace Ové, who'd directed the first Black British feature film *Pressure* in 1977, came in to direct part of the second series, while Denis Bovell, who'd produced Linton Kwesi Johnson's albums, provided the theme tune and the incidental music. There had never been such a project on television; one powered almost exclusively by Black British talent.[38]

Empire Road ended in 1979 after two series, but what Abbensetts and his team achieved was remarkable considering the environment in Britain for Black writers. Between 1970 and 1984 the BBC ran *A Play for Today* – a weekly slot for television plays that helped launch numerous careers, including those of Ken Loach and Alan Bleasdale. Of the more than 300 plays that aired over a fourteen-year period, four productions were from writers of colour. For all its critical acclaim, however, *Empire Road* did not signal the start of a wave of Black British commissions. Channel controllers wouldn't rush to replicate it, and forty years on it stands as an anomaly in British television – a properly backed Black sitcom. As the show was winding down, Hall prepared to appear on the same channel – to make an argument about why programmes like it were so desperately needed.

Lord Reith, the first director general of the BBC and the son of a Free Presbyterian minister from Glasgow, gave the broadcaster its guiding principles, chief among them that broadcasting could be unifying and egalitarian: 'The genius and the fool, the wealthy and the poor listen simultaneously . . . there is no first and third class,' he wrote in his 1924 book *Broadcast Over Britain*. But he was also brazenly elitist, as his remarks from the same year about who should be allowed access to the microphone made clear: the BBC was not to be a platform for all of society – only those who deserve it.

CARM start their *Open Door* by showing a clip from a 1967 interview with Lord Reith conducted by the journalist Malcolm Muggeridge. Muggeridge puts it to the former Director General that during his tenure the broadcaster was perceived as being for 'genteel and respectable elements' of British society. Reith responds with the speed of a boxer throwing an instinctive jab. 'Is there anything wrong with that?' he snaps back.

Then Hall appears, dressed in a suit jacket, red tie and sky-blue shirt, looking almost identical to the portrait Burke took of him in his office. Here, too, he's relaxed and engaging as he introduces the idea of racist depictions in 'harmless' comedy, like *It Aint Half Hot Mum*, where British soldiers make jokes about 'lazy, skiving natives' who, Hall argues, are presented as being 'locked in a deceitful battle of wits against Lord Reith's genteel elements of society.' Even in 1979, more than four decades after Reith stepped down as Director General, taking aim at the man who had shaped the British media landscape was a bold move. Still more provocative to link his comments about 'genteel elements' with an overtly racist comedy like *It Aint Half Hot Mum*. CARM was setting out its stall from the outset: just because *Open Door* was being broadcast on the BBC, the organisation and its biggest names would not be spared Hall's critical gaze.

Robin Day was an erudite, urbane journalist, who'd made his

name by subjecting politicians from Harold Macmillan to President Nasser of Egypt to forensic, unforgiving interviews. His manner could be haughty, and he was rarely seen on screen without his signature polka-dot bowtie. (His fellow broadcaster Ludovic Kennedy described him as 'essentially an establishment man' in his memoir.)[39] By 1979, he'd just been installed as the host of the BBC's current affairs show *Question Time*, and regularly fronted the investigative programme *Panorama*. He was arguably the biggest name at the broadcaster and its voice of authority.

CARM and Hall took aim at Day – and particularly his deference to Enoch Powell, the former Defence Secretary who'd become infamous after his 'Rivers of Blood' speech in 1968, where he predicted race wars in Britain if large-scale immigration continued. Hall's co-host Maggie Steed says that Powell has become the media's superstar on race, with broadcasters listening to his opinion as if it were gospel truth.[40] 'He defines the terms. He sets the agenda. He's helped to ensure that the question is the question of immigration,' she adds. The programme then cuts to a BBC production called *The Question of Immigration*, of which Powell is a special guest and – as Steed and Hall show – is regularly referred to by the host, Day. Just as Reith was linked to casual racism, now the BBC's political star was shown being guided by someone with overtly racist views, rather than doing what he was famous for by pushing back against them.[41]

A staggering amount of ground is covered in the thirty-minute programme: a Brent housing estate where only white residents are given a platform to complain about Blacks; TV executives admitting their shows present characters that are little more than stereotypes; and far-right leader John Kingsley Read's unsubstantiated claims about South Asian people throwing excrement in Blackburn's streets. But the spine of the programme features Birmingham stories, ranging from moral panic around mugging and Black crime to the Rasta outrage. Hall and CARM show a clip from a BBC documentary made after 'Shades of Grey', as Brown walks down a Handsworth street delivering a bitesize version of his infamous report:

> Imagine young West Indians, perhaps born in the early 60s, come on to the labour market just at the worst time – a time of high unemployment, particularly for young people. Then they get perhaps involved with the police, in some act of minor delinquency. The police come round. The parents themselves get het up, reject their children, and this act of rejection is very common, in many ways. So, leaving their parents, they go and shack up with others of their kind, in squats or in communes. On the one hand, searching for purpose, searching for identity. On the other hand, perhaps involved more and more in criminality, acts of violence against the old and defenceless. It's a terrifying scenario.

Much of what Hall had been pushing back against via his work at the CCCS and *Policing The Crisis* is on display: the presentation of Black communities seen exclusively in terms of crime, unemployment, family breakdown and – with the reference to the 'acts against the old and defenceless' – mugging. *It Ain't Half Racist, Mum* ends with an appeal from Steed for viewers to question the media narrative around race, while Hall delivers a cutting monologue.

'Racism has never been put in a critical context by the media in this country,' he starts. 'When it comes to fighting racism, the media are part of the problem. They perpetuate myths and stereotypes about Black people. They lie by omission, distortion and selection. They give racists inflated importance and respectability.' In the space of thirty minutes, many of the arguments that had been reverberating around the academic world of CCCS – and to some extent the streets of Handsworth – were seen by thousands.

When the show aired, it caused a huge internal backlash at the BBC. Robin Day and Ludovic Kennedy, who was also criticised, were appalled. They sought legal advice and eventually pressured senior figures into issuing an apology in a subsequent episode of *Open Door*. Far from taking up the invitation for greater self-awareness and a change of tack, the BBC distanced itself from Hall's arguments. But unlike *Blacks Britannica*, which was never shown in the

UK, the scale of the BBC's reach meant that many people saw or heard about the broadcast. Hall's appearance was crucial to a generation of Black Britons who were trying to figure out their place in the UK.

The artist John Akomfrah was watching that night. He was stunned to see a Black man – still a very rare sight on the BBC – analyse and articulate a problem he himself had become acutely aware of. 'For my generation in the 70s, [Hall] was one of the few people of colour we saw on television who wasn't crooning, dancing or running,' he said. 'His very iconic presence on this most public of platforms suggested all manner of "impossible possibilities". With him and through him we began to ask the indispensable questions: who are we, what are we and what could we become?'[42]

Steel Pulse were aware of Hall; he was respected but ultimately treated with some suspicion, according to Riley. 'This was activism, but it was coming out of a space that we didn't recognise. None of us had gone to university,' says Riley. 'We recognised that he was onside. But we also recognised that he was using a different vernacular for that, which didn't tie in with where we were coming from.'[43] *Handsworth Revolution*, Steel Pulse's most famous record, made in 1977, hinted at their more militant approach – the streets were to be fought over, the frontline was to be defended rather than theorised about.[44] 'He was fighting the cause, but from an academic perspective,' says Burke. 'It's quite the opposite to the man in the street who throws a stone.' While Riley and Steel Pulse might have heard a man talking a different language to them, for Akomfrah and others, Hall was delivering a potent message and showing how to fight back. He made Akomfrah, a young artist just starting out when he watched the *Open Door* episode, believe 'that race wasn't a self-contained fragment on the edge of things but could actually be at the centre of things'.

When I sat down with Vanley Burke at the MAC, it was below a series of towering six-foot photographs in black and white. Known

Participants in the Handsworth Self-Portrait project conducted during 1979

Jah Warriors – Birmingham, 1979

as the Handsworth Self-Portrait project, it was the brainchild of three white photographers – Derek Bishton, John Reardon and Brian Homer – and landed in Handsworth during the summer of 1979. Just down the road from Burke's family store in Handsworth, the trio set up an impromptu sitting space and handed over control to the local community, inviting them to take a self-portrait. Unlike a typical photography studio where people wore their Sunday best, posed formally and projected an idealised version of themselves into the world, the project captured people as they were, often en route to some other engagement.

The frontline that Gilroy spoke about is shown here in all its diversity. Kids with ripped clothes step into the makeshift studio, families with untucked shirts occupy the frame, reggae artists and Rastas take their turn – you can feel the spontaneity and fun of Handsworth in the late 1970s. Like the Burke archive, the music of Steel Pulse, the nuanced drama of *Empire Road* and the robust critiques of Stuart Hall, the project offers another counter narrative to the mainstream view on Birmingham's Black population, and Handsworth specifically.

Burke is now in his seventies; he's an elder statesman of British art, with the honorary degrees and the appearance on *Desert Island Discs* to prove it (he picked records by Linton Kwesi Johnson, Burning Spear and Nina Simone).[45] Barbara Walker became a Turner Prize-nominated artist; Zephaniah's poetry made him a star in the 1980s; Steel Pulse would go on to become the first British reggae act to win a Grammy; Gilroy has spent his career writing celebrated books about race; and Riley joined him in the world of academia. John Akomfrah, the young artist who was inspired after seeing Hall on *Open Door* in 1979, would go on to become a protégé' of the academic eventually representing Britain at the 2024 Venice Biennale. He, along with the rest of the Black Audio Film Collective – a group of university students who had met in Portsmouth – would use Birmingham as the setting for their debut film project *Handsworth Songs*, about the riots of 1985 that swept through the area. There are shots of a young Black woman looking into the camera while conducting work on a production line as Birmingham's industry fades; and the haunting and evocative opening shot of the film is of a lone dreadlocked man trying to evade the police on the streets of Handsworth – six years after 'Shades of Grey' was released.

After 1979, something shifted in the city. Thatcher's election led to an economic agenda that fundamentally changed the once-flourishing voluntary sector. The feel of Handsworth began to change as Thatcher reduced the size of the wider welfare state.[46] The multi-faith were still there but the progressive organisations – like the ones that supported sex workers in Handsworth and Balsall Heath – would slowly disappear. Thatcher's government actually dramatically increased voluntary sector funding – it went up from £93 million in 1979 to £293 million in 1988 – but it was centralised.[47] Local government no longer controlled funding and grants turned into contracts.

Stuart Hall left Birmingham in 1979 for a position at the Open University,[48] where he appeared on people's television screens as the host of free educational programmes. But his time in Birmingham had shaped his worldview: the streets of Handsworth had forged his ideas about what it meant to be Black and British.

He continued to be a presence on British television screens until his death in 2014, arguing for the positive aspects of multiculturalism and promoting a pluralistic view of British identity. 'We need our differences recognised,' he said:

> But, of course, at the same time, we need to feel we can belong . . .
> I think the British have a future only if they can come to terms with the fact Britishness is not one thing and has never been one thing. There have been a million different ways of being British. There have been a million different struggles about Britishness which are only retrospectively smoothly accommodated into the story as if it's unfolding seamlessly.[49]

If anyone knew about those struggles it was Hall, who'd based himself in a city on the frontline of Britain's racial realignment.

The historian Richard Vinen argued that Hall's departure for the capital signalled the moment when London replaced Birmingham as the centre of British radicalism. But that wasn't necessarily the case for Black Britain, as seismic events in July 1981 focused attention away from the capital. The frontline shifted once again; this time it could be found in Liverpool, in one of the oldest Black communities in Europe.

4.
The Ghost of William Huskisson – Liverpool, 1981

On a balmy July evening in 1982, Stephen Nze and his social circle were hanging out in their regular spot outside the Sierra Leone Club, one of more than two dozen Black-run venues that had sprung up in the South Liverpool postcode of Liverpool 8, or L8 for short, over the years.[1] The neighbourhood had become known in the press simply as 'Toxteth' after a summer of violence and protest a year earlier. As Nze and his friends enjoyed an alfresco drink and a smoke, someone turned up in a stolen Ford Cortina with a tow bar on the back.[2] The summer evening turned into night, and the group's attention focused on a statue in the middle of Princes Boulevard, the wide road lined by formerly grand homes that ran through the postcode. 'We called it "the ghost",' says Nze of the statue. 'The ghost of William Huskisson.'

A British politician who came to prominence at the turn of the nineteenth century, the former Liverpool MP was seen as a problematic figure among a Black population who, in many cases, could trace their lineage back to before the abolition of slavery in the mid-1800s. Huskisson had been fickle on the question of slavery: before he moved to the city he'd voted for the abolition of slavery in Britain in 1807 but when he came to Liverpool in 1823, he supported the trade and in so doing helped to make the city's port a thriving hub dominated by slave economic products such as sugar. More than a century and a half after his death, the bronze statue, which featured the politician wrapped in a Roman toga, was a proud symbol of Liverpool's intimate connection to the slave trade.

The group Nze was with started talking about the Huskisson

monument. Some said the MP was an enslaver; others clarified that he hadn't owned enslaved people but had supported the trade as a politician. Regardless, the decision was taken to pull it down. Sixty young people gathered around the statue and a rope was taken and put around Huskisson's neck. It was tied to the Cortina's tow bar and the car was driven away at speed. At first it wouldn't move, the Ford's wheels screeching as they spun wildly on the tarmac. Then there was a loud crack, with the force finally bending the statue. To chants of 'pull it down!' the driver reversed and took another run at it, this time felling the former Liverpool MP and dragging his likeness to the ground to cheers from the assembled crowd. The *Liverpool Echo* would later report that 'the memory of William Huskisson has been brought down to earth with a bump'.

The statue was simply part of the furniture to some – and a caustic affront to others. 'Huskisson didn't belong to us,' Nze later said. 'He belonged to *them*. He was a symbol of the state.' This spectre of slavery had been pulled down by a Black British community that was one of the oldest in the country. Black scousers had settled over multiple generations, dating back to the 1700s. They knew no other country to call home, nor did their parents or, in many cases, grandparents. During the 1980s, Black scousers even started to refer to themselves as 'Liverpool-born Blacks', a term which marked themselves out as distinct from other Black Britons who'd settled later. Their experiences were a bellwether; an indicator for where the newer waves of immigrants who arrived as part of the Windrush Generation were heading. And, in the early 1980s, things weren't looking good.

Black scousers faced challenges that were as stark as any Black community in Europe: unemployment was at 80 per cent for Black youth, the police embraced openly racist tactics, local and national politicians viewed them with suspicion and their image had been shaped by the ideology of eugenicists. 'What you see in Liverpool is a sign of things to come,' warned a Select Committee that visited the city a year before Huskisson fell; while another report said that: 'Liverpool in the 1980s is a sort of model of what British cities in general may be like in the early 2000s.'[3] Huskisson's fate was part of a reaction by Black Britain to the way it had been treated – one that, when it began twelve months earlier, shook the nation.

On 3 July 1981, Leroy Cooper, a young Black artist and poet whose family had a long history of being harassed by the police, was arrested after being manhandled by officers on Selborne Street, Liverpool 8. Three carloads of police had turned up on the street to take Cooper in. The incident was the spark that triggered several nights of unrest.[4] A few hours after the arrest, large groups took to the streets. Hot-wired vehicles were driven into strategic positions on the main thoroughfares, including Upper Parliament Street, then set ablaze. The Rialto, a former cinema that had been transformed into a furniture store, was burned to the ground. Groups chose specific targets, like the exclusive Racquet Club, which hosted the city's elite just a stone's throw away from one of the most deprived areas in Britain. Others, like Stanley House, a community hub, were left alone.

Shops were ransacked, barricades were erected and, for three nights, police were bombarded with bricks and petrol bombs. In total 1,000 officers were deployed and 460 were injured.[5] At one point a JCB was driven into a line of officers. TV cameras captured injured officers arriving at local hospitals, many unable to walk, pushed into the emergency rooms on wheelchairs, with makeshift bandages hanging from their heads. Rumours spread among the police who were being brought in to quell the unrest – apocryphal stories of officers having their legs chopped off.[6] There were even tales of decapitations.[7]

In response, the police were equipped with CS gas canisters. While these had been used in Northern Ireland during the Troubles, it was the first time they'd been deployed on the British mainland. Rubber bullets rained down during clashes that left much of South Liverpool looking like a war zone, and aerial shots showed smoke billowing from dozens of sites across L8. As the unrest spread, the sound of The Specials' 'Ghost Town' – the band's song about

Police officers in riot gear outside a burning shop on Park Road in Liverpool

Thatcher's Britain – could be heard playing on repeat from boom boxes. These were the biggest disturbances mainland Britain had seen since the Luftwaffe's bombing raids during the Second World War. A year before Huskisson was pulled from his plinth, the unrest in Liverpool and elsewhere left Thatcher's government scrambling to come up with a solution to violence that seemed to be out of control.

But Liverpool wasn't only a bellwether city when it came to race. Thatcher's economic policies, which were based around monetarism – an approach that had an unshakeable, if damaging, focus on controlling inflation – were hitting businesses in the city hard. Unemployment soared in the early years of her time in office. Liverpool's docks and their strong union support were repugnant to a politician who despised any form of collectivism, and by 1981 Thatcher's closest allies were ready to write Liverpool off entirely, encouraging instead a policy of 'managed decline' for the city.

*

The Ghost of William Huskisson – Liverpool, 1981

We've already seen some of the factors that led to the eruption in the summer of 1981, and the warning signs were obvious for anyone willing to look. The far-right thuggery that Northern Soul fans had faced; the police's use of Sus and forced confessions in places like Bradford; the violent clashes at the 1976 Notting Hill Carnival; the media's portrayal of entire Black communities, such as Handsworth in Birmingham, as work-shy criminals. High unemployment levels and poor housing; it all made for a combustible mix. The unsustainable pressure captured in films like *Babylon* finally boiled over, while Colin Prescod's ominous predictions in *Blacks Britannica* of a rebellious Black presence that was prepared to revolt had proven accurate.

Before L8 erupted, the country had already witnessed two major moments in the history of Black Britain earlier in 1981 – both had taken place in London. The first was triggered by a fire at a house party in New Cross on 18 January that had claimed the lives of thirteen young Black people. The lack of response from the police and government – in particular, Thatcher's silence[8] – prompted the slogan '13 dead, nothing said'. Those four words became a rallying cry six weeks after the fire, when an estimated 20,000 people marched for eight hours through London in what was known as the Black People's Day of Action. At the time it was the largest demonstration by the Black community in the UK, with coaches bringing protestors from all over the country.

The second turning point happened in Brixton, South London after the Metropolitan Police launched *Operation Swamp 81*. During a ten-day period in April, plainclothes police officers made a hundred arrests in the predominantly Black area of South London, justified – as in Handsworth – as a way of tackling muggings. When rumours that the police had refused to help a Black man who'd been stabbed began circulating during the operation, the following day saw the start of seventy-two hours of disturbances that resulted in £7.5 million worth of damage in the capital.

The problem wasn't confined to one or two pockets; the contagion spread everywhere as spring turned into summer. In the capital, Brixton, Battersea, Dalston, Southall, Streatham and Walthamstow went up. Handsworth in Birmingham, Moss Side in Manchester, Chapeltown in Leeds and Highfields in Leicester saw trouble. Black, white and Asian Britons took to the streets of places as varied as Aldershot, Bedford, Blackburn, Bolton, Cardiff, Cirencester, Chester, Derby, Edinburgh, Ellesmere Port, Halifax, High Wycombe, Huddersfield, Keswick, Luton, Newcastle-upon-Tyne, Nottingham, Portsmouth, Preston, Reading, Sheffield, Southampton, Stockport, and Wolverhampton. Liverpool was part of this wave.

During the height of the unrest, the Metropolitan Police Commissioner, Sir David McNee, told the prime minister he was 'unable to guarantee the security of the royal wedding'[9] of Prince Charles and Lady Diana Spencer a month later without a long list of new equipment, including baton rounds, water cannons and riot helmets – most of which he successfully acquired. That summer across the UK 800 police were injured and more than 3,000 people were arrested. An age of innocence had ended, said the historian Lord Hennessy.[10] 'People thought riots couldn't happen here – but they did.'

Written accounts of the unrest of 1981 have tended to focus on Brixton, the starting point of the summer's disturbances, with the unrest presented as one in a series of events that made 1981 a landmark year for the UK. It wasn't just the unrest that made it remarkable, there was a royal wedding – often depicted as a rare galvanising force in the middle of the tumult. That will usually be coupled with Ian Botham's miraculous performance in the Ashes cricket test against the Australians in Headingley, when 'Beefy' single-handedly delivered the unlikeliest of victories for England against its biggest foe. There might be a cursory mention of Geoffrey Howe's budget, which signalled the end of Keynesian orthodoxy as public expenditure was slashed. The racial unrest is just one story in a year of tumult. The Brixton story is one of the children of the Windrush Generation rebelling against heavy-handed policing and anger at the lack of opportunities or acceptance endured by the post-1948 arrivals.

But the Merseyside story is different. Elsewhere, the eruption in

1981 might have been triggered by the acute problems of the early Thatcher era; in Liverpool, the issues went much, much deeper.

Just off The Strand, the busy road that runs parallel to Liverpool's waterfront, you'll find Our Lady and St Nicholas Church Gardens. A site of worship since the thirteenth century, the church that stands on its grounds has undergone several incarnations. An ornate spire added in the eighteenth century made it, for a while, the tallest building in the city. Today, it's dwarfed by the towering, gleaming office blocks and shopping arcades that dominate Liverpool's skyline. But in its Old Churchyard, a very special piece of history has survived that transformation: the gravestone of 'Adell', a formerly enslaved man who died in 1717 and is considered to be Liverpool's first recorded Black resident.[11] Africans like Adell, who came to Liverpool as enslaved people before settling in the city, created a nascent Black community.

These pioneers settled in a city built on the transatlantic slave trade: between 1700 and 1807, Liverpool ships carried one and a half million Africans across the Atlantic to a life of subjugation. During the American Civil War, when the North fought for emancipation, Liverpool supported the South, which fought to retain slavery. During the conflict, Confederate flags could be seen flying throughout Liverpool. In the city, major civic figures, including MPs, had interests in the slave economy, which was making them – and the city – rich. Powered by the trade in human cargo, Liverpool transformed from a small fishing port to one of the main economic arteries that nurtured the growth of the British Empire. Shortly before the British slave trade was abolished in 1807, around 80 per cent of the industry was controlled by Liverpool, while the city accounted for 40 per cent of the total European trade,[12] with Merseyside merchants enslaving more people than the entire country of France.

The Black communities that followed Adell were always multicultural with Arab, Chinese, African, Caribbean and white – often Irish – residents. Interracial marriage was commonplace. 'My great-grandfather arrived in Liverpool in 1868 from Jamaica,' says Ray Quarless, a fourth-generation Black scouser. 'He married my white great-grandmother in 1870. Then my grandfather comes here from Barbados and meets their daughter. In 1898, they were married, and on it goes.'

Liverpool's unique Black community fascinated many. *Moby Dick* author Herman Melville in 1849 described the city as 'a port in which all climes and countries embrace'. Eighty years later, Bradford's J. B. Priestley came to the city as part of the nationwide tour he embarked on while writing *English Journey*. He marvelled at what he called 'an infant class of half-castes, quadroons, octoroons, with all the latitudes and longitudes confused in them', using terms that were seen as enlightened in the 1930s. In his mind, he'd come across an exotic social experiment. But the community that initially established itself adjacent to the dock, before moving first to Kent Gardens near the waterfront and then, gradually, after the Second World War, to L8, didn't always attract benign voyeurism.

Priestley's words represented the liberal end of the spectrum when it came to opinions on racial mixing in Liverpool. There was another school of thought about race in the city, one that was influenced by eugenics. The ideology, otherwise known as race science – the belief that some races are superior to others – had gained a firm foothold in the city at the University of Liverpool. In the 1920s, Muriel Fletcher – a probation officer and eugenicist who'd trained at the University of Liverpool – produced a paper focused on the 'problem of racially mixed families'.

When the Fletcher Report was released in 1930, it popularised the term 'half-caste' to describe Liverpool's mixed-heritage population and created stereotypes that lodged deeply in the British psyche.[13] Children of interracial relationships were 'genetically abnormal', less intelligent and prone to sexual promiscuity according to the report, which was sent to police, social workers and the media.[14] Bea Freeman, a Black scouser and filmmaker who can trace her family roots in Britain back to the 1800s, said the report's conclusions became lore. 'You got to view the way the establishment saw

Black people in Liverpool,' she told me. 'And that has hardly ever changed.'

The report came in between waves of racial violence in the former slave port. Six decades before the unrest of 1981, there had been major outbreaks of racially fuelled disturbances in the city. In the summer of 1919, Black seamen from West Africa and the Caribbean who'd settled in Liverpool after serving in the merchant navy during the First World War were attacked by white mobs.[15] The violence reached its peak with the death of the sailor Charles Wotten (also known as Wooton), who was forced into the Queens Dock by a gang who threw stones at him while he drowned. That summer of violence was the start of a recurring pattern aimed at Liverpool's Black population that would presage the seismic events of 1981.

Three decades after Wooton's murder, in 1948 – the same year the *Empire Windrush* docked – a seaman's hostel housing Black workers was attacked. But, this time, the more established community was able to fight back.[16] Over the course of three nights during the August bank holiday, small numbers of Black seamen engaged with white mobs, who were now being aided by the local police force. After seventy-two hours of violence, the Colonial Defence Committee was formed to mount legal defences for the seamen. They successfully overturned a conviction for a ship's fireman called Emmanuel Williams who'd been found guilty of assaulting a police officer,[17] while they fought cases for dozens of other men. It's thought to be the first ever 'Defence Committee', a prototype for the groups that campaigned on behalf of other Black Britons who ended up pitted against the state, including the Mangrove Nine in London and George Lindo in Bradford.[18]

After the victories – both on the street and in court – Black Liverpool gained confidence. Post-1948, the numbers of Black people in the city began to grow as those from the Windrush Generation joined the historic, mostly African community. In L8, the diverse clubs began to emerge on Granby Street, Smithdown Lane and Parliament Street,[19] each providing a taste of the country or ethnic group that its name came from. In the Nigerian Yoruba and Ibo clubs, you could get a plate of jollof rice, dodo and moin moin, while Lagosian high-life guitar might soundtrack an evening. In others, jerk chicken and ackee would be served as reggae's low-end frequencies hummed from the speakers.

Less than a decade after the violence of 1948, Liverpool was seen by white authorities as a racial success story,[20] especially after rioting in Notting Hill and Nottingham in 1958 and more protests sparked by Kelso Cochrane's murder in London during the summer of 1959 failed to ignite disturbances in the city. In 1961, church groups backed by local businesses hosted the South Liverpool Festival, boasting that their area – which included L8 – was 'the most racially mixed area of Britain' and they were 'anxious to show how well the races live and work together'.[21] This was the cultural melting pot that produced Lord Woodbine, the Trinidadian calypso star dubbed the 'sixth Beatle' who had a huge influence on Lennon and McCartney's group.[22] Howard Gayle (Liverpool FC) and Michael Trebilcock (Everton FC) became the first Black players for the city's two football clubs. The Mersey Beat poets, who created work about working-class life and had a best-selling anthology in the 1960s, would inspire L8's own writers, including Bobby Nyahoe.[23] An all-Black L8 group, The Chants, would eventually evolve into The Real Thing, a soul-pop act with a string of hits in the 1970s. There were breakthroughs in politics when Glynn George Pratt was elected the first Black councillor on Liverpool and Merseyside County Council in 1972, while two years before Dorothy Kuya was appointed Liverpool's first senior community relations officer.[24] Black scouse talent travelled beyond Merseyside too: boxer John Conteh became an international sports star and friend of Muhammad Ali, while singer Derek Wilkie toured with Little Richard and won plaudits as a theatre performer in Italy.

But the apparent racial harmony was a veneer: in reality, Black scousers were often confined to L8.[25] Those who ventured into town to a club – maybe the ethnically mixed venue The Sink[26] – faced the prospect of racist violence on their way in and when they returned home.[27] In his memoirs, Howard Gayle recalled being warned off spending time in L8 by Liverpool manager Bob Paisley once he'd broken into the side's first team.[28] Increasingly, the residents of L8 felt hemmed in, which bred an insularity. Even Black people from other areas of the city were sometimes treated as outsiders. Joanne Anderson, who grew up in Netherley, in the east of the city, and who would become Liverpool's first Black mayor in 2021, puts that down to the experiences residents of L8 went through during the twentieth century. 'What was going on for people in that community is hard to describe to anyone who was not going through it,' she told me. 'I think that's where they get the mantra of "Yeah, but you're not from *here*."'

If Black families attempted to live in another area of the city, they often met violent opposition to their presence. Maria O'Reilly, an activist who would go on to work in the L8 Law Centre – grew up in Kent Gardens before moving to Kirkby in north Liverpool after she got married. She left within six months. 'My husband was a white lad, they jumped him and battered him,' she said. 'They put all our windows in and left dead birds with nails in outside my front door.' The final straw for O'Reilly was when some men set their dogs on her while she was walking her baby to the local market in a pram.

In 1972, multiple Black families were attacked when skinheads targeted residents on the Falkner Place housing estate, which offered good-quality accommodation and included Black tenants. Skirmishes between the police, skinheads and Black residents – who had erected barricades – raged over five nights. 'Liverpool's Black community is a community of resistance,' Quarless told me. 'You've got 1919, you've got 1948, 1972 and 1981. We've had to deal with that over 80-odd years and that's just the ones that we know about; the ones that are actually recorded.' Liverpool's unique history gave the unrest of 1981 an intensity and fierceness not seen in other places.

A damning Commons committee report on race relations produced in the aftermath of the unrest that raged during the summer of 1981, ventured the reasons behind this: it found that Liverpool was 'the most disturbing case of racial disadvantage in the United Kingdom'[29] and that the deep roots of the city's Black population showed racism 'cannot be expected to disappear by natural causes'.

L8's residents were essentially living a life of segregation and the fact they'd been there for several generations seemed to make no difference. You'd rarely see a Black face in the city centre or beyond the confines of their postcode. The African-American anthropologist Jaqueline Nassy Brown visited Liverpool in 1989 and observed the mental barriers that still existed for residents of L8. 'Among the Blacks I knew, "town" meant one thing: their total exclusion from mainstream Liverpool life, especially in terms of employment.'

In 1973, Dorothy Kuya – from her position as one of the UK's first race relations officers – investigated racial discrimination in Liverpool. She found there were only two school governors, three social workers, three policemen, twenty shopworkers, three street cleaners, two postmen, twenty-one teachers (although seventeen were immigrants rather than British-born), one councillor and two station porters, who were Black[30] out of a population estimated to be around 7,000[31] in a city of half a million people. It was incredibly rare to find any of L8's residents in a position of seniority or one that required interacting with the public. But by the start of the Thatcher era there was another problem in the city, one that would affect all residents of Liverpool, regardless of race.

In the autumn of 1982, the BBC broadcast Alan Bleasdale's *Boys From The Blackstuff*, a five-episode state-of-a-nation drama about a group of scouse workmen who have recently lost their jobs. The series reflected the reality of life in the city: by 1981, around a quarter of Liverpool's population was unemployed.[32] That figure was even higher for young people (31.1 per cent)[33] while estimates put it at around 80 per cent for the young Black population of L8. Areas like L8 had emptied out significantly as the lack of opportunities spread with the postcode's population – plummeting by a third between 1971 and 1981. The once-grand houses on Princes Boulevard began to decay, while empty homes became playgrounds for kids; by 1981 Liverpool's entire population had almost halved to 500,000 from its peak of 900,000 in the 1950s.[34]

The exodus was caused by a deep post-industrial malaise, one that

Thatcher's Chancellor Geoffrey Howe thought might be terminal. Howe's economic agenda didn't help matters on Merseyside. Interest rates were pushed to punitive levels by the treasury at the same time as the arrival of large quantities of North Sea oil had improved the UK's trade position and raised the value of the pound, making exports less competitive. The combination of higher interest rates and the strong pound did for many manufacturers, including a number on Merseyside.

But Howe's response to the unrest of 1981 wasn't a dramatic rethink of the government's approach, instead – during cabinet discussions that were only made public three decades later – he suggested embracing 'managed decline' in the city, believing spending money there was a waste. Turning Liverpool's fortunes around would be like trying to make 'water flow uphill',[35] and the city's unions were blamed for self-inflicted wounds. When they were finally released, many in the city saw Howe's comments as proof of what they'd known for years: Liverpool was being neglected on purpose by central government as animosity grew between Merseyside and Whitehall.

This rebel city with its strong unions and collectivist spirit didn't chime with Thatcher and her individualistic worldview. In the early part of her tenure, Liverpool was a constant thorn in the side of Thatcher's government and had also played its part in the downfall of Callaghan. The starting point for a 1980 protest march against rising unemployment, helmed by Labour, was Liverpool. The Winter of Discontent began with strikes at the Ford plant at Haleswood, just outside of the city, and, months later, the nation recoiled at the images of coffins piled up high during a ten-day gravediggers' strike on Merseyside.

Bleasdale's drama showed the harsh, spirit-sapping reality for Liverpool's unemployed and hinted at the city's former glories. There were iconic shots of the twenty-one-acre Tate & Lyle sugar refinery on the banks of the Mersey, which closed in April 1981, and of the barren docklands – two symbols of the city's decline since Huskisson's heyday. The drama's protagonists – a gang of out-of-work tarmac layers – queue up at the Kafkaesque unemployment office to collect their dole or take on cash-in-hand jobs, while being chased down by 'the sniffers', a group of loathed officials charged with finding benefit cheats. Their relationships collapse and families fall apart as the painful reality of long-term joblessness threatens the men's sanity.[36] The characters represented so many in the city who'd been 'thrown on the scrapheap of life, no longer able to provide for their families'.[37]

Unemployment was seen as one of the main causes of the trouble that erupted in July 1981, and now Thatcher's government was under pressure to do something about it. Her response was to send an ambitious, slick politician – a man who'd made a fortune in property and magazine publishing and had one eye on 10 Downing Street – to find solutions.

Walk through the doors of Thenford House, a Grade I-listed country manor in Thenford, Northamptonshire, and you are immediately confronted by a bust of Michael Heseltine – the house's owner – complete with the Tory politician's trademark swept-back hair. The bust captures the proud attitude of a public figure with a reputation for, if not outright arrogance, then certainly bulletproof self-belief. The Conservative politician Julian Critchley was at school with Heseltine and remembers him mapping out what he wanted from life on the back of an envelope: he would make a fortune in his twenties, become an MP in his thirties, a cabinet minister in his forties and, finally, prime minister in his fifties.[38] By 1981, he'd checked off most of the list.[39]

After a short wait for Lord Heseltine, who is now ninety, he emerges, moving slowly but purposefully, and shakes my hand. 'What are we going to talk about again?' he asks. 'Liverpool and 1981,' I remind him. 'That's right.' He nods his head and silently leads me into his study. Books line the walls of the cosy room overlooking the front of the estate, where two large statues of dogs keep guard. There's a huge painting of a hare that sits above his desk. 'It is a copy of a famous Holbein,' he tells me. This is very much Heseltine's turf – and it's a world away from Liverpool, the city he was sent to help heal four decades ago.

In the aftermath of the unrest, Thatcher decided to despatch her then environment secretary Heseltine to the city, announcing the move on 17 July – almost two weeks after the unrest had erupted.[40] His new role saw him dubbed 'Minister for Merseyside'.[41] Heseltine took an office on the fourth floor of the Liver Building overlooking the River Mersey as he began a three-week 'fact finding mission'. He'd host visitors to hear about their concerns and proposed solutions for the city. Local politicians and business leaders bent his ear, as he tried to formulate a plan for a city on the brink.[42]

In his memoirs, Heseltine writes about the task in front of him.[43] 'I would stand with a glass of wine, looking out at the magnificent view over the river, and ask myself what had gone wrong for this great English city. The Mersey, its lifeblood, flowed as majestically as ever down from the hills. Its monumental Georgian and Victorian buildings, created with such pride, still dominated the skyline. The Liver Building itself, the epicentre of a trading system that had reached out to the four corners of the earth, stood defiant and from my perspective very alone,' he wrote. 'Everything had gone wrong.'

Thatcher had come to the city herself on 13 July and met with a group of young people from L8 and Wally Brown, a community leader who represented the area during the summer of 1981. But it was clear where the prime minister's sympathies lay. When images of the damage were broadcast, she is reported to have responded with: 'Those poor shopkeepers.'[44] Others in her cabinet adopted a more conciliatory tone. The Home Secretary Willie Whitelaw, shaken by what he'd witnessed as he toured the country in 1981, said the government needed to promote mutual tolerance and understanding 'upon which the whole future of British democratic society depends'.[45] But in Thatcher's opinion, despite the violence involving people of all races and ages, some from the oldest Black British population in the country, there simply was no racial element to consider. Brown, who had been trained in community work with Ansel Wong, a race relations advisor on Ken Livingstone's radical Greater London Council, recalls his meeting with Thatcher at the City Hall. 'She wasn't listening,' he told me.

He attempted to explain the challenges the Black community faced in L8, from unemployment to poor housing and the history of police tensions. Thatcher's only response was 'there's no excuse for violence', a line she repeated like a mantra. 'She was dismissive of us,' Brown says. 'We were just like shit on her shoe. She had to speak to us, but she didn't want to.' Thatcher told the young people that their skin colour didn't matter to her, but 'crime did', before urging them not to resort to violence or live in separate communities. Later in her memoirs the prime minister reflected on what she thought had caused the problem, using language that veers into the kind of racist dog whistle that Muriel Fletcher had used to describe Black Liverpool. For Thatcher, the situation was simple: rioters were young men 'whose high animal spirits' had been unleashed to 'wreak havoc'.

Brown, who went on to be chair of the city's Community Relations Council, insisted the biggest issue was policing, pointing out the unrest had started with the heavy-handed arrest of Leroy Cooper. He was so insistent that the prime minister later wrote that she was appalled by the 'hostility to the Chief Constable and the police'. In truth, few Chief Constables during the Thatcher era had healthy relationships with the Black populations they policed, but nowhere was that relationship more fraught than in Liverpool.

Seven years before the summer of 1981, Merseyside welcomed a new Chief Constable. Kenneth Oxford had come up in London's Metropolitan Police after serving with the air force during the Second World War. An imposing, self-assured man, he didn't shy from incendiary comments. 'It was a reaction by a band of thugs and hooligans,' he told news cameras in the aftermath of 1981, 'who just do not want to live to a civilised system.' Many he interacted with deemed him arrogant and a man who cared little what people outside his orbit thought.[46] But some praised him. The *Sunday Times* called him the 'coppers' copper', 'an officer who is always going to be more popular with his men than with outsiders'.

Relations between the community of L8 and the police had been strained well before he arrived. Oxford had succeeded Sir James Haughton, known locally as Sunny Jim the Smiling Assassin thanks to his reputation for polite duplicity. During his tenure in the 1970s, Haughton set up a task force that saw police drive into L8 in Land Rovers and pick up people on Suspected Person Loitering, Liverpool's version of the hated Sus laws. In meetings with community leaders, he would reportedly wear a concerned expression as he listened to accounts of police violence, then turn to his officers as soon as the meeting was over and say, 'Get the vans out.'[47]

Oxford's own relationship with activists in L8 was non-existent. Not only did he carry on Haughton's scorched-earth tactics; in 1978 he gave an interview to the BBC's *The Listener* magazine in which he echoed the sentiments of Muriel Fletcher and the eugenicists, claiming that many of L8's mixed-heritage residents were 'the products of liaisons between Black seamen and white prostitutes'. Though Oxford would later maintain the comments were misquoted or wrongly attributed to him, the interview goes on:

> Naturally, they do not grow up with any kind of recognisable home life. Worse still, after they have done the rounds of homes and institutions, they gradually realise they are nothing. The Negroes will not accept them as Blacks, and the whites assume they are coloureds ... the half-caste community on Merseyside, more particularly Liverpool, is well outside recognised society.[48]

As soon as he arrived in Liverpool, Heseltine made clear that policing did not come under his remit, arguing that it was the preserve of Willie Whitelaw, the Home Secretary. Nevertheless, he met with representatives of L8 at Charles Wootton House, the community facility named after the Black seaman killed by a mob during the 1919 race riots. The meeting was hosted by the L8 Defence Committee, a collection of community activists supporting those facing legal action in the wake of the unrest and presenting an alternative view to the press.

The committee was formidable: there were reports of photographers having their cameras snatched and film destroyed, while other members of the press claimed they were threatened with physical violence. Heseltine remembers palpable tension in the room on arriving at the community meeting in Charles Wootton House. A journalist whispered to him that the group were planning a walk-out. They did, en masse. Another meeting was arranged, again at the Charles Wootton.

'The room was packed,' he recalls in his memoirs.[49] 'Some of those present had cuts and bruises sustained in recent events. I would be the first to admit that it was the most demanding meeting I have ever chaired.' Every row was filled with members from the Black community. The meeting was around an hour old, and members of the audience had spoken about the discrimination they faced, from the police and in employment in the city. Then people – 'movers

Michael Heseltine, the so-called 'Minister for Merseyside' tours Toxteth on 25 July 1981

and shakers' – according to Heseltine, began to walk out again. Once more, the tension rose. 'What people are concerned about is the police, and the policing of this area,' the chair of the defence committee, Rashid Mufti told TV crews after the meeting.[50] 'Mr Heseltine wanted to talk about other things like unemployment, housing and resources, of course people want good housing and jobs, but people weren't talking about that . . . those riots were the result of continual police harassment over years.'

By the time of the meeting, certain members of the defence committee had become minor celebrities, most notably Michael Showers. The son of a Nigerian and a local Black L8 woman, Showers was regularly found at the frontline of protests and was an effective and assured spokesperson for the cause, batting away journalists' questions with ease. When TV crews came to L8, it was often Showers who'd act as their guide. Though he sounded like a radical activist straight out of *Blacks Britannica*, he drove a white Rolls-Royce and eschewed the alternative aesthetic of his peers in favour of a sharp suit. And while Showers might have come across as an activist in interviews, he was also one of the most successful criminals in the history of Merseyside.

He'd started out doing bank jobs, scoping out targets before raiding them and then disappearing abroad (France was his favourite place to spend money, and Paris in particular).[51] By the 1980s Showers had become a major drug trafficker: importing cannabis from Nigeria via Liverpool's docks, which had always been used to bring in illegal cargo.[52] When Heseltine arrived in the city, he said he received an intelligence briefing informing him that Showers was the real power in L8.

While other members of the defence committee – including Alan Gayle, Linda Loy, Rashid Mufti, Solly Bassey, Maria O'Reilly and Wally's brother Manneh – played far bigger roles in the organisation, Heseltine and the city's law enforcement viewed Showers' involvement as an indictment of L8's population as a whole. 'There are no simple generalisations about Toxteth,' Heseltine tells me four decades on. 'Was there discrimination? Yes. Was there poverty? Yes.

But it was also one of the most cash-regenerative bank branches in the National Westminster bank chain. Why? Because it was riddled with crime.' There isn't any evidence to suggest L8 had a crime rate that was higher than other postcodes in Liverpool, but the perception that it did stuck, fuelled not just by events in 1981 but from decades of biased reports and lazy generalisations.

While Heseltine might have been threatened by the actions of the L8 Defence Committee, for the younger generation of L8 activists, they showed how authority – of any level – could be confronted and challenged. 'They set the marker for all of us,' said Quarless, who would go on to found the Steve Biko Housing Association in the city. 'We became quite staunch in our views, and we weren't afraid to confront the establishment. By the time 1981 comes along we could set up organisations, we could get funding, we could co-ordinate and strategise, we could do anything.'

Heseltine's three-week reconnaissance stay in Liverpool in 1981 resulted in a series of headline-grabbing announcements and media events. He arranged a tour of Liverpool for twenty-nine businessmen who were put on a coach and driven through areas of deprivation, such as Everton, and via the defunct Tate & Lyle plant. He thought the private sector would re-energise the city, but many of the leaders on the coach were appalled by the poverty on view. Heseltine and his team created a fourteen-point plan for improving the city, which included redevelopment of the Albert Docks, training schemes for young scousers and the creation of an art gallery that would bring back a great name to the city: Tate Liverpool. A quango called the Taskforce would implement his vision and interact with local government and L8 groups to try and meet their needs.

Heseltine's initial plan impressed many in the city, and in cabinet he pressed the case to save Britain's inner cities. In his report 'It Took a Riot', he asked for £200 million split over two years in order to turn Liverpool around. In private, Thatcher's closest advisors were telling her it was futile to invest. Her Chancellor Geoffrey Howe advocated instead for a policy of 'managed decline', arguing in a private note that Heseltine's plans for a 'massive injection of additional public spending'[53] were folly. In response to his request for investment, Heseltine was given £15 million, with the condition that 'no publicity should be given to this figure'.

Not every aspect of Heseltine's plans was well received. His proposal for an International Garden Festival was met with incredulity by many activists. 'What we needed for our health and wellbeing was trees, and flowers,' says Bea Freeman, who was also part of the L8 Defence Committee. 'And that would stop rioting. Not education or employment – we needed the Garden Festival.' While more than three and a half million visitors attended the event over its five-month stretch in 1984, the festival cost £30 million and created few opportunities for the local population. I ask Heseltine if he knows how many Black people were employed: he can't say. South Liverpool Personnel – the employment agency in L8 that Liz Drysdale worked for – said of the dozens of people they sent for work, only five were employed; other estimates put it as low as two. Claire Dove, who ran South Liverpool Personnel, said the festival felt like a way of making the route into the city centre – which passed by L8 – more attractive rather than helping to create any lasting change in the postcode. 'They put trees down Parliament Street which is the main thoroughfare into town. You put trees up for those people in their cars, so they have a nice vista but hidden behind that are the houses where Black people live. They were using architectural design to make L8 more palatable for the people passing through.'

The legacy of Heseltine's high-profile fourteen-point plan was and remains contested. While government was bringing about change in Liverpool, it was accused of giving with one hand and taking with the other. About £130 million in urban aid and dockland redevelopment assistance had eventually been pumped into Liverpool by 1984 but during the same period it lost about £200 million from Whitehall, with housing subsidies and financial assistance to the council being slashed as Howe squeezed budgets.[54] And despite being the area in the most need of help, L8 was largely ignored by the plans. 'We've got riots in Liverpool 8,' Willy Brown told me, 'but Michael Heseltine is appointed as Minister of Merseyside. Well, Merseyside goes as far as St Helens, it goes over the Wirral – they had nothing to do with the riots. I thought he should have concentrated on Liverpool, or even just Liverpool 8, to sort out the issues here.' Heseltine's biggest projects – the development of a technology park in Wavertree; the renovation of the Albert Dock and the arrival of Tate Liverpool; improvement of a large industrial estate at Knowsley; regeneration of land in front of the Anglican cathedral; council house modernisation – were all concentrated in areas where few Black scousers lived.

In 1985, Channel 4 broadcast a documentary called *They Haven't Done Nothing*. Made by a group of Black scousers and produced by Bea Freeman, the film looked at the aftermath of 1981.[55] Leroy Cooper, the artist whose attempted arrest was blamed for triggering the unrest, appears on Granby Street in dark sunglasses, short dreadlocks, a white shirt and black leather jacket. He recites a poem that offers a bleak view of the options available to the young and unemployed in L8: the dole, 'slave jobs' or crime. 'Blag mask, shotgun – I'll take my chance; it's either five years in Walton or a lifetime in France.' Now he pops up again outside the law courts, impersonating a judge passing sentence on a young Black man: 'You come before me charged with the most serious crime of being Black and alive / you not only have the arrogance to breathe in but you insist on breathing out as well.' It's a funny intervention, but like most good jokes there's a serious point underpinning it. In the early 1980s, Black people, while less than 2 per cent of the general population, were 17 per cent of the prison population while 36 per cent of young prisoners – those aged twenty-one-years-old and younger – were Black.

Freeman's film finds that the country's focus had shifted to other stories – the Falklands War, the miners' strike – while, locally, Liverpool was mired in political infighting and scandal. The City Council had been taken over by Militant Tendency, the Trotskyite group led by Derek Hatton that had infiltrated the Labour Party. While the Conservative central government demanded an ever-smaller state and reduced budgets, Militant Tendency and Hatton refused to cut theirs, and were also at loggerheads with the Labour leader Neil Kinnock, who wanted them out.[56] The city's football fans had a terrible reputation, too, after the Heysel disaster in 1985, which resulted in thirty-nine deaths when Liverpool followers attacked Juventus supporters during the European Cup Final in Brussels, causing a wall to collapse. As Tony Evans puts it in *Two Tribes*, his history of the city and its football culture during the 1980s: 'Few people outside the region had any sympathy for a city with murderous football fans and extremist politics.'

Back in Westminster, Liverpool had slipped down the list of priorities. Heseltine had been promoted to Secretary of State for Defence, where he used his PR skills to neutralise the growing Campaign for Nuclear Disarmament.[57] Thatcher was buoyed by her victory during the swift and decisive Falklands War, and in 1984 she managed to take on and defeat the striking miners a year later, and in so doing accomplished one of her main objectives since taking office in 1979: to reduce the power of the unions. There were other, more lethal issues too; Thatcher narrowly escaped harm from the IRA bomb planted in the Brighton hotel she was staying in during the 1984 Conservative Party conference – a blast that killed five people. Fresh bouts of upheaval broke out in Black communities in Tottenham and in Handsworth during the autumn of 1985, and once again extended to L8. 'At the moment,' Bobby Nyahoe, an L8 community worker and artist, told *The New York Times* in 1985, 'there are no politicians to appeal to who have any sway over anything . . . the normal channels are reduced to chaos.'[58] Despite the trouble in the middle of the decade, however, the problems of Liverpool's Black community had mostly faded from view.

While the government's attention may have moved on, the legacy of 1981 can be seen in the generation of community activists that came from it. Bea Freeman has made half a dozen films about her city that shed light on aspects no one up to that point had bothered to investigate; Ray Quarless has spent decades assisting L8 residents with their housing needs; Claire Dove got hundreds of people into employment; Liz Drysdale went into politics and then ran a day-care centre to help young mothers; Wally Brown continued to do youth work; Maria O'Reilly was in court with L8 residents as they defended themselves. Liverpool's Black population were a minority within a city that was hit as hard as anywhere by the economic turmoil of the 1980s. But the long history of conflict in the city meant they were prepared: the unrest of 1981 was just the latest moment in a unique history, something that people like Heseltine struggled to understand.

L8 wasn't waiting for Heseltine or central government to bring the transformation; they'd started themselves. When Stephen Nze wound up in court accused of pulling down the Huskisson statue, a representative of the L8 Law Centre, a legal advice centre which O'Reilly ran, helped him formulate a successful defence. The Housing Aid Centre on Granby Street provided more legal advice, developed a credit union and offered community transport in the form of a red double-decker London bus. There was the Liverpool Black Organisation; the youth club at the Methodist Church run by Wally Brown; the Charles Wotton i-Tec (a centre that provided IT training); South Liverpool Personnel was an employment agency that had support from the Martin Luther King Foundation; the Liverpool Black Sisters – a Black feminist group that formed in 1979 and started after-school clubs to support Black women in L8. The Black Caucus, a grouping that interacted with the City Council had been taken over by the L8 Defence Committee. The street signs on Granby Street, L8's main thoroughfare, had been painted the Rastafarian colours of red, gold and green by Leroy Cooper. Quarless argues that L8's self-organised infrastructure sent a clear message to the local council and central government: 'We don't need you anymore.'

I spoke to the current mayor of Liverpool, Joanne Anderson, about Heseltine's role in the aftermath of 1981. 'He was raising his profile and using Liverpool [to do that],' she tells me, while acknowledging he did help improve relations between the city and the Conservative Party. Was it possible that Heseltine had been genuinely committed to his task and also seen it as an opportunity to raise his profile with one eye on a future leadership bid? 'I never thought in those terms,' he says, looking at me sternly. 'I do assure you.' He has a comeback for Anderson too: 'It wasn't me who gave me the Freedom of the City,' he says, referring to the honour he received in 2012. 'It was 68 Labour councillors.'

Heseltine never did become prime minister – though responsible for ousting Thatcher through a leadership challenge, he would ultimately lose out on the premiership to John Major in the Conservative Party election of 1990. In her memoir, Thatcher is less than complimentary about his time in the city, arguing that 'most of his efforts only had ephemeral results', and concluding with the words: 'I would not blame him for that: Liverpool has defeated better men than Michael Heseltine.'

Today, much of Heseltine's vision for Liverpool has been realised. The Garden Festival might have been mocked by many but, as Nassy Brown observed, it turned 'the city itself into a proper English place, suitable for investment'. The port has been transformed, with Tate Liverpool sitting in the middle of a shiny new marina in the Albert Dock; the shopping development L1 dominates part of the city centre that overlooks Adell's final resting place; and Everton FC are building their new multi-million-pound stadium by the water. Almost seventy million people visit Liverpool annually, making it one of the most popular cities in the UK for tourism, and in 2008 it was named European Capital of Culture.

I ask Heseltine what he thinks his biggest achievement is, but he refuses to answer. 'You can't single out any one thing; that misses the point,' he says. 'If you want to have dynamic cities, you have to build comprehensively on their strengths, eradicate their weaknesses, seize their opportunities. And this is something you do across the board, not in any one, small compartment.' It's an answer that's typical of the politician who has spent the last four decades lobbying successive governments to invest in his model of urban regeneration that's been implemented in London Docklands in the east of the city and Cardiff's port area. But his claim that regeneration has to happen 'across the board' is something Black scousers will raise an eyebrow at: in the wake of 1981, the wishes of L8 went almost entirely ignored.

Black Liverpool has seen its own changes in the intervening period, and tells a different story to that of the rest of the city: Charles Wootton House is long gone, as are all the historic Black clubs that once lined the area, and so is the L8 Defence Committee. The community has changed, with new influxes of immigration, notably from Somalia, shifting the demographics of the postcode. 'Even though there was poverty, even though there was discrimination, the way that we all came together then – I wish we could do that now,' says Michelle Charters, who was part of the Liverpool Black Women's Group. 'I think that's missing a little bit.' But there is a tangible legacy of those days in the city. Kuumba Imani Millennium Centre, an arts institution that has its roots in the Liverpool Black Sisters group; while other 1981-era organisations, like the Steve Biko Housing Association, remain. Since 2007, Liverpool has been home to the International Slavery Museum, which Charters currently runs. With its permanent home by the docks, the institution ensures Liverpool's Black history is secured in one of the UK's most popular museums.

The grand buildings and streets that Heseltine so admired as he looked out from his perch in the Liver Building are still there, but their connections to the slave trade are being revealed. There has been a sustained and successful campaign, led by Black Liverpudlians, to make known the slave trade connections of places such as Bold Street (named after Jonas Bold, the sugar trader and former mayor of Liverpool) and Seel Street (named in honour of Thomas Seel, an enslaver and merchant). An L8-based history group is looking into more of Liverpool's institutions and unearthing their connections to slavery. If you drive down Princes Avenue, you'll see plaques that honour historical moments from L8's past, fought for and installed by community leaders such as Sonia Bassey.

Perhaps the most obvious legacy of the '81 activists is in the political leadership – the city named its first Black female councillor in 1987, when Liz Drysdale was elected. Today a Black female MP Kim Johnson represents the city's Riverside constituency that includes much of L8, while the outgoing mayor, Joanne Anderson, is also Black. There have been difficulties on the way: Anderson would have been the second Black mayor if Petrona Lashley, a deputy mayor and candidate for the top job in the 1990s, had not been stopped by a media campaign that was widely seen as racist and sexist.[59]

When you compare how many positions of influence are held by Black people in Liverpool and neighbouring Manchester, the difference is startling. Only 4.6 per cent of people in prominent public positions in Manchester are Black, in a city where Black people account for almost 15 per cent of the population.[60] In Liverpool, 5 per cent of leading public positions are held by Black people, a figure roughly in line with the city's 5.2 per cent Black population. A lot of those positions are in politics, with many figures either coming directly from the 1981 generation or growing up in its aftermath.

The improved political representation hasn't served as a panacea. Black youth unemployment is still significantly higher than other groups: in the aftermath of the Covid-19 pandemic, 41.6 per cent of Black people aged 16–24 were unemployed, compared to 12.4 per cent for whites. Despite Sus being abolished four decades ago, Black men are still twice more likely to be stopped by police across Liverpool than their white counterparts, with police using force disproportionately against Black scousers.[61] Shortly after the fortieth anniversary of the 1981 unrest the Merseyside police was described as 'institutionally racist' by the area's police and crime commissioner. For many members of the community there hasn't been enough progress since the summer of 1981.

In Wally Brown's memoirs, he laments the fact Granby Street is now made up of a few shops, and no longer even has a post office or a bank. 'Houses were built,' he wrote.[62] 'But without any community infrastructure.' It's still rare to see Black faces from the L8 community working in the shiny new retail developments like L1 in the city centre, a short walk from Adell's grave. Anna Rothery – the city's first ever Black Lord Mayor – complained that even decades after the disorder of the early 1980s, 'We are still not a visible community. Liverpool is a tale of two cities.'[63] But in Liverpool, the bellwether city for race relations, there were at least some signs that progress – however slow – had been made.

That change reflects and sometimes anticipates the wider national story. When the historic Black community in Brixton revolted in 1981, Britain was forced to pay attention; the impact of that summer was simply too big to ignore. Politics had to change, with the fallout from the disturbances resulting in three Black Labour politicians – Diane Abbott, Bernie Grant and Paul Boateng[64] – being elected six years later. 'Without the uprising in Brixton you wouldn't have had Black people elected to parliament in 1987,' said Abbott on the fortieth anniversary of the unrest. 'Those uprisings made politics pay attention to Black representation, particularly on the left, where people tended to focus on class and thought talking about race was a distraction.'

The ramifications throughout British society were far-reaching. It wasn't just politics that witnessed a watershed: Sus was repealed via the 1981 Criminal Attempts Act – although the Police and Criminal Evidence Act of 1984 would go on to give officers 'stop and search' powers. Black media outlets appeared, such as *The Voice* newspaper and Choice FM, while the public sector began to focus on equal opportunities in an attempt to reduce discrimination. Education finally took the calls from Black teachers and parents about biased curriculums seriously, with the Inner London Education Authority (ILEA), campaigning for the introduction of Black Studies and pushing early calls for curriculums to be decolonised. In 1987, Black History Month would become a permanent fixture in the British calendar, taking place every October.[65] That initiative originated in Ken Livingstone's radical Greater London Council, which continued to support pioneering race relations work until it was abolished in 1986.

*

The Ghost of William Huskisson – Liverpool, 1981

In June 2020, four decades on from the fall of Huskisson, Stephen Nze would turn on the TV and experience a strong sense of déjà vu. On his screen, a crowd cheered as the statue of Edward Colston, the slave owner whose likeness stood in Bristol, was thrown into Bristol Harbour. The ramifications of the Black Lives Matter protests were echoing around the country, just as the unrest in 1981 had done.

Newsreaders said it was a landmark moment, but Nze knew it wasn't the first of its kind. On that summer's evening in Liverpool in 1982 it was members of the local community who took action, inspired by the 1981 movement. 'I was one of those young people at 17 who was influenced by that, I suppose,' Nze said, forty years on. 'Did we plan to do it: no. Did we feel justified doing it: yes. Do we feel justified doing it to this day: yes.'

In 2021, Nze collaborated with the artist Harold Offeh to create an artwork retelling the story of that night. Huskisson's plinth still stands empty on Princes Boulevard, and his statue now resides in Dukes Terrace, a row of grade II listed homes that were originally built for the employees of wealthy merchants; the kind of men Huskisson helped make rich. Perhaps there his ghost can rest easy.

5.
Black Art an'done – Wolverhampton, 1982

Around eighty people answered the call. Some had found out by word of mouth; others through a conversation in a studio space, or via a flyer pressed into an open palm. On Thursday 28 October 1982, dozens of Black artists, students and teachers made their way to a small lecture theatre at Wolverhampton Polytechnic in the West Midlands. Some were enthusiastic, others wary, but all were curious to find out more about what was being billed as the first National Black Art Convention.

The event's organisers weren't learned academics, like Stuart Hall in Birmingham, or the battle-hardened activists who'd helped to free George Lindo in Bradford. They were art students – teenagers or final-year candidates in their early twenties – who, charged with a desire to challenge an art world sealed off to people like them, had banded together under the name of the Blk Art Group.

They were living through an era when Britain's leading art historians had declared 'Africa had no history' before the Europeans arrived.[1] The Black British art of the early 1980s was often dismissed as 'harsh', 'despairing' or coming 'very close to choking on its own anger'. That view had seeped into art schools. When Black art students produced a work about Black themes or subjects, they were met with bemusement or open hostility. These were the children of Windrush: they'd seen the Notting Hill Carnival of 1976 on television and heard Thatcher's 'swamped' comments two years later.[2] Brought up in Britain during the post-war era on the promise of equal rights and opportunity, but finding that reality presented many invisible barriers.

The summer of 1981 – with the violence that moved around the country from Brixton to Liverpool – had represented a collective rejection of the little that Britain had deemed to offer its Black citizens. A year on, and the Blk Art Group wanted to shake the British art world out of its complacency. 'It was about visibility,' Keith Piper, a founding member, told me when outlining the aims of the convention. Being seen by the art establishment, but also by each other.

Many of the young artists in attendance were leading an isolated existence on campus – they were often the sole Black member on their course. The convention offered a chance to come together and forge relationships that would last for decades. They would also debate and in some cases argue fiercely about what Black art should be, a question that felt vital in the wake of 1981. Should their art be political, or could it be abstract or personal too? Did they have a responsibility to respond directly to the restive world that Black Britons faced in the Thatcher era?

The art they created while answering this question produced – arguably for the first time – a Black British visual identity. Their work drew from the imagery of the far right; it took on the themes of slavery and colonialism; it questioned Black women's position in society. Those who attended that autumn day in 1982 would go on to become some of the most celebrated artists of their generation: Turner Prize winners and nominees, Guggenheim scholarship recipients, a Venice Biennale Golden Lion winner among them.

What the Blk Art Group achieved that autumn would change British culture, even if it took many decades for the British art establishment to recognise it. Perhaps fittingly, they did it in a town that was still reverberating from the seismic event of the late 1960s that had reshaped Britain's relationship with race and immigration and put their generation in the firing line.

Fourteen years before the Blk Art Group held their convention, Enoch Powell, MP for Wolverhampton, made his 'Rivers of Blood' speech. Addressing a group of Conservative activists on a Saturday afternoon in Birmingham in April 1968, his twenty-five-minute

A man walks past graffiti in support of Enoch Powell after his 'Rivers of Blood' speech

screed predicted terrifying racial violence if the immigration that had started in 1948 continued. Those present bore witness to the most notorious speech made by a British politician in the twentieth century. Powell – a fifty-six-year-old senior figure in the Conservative Party who'd once run for leader – would claim he was simply prepared to say what others thought in private but dared not utter in public: non-white immigration was a scourge that would destroy Britain.

The shadow defence secretary said he was horrified to speak to an unnamed 'Englishman' from Wolverhampton who told him he thought Britain would soon become a place where the Black man would eventually hold 'the whip hand' over the white man. An old widow allegedly told him she was being harassed, her windows smashed with excrement pushed through her letter box, while on a trip to the shop she was followed by 'wide-grinning piccaninnies'. He rallied against the 'alien element' being introduced to Britain and suggested it wouldn't be enough to simply stop all immigration; he called for voluntary repatriation of immigrants already in the country. We were 'literally mad' as a nation for allowing this to happen and, if it wasn't reversed, the consequences could be a biblical race war. 'As I look ahead,' said Powell, the former classics scholar, 'I am filled with foreboding; like the Roman, I seem to see "the River Tiber foaming with much blood,"' referring to Virgil's *Aeneid*.

The speech came as the Labour government led by Harold Wilson were attempting to beef up the Race Relations Act, introduced three years earlier, with a new bill that focused on making housing and employment more equal. Powell hated the first bill,[3] which made it illegal to promote racial hatred or to discriminate against someone because of their race. Before then it had been perfectly legal to refuse to serve someone in a pub or put up signs outside a lodging house that said 'No dogs, no Blacks, no Irish'.

Powell is often presented as an outlier: colleagues call him 'theatrical' and a 'loner' – a rogue element in the body politic. But his ideas didn't form in a vacuum. Only two months before his speech, the Labour Home Secretary Jim Callaghan argued openly that the 'increased flow' of South Asian migrants from East Africa caused by the 'Africanisation' policy that saw them expelled from Kenya and Uganda by Black nationalist leaders was 'continuing and might become a flood'. The influx, he argued, was 'more than we could absorb' as the controversial 1968 Commonwealth Immigrants Act (an amendment to the 1962 act) was passed – and for the first time denied British citizens entry to the country on the grounds of their race. It did so by requiring entrants to prove a connection to the country by either a parent or grandparent who'd been born in the UK, separating immigrants into two categories: 'belonging', which meant, for example, white Australians whose families had emigrated, and 'non-belonging': Black and brown migrants from former colonies.[4] Callaghan's biographer Kenneth Morgan points out that 'from Callaghan's perspective, Powell's antics were a valuable distraction. They enabled the government to appear, by contrast, sane and balanced.'

Powell knew his speech would ruffle feathers; it was designed to inflame the debate around immigration and racism just as the Race Relations Act was passing through parliament. The night before he reportedly told Clem Jones, the editor of the Wolverhampton *Express & Star* and an old family friend, that he was going to make a speech that would 'fizz like a rocket; but whereas all rockets fall to the earth, this one is going to stay up'. Powell had shifted the tone of British politics almost instantly. No mainstream politician had dared to use the language Powell had, which up until then had been the preserve of fascists like Oswald Mosley.

What the 1968 speech raged against most was the children of immigrants having the exact same rights as white Britons. By accommodating these new Britons, Powell argued, it would be 'ordinary people' in towns like Wolverhampton whose schools would be crammed; maternity wards overcrowded as whites found themselves 'made strangers in their own country'. It was hysterical and outlandish; incendiary and bizarre.[5] And it brazenly played to Britons' fears and ignorance of the new Black citizens who were living among them in greater numbers.

The impact of the speech was instant: Powell was sacked from the shadow cabinet of Edward Heath, his great political rival to whom he'd lost a leadership battle. East London dockers (covertly organised by fascists)[6] called a strike when the news of his dismissal broke, while Powell received 100,000 letters in support and his backers claimed that up to 80 per cent of the British public agreed with his anti-immigration sentiments. Powell was expelled from political life, but Black Britons felt the shockwaves Powell's speech had unleashed.

The academic Stuart Hall, working in Birmingham when Powell made the speech, said he remembered the sudden, shared feeling of fear 'as little groups of Black men and women came together to discuss how to respond to the violence it seemed calculated to unleash'.[7] Graffiti appeared in Black areas of London that read: 'Powell for PM!'; while in Wolverhampton there was a palpable tension among the Black community. A school girl in Powell's constituency was so terrified she was unable to sleep, scared of going

Black Art an'done – Wolverhampton, 1982

into school the day after in case she was lynched.[8] The vision Powell had depicted, of racial armageddon and violence, would hang over Britain well into the Thatcher era and legitimised a powerful idea: Black Britons were an enemy within.

The Blk Art Group was made up of the people Powell so feared: Black British youth claiming their place in Britain. Eddie Chambers – the central galvanising force around which much of the Blk Art Group's activity would rotate – grew up in Wolverhampton in the aftermath of 'Rivers of Blood'. He was organised, driven, and had studied with Keith Piper at Coventry Polytechnic in 1979. When the pair met, Chambers was already in the process of organising a landmark exhibition ('Black Art an'Done') in his hometown as part of a collective called the Wolverhampton Young Black Artists. Held at the Wolverhampton Art Gallery in June 1981, the show featured work by Chambers, Piper, Andrew Hazel, Dominic Dawes and Ian Palmer – a group of Black, male artists who had grown up in the West Midlands. People who walked through the doors of Wolverhampton Art Gallery that summer were faced with art that confronted. The graphic-led work of Piper and Chambers left little doubt as to their concerns. Each artist wrote a statement of intent. 'The Black art student, by his very Blackness, finds himself drawn towards the epicentre of social tension,' Piper wrote. 'He is forced to respond to the urgency of the hour.'

Keith Piper grew up in Sparkbrook, Birmingham and after his foundation course in Coventry had moved to Nottingham where he studied art at Trent Polytechnic. It was in Nottingham that he met Donald Rodney, another art student who was from Smethwick, just north of Birmingham. A flamboyant young artist who wore oversized glasses, he once said he would love to recreate Tate Britain out of sugar cubes as a comment on the art gallery's connection to the sugar trade, which was powered by slavery.

Another Brummie, Marlene Smith, would also join in the summer of 1982 after she saw the group's show at Ikon Gallery in Birmingham. She was the youngest of the Blk Art Group and had only just completed her A Levels. She loved the radical writing of Black feminist bell hooks, and the art produced during the Black Arts Movement of the 1960s, when African-American artists such as Amiri Baraka and Maya Angelou acted as the cultural wing of the Black Power Movement. Smith's mother and Keith Piper's father had worked together in the NHS in Birmingham, where they both spent time as nurses specialising in mental health, and it was her father who'd given Smith a poster for the Blk Art Group's show at the Ikon. The poster was black, with quotes from each member of the group, which had now expanded and featured two female artists: Wenda Leslie and Janet Vernon. The quotes acted as mission statements, and it was Dominic Dawes' that made Smith stop in her tracks. 'I am becoming more aware of how Black people have become victims of this fascist and racist white brutality,' read his statement. 'When I saw the words on the poster the hairs on the back of my neck stood up,' said Smith. 'It was one of those magical goosebumps moments because what they were saying sounded so much like the rhetoric that was being used by the Black Arts Movement in the US.' But it wasn't just US art that the group drew inspiration from, culture from much closer to home in the West Midlands was also shaping their creativity.

When Chambers and Piper met in Coventry, they bonded over a love of art and the city's two-tone scene: a multiracial mash-up of British punk and Jamaican ska. The music was upbeat and hyper, melding the scratchy guitar of punk with the softer melodies of ska, with sardonic lyrics that took aim at life in Thatcher's Britain. They wore sharp suits and pencil ties (the two-tone uniform) and went to see groups like The Selecter and The Beat. 'It had a really important effect on the way that I think Eddie and myself really saw the world politically,' Piper told me when I met him at his studio space in Brixton. 'At that moment, it was very much about the possibilities of this homegrown, politicised form of music coming from these two traditions.'

Like the two-tone bands they loved, their art was direct and often overtly political. They also combined different formats: Chambers' work featured newsprint, photography and text; one work depicts a Black hand grabbing barbed wire with blood running down the wrist. Another of Piper's pieces, 'Go West Young Man', directly addressed the slave trade.[9] Piper takes the famous clarion call for westward expansion in the United States, when citizens were encouraged to 'grow up with the country', and couples it with an image of Black bodies crammed into a slave vessel – a reminder that America's growth came at a human cost. Chambers' most famous work, a deconstructed Union Jack in the shape of a Nazi swastika, summed up life in the aftermath of Powell's speech, where racist attacks in towns like Wolverhampton increased noticeably. For the Blk Art Group, Powell's worldview wasn't an abstract threat, it was tangible and bled into the Black culture that was coming out of the West Midlands in the early 1980s.

At the same time as Chambers and Piper were creating their confrontational art, the Coventry two-tone band The Specials were addressing the wider political landscape in Britain. Their single 'Ghost Town' was released during the disturbances of 1981, hitting number one as the country burned and unemployment shot up to a record high of 14 per cent[10] – conditions that saw Thatcher, only two years into her first term, become the most unpopular leader since the Second World War.[11]

Thatcher's government was in the process of restructuring the British economy as the industrial decline seen in Birmingham, Bradford and Liverpool spread around the country. Britain's industries – from shipbuilding to coal mining to textile mills – had begun to suffer as early as the 1950s, resulting in the loss of hundreds of thousands of jobs two decades before Thatcher saw office. But her first government introduced policies – powered by a belief in monetarism and a small state – that exacerbated the deterioration. Struggling industries wouldn't get government support, as the monetarism doctrine mandated the free market would decide whether companies were worth saving. Under Thatcher's guidance, the UK was to become a country that no longer made things, and instead provided services, the centre of which would be the City of London and the financial markets that would produce obscene amounts of wealth for bankers and traders in the later part of the decade. All of that shifted the economic geography away from places like Wolverhampton and toward the south-east of the country, primarily to the capital and the home counties. It was a painful period, as former industrial giants collapsed or were restructured; and communities that were built around one or maybe two main employers began to adjust to life dominated by long-term unemployment.

In March 1981, as the economic reality of Thatcher's new vision for Britain began to take hold, her approval rating stood at a woeful 16 per cent. Incredibly, just eighteen months later that rating would soar to reach a record high – after a conflict that would redefine her premiership.

On the morning of 2 April 1982, a radio message came into the British military forces, some eighty marine commandos, that a 2,000-strong Argentinian invasion force was incoming to a tiny group of islands just off the coast of the South American country. Sovereignty of the Falkland Islands had been disputed for the 150 years since the British took control of the small but militarily important group of islands in the treacherous seas of the South Atlantic, 8,000 miles from the UK and only 400 miles from the Argentinian coast. Now, the military junta that had seized power of Argentina in 1976 decided it was time to take back the archipelago known in the Spanish-speaking world as the Islas Malvinas. The operation was political: with so much of Britain's navy stationed thousands of miles away, the junta's leadership saw an opportunity to show that they could command respect on the world stage. The move triggered a ten-week conflict that would claim the lives of almost 650 Argentinians and just over 250 Britons.

The Falklands War would dramatically shift people's perceptions of Thatcher. To many, her decision to fight a war on the other side of the world, was a folly – with the Foreign Office advising that the islands would be almost impossible to recapture if taken by the junta. The invasion sent the British navy into panic; sailors flocked to Portsmouth and Plymouth in preparation for deployment of the kind not seen since the Second World War.

The press called for the resignation of the UK's military leadership, who'd been taken completely by surprise, while Thatcher herself was under huge pressure. But she was backed by an enthusiastic, jingoistic tabloid press who covered the conflict as if it were a sporting event. Rupert Murdoch's *The Sun* was the most rabid,[12] inviting readers to sponsor Sidewinder missiles. When the Argentine battleship the *General Belgrano* (carrying 1,000 men) was sunk by a British submarine in May 1982, Murdoch's paper splashed with the celebratory and callous 'GOTCHA' headline.[13]

A few weeks after British troops captured the Falkland Islands' capital Port Stanley in mid-June,[14] Thatcher made a speech in Cheltenham where she not only saluted Britain as once again being a 'competent, courageous and resolute' nation when tested, but also said the war represented something much bigger: the return of Britain as a major nation on the world stage.

'There were those who would not admit it – even perhaps some here today – people who would have strenuously denied the suggestion but – in their heart of hearts – they too had their secret fears that it was true: that Britain was no longer the nation that had built an Empire and ruled a quarter of the world,' she said to a crowd at a Conservative rally.[15] 'Well, they were wrong. The lesson of the Falklands is that Britain has not changed, and that this nation still has those sterling qualities which shine through our history. This generation can match their fathers and grandfathers in ability, in courage, and in resolution. We have not changed.' Her brand of fervent nationalism was potent: the prime minister's approval rating reached a peak of 59 per cent after the conflict, even as many accused her of launching a war to save face as her government faltered.[16] Others have argued Thatcher's popularity was on the rise before the conflict as the economy improved and inflation eased. Either way it was a defining moment of the 1980s, one which the prime minister revelled in.

In truth, Thatcher's Falklands had been incredibly lucky. Many of the Argentinian bombs that fell on British ships failed to detonate because of faulty timers; had the bombs exploded, the land invasion that recaptured the islands would have been impossible.[17] Nevertheless, it was a turning point for Thatcher. The enormous popular support that she enjoyed in the wake of the Falklands meant she was able to silence dissenting voices within her cabinet that disapproved of her economic policies.

But in the industrial towns and cities of the UK, the victory didn't change a bleak economic outlook. The Blk Art Group were watching the war play out with interest. Marlene Smith's cousin was in the army and wrote to her from the Falklands, she and many others in the group saw the conflict as a distraction from the problems in Britain – be that unemployment, Thatcher's approval rating or the racial unrest of 1981.

As Thatcher's Britain emerged, with its winners and losers, the Blk Art Group were driven by an urgency: partly because they were young people with ideas they wanted to get out into the world, and partly out of a need to respond to the frenetic, restive place the UK was in the early 1980s. Playing venues around the country afforded The Specials a unique position from which to sense the national mood. 'You could see that frustration and anger in the audience,' said the band's Jerry Dammers.[18] 'In Glasgow, there were these little old ladies on the streets selling all their household goods, their cups and saucers. It was unbelievable. It was clear that something was very, very wrong.'

The Blk Art Group might have been fuelled by an urgency to engage with the world around them, but there were practical obstacles to overcome. The final core member of the Blk Art Group was Claudette Johnson, who joined after moving to Wolverhampton to study fine art in 1979.[19] Johnson was born in Longsight, Manchester to Jamaican parents and her artistic talent appeared relatively early: in secondary school she had a reputation for being able to sketch portraits of pop stars of the day, and created a small cottage industry out of drawing David Cassidy, David Bowie and Marc Bolan for

Black Art an'done – Wolverhampton, 1982

Claudette Johnson in her studio in London in 1986

her class mates. By the time she arrived at Wolverhampton, Johnson knew she wanted to paint Black figures, but she immediately ran into a problem: a lack of source material. Reference books in the art library didn't feature Black figures, and hiring sitters wasn't financially viable. She broadened her search beyond the art history canon and found Leni Riefenstahl's 1976 book *People of Kau*.

Having made her name as the young director behind Nazi propaganda films like *Triumph of The Will*, a celebration of the 1934 Nuremberg rally, *People of Kau* represented a second act in Riefenstahl's career. It was one of two books she produced about the Nuba tribe of southern Sudan, part of a nimble attempt to reinvent herself as an anthropological photographer.[20] Incredibly, it was a former Nazi collaborator, known as 'Hitler's favourite film-maker',[21] who provided subject matter for Johnson. 'I was trying to find any Black people to use as sources for the work, and that was hard to come by,' Johnson told me. 'Especially anything that has links to Britain.' The fact she had to seek out Riefenstahl's images spoke to a much larger problem at British art schools.

The Blk Art Group finding each other by 1982 was remarkable. Black art students across the country were atomised: often the sole Black representatives on courses taught almost exclusively by white artists, who could be incredibly conservative. Adrian Searle, the white art critic, began teaching at Central St Martins in 1981. Searle remembers being discouraged by other teachers from taking students to the Arnolfini in Bristol, a space that embraced cutting edge experimentation, because he'd be exposing them to 'the wrong kind of art'.[22] When he returned from a trip to New York with pictures of Neo-Geometric Conceptualism work by artists like Jeff Koons, he was warned by a colleague at Coventry Polytechnic not to show them to the students for fear of leading them astray. 'They didn't want to let the bigger world in,' he told me.

Black students creating work that was overtly political, or addressed Blackness, often came up against long-established reactionary forces. In the mid-1960s, the influential historian Hugh Trevor-Roper launched what in today's parlance would be called an attack on wokeness. In the first chapter of his book *The Rise of Christian Europe* he decried 'fashionable' calls for historians to work on African history rather than continue to prioritise Europe. People were seduced by the idea of African history but, he said, 'at present there is none, or very little: there is only the history of the Europeans in Africa. The rest is largely darkness.' The attitude towards Africa and Black culture in general – that it was of little merit – was still dominant when Johnson was at art school, a decade after Trevor-Roper's book had been published. Many Black British artists who studied in the period talk about being isolated, and so were the few Black art teachers.

Gavin Jantjes, the South African artist who moved to the UK in 1982, became the first Black lecturer in art in Britain at what is now the University of the Arts London. Jantjes was clear that he wasn't just there to talk to students about art: he had to diversify the student body and reinvigorate the Eurocentric curriculum. Changing the student body was doable, Jantjes would now sit on the admissions panel and many artists – including Chris Ofili – were given spaces on the university's courses during his time. 'That was easy,' he said. 'Changing the curriculum was different.' His biggest challenge as a teacher was that which Claudette Johnson was facing as a student: a lack of reference materials featuring or discussing Black art. Painstakingly, with two sympathetic colleagues, Jantjes compiled information for students on Black art and artists so there was something for them to use in their studies.

Another issue Black artists faced was that art wasn't seen as a legitimate career path by their parents: cementing your position by moving into classic professions such as medicine or law was a more attractive proposition than the inscrutable world of art. There was also a perception among Black students of art as less radical or interesting than other subjects. 'As a Black art student in Wolverhampton at that time, when I went to the African Caribbean society everyone else was doing sociology or fashion or graphic design,' Claudette Johnson told me. 'Nobody did fine art because it just wasn't the future.'

But for Johnson, the idea of Black radical thought and art converging had taken root. 'It was building from the time I was a foundation student,' says Johnson. 'Certainly, the first two years at Wolverhampton consolidated it, mainly because of mixing with women who were more politically active, who were Marxist socialists. We just talked a lot about race and politics and class culture.' Johnson was now covering the walls outside her studio with her work, often large-scale portraits of Black female figures, their features emphasised to almost caricature-like proportions: such as in 'Trilogy (Part Two) Woman in Black, 1982–86' and 'I Came to Dance', which took its name from a Nils Lofgren song and is a minimalist line drawing of a woman's silhouette.

'I found my visual language and I think that was very apparent,' says Johnson. 'My work was about Black people, and specifically Black women, because I felt that we were kind of at the bottom of the pile. Black men had some currency just because of being male, but Black women didn't seem to have any purchase at all.' But her tutors didn't understand her approach, which was met with bemusement. Like many Black British art students around the country, Johnson wrestled in front of the easel in isolation, expressing a new worldview – powered by Black feminist theory – that was inconceivable for most white art tutors.

It wasn't until her final year at Wolverhampton that Johnson would find a way out of her artistic isolation. Eddie Chambers and Claudette Johnson met after he gave a talk at Wolverhampton University about his art in 1981, shortly after he'd met Piper at Coventry Polytechnic. During the lecture Chambers discussed his ideas for what art should be (confrontational, political, vital) and what it shouldn't be (vague, abstract, self-centred). After the lecture, the two began to talk about their artistic practice and about the realities of being a Black artist, and Johnson took Chambers to her studio. She showed him her work, explained her approach and the new visual language she'd discovered. Finally, here was another Black artist who spoke her language – right there and then, she joined the Blk Art Group.

The group would meet at Chambers' parents' house where Marlene Smith, Donald Rodney, Claudette Johnson and Keith Piper were joined by Eric Pemberton, a youth worker who was a mentor to Chambers and several other Black artists in the West Midlands, including Pogus Caesar and Benjamin Zephaniah. In the summer of 1982, they were discussing an ambitious idea they had: the first Black art convention, a concept that had been percolating for months.

The meetings could be combative. Smith remembers getting into a discussion with Chambers about whether or not the head of the Royal College of Art should be invited. 'We had a long conversation about why he was relevant and what on earth he would possibly have to say to us about the future of Black art,' says Smith. Those questions lingered in the air whenever the group met, but now the group would invite other students and artists to Wolverhampton to discuss what they saw as *the* central question of the era: 'What is Black Art?'

The group created flyers and posters to be sent to community centres and art schools around the country. Lubaina Himid was studying at the Royal College of Art in London at the time and remembers hearing about the event. 'We're talking the 1980s – so posters were like the equivalent of Twitter,' says Himid. 'It could easily have been a flyer coming in my direction.' John Akomfrah was studying in Portsmouth and had just started the Black Audio Film Collective, the group who would go on to make *Handsworth Songs* in 1985. He remembers his fellow member of the collective Trevor Mathison approaching him in their squat with a flyer in his hand shouting, 'Some people are trying to steal our shit!'

The group had been planning their own event – a space for Black artists to respond to the upheaval and anger of 1981. 'When we saw [the flyer] we realised there were people out there who were thinking in the same way,' Akomfrah said. Sonia Boyce, a young student just down the road in the West Midlands town of Stourbridge, also got word, as did Ingrid Pollard, one of the few non-students to attend. The photocopied black and white posters had an evocative call to arms: 'The First National Black Art Convention . . . Watch it, it's happening . . . NOW GO FOR IT!' On 28 October 1982, the Blk Art Group would play host to a new generation of Black artists.

When attendees of the conference arrived in Wolverhampton they were confronted by a tall brutalist building. A boxy, imposing structure made from concrete with huge rectangular windows, since its opening in 1970 the tower had been dedicated to the arts. You approach it from the university campus, taking an underpass that pops out in front of Wolverhampton Wanderers' Molineux Stadium. To the right of the stadium stands the arts tower, overlooked by the ring road. 'It was grim,' says Claudette Johnson, whose studio was on the top floor. In a small theatre at the base of the imposing tower was where the Black artists and students would meet that October day.

On the morning of the convention, Donald Rodney, Claudette Johnson and Marlene Smith were on the door to welcome guests. Smith remembers the physical impression made by the Black Audio Film Collective arriving en masse: 'In my memory, there's this group of young Black radicals wearing black berets and raincoats. But probably what really happened was that one person was wearing a raincoat and one person had a beret on, but I just have this memory of being so impressed with them.' Another person who stood out to her was Sonia Boyce. 'I remember her coming because she had a parasol. So, you know, she looked very arty,' says Smith.

As the attendees arrived they signed in via a guest book. Reading upside down, Smith tried to make out their names. One that she failed to make out was that of Frank Bowling. The Guyanese artist was – even by 1982 – a veteran who'd spent time in New York, won two Guggenheim scholarships, and had the first of many solo exhibitions a full twenty years before the convention took place. Bowling had moved to London as a teenager before enrolling at the Royal College of Art, where his contemporaries included David Hockney.[23] As a young artist Bowling took inspiration from Francis Bacon, picking up his themes of trauma and suffering and putting them through a Black lens – with one critic saying his early 1960s work was made up of 'births, monsters, mirrors, surgeons, beautiful girls on ornate sofas, [and] himself as Othello'.[24] A decade later, Bowling had moved to New York and was creating large-scale abstract works like 'Middle Passage', where he used bright orange, green and yellow which merged into one another over a map of Guyana and pictures of his mother.

Bowling's presence had largely flown over the heads of Smith and others in the group – Sonia Boyce later said that she was completely unaware of who he was. 'Why did I not know this when I was studying at art school, desperate as I was to find possible role models,' she wrote. 'Why was Bowling not on the list of canonical artists to be revered and studied?' – but it was a huge vindication, even if they didn't know it at the time. Most of the artists in attendance in Wolverhampton could only dream of the success Bowling had achieved, and yet here he was to debate the meaning of Black art in Britain. He was intrigued by what this new generation was planning, and – perhaps uniquely among the attendees – was able to link the 1982 convention to an earlier era of Black arts in Britain with its origins in another small living room. This one in Mecklenburgh Square in London's Bloomsbury.[25]

On 16 December 1966, on the same day that fifty Labour MPs wrote to President Johnson to call for an end to US bombing raids of Hanoi, the Caribbean Arts Movement (CAM) was born after the first official meeting of its founding members. Those members were the publisher John La Rose, the poet Edward Kamau Braithwaite and the writer Andrew Salkley, all from the Caribbean diaspora.

Like the Blk Art Group two decades later, CAM would meet to discuss how best to access and reshape the cultural world. The founders, all in their mid-thirties, were particularly concerned with the new generation of Black British artists who were 'living within but apart from British culture'.[26] Black artists were ignored by the mainstream: they couldn't get gallery shows or representation, plays weren't reviewed by critics, writers' work went unpublished.

The group produced a newsletter and a periodical, and engaged in good-natured but often combative debates ranging from the use of patois and regional dialect in their writing, to whether they'd be compromised if they collaborated with the white establishment.[27] Most of the group had grown up in the Caribbean and were taught that their culture was inferior or not of worth. Like the Young Black Artists who had to fight for recognition at art school in the Thatcher era, a key part of CAM's purpose was convincing the artists themselves that their culture mattered.[28]

The fact that the Blk Art Group wasn't aware of CAM or Frank Bowling may be surprising at first, but considering the conditions of the time, it is less so. Black art students weren't only isolated from one another; they were also separated from Black British history – even in their own field of study. Though several members of CAM went on to forge impressive careers, there would've been few art school teachers in the early 1980s able to name one of the artists who took part; it's a history that ran on parallel tracks to the dominant narrative, the lines not truly intersecting until the twenty-first century. Just as the Black dancers from the Northern Soul scene were shifted to the edge of the dance floor, the work of CAM, within a generation, had been largely marginalised.[29]

I grew up in Bradford unaware of George Lindo's case, and

We Were There

Black British students in 1982 didn't know about the efforts of the CAM artists to make their path easier. That missing link is crucial. Together, these stories show the depth and scale of Black people's influence on the UK; in isolation, they can be dismissed as curiosities that don't alter our sense of what constitutes British culture. But connecting those links, highlighting that continuum shows Black British history as a rich and vital component of what makes the country what it is. In October 1982, a new generation would – unbeknown to them – pick up the baton left by CAM.

The First National Black Art Convention started at 11 a.m., an hour after it was supposed to. The microphone cracked and popped as an

Polaroid of the members of Blk Art Group on the day of the convention in 1982 (left to right: Marlene Smith, Keith Piper, Donald Rodney and Eddie Chambers)

audibly nervous Eddie Chambers took to the stage to welcome the audience and briefly tell them about the philosophy of the convention. 'I want you to all ask the questions that are important to you,' he said, in a thick Wolverhampton accent, before handing over to a line-up of speakers who would present their own competing visions of Black art.[30]

The British-Pakistani artist Rasheed Araeen was first up.[31] His most well-known work was 'For Oluwale', a collage created in 1971 about David Oluwale, the Nigerian stowaway who dreamed of becoming an engineer before being hounded to his death by police officers in Leeds in 1969. Mixing newspaper clippings and the iconic mugshot of Oluwale, it was a forerunner to the graphic art made by Piper and Chambers a decade later.

His talk put the Black artist in a radical setting. 'Black art can't be about the past; Black art can't be about magic. It is about the present reality . . . to be Black is to be political,' he concluded. The Q&A session that followed was tense and disjointed as attendees and speakers – including John Akomfrah, Lubaina Himid and Sonia Boyce – struggled to fully understand each other's point of view. 'There were definitely points of disagreement, but there were also these completely different language systems,' says Piper, who remembers the divisions between the Black nationalist groups, the feminist artists, and the groups such as Black Audio Film Collective, who were 'very schooled in cultural theory'. They were literally speaking different dialects.

Neither neat nor orderly, the event was full of competing energies and visions for Black art. A discussion unfolded about whether Black British artists have their own language and whether patois or creole as Caribbean imports count. Anum Iyapo, a poet and artist from a Black nationalist group in north London, takes the microphone: 'If the art that Black people produce does not communicate something which is positive or says something or gives a message,' he says, 'to me it is irrelevant.'

Claudette Johnson is next on with her talk *Images of Black Women in Art*. Johnson had prepared a fifteen-minute presentation about her portraiture, representation of the Black female body, and how it differed from that of European artists. She shares work she has created while at university, and explains that she felt isolated on her course, and that her work was only ever viewed in a 'superficial way'. It's a presentation about art that also doubles as a critique of the ultra-white world of 1980s art schools that many in the audience could identify with.[32] There's a calmness coupled with brutal honesty, a vulnerability even.

The other speakers are clearly reading from prepared notes, but Johnson sounds confident and calm – like someone casually flicking through holiday snaps. 'This is a silk screen from my first year ... [I was] focusing on my own image because there's something very safe about your own images, something very permanent, other things around you are changing or very hostile.' She goes on, clicking onto the next slide: 'This is about feeling peaceful and feeling happy about being a Black woman, because very often I didn't feel that happy about it.'

Once she finishes and the floor is opened to comments, Iyapo addresses Johnson: her approach to Black art doesn't chime with his thesis. He sees no difference between her work and that of Europeans. Their exchange is testy; there are audible groans from the audience as Iyapo speaks.[33] 'That changed everything,' says Himid of Johnson's presentation and the reaction. A breakout group was formed of people who wanted to keep on discussing Johnson's work. After Eric Pemberton closed the discussion, most of the women stood up and left the convention.

Johnson said the interaction and its fallout forced women to choose between a full discussion with everyone at the conference, or being part of something smaller. 'I don't think people should have had to make that choice,' she says. 'On the one hand, it felt strong to be walking away with a group of women who all took each other seriously, but on the other hand it was like being banished.'[34] Himid, Boyce, Pollard and others moved to Johnson's studio in the arts tower. They showed each other slides of their work. 'We could be in a completely different place and actually talk about what we wanted to talk about in an atmosphere where the audience – other Black women – were listening,' says Himid. 'And we just all got up and went.' Without a projector to share their work, they held up to the light the tiny Kodak Ektachrome slides each had brought along and did their best to discern the images. Phone numbers and addresses were exchanged, and within weeks, work was being sent between the women.

Himid considers the point at which the group moved upstairs to Johnson's studio as a definitive moment in Black British art. Here was a space, created out of necessity after a Black female artist's work was dismissed, that could bring together what had been, up to that point, a disparate group. 'We were not part of white feminist groups because they were not interested in what we were doing . . . we'd gone to art school, but in ones and twos and separate from each other [so] we didn't have that sort of a camaraderie with them. We had to make something of our own,' says Himid. 'So that was the moment that several women who had been doing things separately – thinking about how Black women work, and how to push our work forward, were together in the same room and thought, "Oh, well, I can see you're doing it that way." "I want to do it this way." "And you're doing it that way. I think there's probably room for us all to do it."'

Suddenly, paths crossed, conversations started and individual women in male-dominated groups had a nascent community. 'That was the point in which all those ideas could be galvanised,' adds Himid. 'It was perfectly, absolutely fine for you still to belong to the Blk Art Group or whatever other group you wanted to belong to, but I was interested in what women were saying to women.'

The conference would mark a turning point, but not necessarily the one Claudette Johnson had hoped for. She'd imagined the event as a collegiate event where Black artists would come together and collectively forge a way forward. Instead, it was a place of contestation. 'Being part of the Blk Art Group was like finding my family in a way,' she said. 'I had imagined that the whole conference might feel like the extension of that family.' That wasn't to be the case.

The confrontation had been painful but resulted in connections with artists who she'd remain friends with for the rest of her life. The female artists who splintered off after her talk would go on to become some of Britain's most celebrated contemporary artists. But they had to fight to be taken seriously within the nascent movement of the early 1980s.

The fractures that emerged among the Black Art Movement show there was no one Black viewpoint: nationalism, feminism, class, sexuality, method, philosophy, geography were all responsible for creating a group of artists who saw the world differently. The Blk Art Group and others at the convention – most notably Frank Bowling – had shown others that you could have a career as an artist, even if that meant leaving the UK to get recognition. After the event in Wolverhampton, the 1982 generation were about to face the same problem Bowling had come up against in the 1960s: maintaining a place in the British art world.

In 1984 a new arts award was established that shaped the next twenty years of British culture. During its peak in the 1990s and early 2000s, the Turner Prize, named after the British watercolourist J.M.W. Turner and fronted by the Tate gallery, helped to make stars of artists. In its early years, the prize was mostly awarded to painters and sculptors, but as time went on its scope broadened – controversially – to include installations and video art. The most notorious winner was Martin Creed who took home the prize in 2001 for 'Work No 227: The Lights Going On and Off', which consisted of an empty gallery in which the lights did exactly as described, 'plunging you every five seconds into darkness'. The work celebrated by the judges was often abstract, ironic or detached – the opposite of the confrontational political art that Piper and Chambers threw at the world. The artists it recognised most often in the 1990s – Damien Hirst, Douglas Gordon, Rachel Whiteread, Tracey Emin – were the so-called Young British Artists (YBAs). Brash, commercially successful artists who were able to attract the attention of the mainstream press and gallerists such as Charles Saatchi who helped make several of them art world stars.

When the artist and filmmaker Steve McQueen became the second consecutive Black winner, after Chris Ofili in 1998, he was nominated alongside Tracey Emin for her work 'My Bed', which consisted of a dishevelled unmade mattress surrounded by personal items. McQueen's winning work was 'Deadpan', a black-and-white silent film homage to Buster Keaton; while Ofili had taken the prize twelve months earlier for his paintings that incorporated elephant dung and glitter. In an era when the personal, rather than the political, was king; when the question of 'what is Black art?' was overshadowed by 'is the work that wins the Turner Prize even art'?

The Black artists who attended the 1982 Wolverhampton convention sat, for the most part, outside of that world – none were nominated for the Turner Prize in its first twenty-five years. Many found British galleries that were receptive to their work, but few were in the capital. A notable exception was the Black Art Gallery, which opened in 1983 in Finsbury Park, north London, and hosted solo shows by many of the Blk Art Group and their peers.

There had been false dawns: Himid would go back to London after Wolverhampton and put on an exhibition at the Institute of Contemporary Arts (ICA) called *The Thin Black Line* in 1985,[35] but in the late 1980s she was earning a living from curating at Rochdale's Touchstone gallery and then teaching at the University of Central Lancashire, a world away from the Turner and London's art scene. A 1989 exhibition at the Hayward Gallery titled *The Other Story*, curated by Rasheed Araeen, featured Boyce, Piper and Chambers and was Black British arts' biggest show up to that point. The landmark London shows were met with a hostile critical response that often focused on the fact the art was angry or overtly political. A review of *The Thin Black Line* said the show came 'very close to choking on its own anger',[36] while *The Other Story* was criticised for being 'in accord with our country's culture generally – recent Black art is harsher, more hurt, more despairing'.[37]

Throughout the 1980s it was more often in cities like Glasgow and Bradford, or Stoke-on-Trent and Newcastle, where you could see the work of Ingrid Pollard, Gavin Jantjes or Sonia Boyce. Life went on for the collective's original members: Piper continued to work, while Chambers started a Black art archive in Bristol, and wrote several books about Black British art and culture before moving to Texas University to teach. Johnson made her move to the capital and worked with Ingrid Pollard in a workshop in Haggerston, east London, where they created posters and artwork for community groups and other artists. But by the mid-1990s she was no longer earning a living from her art, instead working full time in a project for homeless people. For a few years, she stopped making art altogether. The Blk Art Group were present but on the outskirts of the increasingly glitzy world of commercial art that dominated London.

And then, three decades after the class of 1982 had gathered in Wolverhampton, something changed. In 2017, Lubaina Himid won the Turner Prize. A rule change meant that those over fifty were now eligible. 'Being the first Black woman was bittersweet, because there are many Black women that have been up for it in the recent history of the prize,' she told *Desert Island Discs*, referring to Lynette Yiadom-Boakye and Anthea Hamilton. 'I was happy to win it, but it was bittersweet.' Himid talked about how her peers had been ignored or simply seen as too political. But she also spoke to people who said her win gave them hope for change.

In the aftermath of her victory, it appeared that belief was justified. A couple of years after Himid's win, Frank Bowling was the subject of a Tate Britain retrospective. Incredibly, it was the first of his career in Britain. Since Himid made history, Barbara Walker, Ingrid Pollard, and Veronica Ryan have been nominated for the Turner Prize, with Ryan winning in 2022. In 2021, all the nominees were collectives – some of whom took inspiration from the Blk Art Group. That was the same year Sonia Boyce became the first Black woman to represent the UK at the Venice Biennale, known as the Olympics of the art world, and made more history when she won its top prize, the Golden Lion. It was something the YBA generation had never got close to achieving. John Akomfrah of the Black Audio Film Collective represented Britain in 2024. Johnson has had a career renaissance, with two major retrospectives since 2019 establishing her work as among the most important British figurative paintings of the last fifty years. In 2024, she was also nominated for the Turner Prize.

What changed? The art historian Charles Harrison once wrote that the history of modern art in England is one 'of delayed and mediated responses'. Nowhere is that more evident than in the time it took for the 1982 generation to be recognised. Much of that recognition came in the wake of the Black Lives Matter movement of 2020; a time when street protests following the murder of George Floyd forced conversations about race and discrimination into the mainstream. Arts prizes came under intense scrutiny around their recognition of Black talent. Art that had been deemed too political or abrasive in the YBA era was now en vogue: when I covered the Turner Prize in 2023, Barbara Walker's portraits of Black Britons caught up in the Windrush scandal – which saw people stripped of their citizenship and deported due to bureaucratic errors – covered the walls of the prestigious Towner Eastbourne gallery. It was work that – despite being from a younger artist – loudly echoed the political provocations of the Blk Art Group. Meanwhile, in London's Courtauld Gallery, Claudette Johnson's portraits hung just metres away from Van Goghs and Monets. One of the works was of a young woman from Wolverhampton, eyes down, dancing in front of a reggae sound system in 1978[38] – shortly before Johnson arrived to start her artistic journey.

It's an unseasonably warm autumn morning in Wolverhampton, and around the town centre there are subtle signs this is not an ordinary September day. As people queue up for coffee at Starbucks, a few metres away, robed students fiddle with their hats and pose for selfies in St Peter's churchyard. Parents stand awkwardly in their Sunday best, cigarettes in hand, waiting for the Grand Theatre's doors to open. There's a combination of pride, nerves and intergenerational tension in the air which only graduation day can bring.

Inside the theatre, the procession of university representatives, those awarded honorary degrees and other special guests, winds its way onto the stage as a band plays. Then the music stops, and silence falls in the Grand Theatre. Claudette Johnson is one of the stars of the show. She is about to receive an honorary doctorate from the university she first attended more than four decades prior. 'When I arrived in Wolverhampton as an eighteen-year-old student in 1979 I was still smarting from not gaining a place at Goldsmiths University in London on the fine art course and feeling sorry for myself,' she starts. 'But what my eighteen-year-old self could not have known is that Wolverhampton was to become the nexus for what has come to be known as the Black Art Movement.' It's hard to tell how many of the assembled students and family members know what she's referring to.

Johnson goes on to list the attendees that day: Frank Bowling, Lubaina Himid, Black Audio Film Collective, Ingrid Pollard and Sonia Boyce. 'Wolverhampton did not only provide the gathering point for our current luminaries,' Johnson adds. 'It was also the place that allowed me to find my voice as a young artist trying to make sense of my Black British experience. One that seems to have no precedent. As a first-generation British-born woman of Jamaican parents studying fine art, I was part of a minority within an even smaller minority.' Despite those factors, Johnson and the rest of the Blk Art Group became some of the most influential artists of their generation, emerging from the most unlikely of settings: an industrialised West Midlands town best known in the late 1970s for the glam rock band Slade.

Meanwhile, in Manchester, another Black community were facing a different kind of challenge: their cultural output not only ignored by critics, but under attack from the police and the City Council. The fate of one nightclub, on the edge of the Black neighbourhood of Moss Side, would define an era of groundbreaking music and be a home for politics that would change an entire continent.

6.
The Black Door – Manchester, 1986

In October 2017, Linda Brogan put on a hard hat and started digging. The site of the playwright's archaeological excavation was a night club that had shut its doors three decades earlier. Brogan wanted to burrow into the earth to find artefacts and clues about a place that had been buried to make way for modern Manchester.

The Reno was a small, dark club in a basement underneath a bookies in Moss Side, one of the longest established Black communities in the UK. For the Mancunians who walked through its black door and down the steep stairs into its belly, it conjures myriad images and memories. The club was not glamorous: the toilets were notoriously disgusting, and it could be dangerous for outsiders – you might be relieved of your money if you weren't streetwise. But for its regulars who paid their £2 entry, The Reno offered the cutting edge of Black music and culture.

At a time when informal colour bars operated across venues in the city centre, excluding Black faces, The Reno was a sanctuary for many in Moss Side. It offered food, a fireplace, a side room for pool and card games. The smell of fried plantain, jerk chicken or jollof rice would waft through the venue during the day and early evening, before the club slowly transformed into a club, the aroma of weed replacing that of the food.

The club connected various parts of Black Manchester, from hustlers and criminals to activists and artists. Some of its regulars – and its owner – had connections dating back to the pre-war period, before Windrush, when the city played host to the Pan-African Congress of 1945. African leaders including Kenya's Jomo Kenyatta and Ghana's Kwame Nkrumah met to debate their postcolonial future in a city that represented one of the biggest Black Power bases in the whole of Europe. Black-owned clubs like The Reno could be found up and down Oxford Road, the city's busy central thoroughfare, alongside bookshops and coffee shops that provided Black Mancunians places to read, think and congregate.

In 1986, The Reno would be demolished – it was one of the last remnants of the old Moss Side and Hulme, areas that were razed as part of 'The Manchester Plan', a forty-year project of urban renewal designed to create a modern city. The Reno and its clientele didn't fit with that new vision, which saw hundreds of Black Mancunians forced to sell their homes in the name of progress. But over the two decades of its existence, The Reno had delivered its own vision of the future. The resident DJs, including Persian and Hewan Clarke, played futuristic Black music, from underground soul to the paradigm shift that was house music. The Reno served as a transmitter of Black music, its sounds rippling out across Manchester's cultural landscape and beyond. Without it, the UK wouldn't sound like it does today.

Buried under rubble on the very edge of modern Manchester, with its chrome-and-glass skyscrapers, The Reno is the perfect metaphor for the treatment of Black Manchester's history by the city. If the Northern Soul dancers needed to be pushed back under the spotlight, The Reno needed to be, quite literally, unearthed and placed into the official story of Mancunian culture. What lay under the dirt was special, something worth reviving. 'It was our temple,' Brogan told a journalist during the dig.[1]

The Reno was in the part of Moss Side beyond Raby Street that Brogan considered to be 'naughty'. It was where cool people and the kids from the tenement blocks went, those children whose parents might not have been around to tell them not to go. Brogan's family was a typical one from the area: her mother was Irish, from Limerick, and her father was Jamaican. The family was relatively comfortable; they owned their own home, although relations with her mother's family could be fraught because she'd left her Irish husband and children to start a new life with a Jamaican. Brogan was one of five children and had managed to get a good job working in the accounts team for a department store. She shouldn't really have been going to The Reno, and she knew it. To the teenage Brogan, the girls at the bar with their colourful collars, V-neck jumpers and Levi's 501 jeans 'exuded cool', and as someone searching for her own identity in 1970s Britain, she wanted a part of it. 'You know in *GoodFellas*, when they walk in the club and the biggest and best thing is if someone says hello to you?' says Brogan. 'It was about that recognition.'

But Brogan wasn't the only person who was aware of The Reno's transgressive reputation. She first walked through The Reno's black door in 1976, a year when Swedish pop sensation ABBA and Leicester soft rockers Showaddywaddy were top of the charts – and Manchester received a new Chief Constable named James Anderton. Born in Wigan, Anderton was the son of a miner brought up in a devout Christian household; as a six-year-old, his schedule had included choir practice twice a week, communion services, Sunday school and evensong.

While he shared with Kenneth Oxford, the Chief Constable of Liverpool, a bullet-proof self-confidence, Anderton was driven by something more: a holy mission. Known as 'God's Copper', he once claimed his job was 'an extension of his Christian mission to raise the moral quality of life'.[2] When he took up the post of Chief Constable, Anderton began waging war on those who he considered remorseless sinners.

Anderton's first target was pornographers; he oversaw 284 raids on premises suspected of selling or producing porn during the first year of his tenure.[3] Vehemently homophobic, he would send officers to patrol public toilets where gay men cruised, while in 1986 he called the AIDs crisis a product of 'people swirling about in a human cesspit of their own making'.[4,5] When the popularity of Wigan Casino was at its peak, a horrified Anderton called the event in his hometown a 'post-industrial Gomorrah'.[6]

Anderton developed his hatred of Black music while walking the beat in Moss Side. He policed the illicit blues and shebeens in the area. Once appointed to the top job, The Reno and The Nile were firmly in his sights, with raids a common occurrence during his reign. His officers were notorious in Moss Side for their violence: a cache of knives, coshes and hatchets were found at the area's police station – ironically unearthed by the vice squad who were looking for pornography that had been confiscated on an earlier raid.[7] The right-wing *Daily Telegraph* ran a story that called him 'Britain's toughest policeman'.[8]

Thatcher would repeatedly back Anderton. When his 'human cesspit' comments caused outrage – particularly from the Manchester City Council leader Graham Stringer, whose left-wing Labour administration was seen as not far behind that of Ken Livingstone's Greater London Council in terms of its progressive agenda – it was the prime minister who saved his career. Stringer wrote to then-Home Secretary Douglas Hurd calling for him to reprimand the officer, but Thatcher supported his right to voice his opinions. Stringer's wasn't the only dissenting voice – others close to Thatcher were concerned about the 'religious overtones' of Anderton's rhetoric.[9]

For the Chief Constable, The Reno was little more than a 'vice den'. He would never be able to comprehend the club's importance as a cultural melting pot, and its significance in Manchester's long – and largely forgotten – Black history.

Its owner was a Nigerian, Phil Magbotiwan, who came to Manchester from Lagos in the 1930s, plugging into the network of Black seamen who had gradually moved from their original base – Greengate in Salford – to Moss Side. Like many Black arrivals, Magbotiwan had been attracted to the city by the prospect of work in its factories, and he found employment at Dunlop's rubber manufacturers. He was ambitious and hard-headed. His daughter Lisa Ayegun told me he was fond of saying, 'I can't just live in this country and not have anything.' Possession was important to him and to the hundreds of Black Mancunians who began to buy property in Moss Side and neighbouring Hulme in the 1950s and 60s, taking over large properties on Cecil Street, Princess Road and Denmark Road.

Other Black-owned clubs had sprung up in Manchester before The Reno: there was the Merchant Navy Club, the Morisca Club, the Cotton Club at 28 Ducie Street, and the Kru Club just off Princess Street, which was specifically for members of the Kru ethnic group from West Africa and offered traditional funerals.[10] These clubs were more than just drinking establishments; they were refuges that offered cultural connections for those living thousands of miles from home.

Some of Magbotiwan's own experiences in Manchester showed why the venues were so needed. When contemplating the idea of buying a club, he went to the Little Alex pub, not far from the site of The Reno. The landlord refused to serve him, nodding toward the barrel where people threw their dregs and pint ends. 'Niggers drink out of that,' he was told. Magbotiwan promised the man that one day he'd start his own club, and the man would regret what he'd said.

Magbotiwan used what he'd saved while sleeping on friends' floors to buy his first house on Denmark Road, which he turned into a hostel. He saved again, establishing another. Then he acquired a shop – which sold African produce – and a cafe on Denmark Road, called The Rainy City. Finally, he bought The Reno. He couldn't initially get a licence, so he again turned it into a hostel, offering beds to African seamen who could get a hot meal and buy Johnny Player cigarettes.

But in 1963 he was finally granted a licence and The Reno opened for business. A few weeks after Magbotiwan's doors opened, the landlord of the Little Alex came over to inspect the competition. He walked up to the bar, not realising who the new owner was, and ordered a Red Stripe. While serving him, Magbotiwan asked the man if he remembered his visit to the pub across the road. The man couldn't recall his face at first but then recognised who he was and apologised. 'Anyone can make a mistake,' said Magbotiwan, who forgave the man. The Nigerian was happy – he'd captured a part of Manchester for himself; now he had something of his own.

The Reno was open seven days a week. During the afternoons, it served as a social club, with many of the older African and Caribbean men gathering to play dominos, pool or cards. But on the weekends, it became a bustling club, full of younger Black Mancunians. Anderton might have detested the ungodliness of The Reno, but his officers regularly frequented the club and were happy to take bribes. The club was supposed to close at 2 a.m., but Magbotiwan had an arrangement with a group of officers who would come to the club in the daytime to pick up an envelope filled with money. They'd sometimes go to the Magbotiwans' house. Lisa Ayegun remembers two police officers coming to the door in suits. 'I'd call my dad, and he would say put them in the lounge,' she says. Her father would sit upstairs in his 'money room' before coming down with a payoff that meant they could stay open until 6 a.m. – crucial for the club's success as an after-hours spot. To keep up appearances, the police would occasionally raid the club, which would infuriate Magbotiwan. 'When they'd be gone he'd be like "fucking bastards have had their fucking money",' says Ayegun.

While preventing entry on the basis of skin colour was illegal, Black people – and Black men in particular – were still finding it was impossible to get into many venues in central Manchester in the early 1980s. 'They did it by using simple things,' remembers Bolaji Laurance, whose mother Kath Locke would co-found the Black feminist group the Abasindi Collective. 'You can't come in if you're not with a girl; you can't come in if you've got an Afro or an Afro comb. So The Reno and The Nile became popular simply because nobody could get into [venues in] town.'[11]

In Manchester, there was a divide between The Russell, which was run by a collective of older Caribbean residents who wanted to show Black people could run a successful respectable club, and The Reno – with its clientele pulled from across the social spectrum, from community activists to hustlers. More radical members of the Black Mancunian community like Kath Locke hated some of the conservative Caribbean clubs – not least The Colonial Club, which opened in the early 1950s. Locke, who grew up in a Pan-Africanist household, thought it belonged in another era, not one in which

The Black Door – Manchester, 1986

Black people all over the world were gaining their independence. 'Here we were trying to fight off the shackles of colonialism and they're calling themselves "The Colonial Club",' she once said.[12] Her anger is understandable: that fight for African independence had its roots in Black Manchester.

In 1945, just after the end of the Second World War, Manchester hosted what would arguably be the most important meeting of Black thinkers and politicians of the twentieth century. The fifth Pan-African Congress would reshape an entire continent, connecting political leaders and activists who were envisioning a postcolonial future. Held at Chorlton-on-Medlock town hall in Manchester, the event saw Pan-Africanists – the name for the movement seeking to unite all Black people from the African diaspora – discuss and dissect topics ranging from the mental impact of imperialism to the colour bar in Manchester.

One of the event's architects was T Ras Makonnen, also known as Mak. He was a Guyanese entrepreneur who had come to the city in the late 1930s and quickly founded half a dozen establishments, which mainly served Black American servicemen and Black munitions workers from across the Commonwealth.[13] 'Manchester itself was rather like an African community,' he wrote in his memoirs.[14] 'People were human and warm and you never were made to feel like a stranger.'

His enterprises consisted of restaurants – The Ethiopian Teashop, The Orient, The Belle Etoile – and two clubs: the Cosmopolitan and the Forum, where the Trinidadian calypso star Lord Kitchener regularly played after moving to Manchester. Makonnen also ran a publishing house, The Pan-African Publishing Company, and a bookshop, The Economist.[15] In the novelist Anthony Joseph's fictionalised biography of Lord Kitchener, *Kitch*, he describes the Cosmopolitan as a 'converted dwelling house, four stories high, with dark wooden door frames and heavy pine doors'. It sat across the road from Chorlton-on-Medlock town hall and sounds remarkably like descriptions of The Reno thirty years later.[16] Magbotiwan was following in the footsteps of Mak by channelling his desire for autonomy through club ownership.

The list of attendees at the 1945 event was a who's who from the postcolonial political world: Hastings Banda (Malawi), Kwame Nkrumah (Ghana), Obafemi Awolowo and Nmandi Azikiwe (Nigeria) and Jomo Kenyatta (Kenya) would all go on to lead their nations.

Amy Ashwood Garvey[17] – the first wife of Pan-Africanist leader and figurehead Marcus Garvey, known for advocating a return to Africa for all Black people – chaired the event's opening discussion, titled 'The Colour Problem', and provided a Black feminist perspective throughout the proceedings.

Local Black Mancunians also attended, including the boxer and communist Len Johnson, who would go on to campaign against colour bars in the city. Perhaps the most famous name was W. E. B. Du Bois, the African-American Pan-Africanist whose book *The Souls of Black Folk* – a fourteen-essay collection that unpicked the idea of white supremacy and meditated on the African-American experience – had established him as one of the most important writers of the century.

With so much of the globe just emerging from the grip of the Second World War, the main message coming from the delegates was simple: we've fought and died for you, now live up to your enlightened ideals and give us our independence. The town hall was draped in the flags of the world's only independent Black nations – Liberia, Haiti and Ethiopia – underscoring the event's core ambition. There were parties, dances and dinners as the future leaders of Africa enjoyed Black Mancunian hospitality, while plotting a postcolonial continent.

It was also the first time that Black British ideas about Pan-Africanism had held sway. Previously, the movement had been led by Americans like Du Bois, the force behind the 1900 and 1919 congresses that brought Pan-Africanism to the world's attention. After 1945 it was Africa itself that came to the fore of the movement. But for a moment, just after the war, when Britain was changed by the trauma of conflict and the hope for a better future, Manchester

The Black Door – Manchester, 1986

The audience listening to speakers at the fifth Pan-African Congress, 10 November 1945

became the world focus of Pan-Africanism. The Ghanaian delegate, Joe Appiah – who would go on to help Nkrumah run postcolonial Ghana – described travelling to the event as evoking in him 'all the emotion and sentiments of a Muslim pilgrim to Mecca'.[18]

A picture from the opening of the congress shows Ashwood Garvey on stage with banners behind and in front of her which call for 'Oppressed peoples of the world' to unite, while decrying colour bars. Another optimistically demands that 'Arabs and Jews, Unite against British Imperialism', two years before the Nakba and the creation of Israel. Du Bois was so impressed by the passion of the speakers at the event, that he told *The New York Times*: 'the tempo of coloured people has changed' and that either the British government 'will extend self-government in West Africa and the Caribbean or face open revolt'.

Despite the energy and impetus in the wake of the Congress, it took another fifteen years for many of the nations to gain independence, with the momentum generated in Manchester helping to pressure the British to agree. But the alliances forged at the event ran deep. When Kwame Nkrumah became the first president of postcolonial Ghana in 1960, he invited Du Bois to attend his inauguration and later asked him to live in Ghana. Du Bois accepted the invitation, giving up his American citizenship and moving to the West African nation a year later. He was so revered by the African leader that when Du Bois died in 1963, Nkrumah ensured he had a full state funeral.

Just as Friedrich Engels' time in Manchester and Salford investigating the plight of the mill workers had produced *The Condition of the Working Class in England* and provided some of the intellectual ballast that underpinned the Communist Revolution, the Pan-African Congress helped to shape the African continent. It was the place where the concept of Pan-African socialism – which meshed national independence movements with socialist or communist doctrine – became solidified as the political ideology that would guide many countries as they emerged from colonial rule.

Britain, the US and other former colonial powers were horrified. They plotted to assassinate or overthrow several leaders, often by collaborating with colonial powers and opposition figures. The most famous example is Patrice Lumumba, who was democratically elected in Democratic Republic of Congo before the CIA, former colonial power Belgium and coup leader Joseph-Desire Mobutu, conspired to assassinate him in 1961. Others, including Nkrumah, who was eventually ousted in a coup before dying in exile, were subjected to propaganda campaigns that successfully painted them as corrupt. The idea of a socialist Africa intrigued communist China and Soviet Russia, who also plotted to bend the same countries to their will.

Despite its momentous significance, it wasn't until the 1980s that the fifth Pan-African Congress was recognised at all in the city. Kath Locke – the daughter of a Nigerian who moved in the same circles as Makonnen – successfully campaigned to have a plaque commemorating the event installed at Chorlton-on-Medlock town hall. Despite initial opposition from Manchester Polytechnic, which owned the site, Locke won the argument. 'The Poly, interestingly enough, didn't want to know,' Locke said in an interview shortly before her death in 1992. 'But who cares about them? It's something there for our children to see.'

For centuries, Manchester has been the home of radical movements and pivotal political moments, and the city has proudly marked these. The Chartists movement called for more democratic rights for working-class people – it's taught in schools and has statues that recognise its importance; the Peterloo Massacre, which saw hundreds injured and more than a dozen killed while protesting the lack of political representation in Westminster for working-class people, has been made into a feature film; the Suffragettes, whose protests resulted in women getting the vote, are commemorated by a statue of Emmeline Pankhurst that sits in St Peter's Square; and a statue of Engels stands just a short walk from Manchester Oxford Road train station. The Pan-African Congress deserves equal prominence but was for decades at risk of being forgotten – and would have been without the efforts of Black Mancunians. Like The Reno, it was a hidden part of Manchester's radical past that needed to be unearthed.

The Pan-African Congress's slow fading from view in Manchester tells us something about the city and its relationship to its Black community. Despite being one of the oldest in Europe, with a history that dates back to the city's development as an industrialised centre in the 1800s, the main institutions have largely failed to recognise its significance. The reason for that lies, partly, in Manchester's selective memory.

In the nineteenth century, Manchester was the global capital of cotton manufacturing. Within fifty miles of the city centre – across Lancashire, Derbyshire, and Cheshire – there were almost 2,500 mills employing more than 400,000 people. 'Like Silicon Valley's role as the incubator of the late-twentieth-century tech revolution,' writes the academic Sven Beckert in *Empire of Cotton*,[19] 'the idyllic rolling hills around Manchester emerged in the late eighteenth century as the hotbed of that era's cutting-edge industry – cotton textiles.' The material drove the British economy by the 1800s. The raw product that fuelled the industry was slave-picked cotton, which was in turn powered by the transatlantic slave trade. The Trinidadian writer and the Caribbean country's first prime minister, Eric Williams, argued in his 1944 book *Capitalism and Slavery* that it was the city's 'tremendous dependence on the triangular trade that made Manchester',[20] with the ancestors of future Black Mancunians held in bondage as part of the bargain.

Williams' book was a revelation. He angered many with his argument that the British abolished the slave trade in 1838 principally for economic reasons rather than the moral justifications often cited, and by naming and shaming British enslavers, men such as David Barclay and other industrialists and businessmen who made fortunes from the slavery economy. 'Worthy men, fathers of families and excellent citizens', as he put it. He went even further, claiming that slavery had in effect turbo-charged the industrial revolution. 'The profits obtained provided one of the main streams of that accumulation of capital in England which financed the industrial revolution,' he argued. For Williams, the cotton traders of Manchester were a crucial cog in the larger machinery of the British Empire and its exponential growth.

The city's most prominent nineteenth-century industrialists, Samuel Greg, George Hibbert and Sir George Philips, all traded in cotton and were key players in the city, donating to Manchester University, with Philips helping to fund the *Manchester Guardian*, now the *Guardian* newspaper. They pushed back against the burgeoning abolition movement that saw African Americans, including Sarah Parker Remond and Frederick Douglass – who was a former slave turned anti-slavery campaigner – come to the city. Much like the rest of Britain, which celebrates the decision to end the slave trade without much thought for its earlier participation,

The Black Door – Manchester, 1986

Manchester puts its abolitionist credentials at the centre of its history. The earlier, darker part of the city's history is often obscured in its civic memory.

Mancunian mill workers' acts of solidarity with the enslaved – such as supporting Abraham Lincoln and the north in the American Civil War – are emphasised to show how the city has always been progressive. Current mayor of Greater Manchester Andy Burnham was asked if he thought the north, and particularly Manchester, was different from the south of England: 'Yes,' he responded, 'Manchester mill workers refused to handle slave-picked cotton. Abraham Lincoln wrote to them, praising their sublime heroism. Other ports were flying the Confederate flag. Think about the things that began here: the trades unions, the suffragettes, the co-operative movement. How can you not be inspired by that?'[21]

It was a radical act (although some historians argue the level of support has been exaggerated over time). But while that remarkable act of solidarity is referenced regularly, the contribution of enslaved Black people, many of whom were the ancestors of the Black Mancunians who arrived in the city during the post-war period, is largely ignored. So is the fact the cotton that made the city rich was picked by enslaved people.

In today's Manchester, you can walk down Brazil Street or past the cotton bud fountain in St Ann's Square and have no idea of their links to chattel slavery. You can eat at a swanky restaurant in Manchester's Northern Quarter that uses the city's 'Cottonopolis' nickname in its branding. Walking around Ancoats, a former textile district where cotton warehouses have been turned into luxury flats and co-working spaces, there are no signs of the neighbourhood's connections to slavery – although one such complex is called Colony. There are no statues in honour of radicals like Len Johnson or T Ras Makonnen. But there is a statue of Lincoln, first erected in the city in 1919, which stands as a symbol of Manchester's support for the north in the Civil War. It's by no means a unique situation – few British cities acknowledge their links to chattel slavery or recognise their historic Black residents – but in Manchester in the post-war era, the City Council tried to dismantle Moss Side as it attempted to create a 'modern city'.

One July morning in 1945, Mancunians were invited to the Manchester Art Gallery to see a new vision for their city that had been two years in the making. On the upper floors of the gallery, visitors were met with large-scale maps and diagrams, charts of predicted birth rates and survey results that mapped out the future of their city, from motorways to plans for 'green wedges' of land to break up the concrete sprawl of a new Manchester that would grow from the wreckage caused by the Blitz.

The Manchester Plan, as it would be christened, was an ambitious, scientific approach to urban renewal. In 1941, when the plan was first announced, Lord Reith – who'd left the BBC and was now minister of works and planning in Churchill's war-time administration – told Manchester's leaders to act 'boldly and comprehensively', even as the Second World War raged. Their response would be heavily influenced by modernism, a contemporary design doctrine that emerged in the early twentieth century and embraced functional engineered architecture and infrastructure.

Paul Rotha's 1947 documentary *A City Speaks*, which shows officials working on the new plan, starts with a sweeping aerial shot of Moss Side and Hulme before the clearances. Row upon row of two-up-two-down houses flash up on screen, in tightly packed grids that move inward towards the city centre. This kind of housing was 'cramped, inconvenient and unsightly',[22] according to the Manchester Plan or – as the voiceover in Rotha's film would have it – 'the rotten leftovers of yesterday . . . in our new city to be [they] can have no place'. But within those dense streets was the majority of the city's Black community. And it was their houses that were to be levelled.

The first time I came across Kath Locke was when watching *Blacks Britannica*, where she appears briefly discussing the slum clearance programme – completed by Manchester City Council in the 1960s – that flattened much of Moss Side and Hulme.[23] As images of wrecking balls smashing into red brick houses flash up on screen, Locke is interviewed on a doorstep: 'I was born around here,' she says. 'It's not an ideal community, but it is a community where people know one another and they don't want to move out.' A total of 11,583 houses were selected for clearance in South Manchester between 1965 and 1972, of which 4,613 were located in the two wards of Moss Side.[24] An image of the aftermath shows row after row of demolished houses, as thriving streets that had survived the Blitz became wasteland.

Along with the Pan-African Congress of 1945, the clearance programme constitutes one of the key moments in Manchester's Black history. Born in the same year the African leaders gathered in Manchester, it split the community, destroying whole swathes of Hulme and Moss Side, including 22 Monton Street, where Locke grew up. She and others in the Housing Action Group campaigned for 'phased development'. Under their plan, the worst homes, which were nearly always owned by private landlords, would be knocked down and rebuilt. Homes that were in decent order would be upgraded, instead of demolished.

The alternative plan would see houses redeveloped street by street, so that the community would not have been displaced for long periods and could return once their street was refurbished. But the Corporation of Manchester, which later became the City Council, was not interested. The bulldozers moved in, with clearances continuing throughout the 1960s, and around 4,000 houses destroyed every year.[25] Barry Adamson, the Moss Side musician who was in Magazine and Nick Cave and the Bad Seeds, recalled in his memoir that he saw groups of 'white men with their jauntily angled flat caps' smirking to each other as 'wrecking balls and spades [did] their work' on his parents' home on Upper Medlock Street in Hulme.

Part of the reason the corporation could proceed without significant resistance was the reputation the area had for vice. Moss Side had become the city's red-light district in the 1950s with brothels operating openly. After nearly 200 prosecutions for indecency and disorderly conduct over an eleven-month period in 1950, local church groups appealed for the council and the Home Secretary to 'clean up' the area.[26] Opponents always maintained the problem was 'grossly exaggerated' with some arguing the trade was moved from the city centre to Moss Side intentionally by the police.[27] Either way, the urban renewal project was seen as the perfect vehicle to address the issue – and in the minds of people like Anderton it cemented the area's reputation as an ungodly district in need of his pious intervention.

The most controversial part of the redevelopment plan was the reimbursement that owners were offered as part of the compulsory purchase orders.[28] There had been concerns about Black residents being overcharged by as much as 50 per cent to purchase properties in Moss Side by estate agents, who were selling properties for more than the £500 or £600 usually paid in the area. But now homeowners were rumoured to be offered sums as low as £50, which would only cover a few weeks' rent in the new council-owned properties they were being offered. Newspaper reports at the time were critical of the council's actions, saying that those who had paid off their mortgages and therefore only had modest household bills to consider were being hit by 'severe financial burdens'.[29]

The clearances turned many Black Mancunians from homeowners to council tenants. Before the plan, few Black Mancunians were in council housing, but afterwards, 59 per cent of Black Mancunians were living in council properties, compared to only 45 per cent nationally. The knock-on effect was huge. Black entrepreneurs who wanted to emulate Makonnen and Magbotiwan had been able to build their businesses by using property as collateral. Now that route was blocked. In fact, by 1973 around 80 per cent of Black-owned businesses on Denmark Road and Princess Road and other streets in Moss Side had ceased to operate.[30]

Black residents fought back the most vocally in an effort to preserve their community, which by 1961 was around 5 per cent of Moss Side's population. Much of the community was made up of those who'd emigrated from the Caribbean, including the Guyanese activists and community organisers Elouise and Beresford Edwards, who refused to sell and stayed in their home as others were demolished all around them. But they were only delaying the inevitable. Some Black residents of Moss Side and Hulme were so scarred by the clearance plan and the sums they were offered for their homes that they vowed never to buy a property in Britain again.

In Hulme, the rows of demolished terraced houses were replaced by a large, futuristic housing estate called The Crescents: four towering apartment complexes that curved to mimic the Georgian crescents of Bath and London. In a similar grand manner, each complex was named after a different famous architect, the Scottish designer Robert Adam; Regency architect John Nash; John Charles, who rebuilt the Palace of Westminster and eighteenth-century landscape architect William Kent.

The landings outside the flats were wide enough for a milk float, there were walkways – or streets in the sky – connecting the different sites and communal green spaces that were supposed to compensate for the lack of gardens in the old Moss Side and Hulme houses. They were more spacious than the homes they were replacing, but there was an issue: within a couple of years of their existence, The Crescents were falling apart.

Shoddy workmanship meant that the ventilation ducts didn't work properly, which brought infestations of vermin. The 'streets in the sky' became ideal places for drug dealers to operate and muggings were common. The deck access was wide enough for the milk float, but the lifts rarely worked so milkmen couldn't deliver, while postmen learned to stay away after regularly being relieved of their postbags. The green spaces soon became poorly kept patches of grass. A child died after falling from one of the balconies, which meant the complexes were made 'adult only' in 1974, after many families petitioned to be moved. 'We were packed together like animals, like cattle in a truck,' said the community activist Maria Noble.[31] 'You know you have to move out or destroy yourself, because that is how it got.'

After The Crescents became adult only – just three years after opening – they turned into a surreal incubator for Manchester's cultural underground. There was a theatre troupe that would perform

We Were There

The Crescents in Hulme, 1987

Hamlet on the brutalist steps that littered the complex. Travellers often set up in the site, while The Russell Club – an angular red-brick social club that was adjacent to The Crescents – became the centre of Manchester's alternative music scene. The club had various iterations, including the Public Service Vehicle Club, or PSV, started by Caribbean bus drivers. But its most infamous iteration was when Tony Wilson – the Mancunian Svengali who hosted cultural programmes on Granada TV and started Factory Records – set up The Factory in the club, in an attempt to recreate Andy Warhol's New York Factory in Hulme. While The Factory itself only lasted a few years, the bands who emerged from that scene – Joy Division, New Order, A Certain Ratio and the Happy Mondays – would go on to put Manchester music on the map.

In her history of British council housing, *Estates*, Lynsey Hanley writes that 'it says a lot about the immediate fate of The Crescents that within a decade or so of their completion the upper floors had come instead to be regarded as the epicentre of the city's musical sub-culture'. There was a 24/7 blues club known as The Kitchen, which was made up of two flats that had been knocked into one, like the House of Dreads in Birmingham. The comedian Steve Coogan posed for a famous picture outside The Crescents in a red sports car; Ian Brown, the lead singer of the Stone Roses, spent time in the flats; while the poet Lemn Sissay also lived in them.

But despite the culture that blossomed there, the development was doomed. 'The idea was to get some fresh air into Hulme,' wrote Hanley. 'The reality was an unmitigated disaster.' The initial warnings of the Black community, led by activists like Locke, were ignored and the results were a failed development she'd warned wouldn't work. Their community might not have been perfect, the housing needed to be improved, but to destroy it was an act of vandalism. One that could only come from a council – and a city – that didn't value its Black community. When it was torn down in 1993,[32] the then City Council leader Sir Richard Leese, who would go on to drive much of the city centre's redevelopment in the 2000s, said it was the start of the modern Mancunian era.[33]

The Manchester Plan represented a vision for the future that displaced hundreds of people. The Reno survived the demolition, but other Black clubs, including The Edinburgh by Alexandra Park, were torn down. The heady ideals of the planners who wanted to embrace modernism – and at one point considered introducing helipads around the city, believing helicopter travel would be commonplace – had fallen woefully short.[34] They'd been 'bold and comprehensive', but the top-down approach of the Manchester Corporation and poor execution had splintered one of the oldest Black communities in Europe and left many people worse off. But, despite the tumult that surrounded it, Magbotiwan's club was about to enter its golden era, as the young people of Moss Side – many of whom had been caught up in the churn of urban renewal – looked for a release. The Reno would be that outlet, and a DJ from Jamaica was about to shape Manchester's music scene for decades.

The DJ who gave The Reno its reputation was a man simply known as Persian. The music policy at The Reno when Magbotiwan set it up was initially Blue Beat and ska, but in 1967 Persian was hired as resident DJ and had his own vision. Persian was born into a family of teachers in eastern Kingston, Jamaica, and had inherited his family's love of books. 'I used to wait until my parents went to bed. I would sit up and put the lights on and start reading ... from a young age I was a night person,' he told me. He would read voraciously, switching between the philosophy of Plato and Socrates, and the crime capers of the Hardy Boys. His reading inspired a taste for travel and the desire to experience life beyond Kingston. Persian had two uncles: one lived in Florida and the other in London. 'They both arrived in Jamaica at the same time for the holiday, and both of them asked me if I wanted to come back with them,' he recalls. Persian chose London, moving in with his uncle before relocating to Manchester and Moss Side.

Persian's passion for DJing was ignited at a party in Kingston, where a sound system called B-Rocket was playing. Instead of dancing, Persian studied the DJ and watched in awe as he controlled the dance floor, seeming to know just what record to play and when. As the clock approached midnight, he reached for a record – 'It's Almost Tomorrow' by The Dream Weavers – and followed it with Ray Charles' 'Midnight'. 'I said to myself, "This guy's a genius",' he told me. 'The mixing of those two tracks made me decide that I wanted to be a DJ.'

Persian's skill was in playing mid-tempo soul tracks, often album cuts that others had ignored; tracks like The Crusaders' 'Stomp and Buck Dance' and Earth, Wind and Fire's 'Reasons'; or Bill Summers' 'Summer Fun' and the more sultry 'Weaver of Dreams' by Freddie Hubbard. 'The Reno was deep,' says Hewan Clarke, who would succeed Persian as a resident DJ. 'If there was a new album by Brazilian percussionist Paulinho Da Costa which had a jazz-funk dance track that was popular in the clubs in town, there'd be another track on there with a killer bassline and nice melodic parts,' recalls Clarke. 'Persian would play that kind of stuff.'

Persian's influence was huge. Other Manchester DJs would come down to hear him play, including Clarke, the musical tastemaker

John Grant and former Northern Soul spinner Colin Curtis, who opened the club Rafters in 1978 – one of the first city centre clubs to operate an egalitarian door policy. 'There was one DJ from The Reno who affected what we played and that was Persian,' says Curtis. 'He was a connection between what was happening at The Reno and what was going on in the city centre.' Slowly, the songs that were hits at The Reno started to seep out onto mainstream dance floors across Manchester.

When the Piccadilly Radio station started in 1974, the actor Vanessa Redgrave – who had a foothold in the Manchester Black community after she helped fund the Nello James Centre in Whalley Range, a community hub named after her friend the Trinidadian author C. L. R. James – recommended Persian to its producers. His reputation travelled beyond Manchester after an article in *Blues & Soul* magazine featured Persian and The Reno. Club regulars would often turn up at Spin Inn Records on Cross Street asking for tracks they'd heard him play. Without knowing the name of the artist, they'd often sing to the owner Gary Lane, who'd have to figure out what the record was. 'They would say, "Can I have this? I heard it at The Reno and it goes like *this*,"' recalls Kath Locke's son Bolaji Laurance.[35]

By the middle of Persian's tenure in the mid-1970s, the club's great music and loose, illicit reputation was attracting some famous faces. Muhammad Ali visited the club after Magbotiwan travelled to Canada to watch a fight and told the boxer about Moss Side and his club. His daughter Lisa still wears the golden gloves pendant Ali gave her father on a necklace. There was an apocryphal rumour that Bob Marley once attended. Tony Wilson, who would change the city with his TV show on Granada that gave exposure to bands he'd then release on Factory Records, had his stag do in The Reno. Other Reno regulars included the outlaw snooker player Alex 'Hurricane' Higgins, who would play Magbotiwan at pool. Higgins, whose own hellraiser reputation made him a pariah in polite society, once told Hewan Clarke he preferred socialising with Black people 'because my people don't want me'. The club was for those on the margins of society; Persian saw The Reno as being like a speakeasy that he'd read about and seen in the American prohibition films he'd watched back in Jamaica. It was a place for people to unwind, park their troubles and enjoy his music. But in the summer of 1981, its clientele were about to find themselves on the frontline.

During the summer of 1981, where large-scale civil unrest spread throughout the UK, there were three nights of looting and violence across Moss Side, largely in reaction to the police harassment Black Mancunians were facing. Trouble had originally erupted outside The Nile, the reggae club that was above the betting shop and The Reno, in the early hours of 8 July 1981.

At first Anderton's force used low-profile policing tactics – that included conversations with community leaders rather than confrontation with those on the street. But after the initial twenty-four hours, and following a conversation with the Home Secretary Willie Whitelaw, the Chief Constable shifted to a 'positive action' approach. During the disturbances, Anderton, who referred to the forty-eight-hour period as 'guerilla warfare', had assembled more than 500 officers to clear the streets of Moss Side, headed by his controversial and hated Tactical Action Group who – like Liverpool police's task force – drove around in Land Rovers and were known for their fondness of using Sus laws to detain young Black men.[36]

On the second and third nights, Chief Constable James Anderton's shock-and-awe approach resulted in 150 arrests and horrible injuries. Elouise Edwards and the Abasindi Collective – a Black feminist group who took over a building in Moss Side, running Saturday schools and fought anti-deportation cases – opened their doors to the injured, which included a white apprentice baker who'd been badly beaten by the police and needed to be taken to hospital. 'He said something that has stuck with me forever,' said Edwards in 2011. 'He said: "But you were the people they taught us to hate."' Around 60 per cent of the people arrested during the disturbances were white, yet most of the coverage focused on Black Mancunians. The *Manchester Evening News* put Anderton's 'Guerilla Warfare' line on its front page and suggested the trouble was sparked by outside agitators, a position that police had been pushing but that was never confirmed.

But despite the support Anderton garnered from some in the city's establishment, his force's tactics appalled many in Manchester. Newspapers interviewed Moss Siders who had witnessed the violence and were appalled. One woman told a reporter that she saw a Black man who was trying to get to his house and out of the fray being abused by three officers who called him a 'Black bastard' and warned that if they saw him again they'd 'kick his Black face in'. Anita Thomas, the vice chair of the Moss Side Labour Party, said she intervened when police had isolated a young Black man and was told to 'get back to bed, you trash'.[37]

In the aftermath of the disturbances, the Greater Manchester Council commissioned a QC, Benet Hytner, to produce a report on the events of July 1981. The Hytner Report, as it was known, mostly defended the police actions. It was boycotted by the Moss Side Defence Committee,[38] a community group that included activists such as Elouise Edwards and Gus John, who'd been a key part of Bradford Black's defence of George Lindo. In response to the report, they said that the real issue was Anderton's perception of Moss Side, one that was cemented when he was working as a beat cop in the orbit of The Reno. The activists argued that it was the treatment of Moss Side as a 'dangerous, alien colony, full of actual or potential criminals, which demanded forceful and repressive policing' that had sparked the riots.[39]

The events of July 1981 made The Reno even more important to the young people of Moss Side – a place of safety and escape from the dangers that awaited them on the streets outside their homes. Persian was in Hamburg. He'd taken up a three-month residency at the Third World Club, a forward-thinking soul venue in the German city. On his return from Hamburg, Persian decided to pull out Roberta Flack and Donny Hathaway's 'Back Together Again'. He thought the song – a typically mid-tempo soul affair – would be a tonic for the dancers, many of whom had been caught up in the unrest. As the needle hit the groove and the crowd heard the lyrics, which referred to people persevering through the 'hard times' before being reunited, there was a cheer, and people banged their glasses on the table and slapped the walls of the club: their selector was back.

Persian would spend another two years behind the decks at The Reno; his departure in 1983 marked the end of an era. The midtempo, smoother sounds that he favoured were gradually replaced with new tracks coming over the Atlantic from Chicago. By then Clarke was behind the decks, along with Doctor D, Moses (Magbotiwan's son) and Coolie – a DJ who'd filled in for Persian while he was away in Hamburg.

Linda Brogan went to The Reno one last time in 1986. She'd been a near-weekly regular between 1976 and 1982 – Persian's imperial phase. As she walked in, something felt amiss. 'Persian wasn't there,' she says. 'And the music was different – it was heaving in an odd way.' Her club had disappeared. The basement seemed darker, the crowd was younger and the music was harder. What Brogan had heard was the future: house music had arrived in Manchester – imported by a new generation of DJs. The four-to-the-floor beats sounded like 'Black heavy metal' to her,[40] the antithesis of Persian's downtempo style. What Brogan witnessed wasn't just the birth of house, it was the end of The Reno. The basement club had only one entrance via a set of steep, often slippery stairs; food was cooked on the property and if a fire were to break out and spread, it would mean chaos and, potentially, many casualties. Magbotiwan's daughter, Lisa, believes elements within the council had been trying to get it closed down for years, and finally, in 1986 they succeeded. It was part of yet another reshaping of Moss Side, as Princess Road was extended. But the music that Clarke had introduced wouldn't die with the club, it lived on in Moss Side and Manchester.

There's a photograph of Magbotiwan standing outside the club in the late summer of 1986, shortly before it was torn down. He's wearing his Nigerian attire and is flanked by his daughter Bimpe

The Black Door – Manchester, 1986

Phil Magbotiwan with fellow Nigerian Babalola at the bar in The Reno

and his daughter-in-law Rita. Despite the impending demolition, he looks content. On the hoardings behind them, there's a poster for a gig that's to be held on 27 September 1986 at the Moss Side shopping precinct, constructed as part of the regeneration of the area. Like The Crescents, it ultimately failed but, as with the doomed housing development, it provided a space for Black culture to thrive.

In the winter of 2018, a YouTube clip surfaced and was shared on social media. It showed footage of a small social space called the 8411, which sat above the library in the precinct.[41] The grainy footage lasts less than nine minutes but its existence challenges one of the key origin stories in contemporary British culture. The established folklore is that four intrepid Londoners: Danny Rampling, Johnny Walker, Nicky Holloway and Paul Oakenfold, went to Ibiza in 1987 and imported house music, while providing the building blocks for the rave scene in the UK. But before acid house went mainstream, Manchester's Black dancers were the first to interpret the sounds that Chicago DJs like Ron Hardy and Frankie Knuckles were playing across the Atlantic.

In the 8411 footage, the Chicago house track 'No Way Back' by Adonis Smith is playing over the sound system in a crowded room. Everyone in the crowd is Black, as is the DJ – Mike Shaft. Lads in bright yellow T-shirts and sunglasses shuffle their feet in unison as the camera moves through the club. It's like Tony Palmer's Wigan Casino footage, but heavier, more intense. It would be in the Haçienda that Manchester's reputation as a dance music mecca would be established – but in its early days, it was Hewan Clarke, the club's first resident DJ, who brought many of The Reno regulars with him to nights where they sometimes made up half of the dance floor.[42] The Reno, with Clarke's 'Black heavy metal' that so disturbed Brogan, was the testing ground for the biggest youth movement the UK had seen since the 1960s – acid house and rave.

When Linda Brogan looks back at The Reno it's with a mixture of nostalgia and sadness. Her club had gone by 1986, and her fellow regulars would face testing times in the 1990s as hard drugs – and in particular, heroin – shot through Moss Side.[43] The close ties and intense friendships among the group meant the drug went through The Reno crowd 'like wildfire', Brogan said. When you look at the club's online memorial wall, many of the punters, who would today have been in their fifties and sixties, are long dead – several dying not long after the club was demolished. The people who dug up the club's foundations weren't just former regulars, they were survivors.

After the club closed and the next phase of redevelopment hit Moss Side, the area became plagued by gang war – often fought in the new Alexandra Park Estate, which, with its alleyways and quiet corners, was the perfect place for scores to be settled. Like The Crescents, the estate was created with the promise it would provide a better home for Moss Side's residents. Today, Moss Side remains best known in the popular consciousness for that brief era, with some newspapers still using the 'Gunchester' tag, coined when the violence had spread city-wide; at its peak in 2007, there were 146 reports of shots being fired in the city.[44] What came just before is forgotten. Like the house clearances, the erasure takes with it a vital piece of history: a link between Pan-Africanism, music culture and modern Manchester.

Today, the surviving infrastructure of Black Manchester is once again under threat from yet more redevelopment: by 2025 the Nello James Centre in Whalley Range could be turned into luxury flats;[45] while the West Indian Centre in Hulme has just narrowly avoided being transformed into more student accommodation as the city's universities continue to expand.[46] The Sus laws are gone, but their descendant is Section 60, an order which means that police officers have temporary powers to stop and search people in a defined area within a specific timeframe. It is used regularly.[47] The city's Chief Constable Stephen Watson, is proudly 'anti-woke', telling journalists that his officers shouldn't take the knee in support of anti-racist causes or wear rainbow shoelaces to show solidarity with the city's large LGBT community.[48]

The Manchester Brogan grew up in is long gone. The official history states that after the IRA bombing which destroyed parts of the city centre in 1996, Manchester has been rebuilt: stronger and better.[49] The city received more than £580 million in public and private funding, and its new face was friendlier to businesses, declaring once again it was ready for growth. Under the guidance of City Council leader Sir Richard Leese and his partner Howard Bernstein, developers and foreign investors were courted and the results were spectacular. Cranes began to dominate the city's skyline as glass and chrome apartment towers sprung up, completely altering the feel of Manchester in a few short years.

The transformation left many in lower income brackets behind. An investigation found that of the sixty-one big residential developments granted permission by Manchester's planning committee in 2018 and 2019, not one of the almost 15,000 homes met the government's definition of affordable.[50] 'Sky lounges' and luxury lifestyle experiences sat uncomfortably alongside homelessness stats that showed more and more Mancunians were living on the street.

There are those who would say it's cultural vandalism, that a part of the city which made it special has been erased, replaced with 'boltholes' for Russian and Chinese investors. The real picture is more complicated; yes, the city's property market is making foreign owners rich. But local people have benefited too. Between 2000 and 2021 the total number of jobs in Manchester increased by 49 per cent; across the whole of the UK that figure was 21 per cent.[51] It's been dubbed a growth miracle, one that echoes the vast expansion the city witnessed in the industrial revolution, and makes it an outlier as many other northern cities – still reeling from the damage sustained to their industries during the Thatcher era – struggle to create jobs.

When critics of modern Manchester voice their views, the response from the people who made it, men like Leese and Bernstein, is: 'Do you remember what was there before?' It's a rebuttal that's supposed to conjure images of 1980s Manchester, a dark, grimy city full of failed dreams like The Crescents, the violence of 1981 and – for some – The Reno.

But there's another version of this city, a more complete one, where its Black history, like the Pan-African Congress or the radicalism of Abasindi, sits side by side with the Chartists and the Suffragettes. The city's Black community keeps the memory of people like Elouise Edwards, places like The Reno and events like the Pan-African Congress alive, but the civic memory – the official record – is lacking.

The Reno is the perfect symbol of that contested history. Its origins date back to the historic Black communities that first settled in Salford, Black men and women from East and West Africa and the Caribbean, seafarers mostly. Those pioneers provided a link to the Pan-African Congress and the Manchester of T Ras Makonnen, Black entrepreneurs and political leaders who'd go on to shape postcolonial Africa. In the 1970s it became a haven for a younger generation – those like Linda Brogan who were searching for their own Black British identity, before its final act as an incubator for acid house, a sound that would change Manchester and the UK forever. Among the crowds who stepped through that black door were gangsters, pimps, but also politicians, musicians, sports stars, celebrities and activists. Like Kath Locke said about Moss Side, it wasn't ideal, it wasn't sanitised, but Magbotiwan's club was a hub that linked and nurtured the various strands of Black Manchester.

Standing on the site of The Reno today, a little patch of grass with a foot-high wooden fence that cordons it off from a footpath, it's hard to imagine what once was. The row of shops that sat next to the club are all but gone; as is the reggae club, The Nile, which was upstairs. The only remnants are crumbling buildings and a scrap yard across the road. This feels a world apart from the bright, chrome-filled Manchester that is a few minutes' drive away.

On this patch of grass – flanked by the Heineken brewery's chimneys and Princess Parkway, which hums with traffic coming in and out of the city centre – Brogan, and dozens of former regulars, gathered to help with the dig in 2017. With assistance from the archaeology team at Salford University, the survivors burrowed into the dirt and found the club's foundations. Some people hadn't seen each other for forty years.

Over the course of a couple of weeks, secrets began to emerge as the amateur archaeologists dug up champagne bottles, a pair of flares, discarded records and even a bag of weed. Brogan got the resident DJs back together and invited the old crowd for a party held on the dig site under a marquee. Former regulars chatted about the old days and danced to the tracks they loved from the 1970s played by their DJ – Persian. Pictures from the club's past, including a shot of The Reno's own football team, every member sporting an Afro, were shared online. Brogan interviewed many of them to create an oral history project, while a memorial wall was posted online to commemorate those who'd passed away. For a moment, a forgotten part of Black Manchester's history, one which linked radicals, hustlers and artists, was exhumed.

7.
The Last Fort – 1987

The story of Black Britain we've seen so far has been, primarily, an urban one. Young Black men and women fought for space on the dance floor of Wigan Casino; documentary makers captured the fallout from police corruption in Bradford; and in Birmingham, academics took on the moral panic about the city's Black population created by the British media. Wolverhampton gave birth to an art group that tackled institutional racism, while activists in Liverpool and Manchester fought to secure a presence in the UK's largest urban centres.

It was in cities that Black immigrants decided to create homes. They came not only for the work opportunities but for the existing communities, in some cases centuries old. This chapter is different. It's about a place where there were hardly any Black people in the Thatcher era. A place that, despite large-scale immigration into the UK (Between 1948 and 1971, an estimated 500,000 people born in a Commonwealth country arrived in the UK),[1] remained almost entirely white, and still does to this day: the countryside.

In the mid-1980s, ethnic minorities made up just over 6 per cent of the British population, but in rural areas, that figure was closer to 1.6 per cent. Today, in cities like Manchester, Black Britons account for just under 15 per cent of the population, compared to around 2 per cent in the Thatcher era. But in the countryside, the figure is still the same as it was in the 1980s. Their relatively small presence means that rural Black communities are rarely included in our conversation about race and the UK. If the stories I've selected so far have been obscured by our limited idea of what constitutes Black British history and the ignorance about pivotal cultural moments that took place outside of London, then those of Black rural life are even further removed from the public imagination. In most cases, they're not just hidden; they're almost completely invisible.

But in 1987, one group decided to challenge the status quo: the Black Environmental Network (BEN). Artists and environmentalists, they were Black Britons who loved the countryside, and set out to claim it – or, at the very least, to question the nation's prevailing assumptions about rural life in relation to race – challenging ideas that went to the very heart of what it means to be British. They pressured politicians and environmentalist organisations into recognising the existence of Black people in rural locations and the ways in which their lives were affected by racism. Its members, including Julian Agyeman and the artist Ingrid Pollard, were pioneers whose impact has largely been erased, but whose ideas still shape one of the most contentious debates in contemporary Britain: how do we handle our own history?

The arguments and battles they started are still with us now. When someone brings up the concept of environmental racism, or poorer health outcomes for Black people, it's the work of BEN that set the precedent. They're present each time a countryside estate created by former enslavers attempts to contend with its history, or as organisations like the National Trust grapple with their own connections with colonialism.

At the time, their work produced a fierce backlash by putting Blackness in a space that was – for many – the last bastion of whiteness. During the Thatcher era, this was a place that sat apart from the messy, multiracial reality of inner-city Britain. While many of the UK's cities burned in 1981, the countryside – by and large – remained untouched. But that was only ever an illusion; in reality, the unrest that travelled around Britain from Bristol to Brixton just took a little while to get to the rural idyll, and when it did, it would ignite a debate that is still burning to this day.

In the immediate aftermath of the unrest of 1981, which had seen Britain's racial tensions simmer over to produce an unprecedented summer of violence, the Home Secretary Willie Whitelaw was in shock. A genial man who looked like a Toby jug and was once said to have 'literally sweated good will',[2] Whitelaw travelled around the country, witnessing destruction that left city centres resembling smouldering war zones. The grim images of London, Liverpool and Manchester ablaze, their communities full of hatred for the British state, reminded him of his time in Northern Ireland. After Britain declared direct rule in 1972, Whitelaw was made the first secretary of state for the province and witnessed the Troubles, which saw sectarian violence meted out by militants claiming hundreds of lives every year, up close. He was known for keeping calm in the midst of political warfare and bloody cabinet battles. Yet that summer was one of the biggest challenges he'd faced during his time in office – and it was taking its toll.

After his tour of duty, Whitelaw returned in a daze to his official residence at Dorneywood, near Slough in Buckinghamshire – a beautiful grace-and-favour property surrounded by nature. His wife made him a meal and he gazed out at the cottage garden as he tried to make sense of what he'd seen.

'I remember sitting out after supper on a beautiful hot summer evening, looking at the fields and trees of Burnham Beeches. It was a perfect, peaceful English scene,' he later wrote.[3] 'Was it really the same country as the riot towns and cities which I had visited during the week? Was it really the same vicinity as parts of London a few miles away which at the moment were full of troubles? Surely, I thought, this peaceful countryside represents more accurately the character and mood of the vast majority of the British people.' The view out of his window provided him with inspiration, solace and resolve. But the key guiding message it gave him was that *this* was the real Britain, not the nightmare unfolding in many of the country's cities.

When Whitelaw needed succour, it was the simplicity of a woodland glade he turned to. As the UK burned, the countryside represented safety and order. This was a place seemingly untouched by the chaos of the early Thatcher era: a Britain of strikes, terrorism and racial tension. Whitelaw's line of questioning placed him squarely within a long tradition in England – one where politicians and thinkers place rural Britain on an idealised, almost mythological pedestal.

Sixty years before Whitelaw looked out over Burnham Beeches, the inter-war Conservative prime minister Stanley Baldwin made a speech at the Royal Society of St George's annual dinner. In it he tried to articulate the importance of the countryside to the very concept of England to members of an organisation founded in 1894 to celebrate Englishness. 'To me,' Baldwin began in 1924, 'England is the country, and the country is England. The sounds of England, the tinkle of the hammer on the anvil in the country smithy, the corncrake on a dewy morning, the sound of the scythe against the whetstone, the sight of the plough team coming over the brow of the hill, the sight which has been in England since England was a land, and may be seen in England long after the Empire has perished.'

England and, more specifically, the rural dreamlike version of England that Baldwin conjures is an eternal idyll. The concept generates an emotional response, like few things do in Britain. It's nearly always romanticised but it's also paternalistic, as if this perfect place needs to be protected and kept just as it is.

The great nineteenth-century landscape artist John Constable created arguably *the* iconic vision of the English countryside in 1826 when he produced 'The Cornfield'. Based on his memory of a Suffolk lane he used to walk down as a boy, the painting includes sheep being led by a border collie, verdant verges on either side of the lane that frame a cornfield being worked by farmhands with one tree in the middle distance. Unlike in the work of many artists from the Romantic era, his depiction wasn't of an entirely imagined England populated by mythical creatures: it was rooted in reality, but an idealised one. The antithesis of the city filth produced during the industrial revolution.

One of Stuart Hall's contemporaries in the New Left, the Welsh intellectual Raymond Williams, studied how the countryside was written about in classic English literature. Williams came up with a theory – 'retrospective regret' – to explain a prevalent trope. Authors would pine for a time and place, nearly always in the countryside, which was just out of reach. The good old days of British rural life that were disappearing before their eyes. John Betjeman pined for the 'winding country lanes' of the 1930s; in 1932 the literary critic F. R. Leavis said 'an organic old England' had already disappeared; while in 1911 George Sturt argued that rural England was dying out. Williams believed you could trace the idea all the way back to the Garden of Eden, the original paradise. 'The city is the place of senseless overcrowding, noise, luxury, pride, power whereas the country by comparison is a place of simple innocence, peace,' he said. '"The old values", as it's often put.'[4]

The trope could also be found in contemporary literature, even if it was being satirised. In Kazuo Ishiguro's 1989 novel *Remains of the Day*, Stevens – the butler who much of the story revolves

Farm labourers harvesting bracken on a hill overlooking Lake Windermere at Ambleside in Cumbria

around – admires the Wiltshire countryside from a point just outside Salisbury. 'The English landscape at its finest – such as I saw this morning – possesses a quality that the landscapes of other nations, however more superficially dramatic, inevitably fail to possess,' he says, before calling the English landscape the 'most deeply satisfying in the world', as Ishiguro satirises the obsession. During the First and Second World Wars, images of the countryside were used to inspire patriotism, while soldiers read poetry and prose about English gardens as they hunkered down in Flanders trenches. Prime ministers, soldiers and literary scholars have all reached for this idea of England – whether to explain something profound about national identity or to offer reassurance in the face of horrors.

But the countryside was also an escape, as Raymond Williams found. You go to the country to get away from the city, and in the Thatcher era that also meant escaping from Black Britons. In the 1980s, rural Britain was projected by right-wing politicians, media and conservation groups 'as a secure, nostalgic site infused with cultural and racial sanctity to buttress the influence of immigrants from the old empire,'[5] as one academic put it: a last refuge from modern, urban Britain. The concept of 'white flight' – a phenomenon that saw white residents leave, in their droves, areas with Black immigration – was seen as a predominantly American issue, notably in cities like Detroit or areas such as Watts in South Los Angeles. But now white residents in London boroughs began selling up and moving to Essex, a county known for its beautiful countryside and whiteness.[6] There had been earlier exoduses from neighbourhoods such as Moss Side in Manchester and L8 in Liverpool, as white homeowners sold up and swapped the inner city for the suburbs. In their place came Black Britons: men, women, and children from across the former Commonwealth who began staking their claim in the UK's cities and its institutions. Many didn't consider the countryside as an option. Some did, though. Out in the rural idyll of Baldwin and Whitelaw, there were Black people who were also trying to find their place in Britain.

*

If you went walking in the Lake District in the early 1980s, especially around Loughrigg Fell – a verdant hill that overlooks the village of Ambleside – there's a good chance you would have bumped into Julian Agyeman. A six-foot-two British-Ghanaian ecologist and graduate of Durham University, Agyeman was a teacher at St Aidan's secondary school in Carlisle and would regularly take his classes on field trips to the Lakes. One of his favourites was a walk to the top of Loughrigg Fell, where the class of around twenty students discussed – among other things – how glaciation would have affected the landscape that inspired the Romantic poet William Wordsworth.

But on the trips, he began to notice something odd. While speaking to his class, he would spy groups of walkers stopping on their journey and staring at them. He'd glance down at his gear, including the latest Patagonia shell jacket and Timberland boots, which all looked correct, before surveying the students to see if he was missing something obvious, or even dangerous. Nothing. He concluded that the sight of a group of all-white students being led by a Black man was enough for people to stop their hike, and gawp. 'It happened multiple times,' he told me. What Agyeman experienced was a common phenomenon for Black hill walkers and naturalists. His presence made people stop and stare; as far as they were concerned, he simply wasn't supposed to be there.

Over the period Agyeman was taking his classes out in the Lakes, walking and rambling had never been more popular in Britain, having evolved from niche pursuit to established leisure activity. By 1990, membership of the National Trust topped two million, while there were concerns that overuse of long-distance footpaths was leading to their erosion around the countryside. The huge uptick in people venturing to the countryside created extreme side effects: on bank holidays, the police would close the Kendal exit off the M6, declaring the Lake District was full. More people were flooding to the countryside than ever before, but there was one group that was being left behind: Black Britons. In a Countryside Commission survey of groups who visited rural Britain, 'multiracial' visitors were ranked tenth lowest out of eleven groups, higher only than those from the most deprived council estates.[7]

In the Thatcher era, Black figures in the countryside were treated as alien by the press. Julian McLauchlan was hailed as the 'first Rastafarian shepherd'[8] when he worked at Prince Charles' Highgrove estate. His appointment made headlines around the world, accompanied with an image of him feeding lambs or walking alongside his flock with a shepherd's crook. When a newspaper explored rural racism in Cornwall, they illustrated it with a picture of Ziggy Holder, a West Indian who'd set up a cricket team and was billed as 'the only Black man in Padstow'.[9] Just like the Black artists in Wolverhampton, Agyeman and other Black people in the countryside were atomised, presented as lone representatives of a city dwelling peoples.

Portrait of Julian Agyeman taken by Ingrid Pollard in Essex in front of some oilseed rape fields

When more than one Black or brown person appeared in a rural setting it could trigger outrage. The last Sikh Maharajah, Duleep Singh, lived and was buried in the Suffolk village of Elveden in the nineteenth century. He was a close friend of Queen Victoria and would let his elephants run on the Suffolk beaches. Every year the village would be visited by thousands of Sikhs who paid homage to the spiritual leader, boarding buses from Bradford and Birmingham. But in the late 1980s, in the build-up to the bicentenary of his death, their plans for a large-scale festival met stiff resistance. 'The Sikhs are a bit of a nightmare,' said one resident.[10] 'I suppose we're not used to people like that round here.'

Agyeman had grown up in Hull, raised by his white mother after his father returned to Ghana and, as a child, he developed a love of nature and particularly ornithology. He would set out on bird-watching trips on the weekend, heading toward Cottingham or at Spurn Point in the Humber estuary – a three-and-a-half-mile sand strip where you could spot ringtail hen harriers, woodcocks, snow bunting and red kites. 'It was just my passion,' Agyeman said. He remembers watching Ken Loach's film *Kes*, about a boy from Barnsley called Billy Casper who looks after a kestrel, and thinking it resembled his life.

As in *Kes*, Agyeman's interest in birds puzzled people. A schoolteacher told him he should consider sport because 'a big lad like him' would be good at it. This was the era of the Rugby League star Clive Sullivan, the first-ever Black man to captain a British sports team. Black people were sportsmen, not ornithologists. The teacher was just like the staring ramblers who couldn't comprehend his presence at Loughrigg Fell. All around him, Agyeman's interest in nature was met with perplexed expressions. But he was undeterred. He became a member of the young ornithologist club and developed an interest in the historic Black presence in the countryside. Agyeman remembers being thrilled on learning that in the third century AD there had been a 500-strong Black Roman garrison stationed close to where he taught in Cumbria. 'These were Black Romans, they were Libyans,' he told me. 'They weren't the white bodies that we see on the friezes.' Then, in the early 1980s, a concept came into Agyeman's life that changed the way he thought about his work and hikes in the Lakes.

In 1982, the Reverend Dr Benjamin Chavis, a civil rights activist,[11] coined the term 'environmental racism'. The idea was simple: Black people in the US are exposed to hazardous, toxic waste much more frequently than white Americans; not by accident but by political choice. The environment – nature itself – was being politicised. When Agyeman heard the phrase he was taken back to Loughrigg Fell. He started to think of his experience in the Lake District as an environmental justice issue – one that precluded his comfort and ease in certain spaces.

Agyeman began taking his cues from US environmentalists like Dr Chavis, contemplating questions such as why large roads were more likely to be constructed in lower-income – often Black – neighbourhoods. Or why there were fewer parks and green spaces in those same neighbourhoods. 'It wasn't about birds and bees, necessarily,' he told me. 'It was about structures, amenities and facilities, and linking poor housing to environmental conditions.' He wasn't the only person thinking about these issues. Though he may have appeared a lone figure in the hills of Cumbria, nearby an artist was working on a piece that would come to define Black presence in the countryside for a generation.

Ingrid Pollard – whose family had emigrated to the UK from Georgetown, Guyana in 1956 – was one of the Black artists who answered the call put out by the Blk Art Group in October 1982. She travelled to Wolverhampton for the first-ever National Black Art Convention but, unlike many of the other attendees, Pollard was not a student; she was already living the life of a would-be artist in London.

Slightly older than most of the crowd that congregated in 1982, Pollard was working odd jobs to get by (gardener for the local council, telephonist, assistant at the British Library). A squat in Bromley in South London was where she called home. 'It wasn't some utopian ideal,' Pollard tells me. 'We were poor. Most people were signing on, there were a lot of people in and out of prison.' It could be sketchy and surreal: at one point the housemates were responsible for a couple of horses, and sometimes homeless people would stay downstairs. But there was the occasional escape from London life; Pollard – like Willie Whitelaw – would also find peace in the countryside.

One of her housemates knew the family of social historian G. M. Trevelyan, who had a large house in Langdale Valley in the Lake District, not far from Loughrigg Fell, where Julian Agyeman would take his school class. The housemates had access to a van, and they would travel up and stay a couple of times a year. In the squat, Pollard had begun experimenting with photography and, while on the holidays, she would typically take one roll of film. She'd use her shots sparingly and intentionally, mindful of wasted opportunities at a time when money was hard to come by. It was on these trips that Pollard began to work on a piece that combined ideas of race, countryside and colonialism.

'I grew up on Wordsworth's poetry,' Pollard told an interviewer once.[12] His lyrical poem, 'Daffodils', was her father's favourite, and contained the famous line 'I Wandered Lonely as a Cloud', which inspired ideas of freedom and roaming in the English countryside. 'It was the same with the Pre-Raphaelites, whom I also used to like for their romantic vision of England and Englishness,' added Pollard. 'Like Wordsworth, they went out into the countryside because it freed them to write. But when I went to the Lakes myself, I found I wanted to hide behind a bush.' Pollard would wrestle with these opposing forces in a work called 'Pastoral Interlude', which was constructed over five years.

A series of five hand-tinted silver prints, like five postcards, each featuring a man or woman in a typical rural scene. Pollard photographed a female friend and the son of an acquaintance in different countryside locations, from the Lake District and the Lea Valley, to Derbyshire, East Anglia and St Andrews in Scotland. The pair appear in various settings: wandering in a graveyard, wading in a

The Last Fort – 1987

'The Cost of the English Landscape' by Ingrid Pollard

stream, holding a freshly picked bunch of flowers. They could be part of a photo montage, telling the story of a day spent in the great outdoors.

But there was another dimension to the work. The captions that accompany the images of 'Pastoral Interlude' are reminiscent of the direct, confrontational art made by Eddie Chambers and Keith Piper in Wolverhampton. As the woman looks over a drystone wall a caption reads: '. . . Searching for the seashells; waves lap over my wellington boots, carrying lost souls of brothers & sisters released over the ship side . . .' The next carries another reference to the slave trade, as the man in waders explores a stream: '. . . a lot of what MADE ENGLAND GREAT is founded on the blood of slavery, the sweat of working people . . . an industrial REVOLUTION without the Atlantic Triangle . . .'

Many of the themes that the Blk Art Group tackled are on display. Empire, the slave trade, British nationalism and the legacy of colonialism – but they are framed now in a different context: rural Britain. What Pollard did in 1987 was introduce ideas that are now mainstream but were marginal in the Thatcher era. The work did not only insert Black British people within an unlikely context; it commented on British history, the legacy of colonialism and how that could be found even in the rural idyll. She was also concerned with sustainability and the environment itself. In another piece, 'The Cost of the English Landscape' from 1989, Pollard creates more images – this time of a Black woman going over a stile in the countryside – that she combines with information about a nearby nuclear power plant. Many people misread 'Pastoral Interlude' as a direct comment on racism and the countryside; believing the captions and the images illustrate the same thing: fear and dread.[13] They weren't. Pollard loved the countryside, her trips there were an escape from city life. The images themselves weren't about fear. They were happy, innocent moments with her friends. But at times the whiteness of the environment would affect her. She'd be in Ambleside and notice people staring at her, a not-so-subtle reminder that some did not believe she belonged there.

Another pair of images reference the stereotype of Black people as only residing in cities. 'It's as if the Black experience is only ever lived within an urban environment,' she wrote, before riffing on Wordsworth. 'I thought I liked the Lake District; where I wandered lonely as a Black face in a sea of white.' In the image, Pollard's model is pictured in Nike hi-tops, tan trousers, white windbreaker, green hiking socks and a headscarf, sitting beside a barbed-wire fence with an overcast sky and rolling hills expanding toward the horizon behind her. She's looking off to her right, perhaps at someone or something approaching her. The label next to the work simply reads: '"and what part of Africa do you come from?" inquired the walker . . .', suggesting the kind of interactions Agyeman had on the top of Loughrigg Fell.

By the time 'Pastoral Interlude' was first shown in 1987, Pollard and Agyeman had already met in London. Agyeman had swapped Cumbria for Brixton and was focusing on environmental racism, trying – mostly in vain – to get organisations like the Countryside Commission to take the issue seriously. After meeting Pollard, he now had a fellow traveller and decided to form a group that would push the issue up the agenda. They came together at a time when hardly anyone was discussing the countryside – the nation was transfixed on the city, and the dramatic transformation of one of the country's oldest industries that was reshaping Britain.

A year before Ingrid Pollard showed 'Pastoral Interlude', the City of London – the square mile in the east of the capital, home to the country's financial sector – was turned upside down. Thatcher's government had introduced what came to be known as the Big Bang reforms, which jettisoned the old rules of engagement, and brought about a revolution in banking. From 27 October 1986, fixed commissions on securities trading were eliminated, firms could now operate as brokers and also make trades.[14] A new high-tech computing system was introduced to help modernise the industry and bring it in line with New York. The formerly bustling trading floors stood empty as traders and brokers sat behind computer screens. In an unprecedented move, the London Stock Exchange was opened to foreign firms. The clubby world of London finance – the one of long lunches and deals confirmed by handshakes among old public-school buddies – was blown up overnight.

The changes proved inviting to aggressive American firms, now eager to have a presence in the capital. Young representatives of Goldman Sachs and Lehman Brothers – the bank that would eventually collapse during the 2008 financial crash – brashly arrived in London to snap up City brokerages that had been in business for over a century. Instead of a pragmatic approach based on nurturing relationships over years, now traders hunted for mega deals where their commission would be astronomical. 'You change from long-termism to short-termism,' is how one City veteran who lived through the Big Bang put it. 'From looking after the long-term interests of your client to making the biggest buck out of today's deal.'[15]

The impact was enormous and almost immediate. The volume of trades running through the new high-tech terminals averaged more than $7.4 billion a week after the Big Bang, compared with $4.5 billion the week preceding it. Some estimate the reforms created 1,500 millionaires, as domestic City firms sold up, lured by the staggering sums on offer from the Americans and elsewhere.[16] The deregulation brought in the era of champagne popping on the trading floors when lucrative deals were secured, with the celebrations accompanied by the 'greed is good' mantra that became one of the defining slogans of the 80s. Young Urban Professionals, or Yuppies – city slickers with huge salaries who wore the right brands and ate at the right restaurants – were born.

The Big Bang came a year before Thatcher's third decisive election victory. She hammered Neil Kinnock's Labour, which was struggling to shake off the tag of extremists after the Militant Tendency takeovers of councils in places like Liverpool. Thatcher won 42.3 per cent of the vote in a victory that ushered in her imperial

Internal view of the London Stock Exchange

phase – her main enemies within the Conservative Party had been defeated, and the Falklands had secured her place among the biggest players on the international stage.

But as money was flooding into the capital, and Thatcher revelled in yet another vote of confidence from the electorate, the countryside and rural areas around Britain were in a period of deep decline. A groundbreaking report by the Environment Department and the Rural Development Commission was about to question the popular idea of the countryside as the calm, bucolic antidote to city life. The landmark interviews – conducted with people who actually lived and worked in the countryside around the UK – presented a stark picture.

Four in ten country dwellers lived below the poverty line; one in eight households had no car (despite worsening bus services); one in twelve homes was without a telephone; one in thirteen had structural defects, while one in six didn't have central heating. Jobs were scarce, with wages below the national average. The idea of the friendly village was challenged, too, with one in five families admitting to having problems with neighbours, while 75 per cent reported that they did their shopping at supermarkets, often in distant town centres. The report makes clear that – for many who lived in it – the idealised rural world so loved by Stanley Baldwin, or by Stevens in *Remains of the Day*, simply did not exist. 'We are selling ourselves a myth,' warned the author of the report.[17]

The problems white rural communities were facing were acute, but for Black people, the situation was vastly more challenging. While the Environment Department and Rural Development Commission were putting together the findings of their report, another survey was being conducted. The racial equality work done in the UK up to that point had been almost entirely focused on the country's major cities. The government or a race equality think-tank might commission a report on Birmingham or Bradford; sociologists and anthropologists might arrive in Liverpool to study Black residents – but the research omitted Black Britons in rural areas.

In 1991, following pressure from BEN, the Commission for Racial

Equality sent a man called Eric Jay to Cornwall, Devon, Dorset and Somerset to find out – for the first time – what life was like for Britain's Black countryside residents. Jay was well placed to take the job; he'd started his career as a news reporter, been part of the Normandy beach landings during the Second World War, and gone on to train as a minister in Handsworth, Birmingham.[18] The former preacher found a difficult economic picture: unemployment rates were high, largely thanks to the decline in both agriculture and industrialised ways of working, while migration to the area grew by 6.2 per cent between 1981 and 1989 – much of which came down to second homeowners, who were beginning to price out locals from the property market.

Unlike in Britain's major cities, the South West's Black population was scattered and fragmented, yet the racism that Jay discovered was no less potent than that suffered by their city-dwelling counterparts. He recorded accounts of Black students being turned away from work experience at hair salons by owners who said their presence would affect trade. Black and Asian school teachers faced parents who didn't want them anywhere near their children. Two hotel workers brought successful discrimination cases after they were sacked because racist guests didn't want them maintaining their rooms or providing services.

Jay quotes from a survey of attitudes and opinions among white students, mostly male, in the construction department of a college of further education: 40 per cent of respondents were hostile to the idea of having Black and Asian neighbours. The comments ranged from, 'I would hate to have Black neighbours, because once they move in they take over,' to the quote that inspired the title of the study: 'They could soon be invading us ... keep them in Birmingham.'[19]

There might have been far fewer Black faces in rural areas, but they were being ignored or discriminated against by the state and its service providers. When Jay went to community health councils, police forces and church leaders to ask about their approach to racism, he found that three-quarters of those interviewed were not including racial equality on the agenda. Jay was repeatedly told by complacent officials: 'We have no problem here because we have no Black people.' That denial wasn't benign. Institutions could ignore the prejudice that tiny communities or even single families were facing. But in 1987 the Black Environmental Network was formed with one aim: to force Britain to see the problem of rural racism in its green and pleasant land.

When Julian Agyeman considered Britain in the mid-1980s, he could see the strides forward taken in many areas: politics, housing, education and policing had all been examined in the wake of 1981. The Black Sections movement within the Labour Party had produced three Black MPs at the 1987 general election; the National Federation of Housing Associations told its members they were 'on the frontline in the battle against deprivation and discrimination'; while Black TV makers were producing shows about Black Britain on an unprecedented scale. Policies had been put in place, organisations formed, plans enacted. But the countryside sat outside of that.

Eric Jay's report had highlighted that the experiences of Agyeman and Pollard in the Lake District – the stares and the feeling of not belonging – were not one-offs. They were the tip of an iceberg. Jay's report had shown the reality – the countryside wasn't any less hostile to Black Britons.

The Black Environmental Network was made up of Black nature lovers and environmentalists, including Ingrid Pollard. The fledgling group would lobby hard to start a conversation about rural racism.[20] For Agyeman and the rest of BEN, the countryside needed to be a place where Black Britons felt safe. Agyeman once described the work he was doing with BEN as a 'bridge'[21] – a way of linking two worlds. 'My mother's white English, my father's Black African, I was the bridge in the sense that I'm a product of a bi-racial marriage, so I can see these different worlds, and part of what I was trying to do was think about how they could come together,' he said. 'At the time, I didn't have the wherewithal to know what was happening, but now, reflecting on it, that's exactly the space I was in. And it was quite a lonely space.'

The attitude BEN faced from the Black community itself could be just as indifferent as the countryside agencies the group were looking to influence. The writer Ferdinand Dennis summed up the lack of interest that met Agyeman. 'As a boy I used to read about the verdant, undulating English countryside,' Dennis wrote. 'But somehow I have never been able to appreciate it as an actuality . . . I have no rapport with it. I am an urban person, born in one city and brought up in another. There is an England of farmers and cottages and church-hall meetings and village greens that I will never know.' Agyeman spoke to Black Britons and found that there were four key factors keeping them from the countryside: the cost of getting there from urban centres; a lack of leisure time for many working-class Black people; racist reactions to their presence; and the association, held by some Black people, of the countryside with backwardness or the 'bush' – an uncivilised, dangerous place.[22] It was often frustrating and lonely work. The group would ask the Institute of Race Relations if they had any research on Black rural life, only to be told it wasn't worthwhile conducting. Initially, Agyeman and the others felt they were banging their heads against a brick wall.

The group decided that they needed to focus on identifying the UK's environmental justice issue, just as the Reverend Dr Benjamin Chavis had in America. They went with the idea of rural racism. 'That was an environment,' Agyeman tells me. 'That was a justice issue. I used to talk about how we're confined to cities in many ways. And that when Britain is truly a multicultural land, we will be able to walk on every part of it and not feel like we are outsiders in our own land.' Britain couldn't claim to have a truly equal society until, as Agyeman put it: 'a Black person can stand on the top of Helvellyn or Snowdon and say, "I feel OK".'

Agyeman, Pollard and the Black Environmental Network were starting to attract attention. Newspapers were intrigued. Agyeman wrote for the Black Brixton-based newspaper *The Voice* arguing that the environment and the countryside were issues for the community. The network wanted historic homes with links to slavery to make those connections explicit. Agyeman remembers going to

The Last Fort – 1987

Harewood House in Leeds, a vast country property on the outskirts of the West Yorkshire city. The house was owned by the Lascelles family, who had made a fortune from plantations in the Caribbean. As he walked around, Agyeman spotted a sign that said the 'family had made money from investments in the West Indies'. These euphemisms were offensive to Agyeman and the rest of BEN. Cloaking the horror of slavery in opaque language wasn't good enough. They didn't think it was healthy in a country where many of its newest citizens had direct links to the barbaric practices that had financed and built places like Harewood House, which were now – in their opinion – trying to cover up or at the very least minimise. Many of the ideas they were presenting weren't new: from the margins writers like Eric Williams had been talking about slavery and Britain's detached relationship with it for decades. But the concept of rural racism struck a chord with middle England because it called into question the sanctity of the countryside.

In 1989, the *Daily Telegraph*, the right-wing newspaper favoured by many in the Conservative Party, contacted Agyeman. Its former editor Bill Deedes wanted to interview him. A former MP who came from a family that had produced a member of parliament in every century since 1600, he was part of the establishment. In the piece, titled 'Another Country', Deedes and Agyeman are pictured together walking through a field with a huge tree in the background, Agyeman wearing a pair of slacks and a rain jacket, head down listening to Deedes, who is looking into the distance, wearing a tie and his well-worn Barbour jacket. The photograph is captioned 'Whose idyll?'.

Agyeman hits Deedes with a list of the issues he and BEN have been campaigning on. Black people are only ever being talked about in an urban context, even though 90 per cent of Britain is countryside and only 10 per cent is urban. 'Look at advertising, Bill,' Agyeman continues. 'Look at what you see on television. They portray archaic landscape, never-changing landscape – where there are still buxom wenches milking cows. Whereas in fact, they are factory farms down there. Advertisers like the small field hedgerow.' It's 'the English idyll', Deedes suggests. 'Idyll! Yes,' replies Agyeman. 'So the public is sold the image subliminally. They're told "This is really where your heart is, and when you've made your money in the city, this is where you come back to – where your spirit belongs."'

The pair disagree on how slavery should be addressed. Agyeman wants the dark history of some of the National Trust's country properties to be made explicit, Deedes thinks that's a step too far. 'Why don't they just come out straight and say it was built on the proceeds of slavery?' asks Agyeman. 'A bit of honesty would go a long way towards getting Black people out to see what was there. People like the National Trust could get a lot of sympathy.' At the end of the piece, Deedes offers his own theory on why the countryside matters now, not just for Black Britons, but for the conservative voices who love it and want to preserve it. 'The countryside, it's the last fort and it's under fire,' he argues. 'The British feel a lot has been taken from it in recent years. Our people in the countryside feel that things are going away from them. Now we're to be Europeanised . . . there are two sides to this, nervousness on both sides.' 'Exactly,' Agyeman replies.

For a moment, two seemingly opposing voices are in harmony. Both understand that the idyllic vision of the British countryside is a potent lie. The fragile accord is broken when Deedes suggests that the Black Environmental Network should come out in favour of field sports: 'Blacks for Foxhunting', is the slogan he suggests. There is no reply. But Agyeman 'has a thoughtful look' as he leaves. After the interview, according to Agyeman, Deedes turned to him and said: 'You know what, Julian? I think you've lit a candle. It's not a fire yet. It's a candle.' Agyeman had started a conversation that even a sceptic like Deedes thought could grow into something more substantial.

Despite the interest BEN achieved in the late 1980s, their arguments about Britain's relationship to the countryside and its Black residents fell largely on deaf ears. When Agyeman and others in the group were able to get people's attention, there might be a moment of hope, as in the conversation with Deedes. But getting policymakers to take the matter seriously was nearly impossible. The idea of Black Britons being exclusively city-dwelling was so deeply ingrained, the small group couldn't effectively unpick it.

It wasn't until a decade later, in the aftermath of the murder of a Black teenager, that many countryside institutions began to investigate their relationship to Black Britons. The murder of Stephen Lawrence by white racists in South London in 1993 was arguably *the* pivotal moment in British race relations in the twentieth century. A racist police investigation following the senseless killing failed to produce a successful prosecution because of assumptions made about the victim, and a lack of seriousness when collecting evidence. It outraged not just Black Britons but many in white society.

When Labour was elected in 1997, the Home Secretary Jack Straw agreed to an inquiry into the case, which would become known as the Macpherson Inquiry. Its findings – that the Metropolitan Police force was 'institutionally racist', shook Britain. It wasn't just a watershed for policing but for all institutions, which were once again being pressured to interrogate their own relationships with Black Britain. That fallout would eventually reach the countryside's major institutions, which for the first time were asked serious questions about how they were serving the country's Black population. The National Trust admitted it had no idea how many of its 2.6 million members were Black. 'Perhaps it's the way the Trust is perceived,' said a spokesperson. 'The "shirearchy", country houses and so on – but we just don't get applications from people from ethnic minorities.' The Royal Society for the Protection of Birds, which Agyeman was a member of as a child, admitted that out of the 1,000 people it employed, only 1 per cent – ten people – came from ethnic minority backgrounds. 'Perhaps this just reflects a lack of interest in birdwatching and conservation,' said a spokesperson. Agyeman constantly came up against this attitude; dismissive and uninterested in taking action to change the situation.

Eventually, it became too much: Agyeman would leave for the US to continue his career in academia. Many of the UK's brightest Black thinkers did the same, leading to a brain drain of Black talent.

Academics like Paul Gilroy and Hazel Carby, trailblazing authors like Caryl Phillips and artists like Isaac Julien left Britain in the 1990s for institutions like Yale and Princeton, where their ideas about race and identity were embraced. 'Even to be interested in race,' said Gilroy, shortly after he'd departed, 'let alone to assert its centrality to British nationalism, is to sacrifice the right to be taken seriously.'[23] Agyeman would continue his work on environmental racism in Boston at Tufts University, looking at the ways access to green space and clean air contribute to conditions in Black neighbourhoods.

When he looks back, he recognises that he has achieved more than he ever imagined possible while roving around Spurn Point, a pair of binoculars hanging from his neck, but – tellingly – his successes have mostly come outside of Britain. He left the Black Environmental Network in the early 1990s; it was no longer the political vehicle he'd set up. Its focus had shifted to encouraging diverse groups to use the countryside; he felt it no longer had the urgency and drive of its early years. 'It was Britain's first environmental justice organisation, but I felt that it never really moved on from the rural racism work that we started with,' Agyeman once said. It funded rural field trips for minoritised groups – Muslim women's groups for instance – to go out into the countryside. And although Agyeman thought that was important work, he felt BEN had lost a critical edge. 'Environmental justice work should never be comfortable. If it's comfortable, something's wrong,' he said.[24] Yet, four decades on, the debates Agyeman, Pollard and BEN started in the mid-1980s are being argued all over the UK. Signs that suggest the battles they thought might have been lost are now finally being won.

In June 2020, during the height of the Black Lives Matter protest movement that followed the murder of George Floyd by a police officer in Minneapolis, a programme went out on BBC2 that triggered hundreds of complaints to Ofcom, the television regulator. It's rare any episode generates so much opprobrium, let alone a ten-minute segment on the BBC's long-running magazine show *Countryfile*.

In the episode, the host Dwayne Fields – the first Black Briton to reach the North Pole and a fellow of the Royal Geographical Society, an ambassador for the Scouts, the Woodland Trust and the Ordnance Survey – outlined the main issues facing people of colour in the countryside, many of which Agyeman and Pollard had identified four decades earlier. Black people didn't view the UK countryside as somewhere for them; many said it was not welcoming to outsiders and seemed to be catered towards white, middle-class visitors.

People wrote to the regulator to complain the segment was 'inaccurate' and 'divisive'; others called for the BBC to be defunded. In total, there were 572 complaints. *The Spectator* published a critical article, which argued it was a complex problem and the simple solution that 'white people in the countryside' are racist is 'naturally causing widespread offence'. The *Countryfile* furore was only a small part of a reckoning that ignited during 2020 but had its roots in the debates the Black Environmental Network started in the Thatcher era.

In the latter part of the 2010s, before the BLM protests began, several institutions published reports about their own pasts that made explicit connections to colonialism and the slave trade. In 2018, the University of Glasgow published the results of a year-long investigation into the 'significant financial support' it had received from people whose wealth derived from slavery and announced a £20 million reparations package. Glasgow's council commissioned its own report into the city's ties to transatlantic slavery the following year. In Edinburgh, academics recommended the city apologise for the role it played in sustaining chattel slavery, while in Bristol, the City Council voted for a parliamentary inquiry into slavery reparations.

The *Guardian*, which was founded by Manchester cotton traders, said it would look into its own slavery connections – eventually announcing a £10 million reparations package in 2023. The Bank of England, the insurer Lloyd's, the Royal Palaces, Kew Gardens, the Church of England, the Booker Prize and the University of

Cambridge all launched inquiries into their own slavery connections, following the explosion of the BLM movement. When the National Trust surveyed its own list of properties, the charity found that around a third of its inventory was connected to colonialism.

All of this would have been unthinkable during the 1980s. Now, Harewood House, where Agyeman had come across euphemistic signs about how the estate's former slave owners made their fortune, were engaging fully in the debate. In 2023, the owners unveiled a commissioned portrait of the Black British actor David Harewood, whose ancestors had been enslaved by the Lascelles family. His image sits next to portraits of the very people who held his ancestors in bondage.

But it's not only in grand country homes where you can see the legacy of Agyeman and Pollard. If you head out to the countryside this weekend to the Lake District, the South Downs, the Fens of Lincolnshire or a National Trust property, you may bump into one of the dozens of diverse nature groups that have formed in the last decade. Rhiane Fatinikun founded Black Girls Hike in 2019, when she took a group of fourteen Black women on a walk near Rochdale. She'd been on a train going through the Peak District, watching hikers boarding and disembarking, when the idea came to her. Why not start a group and get out into nature? She set up an Instagram page and organised the first event. A journalist from *The Voice* newspaper attended, and since then she's appeared on *Countryfile* to discuss the group, which is at the vanguard of a renaissance in Black engagement with the outdoors.

The London-based ornithology group Flock Together organises trips in cities and around the country; its social media accounts are full of images of mostly young, diverse people enjoying nature – often staring upwards with binoculars in hand trying to spot a bird, just as Agyeman did around Hull as a child. 'There have been many times where I've been in the countryside and, after I've been on a hike, I would like to go to the pub. But sometimes I think, should I actually walk into this pub? Will I be accepted in this pub? Will I be abused when I go to this pub? By us being together and going into typically white spaces, we find strength and unity and the courage from each other to normalise our presence in these spaces.' Those words come from an interview that Nadeem Perera, co-founder of Flock Together, gave to *Vogue* in 2020.[25] But they could have come from Agyeman in 1987. Four decades later, groups like Flock Together are part of a growing network of outdoor pursuit groups aimed at people of colour all over the UK.

There's Steppas in Coventry, the London Caribbean Trekkers, Bristol Steppin Sistas, Peaks of Colour, The Wanderlust Women, Muslim Hikers, and Black Men Walking. Muslim Hikers have designed their own branded prayer mats, while Fatinikun is a brand ambassador for outdoor clothing giant Berghaus. All these groups, whether they know it or not, are using the footholds first carved out nearly four decades earlier.

When debates about rural racism arise, I often think of an interview Benjamin Zephaniah gave after moving to the fenlands of Lincolnshire. Asked whether he was trying to prove something by living in a rural location after his youth in Handsworth and then London, he said: 'This is what I say to Black people in Britain: do what you want to do. Don't think you can't live in the countryside because you're Black. We need Black people to do everything. All these people that say multiculturalism is bad, it's too late. It has happened. Live with it. We are here and we have to create something new.'[26]

Building something new in a place that many people in Britain believe is perfect as it is. That is the heart of the issue. Feeling comfortable in the countryside isn't a niche concern – as the likes of Stanley Baldwin tell us, it's an essential part of being British, or certainly English. Now, thousands of Black Britons each weekend are doing exactly what Willie Whitelaw did in 1981 as he looked out over the Buckinghamshire woodland, finding solace and succour in nature.

People will fight fiercely to protect their heritage; the concept of who we are and what our collective history is matters. It can be, and often is, weaponised. 'Our way of life' is often under threat if you listen to certain far-right politicians; our heritage, our identity is at stake if we don't repel those who don't share our 'British values'. Those voices don't want the new vision Zephaniah was lobbying for, they want something else: a simplified Britain, which as Raymond Williams said exists almost entirely in people's imagination.

That outlook has a cost, not just for Black Britons who want to access the countryside, but for white residents too. When the first surveys of poverty in the countryside were conducted during the era of BEN, the myth of the rural idyll was exposed. There was poverty and deprivation in those communities, and their situation was not helped by others' romanticised depictions. Change, in some form, had to come to the countryside, even if it didn't map neatly onto the vision of the rural idyll.

We've seen how myths, like the one that was formed around the countryside, can be just as powerful in an urban setting. Manchester's Moss Side and Hulme were demolished, in part, to cleanse them of perceived squalor and the red-light district; Liverpool's Black community could be attacked because it was synonymous with crime in the view of police and politicians. The countryside needed to be protected from Black people because it was 'the last fort', a final bastion, siloed from the forces of multiculturalism.

At around the time the Black Environmental Network was forming, a historic Black community in Wales was reminded about the power of national myths – and how those who wield them can control not just history, but the present and the future.

8.
The Myth and The Bay, Cardiff – 1988

In a small, light-filled office overlooking Butetown – the thin, mile-long stretch of Cardiff dockland that has been home to a Black community for more than 150 years – Gaynor Legall and her colleague Trevor Godbold sit among a treasure trove. They're responsible for Tiger Bay and the World, one of the most extraordinary archives of Black life in Europe, with over 10,000 items, including thousands of photographs and hundreds of hours of oral history interviews.

The archive is entirely analogue and needs to be digitised. When I visit them in spring of 2023, littered around the office are posters and leaflets calling for people to come forward and help identify figures in the photographs, hinting at the mammoth task ahead. Many of the interviewees are long dead, meaning permissions need to be sought from relatives. It's painstaking and thankless work, sustained by grants and volunteers. But the pair are committed.

Godbold loves the depth and nature of the archive, while Legall was born and bred in the area, and became the first Black councillor in Cardiff. This is her history and it's an important one. Butetown was the birthplace of modern British multiculturalism. Along that tiny strip of land abutting the port you could find people from every corner of the globe, living together in a community that looked like nowhere else in the UK.

Shortly after Legall was born in 1950, fifty-seven nationalities were recorded among the 10,000 residents of Butetown, commonly known as Tiger Bay. It wasn't just Black residents like Legall, whose family comes from Belize, living in the area. Legall was raised next to Malaysian and Egyptian families, as well as transient seamen, mostly from the Caribbean. There were Italians and Greeks on the street. A Chinese-Jamaican family were a few doors down from Mrs Rosario from Cape Verde and the Somali boarding house. This international mix created a unique community, one that fascinated the Welsh literary critic Howard Spring. Having worked as an accountant in Mount Stuart Square, in the heart of Butetown, in the 1930s, he would go on to write about the neighbourhood in his memoir, in a passage that would define the area for many years:

> The whole place was a warren of seamen's boarding houses, dubious hotels, ships' chandlers smelling of reap and tarpaulin, . . . dingy chemists' shops stored with doubtful looking pills, herbs, and the works of Aristotle. Children of the strangest colours, fruit of frightful misalliances, staggered half-naked about the streets; and shops were decorated with names that were the epitome of all the clans and classes under the sun. The flags of all nations fluttered on the house fronts; and ever and anon the long bellowing moan of a ship coming into the docks or outward bound seemed the very voice of the meeting place of the seven seas. It was a dirty, rotten and romantic district, an offence and an inspiration, and I loved it.[1]

This small community, with its sounds, smells and customs from across the globe, has drawn interest and attention from its earliest days. It's possibly the most studied Black community in Europe, maybe even the world. Anthropologists have surveyed it. Politicians have reviled it. Officials have called for its residents to be repatriated. Newspapers have romanticised and demonised it, while those who hate it have attempted to burn it to the ground. Few have ever truly understood it.

The ideas and assumptions thrust onto Butetown are important. The myth of the area, which began to form as soon as Black people made it their home, is deeply ingrained in the Welsh psyche. This 'meeting place of the seven seas', as Spring put it, carried with it seafarers' fables – exaggerated yarns with only a kernel of truth at their core. Just as we saw in Moss Side, L8, Manningham and Handsworth, Butetown developed a reputation – created and often promoted by politicians, the press and the police – for violence, vice and drugs. That reputation lingered on into the Thatcher era, long after the dock which had attracted so many Black residents had ceased to function. Butetown underwent its own redevelopment story in the form of a £500 million plan to bring life back to the docks overseen by the Cardiff Bay Development Corporation, with the area's insalubrious reputation used to justify new expensive flats and coffee shops. But the mythology surrounding Butetown and Tiger Bay went further still: in 1988 a court case would show how received ideas could be used to frame people for one of the most notorious murders of the 1980s.

The Tiger Bay and the World archive offers a different view of Butetown to that lodged in the popular consciousness; one shaped exclusively by its residents. The community's position as the original multicultural centre of Britain made it a focal point for a nation's projected fears of what a racially mixed United Kingdom would look like.

The word 'multiculturalism' elicits strong reactions to this day. For those on the left, it's often presented as a strength. Roy Jenkins, the Labour Home Secretary who popularised the term in the 1960s, said it should be seen 'not as a flattening process of uniformity, but cultural diversity, coupled with equal opportunity, in an atmosphere of mutual tolerance'. For those on the right, multiculturalism is often presented as a failure or a betrayal, something foisted on an unsuspecting public who have to bear the burden of foreign customs and cultures that clash with 'British values'. Butetown was the original testing ground for these ideas; and its diverse community was often on the frontline when the prejudice that its presence produced spilled over into violent confrontation.

As I flick through the images dotted around the desks at the archive, and listen to interviews digitised from old cassette tapes, an alternative depiction of Butetown emerges. The myth surrounding the community is devoid of nuance – just as all tall stories are. But in the archive, nuance is all that exists. School photos show children whose parents came from around the globe, all united as Welsh kids in their country's capital. Interviewees recall how challenges faced by the community, from racial violence to poverty, instilled a resolve and cohesion within a place that was often segregated from the rest of Cardiff. This alternative story is one of success and integration, but also defiance and survival in a port that looked out across the Bristol Channel and pulled people in from across the whole of the British Empire.

One single commodity was, primarily, responsible for the creation of a Black community in Butetown: coal. By 1900, twenty-four million tons a year was exported from the port,[2] much of it dug out from the rich reserves of South Wales, which sat only ten miles from Cardiff. At the end of the nineteenth century, as thousands flocked to the Welsh capital for work on ships or the boarding houses, cafes, pubs and other businesses that popped up to service the new arrivals, the area around Cardiff Bay was being compared to the Gold Rush towns of California in the 1850s.

Cardiff is a young city. Its population grew tenfold from 1,800 residents in 1850 to 180,000 in 1911 – during a century when the Welsh capital boasted the largest coal port in the world. At its peak, the port was responsible for exporting an estimated quarter of the world's light and energy sources. Its rapid growth made the port's owner, the Marquess of Bute, one of the wealthiest on the planet, and his name was given to the area that directly abutted the waterfront.

Arabs, West Africans, Somalis, West Indians and Europeans all came to work on the ships that took Welsh coal – and eventually steel – all over the globe. The influx to Butetown brought Arab bazaars, gambling houses and Chinese opium dens. Sex work was commonplace, as was petty crime, while violence among the seamen could be ferocious, with knives often pulled during disputes. By 1914, the first year of the First World War, it was estimated that 700 Black people lived in Cardiff, with many more there on a temporary basis, coming and going on the ships that unloaded in the city's port. This was the frenetic world that Howard Spring was so struck by – but the multiracial frontier community horrified many.

The Myth and The Bay, Cardiff – 1988

The growing Black presence in Wales had not gone unnoticed. This was the early twentieth century, a time of race science and the obsession with interracial relationships and their offspring. It wasn't until the end of the Second World War, when the horrific genocidal consequences of social engineering were realised with the extermination of six million Jews, that the pseudoscience of Muriel Fletcher and the eugenicists finally became unfashionable. The view that the white race, and particularly the middle class, was superior to all others, was not confined to the right of the political spectrum. In the early twentieth century, economists and social reformers including Sidney and Beatrice Webb, George Bernard Shaw, John Maynard Keynes and Marie Stopes all supported eugenics and committed to

Two friends playing outside in the dockland area of Cardiff

a goal of, as one writer put it, a 'Darwinian commitment to improving the quality of the nation's genetic stock'. Butetown represented the antithesis of what the left-wing eugenicists were petitioning for: far from an organised, carefully constructed or engineered community where those of 'good stock' had the chance to 'breed' with others of their standing.[3] Rather, a free-for-all where people from all over the world mixed.

The area's unofficial boundary that separated it from the rest of Cardiff was a bridge – part of the railway that connected the Welsh capital with London. The bridge was a marker, likened by some to the Mason–Dixon line demarcating Southern and Northern US states. In Cardiff, the bridge told people when they were entering Butetown, or Tiger Bay, as it had been christened by Portuguese sailors. The separation pleased many. The author of a letter published by the *South Wales Daily News* on 28 November 1893 claimed that they'd never seen 'so Black a blot on an otherwise fair and thriving town as the so-called Tiger Bay is on Cardiff', before suggesting a fire like the Great Fire of London that wiped out the plague and made 85 per cent of the population homeless in 1666 'would be a godsend'.[4] The angry sentiments seen in the *South Wales Daily News* didn't dissipate. There were flare-ups between the residents of Butetown as more people came to the docks over the course of the First World War. These would build to a crescendo of violence aimed at Cardiff's new Black population.

In the summer of 1919, a dark mood descended on the port towns around the UK, from South Shields in the Northeast and Liverpool on the banks of the River Mersey, to Glasgow north of the border and Bristol in the Southwest. Around the country there was a general air of xenophobia, with 'alien purchasers' blamed for hiking rents, with Russian Jews often blamed, while the Chinese were also accused of usurping white workers and painted as 'alien job seekers'. The ports, the focal point for many of these rumours, were about to witness the biggest outpouring of racial violence the country had ever seen.

Tensions between new Black arrivals – seamen who had come to fill vacancies created during the war mostly as part of the merchant navy – and returning demobbed servicemen were growing. Between November 1918 and March 1919, 2.1 million troops had left the armed forces, and when they came home the men often faced difficulties as a worldwide recession crippled the economy. More than 1,350 of the returning seamen were unemployed in South Wales by mid-1919, while there were 300,000 disabled ex-combatants who were out of work.[5] The picture was no better for the Black seamen who'd joined the war effort, with around 1,200 unemployed. Resentment festered, powered by three issues: white seamen were paid much less in the Royal Navy than the Black and Arab seamen in the merchant navy; there was an acute housing shortage in port cities; and the anger of some white seamen when confronted with local women who had started relationships with Black men. In early June 1919, those factors would combine to spark an explosion.

The first problems in Wales started in Newport on 6 June 1919, after a Black seaman allegedly put his arms around a white woman and made offensive remarks. After rumours of the incident spread, houses where Black people lived had their windows broken, while a crowd of over a thousand looted two homes, and Black residents defended themselves with pokers and pistols. Five days later, there was a deadly confrontation between a Black seaman and a white sailor in Barry, which resulted in a large mob going through the town looking for Black people.[6]

The outbreak of violence in Cardiff was the most extreme. The Black population in the city was now at 3,000, having grown exponentially during the war as more Africans, Arabs and seamen from the Caribbean came to the docks. On 11 June 1919, a car carrying Black men and their white spouses was encircled, while a fight broke out between whites and Blacks on Canal Parade Bridge. The police attempted to stop a mob from reaching Butetown, but eventually, they broke through, ransacking shops and burning down a lodging house on Homfray Street. 'Many were willing and even eager to participate in the negro-hunting, which had developed into something like a fever,' wrote the *Western Mail* as the violence broke out. *The Times*, meanwhile, casually referred to the area where the trouble took place as 'Nigger Town'.[7]

On the second day, as rumours of the violence being part of a Bolshevik plot inspired by the Russian revolution of two years earlier began to circulate, a company of the Welsh Regiment was sent into the area. On Millicent Street, a house with eight Black occupants was attacked. The men who were trapped inside fired a pistol on the crowd outside, with one bullet hitting a man who was taken away in 'dying condition'. Rioters used a table as a shield and made their way upstairs, fighting the house's inhabitants, who used razor blades and their fists to defend themselves. A fire broke out inside, and the mob waited for the men to leave the relative safety of the house.[8] By the time the fighting in the city stopped, four people had died and thousands of pounds worth of damage had been done to Black property.

The political response was two-fold: voluntary repatriation of Black seamen resulted in 600 Black residents leaving Cardiff by September 1919.[9] Lord Mayor of Cardiff advocated for repatriation, while the chief immigration officer said 'it would be safer and better to place all these men in concentration camps' if they refused to leave. The repatriation scheme started with sixty-three Indians and fifty men from Yemen boarding the SS *Kurmask*, while the SS *Santille* left Cardiff for Jamaica with 147 repatriates on board. Many passengers arrived in Kingston and looked for white-owned houses to loot and businesses to ransack – the legacy of racial violence in South Wales leading to reprisals in the Jamaican capital.

The second response to the violence was a new piece of draconian immigration legislation, aimed not at the white mobs – who the police recognised were responsible for the rioting – but the community they'd attacked.[10] The 1919 Alien Act was brought in to stop the flow of seamen into ports like Cardiff, making it mandatory for them to register and limiting where they could live.[11] Six years later, the 1925 Alien Act forced all seamen to carry an identity card, known as a 'certificate of nationality and identity issued to a British Colonial Seaman'. Inside was a passport-size photograph, description of eye and skin colour, height and a signature and thumb print. Without it the seamen couldn't get a job, and it was a measure which treated them like criminals. The implementation of the act was supposed to target foreign seamen but in reality, it disenfranchised British-born Black people, around 3,000 of whom had their British citizenship revoked, according to an exposé by the League of Coloured Peoples, a British civil rights organisation.

The aftermath of the violence that broke out over the summer of 1919 made clear that residents of Butetown were not considered British. They were foreign objects in the body politic that needed to be removed, forcibly if necessary. In an era when eugenicist thought was *de rigueur*, it's no surprise that the reaction was to 'get rid' of the Black population rather than seek to address the racism that had caused the violence. But not all the Black population of Butetown decided to leave. The vast majority decided to stay in their homes by the port that had made Cardiff rich. And sailors who'd had their citizenship revoked during the 1920s and 1930s fought back, just like the community had in 1919.

The intensity of the violence seen in 1919, and the reprisals that followed, is still shocking today. But this key event in British history contained the same combustible material that would fuel British racial politics for the rest of the twentieth century: from the fascism of Oswald Mosley and the National Front, to the bleak predictions of Enoch Powell and Margaret Thatcher's 'swamped' dog whistles.

Among the mob that had attacked Butetown there was an obsession with interracial relationships and the idea that Black Britons were doing better than them. The worldwide recession after the First World War had reduced demand for the produce coming in and out of British docks, and people – of all backgrounds – were struggling to find employment. The leaders of the violence asked the *Western Mail*, 'Why should these coloured men be able to get work when it is refused to us?', while the interracial relations between the Black seamen and white women were 'referred to darkly'. The shortage of good quality housing for those in low paid jobs living in cities like Liverpool and Cardiff also contributed to the fuel that ignited the violence.

We've seen these ingredients already. Remember Bradford, the Worstedopolis where textile was king and foreign investors flooded to make fortunes; or Birmingham 'the toy shop of Europe' with its foundries and car manufacturers. When both cities' fortunes changed, recent Black arrivals became the scapegoats, with explosive consequences. The same had happened in Cardiff half a century earlier yet these dramatic events are largely forgotten. The year 1919 is synonymous with the Spanish flu that wrought devastation after the end of the First World War, not racial violence on British shores. Like the George Lindo case or the Pan-African Congress, the memory is kept alive by those who know this secret history, either via family connections or academic research.

But while many in Britain quickly forgot about the violence of 1919, tales of it seeped into Butetown folklore. Legall remembers her grandmother telling her how she collected bricks and stones to dump on the mob if they tried to enter their home, while others told tales of women carrying guns and knives under their pinafores. Incredibly, it seemed to instil a greater sense of patriotism in the people who stayed: when war broke out again, many men from Butetown signed up, heading out on vessels not to transport coal but to fight a war. 'We have shed blood for this country, between 1939 to 1945 the docks were like something from ancient Egypt,' said Keith Abdi, a local activist who grew up alongside Legall.[12] 'One person out of every family was killed or torpedoed . . . We didn't fight fascism on a beach called Dunkirk or in Berlin, we fought [on the sea]. The number of West African, Arab and Somali seamen who went down and had no family – their names can't be recorded. But the people who had family, one person from every family was lost.' The events of June 1919 had been horrific – and they'd proved to be unifying; the community had been tested and it had responded.

Howard Spring's depiction of Butetown post-1919 remains probably the best known to this day. But perhaps the most disturbing comes from the man once in charge of policing the district. In 1929, Chief Constable James Arthur Wilson complained to the Home Office about the racial mixing that was taking place in Butetown's cafes. While he acknowledged that the Black seamen who lived in Cardiff 'observe our laws' he believed they were not 'imbued with our moral code' and had not assimilated. 'They come into contact with the female sex of the white race, and their progeny are half-caste with the vicious hereditary taint of their parents. They are dissolute thieves, inveterate gamesters, the associates of prostitutes and strongly suspected of living on their immoral earnings,' he wrote in a report that was extracted in the *Western Mail* on 23 January 1929, his words presaging those of Kenneth Oxford, Liverpool's Chief Constable a few years before the unrest of 1981.[13]

In 1946, David Martin's novel *Tiger Bay* – about a Welsh girl from the Valleys who falls out with her family and drifts to Butetown, where she has a relationship with a Somali man – added to the mystique. Some traded off the area's reputation, like Shirley Bassey, who was a toddler when she moved away from the district, but who would be regularly referred to as 'the girl from Tiger Bay' early on in her career, conferring her with an exotic edge. The area's reputation was still alive in 1970, when the *South Wales Echo* commissioned a nine-part series with headlines that touched on every stereotype it was known for: 'PUB BRAWLS, PIMPS AND OPIUM DENS . . . BUT FOR MANY IT WAS UTOPIA', 'GIRLS SOLD TO VICE DENS AT 2S A HEAD' and 'THE SEAMAN WHO WAS ALWAYS ROBBED BY THE SAME GIRL'.

Butetown didn't just attract attention from sensationalist media outlets looking to sell newspapers; its intense mix of nationalities and reputation as a cultural melting pot turned the heads of another group: anthropologists.

In 1941, an unlikely figure turned up in Butetown. Kenneth Little – a small bald man with piercing eyes often hidden behind wingtip spectacles – was part of a new branch of anthropology that was interested in the field of race relations. Little had trained under

Raymond Firth, the founding father of British anthropology, and was the son of a ship broker from Liverpool. Though he was raised in a city with one of the oldest Black communities in Europe, Little had never met a Black person until he went to Cambridge University. It was this African friend who first told him about the everyday racism Black people faced in Britain, and inadvertently set him down a path that led him to Cardiff.

While studying under Firth, who was famed for his surveys of Māori culture in his native New Zealand, Little embarked on a five-year PhD project that would eventually be called *Negroes in Britain*. He chose Butetown as his base because of the intensity of the racial mixing. Its tightly packed streets, where it was said there were more than 140 people to the acre, were a dream for an anthropologist. 'The Tiger Bay community offered, in a sense, a challenge that I was unable to resist,' he once said.

Little was eccentric and entrepreneurial. In the midst of his Cardiff research, he managed to blag his way into the BBC as an expert host for a radio programme about the colour bar – the programme was eventually shelved by nervous producers. At his home in Edinburgh, he also hosted late-night African drumming sessions that attracted the attention of the police. He took that intensity and charm to Cardiff with him and began to poke his head into every corner. He produced detailed accounts of the cafes that lined Bute Street and operated as brothels, often run by Maltese businessmen. He created a map detailing the different areas of Butetown where 'Arabs', 'Greeks and Cypriots' and 'Spaniards' held sway. Little observed the workings of the Sons of Africa – a mutual aid association, which, despite its name, was open to anyone, including women, and provided financial assistance for those who needed hospital treatment.

The report now makes for uncomfortable reading, with Little repeating many racist stereotypes about Butetown's residents. Mixed-race members of the community were deemed by Little to be 'marginal men', doomed to sit outside both Welsh culture and the 'inferior' ethnic community of their parents from overseas. He thought they had a 'light-hearted attitude towards life, and a suggestion of irresponsibility', while the womenfolk who had relationships with Black men were usually of 'poor class'. But in comparison to what had come before it was incredibly liberal. Little was at the vanguard of a movement that wrestled control of ideas about race away from eugenicists like Muriel Fletcher.[14] What Little and his peers did was switch the proposition: the problem wasn't the fact Black people had made Britain their home, it was the fact they were being marginalised. He wrote that 'racial relationships are to be conceived of as a function of the wider socio-politico-economic system in which they occur', rather than an exotic part of British life that was separate from and unaffected by events in the rest of the country. In a move that was decades ahead of its time, Little argued racism was a white problem.

Negroes in Britain made Little a star in the UK's nascent race relations world. He spoke at the headquarters of the Royal Commonwealth Society to raise awareness about racism in schools[15] and petitioned for American films depicting Black people as 'servants, pugilists, or as eyeball-rolling "coons"' to be censored by the Colonial Office.[16] He criticised the BBC's approach to covering race as 'haphazard and unprofessional'[17] and spent time discussing race with the African-American author James Baldwin. He would remain an advisor to the Home Office on race relations into the 1970s, but in Butetown few people were toasting his name.

Little's study, while raising awareness about the challenges facing the Black community, also painted that community in a cold and often critical light. Residents had opened their doors to Little and felt betrayed when he wrote about sex workers, pimps and 'tragic', mixed-race children. For many Butetown residents, this was their golden era. The area was politically charged with communists, Pan-Africanists, Black Nationalists and Christian groups all vying for attention, while The Rainbow Club – a multiracial social club – had opened and was typical of Butetown's refusal to allow segregation among its residents. Footage from the time shows Black, white and Arab weddings, processions celebrating religious ceremonies[18] flowing through Cardiff's streets, while school children sing as the Pakistani flag flies next to the Y Ddraig Goch of Wales.[19] Little's report, despite its detail and his own good intentions, missed this warmth and complexity. Butetown residents felt like he'd taken police statements at face value, while ignoring complaints of racism at the docks, where Black seamen were often prevented from getting work. 'People still talk about it to this day,' Legall told me.

The residents' biggest complaint about Little's work was its failure to address the poverty and lack of services they faced. Poor-quality housing blighted the area: damp was rife in the properties, and Butetown had a tuberculosis rate higher than anywhere else in Cardiff. People had let Little into their homes and social circles, and in return he'd created a report that gave a negative impression to outsiders.

While his work might have been rejected by the local community, Little's *Negroes in Britain* was eagerly sought out by other anthropologists and policymakers. The Labour MP for Cardiff South East Jim Callaghan[20] was, according to Little, 'one of the first people to question me further' when the book came out in 1947.[21] For them it seemed to confirm what many already knew: Butetown was a fascinating but deeply troubling anomaly; one that needed to be fixed.

Negroes in Britain was published a year before HMT *Windrush* docked in Tilbury, Essex; two years after the end of the Second World War and the Pan-African Congress; in Manchester; and three years after Eric Williams' book *Capitalism and Slavery* had firmly linked the rise of Britain with the profits it made from the transatlantic trade in human beings. Black Britons around the country were involved in conversations about their future in the UK, as well as about a future postcolonial Africa, and the racism that had supported imperialism. And it would be a Pan-Africanist sociologist who would come to Cardiff to produce a response to *Negroes in Britain*.

In 1945, St Clair Drake – a handsome African American with delicate features who looked more like a film star than an academic – had published *Black Metropolis: A Study of Negro Life in a Northern City*, with his colleague at the University of Chicago, Horace Cayton. A Black Quaker, Drake 'narrowly missed the lynching rope'[22] several times on his travels south of the Mason–Dixon Line with Black militants and peace activists during the civil rights era, while his convictions saw him serve in the merchant navy during the Second World War to avoid segregation.

Black Metropolis was groundbreaking, substantial (at more than 800 pages) and provocative. The pair of sociologists studied Bronzeville, a Black neighbourhood on Chicago's Southside, and wrote of 'the invisible barbed-wire fence of restrictive covenants' that surrounded the ghetto: an image which deliberately evoked the Third Reich.[23] Just as in Butetown, Chicago had been through a race riot two decades earlier in which thirty-eight people died, and like in Britain's ports, housing and employment discrimination were the issues that blighted Black communities. Drake was aware of Butetown because of Little's landmark study and had links to Britain through the Pan-Africanist network, including W. E. B. Du Bois and Kwame Nkrumah, for whom Drake would serve as an advisor in the early years of his presidency in postcolonial Ghana.

In 1948, he took up residence at 251 Bute Street.[24] Like Little, he came to South Wales to interview residents and observe the social life of the area. But Drake's observations went deeper, often drawing meaning from everyday social dynamics. For example, gambling wasn't just a vice that afflicted the area; Drake saw it as popular because 'it reduced semantic difficulties to a minimum and made participation and communication possible for everyone'. Gambling houses were so well frequented because anyone, regardless of background, could take part. Rather than a sign of wayward living, for St Clair, gambling was a vital part of life in Butetown – it helped hold the place together.

He noticed how athletics and cricket teams were important points of social pride; successful athletes such as the heavyweight boxing champion Joey Erskine were heroes, their accolades discussed and dissected by the community. Posters featuring Paul Robeson – the African-American actor and activist who'd starred in the film *Proud*

Valley as David Goliath, an unemployed Black seaman who arrives in a South Wales mining community and eventually becomes accepted in the community – hung on cafe walls.

Drake noted tensions between two voluntary organisations: the Colonial Defence Association, a communist-backed workers' rights group, and the anti-communist Loudoun Square Coloured Mission. He observed community pushback against a Maltese seaman club, which some argued would be a first step toward segregation in Butetown. He noted that mixed-race Butetown residents had difficulty in finding work on ships or in domestic service or in factories, where white co-workers refused to work with them. The impact of the African American soldiers who'd come to the area during the Second World War was still felt, as he constantly fielded requests for American magazines like *Jet* and *Ebony*.

When he noted that the most popular pastime was 'standing around talking', he didn't leave it at that, but instead outlined what people were discussing. Popular topics ranged from British politics and 'the inequities of the "colour-conscious" and "imperialistic British"' to the exploits of local sporting heroes and the state of the declining shipping industry.[25] These conversations weren't just idle chat, but part of the social fabric of a politically tuned-in community.

Drake produced a complex flow-chart showing how the voluntary organisations, religious groups, different ethnic groups and local government interacted. In a section which seems to deliberately upend the stereotypes that Howard Spring imposed on the area, Drake wrote that: 'Butetown is more than the crowds of children pushing and shoving on the playground. It is more than the strollers wandering around from street to street, or the little knots of people here and there gambling or gossiping. It is more than the dirt and disorder which first strike the casual observer's eye.'

Butetown offered something more significant than a superficial look could ever perceive; in Drake's view the residents were creating a 'new sub-culture', one that merged foreign customs with those of South Wales.

What the American was doing in South Wales mattered. His

subjects were more than just cyphers who made up numbers in charts and graphs; they were three-dimensional and politically engaged. His report (also his doctoral thesis) would be published under the title 'Value Systems, Social Structure and Race Relations in the British Isles in 1954', and offered a counter to the simplified, sensationalist narrative that surrounded the docklands. He also published an account in the NAACP's magazine *The Crisis* in which he wrote: 'One could see the determination in all the British-born coloured youth, as they face life in a new Socialist Britain, to reject the status of "half-caste" that some Britishers have imposed on them and to operate as full men and women.'[26] Drake saw what others, including Little, had missed: Butetown was a prototype for multicultural Britain; ahead of its time and deeply misunderstood. The myth of Tiger Bay was dangerous.

As innovative as Drake's report was, it didn't change the mainstream view of Butetown: many more people were familiar with the conclusions of *Negroes in Britain*. And, just as the anthropologists were leaving, the area's reputation for vice and violence gave the green light for a period of urban renewal that would change it beyond all recognition.

In the 1960s, the urban renewal surge that had already seen cities like Manchester rebuilt after the destruction of the Second World War finally came to Cardiff, which had endured less damage in the bombing raids. As with the Manchester Plan, the city's council was determined to rid itself of 'slums' and create a new, functional metropolis built on the tenets of modernism.

Council leaders warned that their city was 'worn out, inconvenient, drab, and down-right dangerous'. Their answer was Centreplan 70, a futuristic vision for the city where much of the old Cardiff would be destroyed and replaced entirely.[27] Huge twenty-one-storey modernist tower blocks would shoot into the sky; the churches were to be demolished and rebuilt in the 'church precinct'; and planners proudly insisted the city's residents would never be more than 200 yards from a car park.

Like the eugenicists who insisted on careful social engineering, the council envisioned all elements of life being organised, neat and contained. There would be an 88,700 square foot 'entertainment centre' with a casino and ballroom, a 20,000 square foot 'design centre', a huge central library, concert hall, three bus stations and a theatre. It was ambitious and driven by a sense of urgency, with promotional material claiming: 'If Cardiff fails to fulfil its regional role for business, commerce, education, entertainment and central and local government, then not only Cardiff but the whole of Wales will suffer.' In truth, the city was already in deep decline.

By the late 1960s, the coal industry that had given rise to the Cardiff 'Gold Rush' was in retreat. In 1964, the final shipment of Welsh coal left the docks in Butetown, with the steelworks that sat on the docks closing in 1978, the year before Thatcher took office.[28] By then, the docks were barely recognisable from their peak in the early twentieth century: in 1920, 115 shipping companies owned a total of 382 vessels; by the end of the 1960s there were only twenty-one ships left.[29] As the numbers of vessels coming into the bay declined, Butetown changed too. The shops that had once serviced the ships and their crews closed, as did the notorious cafes, taking with them something of the area's distinctiveness. Soon there were no longer 'little shops where you feel you're nearer Constantinople than Cardiff,' reported the *South Wales Echo* in 1970. Cardiff was heavily dependent on both coal and steel, and the deindustrialisation in South Wales was a precursor to a much bigger shift that would happen throughout the UK during the Thatcher era, and had also hit cities like Bradford, Birmingham and Liverpool.

Despite the demise of the port, coal mining was still the biggest employer in Wales and as new plans were being formulated for Cardiff's future, Thatcher was preparing to wage war with Arthur Scargill and the miners' unions. For a twelve-month period between 1984 and 1985, the coal industry and Thatcher's government were locked in a bitter dispute over pay and planned pit closures. Thousands of miners went on strike, bringing coal production to a standstill. It was one of the definitive battles of the period. Instead of negotiating, Thatcher's government decided to try to crush the power of the unions that had hobbled Edward Heath in the 1970s.

Picket lines were formed and miners who refused to strike became 'scabs', pariahs in communities they'd grown up in. Scandal and confrontation followed as police clashed with striking miners near Rotherham in South Yorkshire on 18 June 1984, during what would become known as the Battle of Orgreave. Police charged at the miners with horses, used truncheons and arrested fifty-five men, claiming they'd started a riot.[30] The prosecutions were later thrown out: the miners' legal team claimed the police incited the incident and then attempted to cover up their failings. But the saga was the beginning of the end for the industry.

Thatcher had stockpiled coal in case there was a strike, and slowly more striking miners went back to work, many frustrated at the unions not calling a nationwide ballot on the issue. After the decision was taken to go back to work in March 1985, with a defiant Scargill saying he would carry on the fight, many pits began to close and followed the fate of Cardiff's docks as they slipped into a period of sharp decline.[31] The battle was hugely symbolic. Thatcher argued that the mines were no longer economically viable, painting those out on strike as desperately clinging on to an obsolete past. 'The miners were cast in the role of the last actors in a doomed proletarian romance,' is how Mark Fisher put it.

The full ambition of the Centreplan 70 wasn't realised, but Butetown was transformed, with the 'smoky grid' of two-storey homes demolished en masse.[32] Loudon Square, which once housed the ship owners and captains, and featured grand Dutch-gabled terraced houses that surrounded a park, was knocked down. In its place were rows of grey maisonettes and low-rise houses, arranged in horizontal and vertical rows that looked like drab Tetris blocks.

Bute Street, where St Clair Drake was based during his time in the city, was mostly razed. More than ninety pubs, social spaces where so many of the interactions that Drake observed took place, were destroyed. Green space had disappeared, replaced with concrete, car parking and kerbsides. As in Manchester, the

We Were There

The Queen, Prince Phillip and Prince Charles travel along Bute Street in May 1999 on their way to officially open the National Assembly for Wales for the first time after Wales voted for Devolution in September 1997.

City Council issued compulsory purchase orders to those whose homes were to be demolished, which left some people in an untenable position.

Homeowners who'd bought their properties on fifteen-year mortgages with money loaned by the council would be left paying for a property that would no longer exist, turned into a pile of rubble by the dockland.[33] 'They said it was a slum and all the lies you can imagine,' said local historian Neil Sinclair.[34] 'From an insider's perspective, we were targeted, something to be got rid of. Rather than renovate housing in stages as they'd done in neighbouring Grangetown, for instance, they wanted us gone, and one way to do that was to knock it all down. All they succeeded in doing was destroying the architectural legacy of the Marquess of Bute for Cardiff and for Welsh history. Replace it with the first council estate to be dropped on to an inter-generational, multicultural, multiethnic, multiecumenical community. It was a tragedy.'

Butetown features in a documentary film about the Centreplan

70 project.³⁵ Councillors who commissioned the plan crouch over a scale model of the new Cardiff, wearing smiles and suits as shots of glimmering office blocks are juxtaposed with old drawings of the port and modern-day images of the sun setting on the dock. Its message is clear: the new plan and its vision was the future, the old Butetown and the dock which had attracted its unique community was to be confined firmly to the past. But not everyone saw it like that. 'Those horrible flats are the worst thing to happen to me in the last 20 years,' said Butetown resident Olwen Watkins in 1984. 'It robbed people of something . . . a sense of community life. It has closed people off from each other. Life had been richer.' Just as in Manchester, where the Black community of Moss Side and Hulme was forcibly moved, so the residents of Butetown were offered council housing elsewhere. Meanwhile, those who stayed were said to be 'marooned in a sea of industrial dereliction'. While the Centreplan 70 project ultimately failed because of budget constraints, in the Thatcher era Cardiff would be transformed by another ambitious regeneration plan.

A year after Thatcher walked into Downing Street, a new kind of British corporation came to life in London's Docklands. In November 1980, Thatcher's government pushed through the creation of the London Docklands Development Corporation (LDDC) – an organisation that would be funded by the government but would essentially cede power to developers who had an eye on the capital's vast derelict waterfront area in the east. The only person they would be answerable to was the environment secretary, Michael Heseltine, who in 1981 would recycle the idea on the banks of the River Mersey. With the state seen as an obstruction to progress by Thatcher's administration, the new development area was billed as a 'government-free zone' by Chancellor Geoffrey Howe.

The corporation mowed over any opposition. Compulsory purchase orders were issued for properties that stood in the LDDC's way, other sites were deemed unsafe or eyesores that needed to be demolished.³⁶ By the end of the 1980s the LDDC had transformed the docklands: London City Airport opened in 1987; the modern

Savage Gardens housing estate was built in Beckton; Docklands Light Rail opened; while Limehouse Studios brought TV productions, including the satirical puppet show *Spitting Image*, to the area. The metal and chrome skyscrapers of Canary Wharf, a financial district that provides 120,000 jobs and oversees the movement of countless billions a year, is the corporation's most obvious legacy.[37]

In December 1986, the Cardiff Bay Development Corporation was launched. Taking its cues from the LDDC, its focus was on a 2,700-acre area around the docks that bordered Butetown. The CBDC's goal was different to that of the utopian ideals of the Centreplan 70. Rather than seeking to improve life for Butetown's residents, the organisation aimed to establish Cardiff internationally as a 'superlative maritime city' – one that would look to Sydney, Copenhagen and Oslo for inspiration. A key aspect of the plan was the creation of a barrage to tame the tidal waters of the River Taff. When the tide went out a huge spread of mudflats were revealed, and the CBDC's plan relied on the barrage to create a tranquil marina. The American port city of Baltimore was another inspiration for the corporation; representatives travelled to the city on a fact-finding mission to learn from that redevelopment's emphasis on 'a reclaimed waterfront, iconic buildings and designer spaces to serve as an urban playground for affluent residents and tourists.'

The plan and its promotional material rarely mentioned Butetown and the 3,000 residents that sat within its borders. As had happened with the LDDC, local opposition to plans was disregarded, although arguments over the environmental impact of the scheme held it up for six years. People from Butetown were distrustful of the plan – the memory of the 1960s slum clearances and the friends that they'd lost was still alive for many. At a meeting with the community, a representative from the developers said 'This [development] is what's going to happen, and it would be much better off if we could do this [the meeting] in a sort of a peaceful atmosphere', only for an enraged resident to stand up and say, 'What you don't realise, is that we are the moderates – the others are outside setting fire to your car.'[38] Legall ascribes the response to the wariness of a community that has had to live with redevelopment for over fifty years, with projects stopping and starting, reshaping the community. 'There is this threat because of redevelopment,' she said. 'If there is constant change and churn, it makes you feel unstable, insecure.'

A year after the corporation was established, the most violent murder to happen in the UK for over a decade took place in Butetown. It undermined the corporation's attempt to present the docks in a shiny new light, and showed just how powerful the mythology that had developed around the area really was.

On Valentine's Day 1988, the murder of twenty-year-old Lynette White stunned Butetown. The young sex worker was stabbed more than fifty times and her throat slit. The nation hadn't seen a crime this violent since the Yorkshire Ripper cases of the 1970s. Eyewitness accounts provided the police with a suspect profile: a white man in his mid-thirties who had been seen on the doorstep next to the scene of the murder, shaking, crying and with blood on his hands. Detective Chief Superintendent John Williams of the South Wales Police led the initial investigation; at its peak, he would oversee a team of sixty-two officers and other personnel. A running enthusiast with dark eyes, a bald head and a calm disposition, Williams went on the BBC's *Crimewatch* programme and appealed for any sex workers in the area to talk. 'They are the people who may hold the key to this terrible murder,' he told cameras. But people weren't talking, no one was.

The police's relationship with Butetown had been fractious for decades. By the late 1980s, the Cardiff police force was notorious for its hard-man approach – not just on the docks, but across the city. If officers thought someone had committed a crime, they would arrest the suspect and build the case around that hunch. Racist and misogynist attitudes were ingrained, especially toward the residents of Butetown. The police said they came up against a 'wall of silence', not just from the sex workers but from the Black community of Butetown. Door-to-doors gave them no leads. In an area where there were illegal gambling houses and a history of police harassment – from the implementation of the Alien Act of 1919 to the words of Chief Constable Wilson – their presence was a nuisance.

But amid the investigation, some people were talking. The residents of Butetown were having discussions, not about White but about the history of their area. A year before the murder, another African American anthropologist came to South Wales. Glenn Jordan studied under St Clair Drake at Stanford University, and would follow in his footsteps, moving to Butetown to survey the unique Black community. He began hosting an oral history class at the local community centre, inviting people to come and share their stories, which were recorded on hundreds of cassettes. The Tiger Bay and the World archive, today looked after by Gaynor Legall and Trevor Godbold, was his creation, painstakingly compiled over decades. 'I wanted to empower people to control their own history,' he once said. 'I also believe it is morally right to preserve the history of ordinary working-class people, many of them immigrants who suffered and died helping make Cardiff a great city. Future generations should be able to learn about their experiences – not just about the history of coal merchants and the lords of Bute.'

As Jordan was slowly building up his alternative history of Butetown, pressure was beginning to mount on Williams and South Wales Police. The grizzly, unsolved murder had taken place right in the heart of the proposed development zone, while the police had searched for a man who matched the initial profile in vain. They then changed tack and started to pick up Black men from Butetown for questioning, as rumours and suspicions began to circulate around the community.

White's boyfriend at the time of her death was a Black man called Stephen Miller, a small-time hustler from London. Police had questioned him early on in their investigation, and ruled him out when he produced an alibi, and after confirming his blood type didn't match the one found at the scene. But as Christmas approached in 1988 – and with the plans for a new Oslo-style Cardiff Bay released into the world – the police changed the focus of the investigation and made a series of arrests. Miller and his brother, who was released after producing an alibi, were arrested in London and taken to Cardiff in a police convoy. And four local Black men – Ronald Actie, John Actie, Yusef Abdullahi and Tony Paris – were picked up in Wales. Together, they would become known as the Cardiff Five. The police had produced new evidence – interviews with two sex workers, Leanne Vilday and Angela Psaila, who accused the five men not just of killing White but of taking part in a ritualistic murder. All the men denied the murder, but their alibis were disregarded, and all were subjected to a relentless series of interviews.[39]

Miller received the most intense questioning. Just twenty-one at the time, and with an IQ of 75, he would be questioned on nineteen occasions and deny being at the murder scene 303 times. Eventually, worn down by the interrogations and led by the officers, Miller gave an account of events that came close to the one suggested by Vilday and Psaila.[40] With Miller's confession, which came a decade after George Lindo's forced admission of guilt, the police had enough to charge the men with White's murder. A delighted Williams spoke to journalists after the news broke. 'We knew that the answer lay somewhere there, in the docks,' he said.

The trial took place in Swansea before an all-white jury. The men were painted as animals by the prosecution, whose opening statement used lines that could have been lifted straight from the sensationalist *South Wales Echo* stories about Butetown.

David Elfer QC talked about the docks as somewhere people lived outside of normal society and knives were 'worn like jewellery'. He described the area as an upside-down world. 'When we go home from work, they get up and go to clubs,' he said. 'Then when we get up to go to work, they return home to sleep.' When Psaila was interrogated, she referred to the men as 'monkeys', while officers sniggered at the defendants in the dock.

The defence attempted to have the confessions ruled inadmissible but failed. Stephen Miller, Tony Paris and Yusef Abdullahi received life sentences. As with the George Lindo case in 1978, a local campaign was organised for the men, now known as the Cardiff Three. It gained international traction, with civil rights campaigner Reverend Al Sharpton visiting Cardiff and taking part in a march from Butetown to the prison the men were held in.

It's never been established if the corporation's big plans for Cardiff Bay put political pressure on the police to get a conviction, whatever the cost. While the police force appeared to be acting from – and reinforcing – preconceived ideas about the inhabitants of Butetown, Glenn Jordan's project was painting an alternative picture at exactly the same time. More people were coming forward and telling him about their experiences of 1919 and the barren postwar years that followed. Stories emerged of hardship and resilience that Jordan – an outsider – saw as part of a pattern that stretched back to the 1850s and the Gold Rush era. 'Black people have either been stuck in dying and marginal industries or forced into subordinate positions in thriving ones,' he said. 'Butetown is not just suffering from a recent recession. It has been in a permanent slump for well over half a century.'

The Cardiff Three would eventually walk free in 1992, after an appeal led by Michael Mansfield QC who'd worked on previous miscarriage of justice cases including the Tottenham Three, convicted for the murder of PC Blakelock during the Broadwater Farm uprising of 1985, and the Birmingham Six, a group of Irish men who spent sixteen years behind bars for two IRA pub bombings in 1974. An independent review of the Cardiff case found it to be 'one of the worst miscarriages of justice in the history of our criminal justice system.'[41] It was a miscarriage made possible thanks, in part, to the myth of Butetown as a violent, exotic township.

Myths are potent. They can make the impossible seem, if only for an instant, plausible. Butetown's own lore has always possessed an uncanny pull. It was multicultural Britain – before the term entered the popular lexicon. 'Although we had living amongst us thieves and murderers and prostitutes,' Legall tells me, 'most of the people were ordinary, working-class, hardworking people. It was safe, we didn't face the racism in Tiger Bay that we did when we went into town.' Butetown was far from perfect. But it was unique. I can understand why Kenneth Little saw it as 'irresistible' and why St Clair Drake wanted to look deeper into its workings. And I understand too why, with its racial mix and lack of resemblance to the rest of Cardiff or the country, its emergence in the era of eugenics was repulsive to so many.

The area is often described as a kaleidoscope, offering endless combinations of vivid images and colours. Look once and you might see the violence and the vice of the frontier period. Look again and it's the food, culture and shops that lured people in. Twist it a third time and perhaps you'd see a model for how people of different backgrounds could live together. 'The social history of Butetown provides us with valuable lessons about how to live with others,' Glenn Jordan once said. 'With people of different skin colours, beliefs and ways of life – in an atmosphere of tolerance, respect and harmony.' What I found when looking through the pictures and listening to the interviews compiled in the Tiger Bay and the World archive was a story of community – a complex one with dark moments but a togetherness born out of necessity.

Today cranes punctuate the city's skyline, particularly by the docklands. As I walk down from the train station and approach Butetown, huge housing redevelopments butt up against each other. Their names suggest maritime grandeur. There's 'Atlantic Wharf', a major project that promises an arena and hotels while pledging it will become 'a new city destination where people come to work, have fun and relax'[42] and the £55 million 'Anchorworks' housing development that will bring more than 400 high-end homes by the end of 2024.[43] A few hundred metres up the road there's another large-scale development, 'The Embankment', which promises up to 2,500 new homes on a forty-acre site.[44] In 2027, yet another housing development will be completed: the 'Central Quay' project, with 700 apartments.[45] Work has begun on a new railway station in Butetown that will improve the area's public transport network.[46]

But as the cranes go up and the concrete foundations are laid, you can't help the feeling that Butetown is being boxed in, rather than integrated into the plans.[47] Local politicians have called for developers to engage with the community in a way that the corporation didn't in the 1980s. Jobs and apprenticeships have been promised. But there's a 'wait and see' attitude from community leaders wary of the pledges made in earlier development phases. Butetown councillor Saeed Ebrahim looked back at the 1980s development and saw it as a missed opportunity; one that needs to be learned from. 'There was a big opportunity wasted in [not] joining up what was existing and what was new,' he said in 2018.[48] The building work is helping to tell a new tale about the area; one with a legacy rooted in the redevelopments of the 1960s and 1980s.

Legall, Godbold and the archive are surrounded by the new Cardiff emerging beside the docks. I ask Legall what her dream home for the archive would be. She talks about the Rhondda Heritage Park, an interactive visitor space that replicates life in the coal industry of South Wales. There are rides that simulate diving deep underground; it's a history you can almost touch and taste. Legall would love to see something similar devised from the material in the Butetown archive, so visitors might walk around the bazaars, take in the sounds of musicians and witness the men going to work on the ships. 'You could replicate the boarding houses and listen to people talking to each other about their lives,' she says, just as St Clair Drake did. Perhaps her childhood street, with its residents from all over the world, could be recreated.

But that's all a dream at the moment and for now Legall's main worry is how the archive will be used. As it stands, Legall and Godbold determine who gets access. Both are aware of the history not only of the area but how Butetown has been written about by authors, anthropologists and politicians. But the archive's future is secure. Legall tells me institutions want the archive, but that's not really the point. She believes it should stay within the community, one that has a remarkable story of resilience.

In Cardiff, the myths surrounding Butetown produced one of the biggest scandals of the 1980s. The wrongful imprisonment of a group of men for a murder they didn't commit was the result not just of desperate policing, but of decades worth of lies, fabrications and half-truths used to paint a Black population as a problem. Just one year later, in Scotland, another British blind spot on race would spark a battle north of the border.

9.
The English Disease, Edinburgh – 1989

At the dawn of the Thatcher era, the most famous Black Scot in the country was a character in a TV prison comedy. Tony Osoba played Jock McLaren in *Porridge*, Ronnie Barker's show about crafty inmates that ran from 1974 to 1977. At a time when hard-hitting prison dramas such as *Law and Order* and Alan Clarke's *Scum* were grabbing British viewers by the throat, and showing the horrors of the British justice system, *Porridge* was subtly undermining the credibility of that same system by using humour. Osoba's angry, acerbic character was typical of the comedy, which had viewers rooting for and laughing along with its cast of anti-heroes. He was also, crucially, Black and unmistakably Scottish.

Other TV shows, including *Rising Damp* and Michael Abbensetts' *Empire Road*, had featured mould-breaking Black characters, but all of them were based in England. Jock McLaren was an exception – and would remain so for a long time. A decade on from the last episode of *Porridge*, Black Scottish cultural figures of any sort remained elusive.

The Black population in Scotland during the Thatcher era was tiny, even smaller than that of the countryside. The 1991 census – which included respondents' ethnic origin rather than place of birth for the first time – revealed that there were around 50,000 Black, South Asian and Chinese Scots living north of the border, accounting for 1 per cent of the population. The vast majority were of Pakistani or Indian origin, about 20 per cent were Chinese and a small fraction were Black. Almost two-thirds of Scotland's ethnic minority populations were living in Glasgow and Edinburgh. Unlike in Cardiff's Butetown or Manchester's Moss Side, where the Black and brown community was often concentrated in one area of the city, here ethnic minority populations could be so small that they occupied just a few streets or houses.

Scotland's knotty relationship with Black people dates back centuries, to the time of the Stuarts when there were enslaved Africans in the court of James IV in Edinburgh. The king also sent privateers to intercept Portuguese ships carrying enslaved people, while Scottish merchants were partly responsible for hugely expanding British slave trading in the 1700s.[1] But in the late 1980s Scotland was largely oblivious to its slave-owning past. The subject wasn't taught in schools or discussed publicly, while the problem of racism was often defined by Scottish journalists as the 'English disease' – an acknowledgement of the rise of English nationalism weaponised by football hooligans under the influence of far-right groups such as the National Front, and pandered to by mainstream politicians.

The Scots had themselves been exploited and brought to heel by the English; even, some would argue, been colonised. This history created a potent orthodoxy: Scots could not be racist because – as well as there being no ethnic minorities in the country – they themselves had been the victims of English bigotry for centuries.

The truth was more complicated. Unlike India, Jamaica or Anglophone African countries like Ghana and Sierra Leone, Scotland hadn't actually been colonised. When the English and Scottish crowns unified in 1603, it was the Scottish Stuart dynasty that was the dominant partner. That royal alliance was followed by a contentious political union in 1707, which faced rebellions in some parts of the country, and had widespread support in others. The two states were fused – it may have been an awkward marriage, but this was not the outright subjugation other nations faced under the British.

Scotland underwent instead a soft colonisation. The country's education and legal system remained separate, but its ruling classes became closely aligned with the English, while Scottish MPs took their seats in Westminster. Expensive and exclusive public schools were set up. Members of the royal family were educated north of the border, while the Scottish elites followed suit. The royal family's

Balmoral Castle and estate in Aberdeenshire is a symbolic reminder of the ties between Scotland and England. Culturally, England began to influence its northern neighbour.

While many Scottish nationalists complain about English dominance, Scots were often part of colonising forces, whether to neighbouring Ireland, when Scottish 'settlers' were awarded land confiscated from Catholics during the plantation of Ulster in the fifteenth century, or to the fledgling settlements in America. The idea of racism as an 'English disease' cooked up by far-right fanatics south of the border doesn't stand up to scrutiny. There had been plenty of fascist activity in Scotland in the twentieth century: Mosley's British Union of Fascists held protests in Edinburgh, while Hugh MacDiarmid, the poet and Scottish nationalist, flirted with fascism[2] and some nationalist MPs had close connections to German far-right groups.[3] But the powerful unalloyed narrative of a colonised nation under the boot of the Auld Enemy endured well into the Thatcher era.

Chris Bramble, a British-Guyanese ceramicist who studied at the Glasgow School of Art in the 1980s, remembers being in a pub and ending up on the receiving end of a rant by a fellow punter about the English. 'They'd talk about how the Scots Guards [a Scottish regiment of the British army] were sent out first as cannon fodder,' he told me,[4] while another favourite topic of conversation was the Battle of Culloden, where the Jacobite rebellion intent on destroying the union was put down by an English army during a bloody massacre in 1745. Renton, the sardonic heroin addict from Irvine Welsh's 1993 novel *Trainspotting*, delivered a speech that summed up the dynamic: 'Ah don't hate the English. They're just wankers. We are colonised by wankers. We can't even pick a decent culture to be colonised by. No. We're ruled by effete arseholes. What does that make us?' When James Kelman won the Booker Prize in 1994 for his book about the life of a Glaswegian drunk, he said his work – written in Scots dialect – was part of a tradition of 'decolonisation and self-determination'. This was a nation that knew what it felt like to be looked down upon and dispossessed, and that made racism – of the kind seen in England – impossible. 'The Scots tolerance of racial minorities stems from the compassion that the underdog feels for the underdog,' wrote one Scottish journalist. 'The Scots are too busy hating the English to have time for any other abuse.'[5]

South of the border, 1981 had been a year of racial awakening. The widespread disorder in cities including London, Manchester, Liverpool and Bristol forced a conversation on racist police practices, unemployment and lack of investment in Black areas. It had even made it into the countryside via the actions of the Black Environmental Network. Debates raged and the problem was named. But Scotland had not gone through the same turmoil and hand-wringing. The events of 1981 only appeared to confirm the orthodoxy: racism was an English problem created by the colonisers. But the events of one January night in 1989 would jolt the nation out of its complacency.

On 16 January 1989, Axmed Abuukar Sheekh Maxamed was making his way home after a night out in Edinburgh. The Somali was walking along the Cowgate, one of the many historic streets that today helps to attract more than 3.5 million tourists to the Scottish capital every year. The Cowgate is a narrow road with buildings that shoot up high on either side, creating a funnel through which traders would usher their cattle to market.

Sheekh was with his cousin, Abdiriziak Yusuf. Both were refugees who had fled the military regime of the dictator Mohamed Said Barre. Sheekh had left behind his family in Mogadishu and made his journey to the UK in 1987.

Not much is known about his route to Europe, but when he arrived in Britain, Sheekh was initially detained for three months on the notorious *Earl William* prison ship at the port of Harwich, Essex.[6] The converted car ferry made headlines first when its passengers launched a hunger strike and then when it ran aground during the great storm of 1987, with dozens of Tamils who'd fled civil war in Sri Lanka on board. After the ship was retrieved, the detainees were given permission to leave. While Sheekh waited for his asylum

Axmed Abuukar Sheekh Maxamed

claim to be processed, he moved to Edinburgh. He told his English teachers that he thought it would be safer than London, despite there being a more established Somali community in the English capital. Scotland, he thought, would be quieter and friendlier.

Abdourahim Said Bakar was another African in Edinburgh. He came from the Comoros Islands and had been in Scotland since 1982, initially teaching French before working as an education researcher at universities in Glasgow and Edinburgh. He knew Sheekh through the small, transient group of African students who congregated in the Scottish capital and mixed with the handful of asylum seekers who'd made Edinburgh their home during the late 1980s. Sheekh was unassuming and quiet – at gatherings he'd sit on the margins, before tentatively engaging people in one-on-one conversations with his limited English.

He might have been softly spoken, but it didn't take him long to make friends in Edinburgh. Said Bakar and the African students would socialise at one another's houses or flats, and sometimes Sheekh would show a more outgoing side to his personality. He cared passionately about the anti-apartheid movement and would speak at length about his concerns for the Kurds, who were being massacred by the Baathist regime in Iraq.[7] He saw the similarities between Scottish and Somali society, where both were traditionally built on clan-based power structures. Sheekh told his friends about a desire to become a doctor and eventually return to Somalia; he loved his country, its language and culture and would occasionally sing Somali folk songs in Aramaic. 'Axmed was trying to learn another language to survive in Scotland,' Said Bakar told me. 'But without forgetting his own.'

On that cold January night, Sheekh and Yusuf ran into a group of Hibernian football casuals, including Terence Reilly and Francis Glancy, who had been causing trouble around Edinburgh that evening. They'd accosted a couple on the Grassmarket, another major thoroughfare that connects to the Cowgate, brandishing a knife. Then they assaulted two men in Tollcross, an area that sits in the shadow of Edinburgh Castle. It was around 4 a.m. when the group confronted the two Somalis. The street where cattle was once driven to market, and that is now lined by student accommodation, hostels and bars, witnessed a deadly chase.

The football casuals began by hurling racist abuse, before attacking the men. Yusuf was stabbed in the stomach but managed to make an escape, while Sheekh was cornered in a phone box, where he'd attempted to hide. He was kicked, punched and repeatedly stabbed – a style of attack that would be tragically echoed in the murder of the Black teenager Stephen Lawrence in South London four years later.

A taxi driver saw Sheekh after the sustained assault and called an ambulance. Surgeons performed two emergency operations, but were unable to stop the bleeding, and Sheekh died of his injuries at Edinburgh Royal Infirmary. He'd dreamed of studying to become a doctor, now his body lay in the morgue of the hospital where he would have trained, in a city where he thought he'd finally found safety.

The next day, word of the murder started to spread. Joan Weir,

Sheekh's English teacher at Stevenson College in west Edinburgh, which had a programme that supported asylum seekers, was at work. She walked into an office in the city library where she was part of the racial equality team and met her friend Joyce Cochrane, who was married to Said Bakar. 'Joyce said, "Axmed's been killed",' she told me. Weir then informed others she knew in her network, such as Rowena Arshad, a British-Malaysian youth worker, who in turn told others.

As the news filtered out, a ripple of horror spread throughout the small Black and Asian communities of Edinburgh, Glasgow and Aberdeen. Weir and other white Scots asked themselves how something like this could happen. But the murder was not a surprise to Black and Asian Scots like Arshad and Said Bakar, who'd been warning of just these consequences if the country did not confront its problem with racism.[8]

Look around Scotland's main cities and you'll see dozens of reminders about the country's connections to slavery. Much of Glasgow's and Edinburgh's civic infrastructure, including their universities, was funded at least in part by money made from the slavery economy. In Edinburgh, the towering Melville Monument in St Andrew Square honours Henry Dundas, an eighteenth-century politician who, like William Huskisson in Liverpool, argued in favour of the slave trade. The Free Church of Scotland with its headquarters on The Mound received money from pro-slavery churches in North America; while Bute House on Charlotte Square is said to be 'inhabited by the ghosts of slavery', because its former owners received large sums of compensation as part of the agreement to abolish slavery.[9] These sites can be found all over major British cities; the idea of Scottish exceptionalism when it comes to racism was partly rooted in a lie, or a 'cloud of amnesia' as one academic put it.[10]

There have always been voices that challenged Scotland on its race record. In 1919, as in other British port cities like Liverpool and Cardiff, there was racially motivated violence in Glasgow.[11] Black and white seamen fought in the streets with more than two dozen Black sailors taken into 'protective custody' by the police, who would go on to charge only Black men in the wake of the violence. The African Races Association of Glasgow – whose members included the South African academic and political leader Silas Modiri Molema – protested, and sent a letter to newspapers that referenced the sacrifices Black Britons had made during the First World War. 'Did not some of these men fight on the same battlefields with white men to defeat the enemy and make secure the British Empire? Why couldn't they work now in the same factories as white men,' they asked.[12] 'Is the treatment meted out to them now compatible with the British teaching of justice and equity, or is it an exhibition of British gratitude?'

Throughout the early part of the twentieth century, Scotland witnessed many of the same racial battles as the rest of the country. In 1927, African, Caribbean and Indian students successfully challenged the introduction of colour bars in Edinburgh's cafes and dance halls.[13] When more Blacks and Asians were denied service at city-centre bars in 1931 a boycott was organised.[14] In the same year, at the annual conference of the students' representative councils in Glasgow, it was recognised that 'overseas students in this country were living in comparative isolation, while many were suffering considerable disability on account of their colour.'[15] But the Black Scottish presence wasn't just made up of students, there was an older community – as in Cardiff and Liverpool – that had settled in Leith by Edinburgh's docks.

Two years after Sheekh's murder, Maureen Blackwood's documentary *A Family Called Abrew* was released.[16] Tracing the story of a family that had been based in Scotland since the end of the nineteenth century, it showed the reality of life for Black Scots in the colour-bar era. The eponymous family was based in Leith and was full of sportsmen and entertainers. There was Lottie, a dancer who was born in Edinburgh and worked all over the UK during the interwar period. Her brother Charlie, whose accent is pure Leith – rich and dense, almost leaving a trace of itself in the air after he finishes a sentence – would have liked to be a ship's engineer. But as a young Black man he couldn't get a job in the industry and instead, like his older brother Manuel, ended up boxing. The family carved out a living in the world of prize fighting and entertainment. Blackwood's story takes place in the shadows and margins of Britain like in Soho nightclubs and smoky boxing rings, as well as the stage and screen, where the family work as extras alongside Paul Robeson.

The Abrews' home in Leith became a meeting place for Black arrivals in Edinburgh; seafarers would seek out the family after being told about them by dock workers. In 1941, a significant, but mostly forgotten, group of men, known as the British Honduran Forestry Unit, added to that number.[17] Around 900 lumberjacks came to Scotland from Belize to support the war effort, which was in desperate need of timber.[18] One of the arrivals, Sam Martinez,[19] was sent to Ullapool in north-west Scotland to cut down trees, while men were put to work in towns around Edinburgh like Duns and Tranent, and others were sent to Highland villages, including Golspie and Kinlochewe.[20] It was tough work, and the men were ill-equipped

Two Belizean lumberjacks (left to right: W. Ellis and G. Gabourel) hard at work in East Linton, Scotland, during 1943

for the harsh Scottish winters. 'None of us expected chandeliers, but our situation was much worse than we expected,' wrote Amos Ford, who published an account of his time as a lumberjack.[21] 'We were treated as lackeys.' Many returned to Belize at the end of the war, but some stayed and made Scotland their home.[22]

Despite this long and chequered history with Black people, Scottish people struggled to see Black Scots like Martinez and the Abrews as countrymen. 'For most people, being Scottish is synonymous with being white,' said one Asian Scot.[23] 'So when I'm in Scotland I'm Asian, but anywhere else, including England, I'm Scottish.' Jackie Kay, the Black Scottish writer and poet, told me that she's been asked countless times, by fellow Scots, if she's 'visiting from America' – despite her strong Glaswegian accent. This only changed once she became the national poet of Scotland, and her profile rose significantly. 'It took me, really, till I was 56 to feel I belong to my country or feel like my country recognised me as belonging to it.'

This denial of a national identity for Black Scots raised questions of belonging for many. It also spoke to something more sinister that was beginning to emerge in Scottish life during the decade leading up to Sheekh's murder.

Rowena Arshad and her young family lived in a tenement building on Marlborough Street, just to the east of Leith, next to Edinburgh's docks.[24] The daughter of a Malaysian couple who'd met in Liverpool while studying – her mother was Chinese Christian, her father was an Indian Muslim – Arshad had left her Northamptonshire home after marrying a Scottish man. They initially moved north of the border in 1985 and three years later moved to Leith. There, Arshad noticed that her ground floor garden always seemed to have rubbish in it. Initially, she put it down to the wind blowing it their way. 'That's how you survive: you rationalise things,' she told me. But before too long it became clear that people were deliberately dumping their waste in her garden. Soon after moving in, the family's car was keyed. Another time, her daughter was playing in the front yard when a glass milk bottle dropped down from the top floor. It missed her, but shattered everywhere. 'I hated walking down that street,' she told me.

The journalist and academic, Gary Younge, moved to Edinburgh in 1987 to study French and Russian at Heriot-Watt University and experienced his own brush with the kind of racial violence that proved fatal for Sheekh. He was walking up Kings Stable Road in the city centre in 1988 when a car sped up as it approached him and almost hit him. Younge stuck up two fingers at the driver and passenger. The passenger got out with a baseball bat and started hitting it against his palm. Younge ran, and the skinhead gave chase up Lothian Road – a busy main road in the city centre. It was around 7 p.m. and there were lots of people in the street; they moved aside as Younge ran through them, chased by the man. No one stepped in. 'I just ran for my life,' says Younge.

In the spring of 1989, just months after his friend Sheekh was murdered, Said Bakar would also be confronted by Hibernian supporters, who threatened him with a knife. He and Cochrane were walking near Hibernian's stadium at Easter Road when the attack happened. 'I remember running and screaming for help on Montgomery Street and eventually someone called the police,' recalled Cochrane. 'But it seemed like an age before people would do anything.' The most common response to Black people who mentioned these attacks was silence or disbelief.

Scotland had an established anti-racist movement – but it was a movement largely concerned with examining foreign racism, rather than homegrown prejudice. In 1986, Edinburgh was due to host the Commonwealth Games, an event which had been successfully held in the city sixteen years earlier. Much of the infrastructure was still in place, although funding was a serious challenge, with a large shortfall that organisers struggled to fill.[25] But there was another problem: most of the nations wanted a boycott of South Africa because of its detention of Nelson Mandela and its racist apartheid system.

With the organisers refusing to bar South African athletes, thirty-two of the fifty-nine eligible countries declined to take part – many of them from the Caribbean and Africa. It was the lowest turnout of athletes since the 1950 event and resulted in fewer broadcasting rights and a drop in sponsorship, which contributed to the substantial debt. The financial situation was bad enough, but the optics were terrible. The notable absence of ethnic diversity at the 1986 Games was a 'major embarrassment in the modern era,' wrote the *Scotsman*.

Margaret Thatcher recalled the issue in her diaries. 'The media and the opposition were by now quite obsessive about South Africa,' she wrote, claiming that the views of the commentators were unrepresentative of what the general public felt. When the games were held, she visited Edinburgh and the Games village that housed the remaining competitors with her husband Denis, where she was met with 'a few catcalls and some sour criticism'. She later observed: 'I did not disagree with Denis when he remarked that this was "one of the most poisonous visits" we had ever made.'

The anti-racist movement also attracted attention from the Scottish far right, especially the British National Party, which was beginning to assert its authority as the leading far-right political movement in the UK after the decline of the National Front that had never recovered from its 1979 election disaster, although it was still active. Leafleting increased – as did racist attacks, with a Scottish Council for Racial Equality survey in 1988 claiming 58 per cent of Indians reported being physically assaulted.[26] The far right's main recruitment targets were Rangers football supporters in Glasgow, for two reasons: their sympathy with Orange Loyalism and history of anti-Catholic bigotry. Searchlight described far-right activity around Ranger's Ibrox stadium as 'kicking at a door that's already open'. Edinburgh's football teams were also on the radar. Reilly and Glancy were members of the Capital City Service, a Hibernian firm; while at the city's other club, Hearts, posters supporting the Ku Klux Klan appeared outside its Tynecastle Park ground in 1989.[27] The weekend activities of many Black and Asian families were determined by football fixtures: if they lived in the vicinity of Ibrox when Rangers had a home game they simply didn't leave the house.

The far right was also politically active. In 1988, councillors at Glasgow City Chambers hosted a national conference on local government and anti-apartheid initiatives. On the way into the event attendees were met by a 'whole team of young, smartly dressed men with very short hair' carrying placards saying, 'Hang Nelson Mandela'. 'They heckled everyone going into the conference and pushed and jostled delegates where they could. It was a frightening atmosphere,' said a race relations officer.[28] 'I have never seen such a public grouping of fascists in Glasgow before. Now and then incidents like that give you a glimpse of what's happening underneath.'

As far-right nationalism came to the surface, another political movement was beginning to break new ground north of the border, powered by anti-colonialist sentiment. The political group that emerged from it called itself the Scottish National Party, and before long it would come to transform the country.

Unlike in England, where the Conservative Party dominated politics throughout the 1980s, north of the border, Labour was the dominant force. In her memoirs, Thatcher dedicates a whole section to Scotland, where she tries to understand why there was no 'Tartan Thatcherite revolution'. Attempting to unpick why the Conservative share of the vote in Scotland had slumped from 50 per cent in 1955 to 24 per cent in 1987, she points to crumbling unionist support and the high proportion of people (around half the population) living in council housing.[29] 'In short the conditions of dependency were strongly present,' she concluded. 'And the conditions of dependency are conditions for socialism.'

The truth was more complicated. Neil Kinnock, who proved to be a difficult sell for Labour when it came to English voters, was much better received in Scotland. As a Welshman, he was seen as a fellow victim of colonisation.[30] Thatcher had always struggled with Scottish Conservatives, whom she distrusted because of their historic support for nationalism north of the border.[31] She despised the idea of devolution, wanting to maintain home rule and a federalised system, where Westminster – not a Scottish assembly – dictated national policy for Scotland. But Thatcher and her ideas were up against Scottish nationalism, a movement in the midst of a transformation.

The Scottish National Party won its first seat at a general election in 1970. Over the decade that followed, the SNP went from being seen as 'an affair of cranks in kilts and poets in pubs'[32] to a serious political proposition, helped in large part by the discovery of oil in the North Sea, which gave the party a tool to use in its bid for economic credibility. When the Arab-Israeli Yom Kippur War erupted in 1973 and sent oil prices soaring, the SNP had the perfect news story with which to illustrate the potential power of what it called 'Scotland's Oil'.[33]

During the Thatcher era, the party started to create a progressive form of nationalism, one where – unlike in England – race was not seen as a barrier to entry. The SNP laid out its inclusive view when it described Scottish people as 'all those who stay and work in Scotland and who want to contribute to the Scottish community'. The SNP's nationalism explicitly renounced ethnic nativism and championed 'a pro-immigration civic nationalism', argues the academic Colin Kidd, who writes that, 'Scottish nationalism is much more sophisticated than its boorish English cousin.'[34]

Within this political environment that rejected Thatcherism and embraced progressive nationalism,[35] Gary Younge and other Black Britons living in Scotland saw the potential for anti-racist work in the country. The idea that the land north of the border was a racial utopia was clearly nonsense, but tied up in that myth were tangibles that offered reasons to be optimistic.

Support for causes such as the anti-apartheid movement and the Palestinian struggle for statehood had greater mainstream support than they did in England. As a member of the Labour Club, Younge saw how Labour Party Black Sections (a group within the party that called for more Black representation) faced less resistance north of the border. He noticed that the sectarian line that divided Celtic and Rangers fans largely separated people politically too, between those more inclined to far-left and far-right politics.[36] There was a history of anti-Catholic bigotry in Scotland, with those of Irish Catholic descent often facing discrimination while at school or in the workplace. That experience, which many Scottish Catholics would refer to as racism, made some Scots hyper aware of prejudice and keen to stand against it. Compared to Younge's white peers in Stevenage, who largely rejected left-wing politics and were more closely aligned to the tenets of Thatcherism, in Scotland he saw a country that was at least *open* to the idea of anti-racism. The situation wasn't perfect, but he and others did sense opportunities to build a coalition – one that would force a conversation about race Scotland didn't know it needed.

One of the most disturbing aspects of the Sheekh case was the police's refusal to describe the attack as a racist incident. Senior officials would say there wasn't enough evidence to have it recorded as such, but a report by the Runnymede Trust released a year after Sheekh had been killed illustrated the extent of the problem across Scotland. Sheekh's murder was a nadir, but it was in no way an isolated act of racial violence.

The report showed that between 1988 and 1990 there was a 100 per cent increase in racist assaults in the Edinburgh region and a 283 per cent rise in Strathclyde, which includes Glasgow. The Runnymede Report quantified the experiences that Arshad, Younge and others were having in Scotland – of foot chases, baseball bats and broken milk bottles. If this murder wasn't categorised as racially motivated, Rowena Arshad and other activists knew it wouldn't be the last they'd have to deal with.

After Sheekh's murder, Arshad understood she needed to build a wider coalition to force the police to change their stance and recognise that racism had played a part in what had happened. Arshad had already founded the Scottish Black Women's Group, where she met other Black and Asian women in Scotland, like Philomena De Lima, who'd moved to the country in the wave of East African immigration in the 1970s, and Mukami McCrum, a Kenyan activist and academic. The group had experience of organising in

Scotland: members had campaigned to get a refuge for Black and Asian Scottish women, one where there wasn't a policy of promoting reconciliation between women and their abusive partners. The Lothian Black Forum would be that vehicle for change.

Arshad invited white women, as well as Black and Asian men, to join as allies: Joan Weir, Tarlochan Gata-Aura, who was part of Bradford's Asian Youth Movement, youth worker Carl Young, Said Bakar and Gary Younge all became involved. 'There comes a time when people say enough is enough,' Gata-Aura told reporters shortly after the group formed. 'There has been a significant change within the Black community – a tremendous feeling that something has to be done. The myth that racism is not a problem in Scotland has been blown to smithereens as a result of recent events.'[37] The Lothian Black Forum decided to call a public meeting at Drummond Community High School near Leith.[38] On the day of the event there was standing room only, as Edinburgh's anti-racist groups, anti-apartheid campaigners, and Black Scots gathered to discuss what could be done.

Gary Younge attended and decided to speak, to tell his story of Scottish racism. Even as a student, Younge was comfortable speaking in public, but he'd felt on edge before deciding to stand up and tell the story of being chased down Lothian Road a few months before Sheekh's murder. Rather than being dismissed, those in attendance listened to him. He remembers Arshad introducing the idea of 'a conspiracy of silence' among Scottish society when it came to racism. 'People were shocked,' says Arshad. 'I think that was important because a lot of these white liberal, anti-racist activists, they would campaign against apartheid but didn't really know many Black people and their lived experience.' Many white Scots in the crowd heard – perhaps for the first time – just how dangerous life had become for their Black compatriots. 'It was a wake-up call for some of them,' Arshad told me.

Reilly and Glancy had been charged with the murder and their trial would take place in May 1989. When the trial started, members of the Lothian Black Forum attended to show their support and monitor proceedings. Glancy and Reilly's supporters were not separated from Sheekh's, so those who attended, such as McCrum and Said Bakar, were sat a few metres away from some of the group who'd been accused of the attack on 16 January. It was a charged and often unruly atmosphere, and it wasn't unusual for the Sheekh supporters to be racially abused while in the courtroom itself. From early in the proceedings, the Lothian Black Forum members were worried about how the trial was going.

In the words of Joan Weir, the prosecution was 'all over the place'. She didn't have much confidence in the police after witnessing their treatment of Abdiriziak Yusuf, Sheekh's cousin who had also been attacked and was repeatedly interviewed by officers afterwards. They seemed disinterested and in a rush to get on with the rest of their day. He needed an interpreter, which seemed to annoy officers. Worst of all, they showed minimal compassion toward a young man, and an asylum seeker, who'd watched his cousin be murdered. 'I thought they were so unsympathetic – in fact I was horrified, really horrified at the whole attitude,' said Weir. There were other worrying signs: there was no DNA evidence, while the defence used a simple but effective tactic of trying to instil doubt about whether either Glancy or Reilly had been in possession of a knife. Five days into the eight-day trial, the crown dropped charges against Glancy and called him as a witness; now the sole focus was Reilly.

The details that emerged made the police's decision to categorically deny there was a racist motive even harder for the Lothian Black Forum to accept. During the trial, a detective sergeant told the court how he'd taken possession of several letters written by Reilly while in Saughton Prison in the west of the city. On the flap of one envelope were written the words: 'What is Black and red and runs at 50mph? That nigger that died.' On another he wrote a series of far-right slogans: 'Britain for the British', 'CCS' (an acronym of the Capital City Service firm he was part of) and 'NF'. The prosecution said that, when charged, Reilly had stated he didn't have a knife on the night of 16 January, but the court was told that in one letter he wrote 'I know I had a knife on me that night, but like I said

I killed no-one.' In another letter to the outside world, he wrote 'Honest, I am easy, although I never killed that nigger.'

The lack of DNA and the lacklustre prosecution led to an inevitable conclusion: Reilly was found not guilty of murder and attempted murder, although he was found guilty of repeatedly kicking and punching Sheekh. Reilly was jailed for twenty-one months but that was for confronting the couple on the Grassmarket with a knife, and the Tollcross assault.

Despite the damning facts emerging from the courtroom, newspapers were not interested in covering the trial. In January, the murder itself passed mostly without comment from either Scottish or English papers. Five months later, the trial offered a heady mix of death, racism and football hooliganism, which both tabloids and broadsheets were ordinarily keen to cover. But not this time. For once the old, macabre newspaper maxim of 'if it bleeds, it leads' was ignored.

'Newspapers love murder trials. They are packed with drama and make for exciting, voyeuristic reading. This one should have been no exception,' wrote Callum MacRae, an *Observer Scotland* reporter who did cover the trial. 'But something strange happened, something frightening. Not one national daily newspaper, Scottish or British, quality or tabloid, reported a single word. The death of Axmed Sheekh and the trial of those accused of his murder was simply not news ... The unpalatable fact is that for most newspapers Sheekh's death failed the "news value" test. And "news value" in this context at least, reflects the priorities of society.'

Sheekh's supporters were stunned. If Axmed's murder had spread fear among the members of the Lothian Black Forum, now anger was coming to the fore. 'It looks as though they have been given a free hand to go about bashing or murdering Black people knowing that nothing will be done about it,' said Said Bakar after the verdict. 'It is as if the death of a Black person is not important. If this incident had Scottish-wide coverage, maybe some people would have started to think about the level of racism in the country.'

Reilly's not guilty verdict was a huge blow. The Lothian Black

We Were There

Forum decided to respond with a rally, held in Edinburgh. The group called for attendees to assemble at 1 p.m. at the Grassmarket, from where they would walk past the site of the murder and invite people to lay flowers. They then planned to walk up Blair Street, past the high court, before holding a rally at The Mound. It would be a peaceful demonstration from their anti-racist coalition, and it attracted the attention of the far right. Letters addressed to Mr and Mrs B Nigger would drop into the mailbox accompanied with threats of violence toward the group if they continued.

But as well as receiving threats, the group also had unlikely offers of support. Ahead of the march, they were contacted by the James Connolly Society, an organisation with Irish republican connections, named after the Edinburgh-born socialist and trade unionist who fought the British in the 1916 Irish rebellion and was subsequently executed. They were known for their violent clashes with loyalist groups that often flared up around marching season in the Scottish capital. With the safety of those attending the march a pressing concern, the Lothian Black Forum accepted the invitation.

As well as the James Connolly Society, the group was supported by the anti-apartheid protestors and trade unions, including the Edinburgh Workers Association and the Trade Union Association.[39] The coalition that Younge and others had hoped for would assemble.

In total more than 1,500 people attended the rally. The far right did show up, shouting and jostling as they had with the anti-apartheid conference in Glasgow, but the unions and the James Connolly Society acted as a shield between them and the Lothian Black Forum members. It was the largest anti-racism march in Scotland's history.

The significance of the event could not be denied. The Lothian Black Forum had managed to get groups who, up until a few months earlier, hadn't even been willing to accept Scotland had a race problem to confront the issue on the streets. While the march was largely ignored by the press, the group had caught the attention of some politicians.

Alistair Darling, who would go on to become Chancellor in Gordon Brown's cabinet, was Labour's home affairs spokesperson on race relations and the MP for Edinburgh Central, which covered the Cowgate. In August, he wrote to the Lord Advocate – Lord Fraser of Carmyllie, the most senior law officer in Scotland – to point out that no one had been convicted of the killing, 'and asking what he would be doing about it'. The response from Lord Fraser was that 'there is nothing on the present basis which should suggest that further inquiries are appropriate,' while Chief Inspector Jim Scott of Lothian and Borders police added: 'I don't think there is any proof that this was a racist murder.'

The response from the Lothian Black Forum was swift. Gata-Aura said the remarks epitomised the force's 'lack of seriousness' about racist violence. He referred to a passage in the Lothian and Borders police annual report of 1988, written by the Chief Constable William Sutherland, in which he said that, although incidents of a racial nature continued to occur – the annual report recorded 87 racial incidents – 'the number of confirmed racial incidents recorded and dealt with by my officers showed a decrease'. 'If they are claiming that the killing of Axmed Sheekh was not racist, it is hardly surprising that the number of recorded racist incidents has decreased,' Gata-Aura retorted.[40]

Looking back at Scotland in the late 1980s, the level of denial when it came to racism was extraordinary. The dramatic uptick in violence aimed at Black and Asian Scots was as intense as the far-right attacks seen in England during the 1970s, when the National Front was at its peak. The term 'gaslighting' is used to describe the act of manipulating another person by making them doubt what they know to be true, often in the context of a romantic relationship: an abuser who uses lies to coerce or control a partner. But a gaslighting dynamic was at play in Scotland during 1989. If the police could deny the problem existed, then they wouldn't have to fix it; if the old orthodoxy of the 'English disease' held true, racism could not be part of the Scottish character. But the political pressure applied through the efforts of the Lothian Black Forum was working. Darling's intervention created additional pressure, and the police were having to justify their decision.

In the autumn, a month after Darling's letter to the Lord Advocate, something unexpected happened. On 16 September Chief Superintendent Ian McPherson confirmed the Sheekh killing was now listed as a racist incident.[41] In January 1990, almost a year to the day since Sheekh's murder, McPherson defended the delay in defining Sheekh's murder as a 'racist incident'. He made the comments on the BBC's *Focal Point* programme, which ran a special on racism in Scotland – itself an important moment for the Scottish media.

'It was not a sudden change of tack,' he insisted. 'It is good practice to wait until all the proceedings are finished to allow you to make a total assessment of the situation. And it was at that stage that we were able to categorise it and confirm that it was recorded in our system as a racial incident.' Buried in the officious language was the admission of something huge. Arshad's response to the decision was muted. Yes, it marked a victory for the group, but her mind lingered on the trial and lack of conviction. 'We have to ask what effect the weight of that statement would have had on the case, and the way the evidence would have been viewed,' she said.[42] Nevertheless, it was a victory for the Lothian Black Forum. The pressure, the protest and the persistence had paid off.

I remember, as a nine-year-old, hearing the news of Stephen Lawrence's murder. His portrait flashing up on the BBC News: a smiling teenager with a raised fist, a young man wearing a striped T-shirt, a house plant in the background. Seeing his parents Doreen and Neville, everyday people thrust into a maelstrom, a nightmare. The court case, the accused – spoiling for a fight, chests out. Macpherson, the Met, 'institutionally racist'. Images, names and phrases few people of my generation will ever forget. Stephen Lawrence's murder in Eltham, south-east London in 1993 fundamentally shifted the conversation on race and racism in England. The findings of the 1999 Macpherson Inquiry into the murder and its subsequent investigation were categorical: the Metropolitan Police were institutionally racist. The lethargic, shoddy investigation that failed to produce a conviction was hampered by corruption and racist assumptions.

Lawrence's murder was horrific, but the police and the court's attitude were a betrayal.

Sheekh's death had already sparked a similar conversation in Scotland: a difficult, stilted, uncomfortable discussion, but a necessary one. Four years before Lawrence's murder, the Lothian Black Forum had started a dialogue that forced Sheekh's name into Scottish consciousness. Later, after the Stephen Lawrence inquiry and the Macpherson Report, the Institute of Race Relations would create *Homebeats*: an anti-racism teaching resource, distributed on CD-ROM, aimed at schools who were looking to update their anti-racist policies. Glasgow City Council used it in all thirty-three of its secondary schools, where it informed children that the killing of Sheekh 'shattered the complacent assumption that racism was an "English disease".'[43]

The Lothian Black Forum continued to operate, first helping the Sheekh family in Somalia seek compensation and then broadening its remit to support the wider Black community in Scotland.[44] On the tenth anniversary of Sheekh's murder, there was another march held in his memory, with McCrum and other Lothian Black Forum members leading a silent vigil of some 300 people. In the intervening decade, several groups had sprung up in Scotland, taking the LBF's lead and tackling racism north of the border. There was the Lothian Campaign Against Racism and Fascism; members of the James Connolly Society led the Scottish Campaign Against Racism and Fascism, which focused on the football terraces. In Edinburgh, there were local groups such as Muirhouse Against Racism and the Wester Hailes Anti-Racism project, while the Scottish TUC helped set up similar organisations on the west coast. The Lothian Black Forum, far from being an outlier, was now joined by dozens of similar projects around the country, which spread the idea of Scottish anti-racism beyond its traditional base of the middle-class anti-apartheid movement.

Sheekh's name might not be known as widely as it should, but the legacy of resistance that developed in the wake of his murder is still felt north of the border. In May 2021, Home Office officials attempted to detain two Sikh men living in the Pollokshields area of Glasgow. The men had resided in the UK for a decade but had not been given permanent leave to remain and could – potentially – face deportation. Locals quickly organised and surrounded the Home Office van on Kenmure Street, where the men were living, to prevent it from leaving. As the day wore on, the crowd grew, and Police Scotland responded by bringing in horses and officers with riot gear. After an eight-hour standoff, the men were released. One man who took part said: 'I put my shoes on and sprinted out. I just thought: You're not going to do that in front of me. There is due process and this is not it.'[45]

When the national conversation about Britain's connections to slavery began to get louder in the 2010s, Scottish institutions put down markers that differentiated them from their English counterparts. In 2018, the University of Glasgow published the results of a year-long investigation into the 'significant financial support' it had received from people whose wealth derived from slavery and announced a £20 million reparations package – the most significant of its kind in the UK. The institution acknowledged it received around £200 million from the slavery economy during the eighteenth and nineteenth centuries, while many other English universities dithered and deflected.

Around the same time, Glaswegian activists put up new street signs honouring civil rights figures next to those which were named after Scottish slave traders: Wilson Street (named after merchant Jonathan Wilson) became Rosa Park Street; while Glassford Street (the tobacco lord who owned plantations in Virginia and Maryland) became Fred Hampton Street.[46] Jackie Kay, who in 2019 warned that Scotland had to 'grow up' and take more responsibility for the treatment of Black and ethnic minority people, told me that the shift in acknowledging the country's slave-owning past was a result of decades of work, dating back to the time of Sheekh's murder. Kay wrote a poem 'Flag Up Scotland, Jamaica' to mark the University of Glasgow's reparation announcement with the lines: 'Here's the redress that's long been owed/ Here's the first step on the road.'

The English Disease, Edinburgh – 1989

There are signs of significant progress since 1989, most echoing arguments from the time of Sheekh's murder. In May 2023, Police Scotland's Chief Constable Sir Iain Livingstone made a landmark statement after a series of high-profile cases of misogynistic bullying and deaths in police custody involving Black and Asian people, including thirty-one-year-old father of two, Sheku Bayoh, who'd fled Sierra Leone as a child, and had been living in Fife for more than two decades. Bayoh died after being restrained by officers on a Kirkcaldy street in 2015.[47] After an inquiry, which Bayoh's family had to fight fiercely to establish, Livingstone publicly admitted the force he led was institutionally racist and discriminatory. The family of Bayoh praised the announcement. Through their lawyer the family said they wanted to 'thank the chief constable for raising his voice for the truth and being brave enough to say what Black and Asian communities have known for decades'. That victory did not come easy.

Scotland has had a first minister who is the son of Pakistani immigrants. In 2023, Humza Yousaf took over from Nicola Sturgeon as first minister of Scotland, a position he held for a year. In 2011, when Yousaf first became a member of the Scottish parliament he swore his oath of allegiance in Urdu, wearing traditional attire decorated with a band of tartan, symbolic of the Scottish and Pakistani traditions he embodied. Throughout his political career, Humza has wheeled out a well-polished anecdote about his father's nationalist awakening. 'My dad just assumed that Scotland was independent,' he says,[48] 'and it was only when he was told that we're not, he thought, "Well, that's not right", and so decided to join [the SNP].'[49] If you take Yousaf (who was the party's only non-white cabinet member for years) out of the equation, the SNP is still very low on senior politicians of colour, but today, Scotland is closer to the country Axmed Sheekh thought he was moving to in the late 1980s, even if some stereotypes take a long time to die. After the announcement from Police Scotland, the satirical magazine *Private Eye* published a cartoon: a frowning police officer, surrounded by microphones is asked 'Are the Scottish police racist?' His reply? 'Aye, it's true . . . we all hate the English.'[50]

In 2012, two of the men who attacked Stephen Lawrence were tried and found guilty of his murder. In the wake of the high-profile story, pressure built for Axmed Sheekh's case to be re-examined but, to date, no one has ever been charged with his murder. His death was nevertheless a turning point in Scottish life. The coalition built by the Lothian Black Forum showed that thousands were prepared to acknowledge and march in the name of anti-racism north of the border. Just as the George Lindo campaign forced a discussion about police tactics and forced confessions in Bradford, the Sheekh case destroyed the concept of Scottish exceptionalism, rooted in an idea that as the 'colonised', they could never be racist. In its place, came the idea that those who had themselves fought imperialism could take a different direction than Thatcher's government when it came to race and immigration. Their nationalism could be a civic one, open – in theory – to all. Today, you can see the legacy in every deportation protest and the far more welcoming approach to refugees north of the border, which can be seen in the policy – New Scots – that states people like Sheekh 'should be integrated into our communities from day one'.

After Sheekh's death, Joan Weir and some of the small Somali community in Edinburgh arranged for him to be buried in the Muslim section of Rosebank Cemetery in Pilrig. A short ceremony commemorated the life of a young man who'd come to build a life for himself in a country that was not his own. In 2013, Axmed's younger brother Omar, who also came to the UK, and Weir released the Sheekh family's final statement on the case after years of trying to get a retrial:

> Now it is time for the family to draw a line under the public aspects of this tragedy, but we call on other individuals and agencies to ensure the continued development and monitoring of such improvements.

Words from Axmed's family's document produced in 1990 still resonate:

The English Disease, Edinburgh – 1989

We will continue to feel that Axmed died quite senselessly, but there may be some consolation if we can feel our questions in some small way will lead to changes resulting not only in a greater chance for justice for Black people suffering racism, but for the eradication of racism in Scotland.

Omar Abukar and Joan Weir
Bristol and Edinburgh
October 2013

10.
People of the Future – 1990

A decade on from Tony Palmer's trip to Wigan Casino in 1977, the Britain he'd sought out had, in many ways, disappeared. Northern Soul carried on, but the scene was nowhere near the juggernaut it had been in the mid-1970s; Steve Caesar, Rhonda Finlayson, Ian Obeng and the other Black dancers who stood under the glow of Wigan Casino's lights had long moved on. The venue had become a car park, and several of the other clubs on the circuit were defunct – but it wasn't just the Northern Soul scene that had suffered.

By the end of the 1980s, Margaret Thatcher's political vision had been realised, and the country was transformed. The economic map of the UK had been redrawn, with the industrialised heartlands of the north and Midlands hit hardest by Thatcher's economic agenda, which involved switching focus and power to the City of London and the south-east with the Big Bang reforms in 1986. Yuppies were born and the dockland areas of London, Liverpool and Cardiff transformed by the development corporations that turned them from ghosts of the industrialised age to playgrounds for property speculators and the newly rich.

It was an era when the power of the individual usurped the might of the collective. The union power that had produced the Winter of Discontent had been fatally wounded by the miners' strike defeat; and the far right found itself once again in the margins, with internal squabbles and schisms defining their increasingly insular world. Thatcher would argue that it was her grand plan that had awakened a sleeping giant, giving Britain back its bite and prestige.

Stuart Hall was one of Thatcher's loudest critics. At the start of the Thatcher era, in 1979, Hall wrote one of his best-known essays,

'The Great Moving Right Show', in which he argued that the country had been shifting towards the right since the late 1960s. But it was Thatcher who had given that movement 'a powerful impetus and a distinctive personal stamp', while she helped the right 're-establish its monopoly over "good ideas" . . . "capitalism" and "the free market" have come back into common usage as terms of positive approval.' Hall could see what made Thatcher successful: she was able to win the 'battle of ideas', and convince millions of British people to come on the journey with her and the Conservative Party.

There were others who painted Thatcher as a pantomime villain. The novelist Angela Carter described Thatcher in 1988 as part-nanny, part-Elizabeth I as Gloriana and part-Countess Dracula, adding that she 'coos like a dove, hisses like a serpent, bays like a hound'. Salman Rushdie was horrified by the Britain that had emerged in the 1980s. 'There are, of course, many Britains, and many of them – the sceptical, questioning, radical, reformist, libertarian, non-conformist Britains – I have always admired greatly,' he wrote. 'But these Britains are presently in retreat, even in disarray; while nanny-Britain, strait-laced Victorian values Britain, thin-lipped jingoist Britain, is in charge. Dark goddesses rule; brightness falls from the air.'

But amid the tumult of the Thatcher era, Black Britain had also been transformed. Culturally and politically, Black Britain had found a new confidence – the social unrest and protest of the decade had not only produced victories like the Lindo case, but it had also instilled a resilience and networks that spread around the country. Black-led protests across various cities and towns in 1981 had produced landmark moments: from the outlawing of Sus to the 1987 general election when three Black Labour MPs – Diane Abbott, Paul Boateng and Bernie Grant – were elected to the Houses of Parliament. The activists and academics of the 1970s had become the TV producers of the late 1980s. Colin Prescod, the dreadlocked academic of *Blacks Britannica* was now at Channel 4, producing films about the history of Butetown; Darcus Howe had become a mainstay of British TV and radio, taking his critiques of the British state from the street to the screen. Weekly shows, including *Ebony on the*

Road and *Black Bag* produced deep dives into communities around the UK and told stories that captivated Black Britain, including the Cardiff Three scandal. Never had Black life been so present in the British mainstream. At the same time, Black Britain continued to influence underground currents – and it was on dance floors where once again culture was being reshaped.

A couple of years after Linda Brogan walked into The Reno in Manchester and heard 'Black heavy metal' being played by the DJ Hewan Clarke, house music had gone through a Day-Glo filter and become acid house. Acid house developed out of the African American house music scene in Chicago. Powered by a signature squelchy bassline produced by the Roland TB 303, a piece of equipment that a young producer called DJ Pierre had manipulated into creating new sounds. When he and two friends – known collectively as Phuture – first played their song 'Acid Tracks' at the cutting-edge Chicago club Music Box, they cleared the dance floor. But the resident DJ Ron Hardy kept on playing it and by the fourth time, this mutated, throbbing track had won the crowd over. This new, harder sound was dubbed acid house. It would cross the Atlantic and find a receptive audience in small, forward-thinking clubs like Manchester's The Reno. But it was another venue in the same city that would become its spiritual home.

When the Haçienda opened in Manchester in 1982, its owner Tony Wilson – the Mancunian Svengali who started Factory Records and was a semi-regular face at The Reno – told his new resident DJ, Hewan Clarke, he wanted Black music to be played. Clarke was confused – this was a venue where indie bands and counter-cultural figures like beat poet William Burroughs were often booked – but Wilson insisted. His rationale was that Black music was going to become 'an essential part in white musical culture in the future'. In 1982, a time where physical and psychological barriers were in place across British culture dividing racial groups, the idea seemed farfetched and radical. 'He actually said that to me,' recalled Clarke.[1] 'I was like, I can't see this happening, but it did.'

In the first four years of the club's life, its clientele was racially mixed, with a prominent Black presence. But by the second half of the decade, the Haçienda's original Black-led dance floor had become engulfed by an almost entirely white crowd. The newcomers wore baggy clothes, blew whistles and were powered by the latest drug of choice: ecstasy. Mike Pickering, another resident DJ, talked about witnessing the club's demographic change before his eyes. 'Once it exploded, it was weird, you could watch from Friday to Friday and see the crowd change in colour,' he said.[2] 'In those days, most of the Black kids would smoke weed, but they weren't into chemicals. But then when ecstasy came in, it wiped it all out. It was so quick. It was over about four or five weeks.'

Rave took the music out of clubs and into ad-hoc party venues in farmers' fields, abandoned warehouses and even airstrips. By the summer of 1989, thousands of people were travelling around the UK each weekend to search out gatherings. Tabloid hysteria and a moral panic quickly followed: *The Sun*'s medical correspondent claimed people who went raving could 'end up in a mental hospital for life' and would almost certainly be sexually assaulted, while the same newspaper led with a front-page splash 'SPACED OUT!' when 11,000 ravers turned up at the White Waltham airfield in June 1989. The countryside around the M25 was a notorious hub for the parties, but there were other centres, such as Blackburn, with its old defunct mills providing ideal locations for impromptu parties that could rage all weekend.[3] The first ecstasy deaths followed and added to the media furore.

The phenomenon could not be stopped. It was a dramatic shift that came towards the end of a decade where Thatcher had transformed British life. After an era where libertarian economics, the Falklands War, the miners' strikes, climbing unemployment and race-fuelled unrest had drastically altered the country's political alignment, now for some young people the despondency of the early 1980s was being replaced with a colourful, hedonistic counter-cultural alternative. And although Black dancers might have been elbowed off the dance floor at the Haçienda, Black artists were still central to the scene. It wasn't long before cutting-edge musicians in the north of England had developed Bleep and Bass, a sound that would dominate the nascent acid house and rave scene.

In Bradford, Unique 3 made the first ever Bleep and Bass tune, 'The Theme' – a stark, trippy track with pulverising bass that came out in October 1988. Nightmares on Wax, a West Yorkshire duo, would create their own bass-heavy retort called 'Dextrous', while Sheffield became the epicentre of the scene with the Warp label providing a home for many artists. Nearly all the Bleep and Bass producers were Black: out of Unique 3's four members, three were Black – so were both of Nightmares on Wax. Warp's go-to producer and engineer was another Black British musician, Rob Gordon. In Leeds, the original line-up of the LFO group included Martin Williams, who set up a studio with another Black friend, Homer Harriott. The pair went on to produce records for Ability II, Juno and Ital Rockers, who were all Black. A Guy Called Gerald's 'Voodoo Ray' – created by Gerald Simpson from Hulme, in Manchester – was the scene's biggest track, becoming one of the Haçienda's anthems at the same time many Black dancers were leaving the dance floor.[4]

Nightmares on Wax (left to right: George Evelyn and Kevin Harper) pose outside Warp Records in Sheffield

While the musicians who made Bleep and Bass were overwhelmingly working-class Black kids, the tracks they made signalled a cultural shift: here was music that mixed American hip-hop and house sounds with the homegrown reggae culture that had emerged in the 1970s. The young producers didn't apply the purist, racially segregated mindset that dominated the 1970s; now these aural elements sat side by side, fused together by a new generation increasingly calling themselves Black British. Nightmares on Wax, Unique 3 and the other Bleep and Bass producers were taking American music and reinterpreting it in a Black British form.

The influence of sound systems meant the low-end sounds had to be huge in order for it to work on the speakers designed to produce rib-rattling bass, while the use of MCs was arguably much closer to the Jamaican tradition of 'toasting' than the US creation of the rapper. The beats that undergirded the music had a slight swing – there wasn't the same strict four-to-the-floor beat of house: you could feel the influence of music imported from the Caribbean in Bleep and Bass, such as the broken rhythms of early dancehall. These building blocks have been used in every British form of dance music since: Jungle, Drum'n'Bass, 2-Step Garage, Bassline, Grime, Afro-bashment and British Jazz – all use that aural palette to paint with. This genre, which emerged from Yorkshire, ushered in a new era and laid down the foundations of every British sub-genre that has emerged since. But it wasn't just music that the scene was changing.

The music critic and cultural historian Simon Reynolds wrote about hearing Unique 3's follow up to 'The Theme', the colossal 'Weight of the Bass', in his classic history of rave, *Energy Flash*, saying it conjured 'the unlikely vision of dreadlocked roots rockers on E' and 'rude-boys swapping their guns for fluorescent lightsticks'. The divisions that had existed in culture and society – ones that placed white and Black culture in different worlds – were beginning to melt away.

Ecstasy, the drug fuelling the scene, encouraged not just dancing but also increased levels of empathy. Developed by German scientists in the 1910s, Ecstasy, MDMA or 3,4 methylenedioxymethamphetamine was a stimulant. But unlike the amphetamines that some Northern Soul dancers relied on, it also had psychedelic qualities that expanded the mind and altered a user's mood. Not every raver took ecstasy, but for those who did, it could be a revolutionary experience.

George Evelyn of Nightmares on Wax remembers being at a rave in Leeds and seeing members of the Leeds Service Crew, a notorious firm of Leeds United hooligans. As a younger teenager Evelyn would narrowly avoid kick-ins from the group whenever he ventured into Leeds city centre. Now here they were, dancing to his music and embracing him. 'All of a sudden we were seeing the same people we were scared of,' said Evelyn. 'Service Crew were on the dance floor with sunglasses hugging my mates from the hood; the optics and dynamics started to change.' For Evelyn, during the late 1980s, Britain began to open up. The old barriers, physical and psychological, were starting to collapse – fuelled in part by acid house epiphanies.

It wasn't just on dance floors where Black British culture was influencing the wider world around it. In the heartlands of northern England, in the same towns and cities where Bleep and Bass had emerged, another revolution was taking place. As the Thatcher era ended, the rise of two Black sportsmen also signalled a shift in Britain as the most northern of sports – Rugby League – was reinvented by a Londoner and a maverick from Leeds. Like the Bleep and Bass producers, the players would take a unique approach to their craft, imbuing it with flair and panache.

Tuning into BBC One on Saturday afternoon in the 1980s meant one thing for sports fans: four hours of *Grandstand*. From its debut in 1958,[5] the public broadcaster's weekend sports magazine show quickly became an institution. Horse racing, gymnastics, football and golf – the gamut of British sporting life was covered by genial hosts like Peter Dimmock and David Coleman. Its appeal lay in its broad coverage of sporting events, from big hitters like the Grand National, which would attract ten million viewers every April, to lesser-known competitions and more obscure sports. Rugby

League – the hyper-masculine, thirteen-man code of the sport played in towns and cities dotted across the M62 in the north of England – was one such sport.

League had always been a rebel sport. It broke away from the amateur fifteen-man union code in 1895 over a dispute about pay. The northern union teams paid players to take time off work, while the mostly southern-based authorities insisted it should be a wholly amateur sport. Class was and still is the great divider between the two codes. Union was a gentleman's game, played by those who worked as solicitors and headmasters during the week; while league was for the working classes, men who might go down the pit, as a secondary source of income.

In the 1963 film *This Sporting Life*, Richard Harris's character – a taciturn, violent miner who plays league on the weekend – is asked if he's one of the team's stars. Harris's Frank Machin replies, 'This sport doesn't have stars, that's soccer.' When asked what this sport has, he deadpans, 'People like me.' Rugby League feeds into the national mythology that would have the north of England as inherently tougher, perhaps more honest, than the south.

Grandstand's coverage helped take league out of its northern heartlands in Lancashire and Yorkshire, beaming it into the homes of millions around the country. In 1983, *Grandstand* covered the Challenge Cup semi-final as Bradford Northern played against Featherstone Rovers for a place in the final of the sport's most prestigious competition. It was a match that would announce the arrival of a once-in-a-generation talent.

Ellery Hanley was the son of immigrants from St Kitts who'd settled in Leeds. He struggled in mainstream education, eventually ending up at Shadwell, a school for pupils who had been excluded from mainstream education in his hometown. Henderson Gill, another Black Rugby League star, went to the school with Hanley, and described it as a 'mini-Borstal' – a place where students needed serious mental strength to survive. If they misbehaved, it could be months before they were allowed to leave the facility. But the pair had an escape while at the school in the form of Rugby

League. They were a phenomenon: with both being selected for England school boys before signing with leading league club Bradford Northern in 1978.

Hanley, despite his talent, couldn't stay out of trouble. 'When I look back on those times and the way I behaved, I am not disgusted, because I feel I learnt from it,' he said in a rare interview about the period. 'It was a good couple of years before it came home to me that I either had to pull my thumb out and change my ways, or waste the chances on offer . . . I've learnt in the hard times. They've stood me in good stead.'[6] In his early career, he regularly faced abuse from the stands, with supporters taunting him about his criminal record. Journalists mentioned it so often he refused to be interviewed. 'Brooding, malevolent, venomous,' is how the sportswriter Simon Barnes summed up Hanley. 'He is a grim, driving figure . . . perhaps the most intense ball-player I have ever seen. That is the only way he has ever allowed the world to see him: as opponents do, fearsome, smouldering, utterly unforgiving.'

On 26 March 1983, as millions watched at home, he picked the ball up eighty-five yards from Featherstone's try line. In front of him were three defenders, which would ordinarily be enough to deter a player from trying to break the line. Hanley ran towards the first defender at full tilt, knocking him off balance. The second defender appeared, and Hanley shoved him into the first man, who crashed to the ground like a bowling pin. As the full back – the last line of defence and usually one of the best tacklers in the team – closes in, Hanley dips his head, anticipating the tackle, and seems to find another gear, sending the defender sprawling as he races clear. Then it's a straight sprint to the line, which Hanley wins comfortably. The whole thing is over in around fifteen seconds. Like with many of his greatest tries, it doesn't seem possible. He 'earned every decibel of the thunderous ovation his effort received,'[7] wrote the *Guardian*'s Paul Fitzpatrick. Bradford would lose the game, but Hanley had arrived.[8]

By the mid-1980s, his skill and star power had helped to drag the sport out of a malaise that had consumed it for the greater part of twenty years. In the preceding decade, crowds had drifted away. League had become a caricature of itself with one writer describing it as looking like a mix between *It's a Knock Out* and mud wrestling'.⁹ Like the stodgy, old-fashioned night clubs that acid house was eclipsing, Rugby League was about to be transformed in the 1980s. Hanley was the spark. He was explosive, unpredictable and created opportunities out of nothing. When he broke into the Bradford side, he became a score-trying phenomenon: during the 1984–5 season he scored fifty-five tries in thirty-seven appearances, becoming the first man to score fifty tries in a season since the early 1960s.

He was also divisive: people *had* to see him, even if it was to jeer him. When he returned to Bradford after signing for Wigan, it brought the biggest crowd Odsal Stadium had seen in twenty years.[10] His record-breaking performances were bigger than just numbers though. 'Ellery's feat seemed to signify that Rugby League had recovered from its seemingly terminal decline,' argued Rugby League historian, Tony Collins. He was the most gifted player of his generation, seemingly peerless.

As Ellery Hanley was breathing new life into Rugby League, a coach was looking for his own revolutionary talent. Doug Laughton, a former Great Britain player now coaching Widnes and known for his guile and toughness, was on the hunt for players who might be hiding in plain sight. Code-switching – the term used to describe players moving between the two forms of rugby – was controversial, but Laughton had perfected the art of bringing over the best from the other side. He'd managed to lure union players, such as the Scottish winger and full back Alan Tait and the Welsh international half back Jonathan Davies to add flair to his combative, hard-to-beat Widnes side. But he was after another player, someone who could provide him with tries: a winger. Scouts were talking about a player who was carving up the rugby sevens scene, the frantic small-sided version of union – a British-Nigerian called Martin Offiah.[11] As soon as Laughton saw Offiah play, he felt there was something special about him. 'It was like discovering the Rock of Gibraltar, Galileo,

Nijinsky, you name it,' he wrote in his memoir. 'I've got it here with this one,'[12] he told himself.[13]

Like Hanley, Offiah's early years had been challenging. When his parents arrived in London from Nigeria in the 1960s, they did what hundreds of other West Africans did: sent their son to live with white foster parents. 'Farming' was often used as parents established themselves in their new home or concentrated on studying. It's thought that up to 70,000 children were looked after in this capacity from the time the first advert for foster parents appeared in 1955 to when the practice ended forty years later.[14] Offiah was 'farmed' until he was three.

After reuniting with her son, Offiah's mother secured him a place at the prestigious Woolverstone Hall in Suffolk, a progressive institution in a semi-rural setting that offered boarding for state school students. A BBC documentary dubbed the school 'the poor man's Eton',[15] painting it as an educational anomaly in post-war Britain, one that took pride in moulding 'inner city' kids, many of whom were Black. Offiah swapped Hackney for Suffolk and thrived there. He fell in love with Rugby Union at Woolverstone and dreamed of playing for England, something no Black player had done since James Peters in 1906.

While it was a rare sight to see a Black player in a Rugby Union team, especially at the highest levels, Rugby League offered a different picture. Arguably, there is no sport that has been more welcoming to Black British talent as Rugby League. Players such as Billy Boston, a Welsh winger from Tiger Bay, was a phenomenon at Wigan in the 1950s; he set scoring records and has a statue in the town in his honour.[16] Colin Dixon and Johnny Freeman were crowd favourites at Halifax. Roy Francis became the first Black coach of a British professional sports team when he took charge of Hull FC in 1954. In 1972, Clive Sullivan captained Great Britain to World Cup success – the first time any Black sportsperson had worn the armband of a British team.[17] When Hanley, Offiah and Gill broke through in the 1980s, it was, to an extent, business as usual. But their arrival coincided with a time when sport was changing.

British sports often sidelined or brazenly ignored Black British talent. The England football team only welcomed its first Black player, Nottingham-born Viv Anderson, in 1978. (Paul Ince would become the first Black captain in 1993.) When John Barnes played for England's football team against Brazil in 1984, scoring a wonder goal in a 2-0 victory at the Maracanã Stadium in Rio de Janeiro, England fans chanted 'we only won 1-0' – refusing to acknowledge Barnes' brilliance on account of his race. Cricket was one of the most popular sports in the Thatcher era; but many Black Britons supported the West Indies, one of the dominant forces in world cricket, who'd destroyed England in a heated 1976 series. That tour had been tainted by comments by the England captain Tony Grieg, who'd insisted his side would make the former colonial subject 'grovel'. The West Indies, led by a blistering pace attack and the batting of Viv Richards, won 3-0. Black British cricket fans had to wait until 1980 for Roland Butcher to become England's first-ever capped Black player. Like cricket, Rugby Union was still governed by arcane and sometimes overtly racist public school attitudes that stopped Black players from getting opportunities. Players were often quietly ignored. In 1988, Chris Oti became the first Black player to pull on the white shirt of England in over eighty years; Jeremy Guscott would follow shortly afterwards – but by then, Offiah was up north.

When I met Offiah, I asked him about swapping Hackney for the north-west. It must have been a huge adjustment? 'I was used to culture shocks,' he said, mentioning his time in foster care and boarding school. When he got to Widnes, the small industrial town on the edge of Merseyside, Offiah was struck by the cobbled streets and smokestacks from the chemical plant. It reminded him of *Coronation Street*. Widnes was a world away from Hackney, but life as a farmed child and a student at Woolverstone had taught him to adjust.

Despite having never played Rugby League before signing for Widnes, Offiah was a natural. Like Hanley, he could conjure tries out of nothing. He was fast, read the game well and would take on opponents when others might pass. Mike Ford remembers playing against Offiah during that first season. Ford was a stand-off, a creative player that operates like the team's quarterback orchestrating its attack, but one who prided himself on doing his part defensively. He wasn't the fastest but could usually get his angles right, cutting off the field and at least attempting to tackle even the most rapid opponents. As Offiah came towards him, Ford remembers thinking he had him. 'I never touched him; never got anywhere near him,' he told me. 'And it was the first time that happened to me.'

Ford wasn't the only one to be humbled by the new arrival, who seemed to save his best performances for the biggest stages. Offiah scored a hat-trick against St Helens to help Widnes win their first championship in a decade; then the team beat St Helens again in the Premiership Final, with Offiah being named Man of Steel – the award for most valuable player. Offiah touched down forty-four in his first season making him the top scorer in the league and taking the title from Hanley, who had held it for the previous four seasons. Laughton's gamble had paid off.

Offiah was turning heads off the pitch too. He seemed to know he had star power that could sell. That didn't always sit well with the game's old guard. Alex Murphy, who'd briefly coached Wigan, had a column in the *Daily Mirror* in which he would regularly question Offiah's quality. His Widnes teammates weren't always welcoming either. Offiah was bought a BMW by the club after his scoring exploits. One day a stain appeared on the bonnet that Offiah couldn't get rid of. 'Someone had taken a shit on my car,' he told me. Despite the scatological initiation, Offiah's first season was a sensation. 'There has never been such a Rugby League debut,' declared *The Observer*.[18] His and Hanley's success – and confidence – was echoed in other cultural movements around the country.

Like the Rugby League players, during the late 1980s, the Bleep and Bass producers were pushing each other to greater heights.

The DJ Winston Hazel grew up in Sheffield, as part of a largely Jamaican community based around Havelock Square. His family rented a room in a big house that ran a regular weekend party called

Sunny's Blues. 'You lived a life of reggae sonics,' he tells me when we meet in Sheffield. Lying in bed as a child he felt his ribs tickled by the low-end frequencies emanating from the blues. Many of the Bleep and Bass producers had grown up with sound system culture. Evelyn had started his own sound, called Echo 45, made from shoe boxes and recycled speakers from old TVs.

The reggae parties were a fixture of what Hazel calls the 'Black ring of security' that surrounded him in his youth – church, soul nights, blues, community centres. These were largely Black-only spaces, one where he felt safe but restricted. 'You were expected to act and be a certain way,' he tells me. 'And if you started to live outside of that, there were constant unknown pressures that kept dragging you back.' Hazel found it suffocating; his interests stretched beyond the cultural landscape of Black Sheffield. But with the arrival of acid house, he, like many young Britons, spotted an opportunity to rebel.

Sheffield's nightlife was deeply segregated in the Thatcher era. Hazel would play for the Black crowd at Turn-Ups club, while across the city his friend and future DJing partner Richard Barratt, AKA Parrot, was a resident at the largely white Mona Lisa's. Their solution was to start their own night: Jive Turkey. The night, which opened in 1985 and would run until 1992, melded the hip-hop, street soul, techno, electro and house that Hazel and Parrot revered.[19] When pop critic Jon Savage went to see what the fuss was about on a cold November night in 1988, he found 'local Blacks in flying jackets and Davy Crockett caps dancing next to young whites in Levi's and short, razored hair'.[20]

Jive Turkey attracted fellow travellers like Nightmares on Wax, who were regulars. Now after their early studio experimentations, the pair wanted proof of concept. The litmus test for any dance music producer was whether your records would sell, so George Evelyn borrowed £400 from his brother and pressed up 2,000 white-label copies of a Nightmares on Wax track called 'Dextrous'. Unlike the organised chaos of their early productions like 'Let It Roll', 'Dextrous' was pared back, with a huge bassline echoing the bleeping keyboard line and rattling percussion. Evelyn rented a red Nissan Micra and hit the road. He went to Fon Records in Sheffield, where Hazel was working as a buyer, then drove down the M1 to London. He played 'Dextrous' for one of Norman Jay's protégés, Trevor Nelson, who immediately bought copies; as did Dave Dorell, another tastemaker in the capital, and he met Paul 'Trouble' Anderson who could make or break a track. In a couple of weeks, Evelyn and Harper had sold all 2,000 records. 'Dextrous' became an underground sensation, and put Nightmares on Wax on the radar of a record store owner in Sheffield.

Warp Records started life as a shop (originally called Fon), opening in 1986, a year after Jive Turkey launched. Steve Beckett's store became a hub in the birth of Bleep and Bass. The label was started in part thanks to the Tory government's Enterprise Allowance Scheme, which offered a guaranteed income of £40 a week for up to twelve months for anybody who could show they were starting a small business. The scheme's beneficiaries included many of the Young British Artists who succeeded the Blk Art Group, while Jazzie B of Soul II Soul used it to bankroll his shop in Camden, north London, that sold the band's merch and clothing line.[21] Sporting a new confident Black British aesthetic of dreadlocks, dark sunglasses and designer shirts, Soul II Soul produced slick British R'n'B, otherwise known as street soul, that saw success on both sides of the Atlantic. Jazzie B's entrepreneurial nous was in step with Thatcher's vision for a generation of go-getting self-starters. 'I want to see more young business people, more people doing what we're doing here in the shop,' said Jazzie B. 'I want to see more of us in the charts, more of us in the media's eye.'

It's often suggested by cultural journalists that the scheme inadvertently helped create much of the late 1980s indie music boom in Britain, as bands and artists like Jarvis Cocker from Pulp, Shaun Ryder of the Happy Mondays, Alan McGee of Creation Records and Laurence Bell of Domino all signed up; while artists including Tracey Emin, Rachel Whiteread, Jeremy Deller and Edmund de Waal cashed in too.[22] But it also helped bolster Bleep and Bass.

Nightmares on Wax used another government scheme to book studio space to work on their early tracks.

Warp Records became a focal point for the Bleep and Bass producers who, like Nightmares on Wax, wanted to see if their sounds would sell. This was different to the Black British music that had come before. The advent of cheap and intuitive hardware meant people like Evelyn and Harper could make their own tracks in their bedrooms, while the existence of government grants gave them access to mastering facilities. Unlike the Black British soul acts – like The Real Thing or Sweet Sensation – they weren't, initially at least, beholden to record labels. They could press their own short runs and ferry them to shops, as Evelyn had done. It was Thatcherite entrepreneurialism remixed in the illegal warehouse parties of acid house. 'We're right in the middle of this revolution and all these DJs would come into the shop, buying their tunes for the weekend, but at the same time they're all trying to make their own tracks,' said Steve Beckett of the deluge of new music coming into his shop. 'You'd get people like Nightmares On Wax and DJ Martin from LFO coming in with their own tunes, and we'd try them out in the club at the weekend and the audience would go insane.'

After the white-label copies of 'Dextrous' sold out, Beckett approached Nightmares on Wax and proposed doing an official release. Warp had already put out one single – 'Track With No Name' by Winston Hazel's group Forgemasters – but 'Dextrous' would prove to be a quantum leap for the fledgling label. It sold 40,000 copies and went into the Top 40; then LFO's track 'LFO' raised the stakes again. 'That was the one that turned us into a "real label",' said Beckett. 'We just weren't prepared for what would happen with that record. It was at the time when a single could come out and keep sneaking up and up; at first it was just into the top 40, next week it was in the top 20, then it was twelve. We sold 130,000 12's, which was just unbelievable.'[23] Nightmares on Wax and Beckett had proof now: Bleep and Bass sold shedloads. Throughout 1989, the scene burst through the 'Black ring of security' where it had started, landing in the charts just as Hanley and Offiah were

We Were There

Winston Hazel (left) and DJ Parrot of Jive Turkey and Forgemasters

making their own leap, becoming something few Black Britons had ever become: celebrities.

In the 1980s, the limitations of the media inadvertently made Rugby League players household names. With many of their most impressive sporting displays broadcast on *Grandstand* – which continued to show the marquee moments of the Rugby League calendar, including the Challenge Cup Final – Hanley's and Offiah's exploits reached huge audiences. Without the help of social media or any platform other than print media and four terrestrial TV channels, they carved out their image. As the Thatcher era drew to a close, Offiah and Hanley were mixing with rock stars and had greater name recognition than that of many professional footballers.

At the end of the 1988 season, Hanley, Gill and Offiah starred in a testing tour of Australia, a side Great Britain hadn't beaten down under since 1974. The 1988 tour was special. It featured six Black players, the most diverse touring party Great Britain had ever seen.[24] There was Hanley, who captained the side, Offiah, Leeds players Carl Gibson and Roy Powell, Welsh half back Phil Ford, and Henderson Gill.

People of the Future – 1990

English Rugby League tourists Roy Powell (left) and Henderson Gill have photos taken for their family albums at the new Sydney Football Stadium by teammate Carl Gibson

The tour got off to a disappointing start with a narrow loss in the first test, followed up with a more convincing defeat in the second. But in the third game against the Australians, Hanley's team delivered, winning 26-12, with Offiah, Gill and Phil Ford all scoring. When Gill scored, he leapt up and started to dance, rotating his hips, prompting the commentator to shout, 'He's doing a bit of a boogie!', as the travelling fans waved Union Jacks in celebration. The dancing would become known as the 'downtown boogie', and the try helped the Lions to their first win over the Australians, home or away, since 1978.[25]

When the final hooter sounded, the camera focused on Offiah and Hanley as the two star players embraced. The 1988 tour had given Hanley and Offiah an opportunity to get to know each other. Until then, their interactions had been limited to the field: tackles and shimmies, quick handshakes afterwards. The pair roomed together. They played chess, talked about music – they were both soul heads – and, crucially, discussed the business side of the game.

When Offiah signed for Widnes, he'd committed to a nine-year contract, a ridiculous length that, after the £25,000 up front, left him with a relatively paltry sum of £5,000 per year. Offiah wasn't happy and wanted out. It was Hanley who would show him the way.

Hanley was well known as not only an exceptional player but a shrewd negotiator, with almost as many column inches dedicated to how much he was paid as to his feats on the pitch. Before the tour he'd fallen out with the head coach at Wigan and went onto the transfer market for a world record fee of £225,000, a sum no one could pay – although Warrington flirted with the idea. After the 1988 tour, Hanley would return to Australia to play first for Balmain and then the Western Suburbs, where he earned £3,000 per match[26] – an astronomical fee for Rugby League but one he justified by guiding Balmain to a Grand Final.[27] Like the Bleep and Bass producers, Hanley had taken control of his career, understanding that the player was a brand, one with incredible value.

'Remember,' he'd tell Offiah in their Australian hotel room. 'You're a valuable asset. Without you, they are nothing. They put you in the Halifax team, then Halifax win. They put you in at Widnes, then Widnes win. I don't care how great they think they are, without you putting that ball down over the line and scoring tries, they do not win.' Hanley the businessman was just as unrelenting as the player. And the advice he gave Offiah revealed an athlete who knew his worth in an era when Black talent was starting to call the shots.

Offiah was one of the few players who had an agent, while Hanley had signed with Ambrose Mendy, another agent who also looked after other high-profile sports stars, including footballers Paul Ince and John Fashanu, Olympic sprinter Linford Christie and boxer Nigel Benn, collectively known as the Black Pack. Mendy was streetwise, quick witted and knew when an opportunity presented itself. He was branded a Buppie (a Black Yuppie) and seemed to embody a Black embrace of Thatcherism. His office was a converted loft space in London Bridge, he owned a huge house with a swimming pool in Wanstead, drove a Mercedes and would charm journalists with great quotes. 'It's a dog-eat-dog bullshit society,' he once said, 'so you've got to take as much as you can for as little as you can fairly give.'[28] Mendy spotted that Black British celebrities were emerging as a force not just in sports, but in other areas of popular culture.

In the earlier part of the Thatcher era, only a handful of Black names had mainstream recognition – comedian Lenny Henry was a household name, as was boxer Frank Bruno, while newsreaders Sir Trevor MacDonald and Moira Stuart spoke to huge audiences every night. But by 1986 things were changing. Fashion, for decades a place where Black women were all but invisible, was now championing a Black British supermodel: Naomi Campbell who, along with Linda Evangelista, Cindy Crawford and Christy Turlington, dominated catwalks and campaigns during the 1980s and 90s. At the turn of the decade, Evangelista was quoted as saying she 'wouldn't get out of bed for less than $10,000' – a line she has since denied, but it reinforced her and Campbell's status as truly global stars who could demand astronomical sums. Sade, the British-Nigerian soul singer, had also become a worldwide star by 1986 with her sultry, elegant tracks defining the era's soul sound, along with Soul II Soul. Her first two albums sold two million copies each. In Spike Lee's 1989 film *Do The Right Thing*, a drama about racial tensions in Brooklyn, a DJ shouts out the artists he loves – Sade and the Birmingham reggae act Steel Pulse are the only two British acts named.

Martin Offiah and Ellery Hanley – two players in a relatively little-known sport – were part of that wave of Black celebrity. By the turn of the decade, the pair featured on the nation's TV screens, transcending the sports world of *Grandstand*. They appeared side by side on the ITV gameshow, *Gladiators*, in which contestants braved a demanding assault course and competed against professional athletes – a programme watched by fourteen million people across the country at its peak. The pair were often seen together at boxing matches, invited backstage to hang out with socialite Patsy Kensit and musician Liam Gallagher. Offiah accepted a string of modelling jobs, including a nude shoot for *Cosmopolitan* magazine, for which he was ridiculed within Rugby League, the most macho of sports.[29]

He also did interviews with *The Voice*, a Black British newspaper which brought him to the attention of readers who might never have heard of Rugby League. Hanley had real cachet too. When the World League of American Football started a franchise in the UK called the London Monarchs, it was Hanley who they approached to be their star player. The move didn't work out, but it was proof of what he'd told Offiah: they were valuable assets.

While Hanley helped snap the sport out of a malaise, Offiah was committed to take it out of its comfort zone and the Widnes player was slowly moving out of the shadow of Hanley by the turn of the decade. Hanley might have been the one to open Offiah's eyes to his worth as a brand, but Offiah was a quick study. 'I spent a lot of time in Leeds. He had the flash car, he had a villa in Leeds, he had all the trappings,' Offiah says of Hanley. 'He had a sauna and steam room in his own house – this was something to aspire to. Then I went on to better him: I had a house with an indoor swimming pool, a steam room and a jacuzzi.' He signed a lucrative sponsorship deal

Martin Offiah (left) and Ellery Hanley celebrate after their 26-12 victory against Australia on 9 July 1988

with Nike, and featured in an advert campaign that also starred basketball superstar Michael Jordan: the biggest sporting figure of the 90s.[30] The poster showed Offiah running with a ball under his arm, both his legs a blur beneath him with the tagline: 'Your Hands Can't Catch What Your Eyes Can't See'.[31]

As Offiah, Hanley and the Bleep and Bass producers carved out a new space for Black Britons, Margaret Thatcher's hold over the Conservative Party was slipping. The seemingly unstoppable prime minister would be brought down by internal wrangling over Europe, aided by resentment of her domineering leadership style. The leader who had won three elections, torn up the post-war consensus and reshaped Britain, resigned after a row over whether the UK should join the single currency – the idea that European nations should replace their legal tender with one unifying currency called the Euro.

Her once-loyal Chancellor Geoffrey Howe, who'd been sidelined and was often on the receiving end of dressing downs in cabinet, would signal the beginning of the end with his resignation.[32] After clashing with Thatcher over the policy, which he was in favour of, Howe delivered a fatal attack on Thatcher in the House of Commons. Howe used a cricket metaphor to illustrate his frustration with Thatcher's public hostility to Europe, which he saw as thwarting the work he and others were doing to build connections on the continent. 'Mr Speaker. I believe the chancellor and the governor [of the Bank of England] are cricketing enthusiasts, so I hope there is no monopoly on cricketing metaphors,' he said. 'It is rather like sending your opening batsmen to the crease only for them to find, the moment the first balls are bowled, that their bats have been broken before the game, by the team captain.'

In the following days, terrible polling put the Conservatives 21 per cent behind Neil Kinnock's Labour. There was a brief leadership contest, in which Thatcher gained more votes than her rival – the former 'Minister for Merseyside' Michael Heseltine – but not enough votes to produce a comprehensive victory. After a showdown with advisors and allies, in which it became apparent that the

Iron Lady no longer had the backing of her lieutenants – many of whom thought she might lose a second round against Heseltine – it was clear she would not survive. Within nine days of Howe's address, Thatcher had resigned, and an era was over.

On her final day in Number 10, Thatcher found out just how quickly politics moves on. 'Early that morning I went down from the flat to my study for the last time to check that nothing had been left behind,' she wrote in her memoir. 'It was a shock to find that I could not get in because the key had already been taken off my key-ring.'[33] When Thatcher left 10 Downing Street the sound of Bleep and Bass was reverberating around the country. The week she departed, 808 State – the group that Gerald Simpson was part of – were hovering around the Top 10 with their track 'Cubik'. She was succeeded as prime minister not by Heseltine, but by John Major.

Some in Black Britain embraced Thatcher's worldview and vision for the country. Shortly after her death in 2013, Jazzie B said in an interview, 'It's quite interesting that in the aftermath of Thatcher's death, I'm reminded that, technically speaking, she legitimised people like me. We set up a small business in an institutionally racist environment where it was difficult to get a job you wanted. The idea was to do it yourself.'[34] The confidence and swagger of Black Britons like Ambrose Mendy and Martin Offiah fit in with the image of Thatcherism, but the fundamental question of whether Black people could ever be truly British – already alive before she came into office – was still being fiercely contested at the end of the Thatcher era.

Diane Abbott, Paul Boateng and Bernie Grant's election victories in 1987 were a landmark for Labour, but by 1990 there were still no Black Conservative members of the House of Commons. In an effort to address the dearth of Black Tories, the Conservative Party central office suggested the Birmingham-based lawyer John Taylor to the Cheltenham branch as the candidate in their constituency for the next general election. Taylor had served as a councillor in Birmingham, and spent time in Whitehall, where he worked as an advisor for the Home Office. But a row was sparked when local businessman Bill Galbraith, who was a cousin of Britain's junior Scottish secretary, described Taylor in public as a 'bloody nigger'.[35] He refused to withdraw his remarks, saying 'I don't think having [a Black] as candidate is good for our town.'[36]

A few months before a tearful Thatcher left Downing Street for good, one of her closest allies and a hardliner on race, Norman Tebbit, gave an interview where he voiced the tenuous status of Black Britishness. Tebbit was asked about an *Independent on Sunday* poll that showed huge anti-immigration sentiment in the country, results he said which could lead to unrest. 'Where you have a clash of history, a clash of religion, a clash of race,' he said, 'then it's all too easy for there to be an actual clash of violence. A nation is a nation because of what it shares in common.'[37]

He devised the 'cricket test', as it would come to be known, a crude measurement of whether an immigrant was loyal to Britain or their (or their parents') home country. Would they support England's cricket team rather than India, Pakistan or the West Indies? 'Which side do they cheer for? It's an interesting test. Are you still harking back to where you came from or where you are?' The question was as blunt as his 'get on your bike' speech after the unrest of 1981 – but it spoke to an attitude that was prevalent in British life: Black people would be tolerated as long as they assimilated.

There were still reminders that even those who had found success could be targeted. The Olympic sprinter Linford Christie was subjected to a prolonged campaign by *The Sun* newspaper that constantly wrote articles about the size of his 'lunchbox', referring to his penis. Meanwhile, gay footballer Justin Fashanu faced heavy criticism from *The Voice* newspaper after coming out. Tragically, he died by suicide in 1998.

Bleep and Bass's emergence during the acid house and rave boom, and the success of Martin Offiah and Ellery Hanley, showed that there was another vision of Britain evolving alongside and at odds with Tebbit's limited view. You didn't have to compromise your culture; you could add it to what already existed. By the end of the 1980s, music producers like Nightmares on Wax no longer found themselves atomised, as Black artists had done during the early part of the decade. They'd been embraced in a scene where racial boundaries could be circumvented. Black British culture was becoming British culture; an organic, multicultural version pliant enough to absorb and be reshaped by influences from across the globe. It's the Britain we see now in most of our major cities, it's the music we hear on our radio stations and on the stages at our biggest festivals.

In the same interview in which he reflects on Margaret Thatcher's death, Jazzie B was asked about the success he experienced as a musician. 'It wasn't just that Soul II Soul could only have happened in Britain, it could only have happened in London. It's the shop window for the rest of the world,' he said. His answer is telling. This London-centric view of Black British culture and its influence is still prevalent. It maintains that the capital represents the centre of Black Britishness, from where it gets beamed out to the rest of the country and around the world. But his answer ignores the fact that Bleep and Bass was selling thousands of records at the same time his group emerged, and that Unique 3 were signed to the same label. During the Thatcher era, Black British culture was reshaping every corner of the country – from Cardiff and Wolverhampton to Bradford and the Lake District. Often, it would be met with resistance from institutions and other artistic movements, but each of those battles created an opening. 'We throw stones and then a door opens and a few people are pulled through,' Vanley Burke told me about the activism he captured in Birmingham during the 1970s. 'Then the door is slammed and we throw some more stones and it continues.' By the end of the 1980s, thanks to the confidence and persistence of Black Britain, the hinges of that door were starting to loosen.

In June 2019, I stood in a parched Somerset field. Night had fallen, and there was a palpable shift in the atmosphere at Glastonbury Festival. As the sun went down, I was among thousands of people trying to find a space in front of the Other Stage, squeezing in where they could; the English electronic duo The Chemical Brothers were about to come on for their headlining set.

After a long, meandering intro, bright purple visuals kick in: huge polygon figures sprint towards the audience as the juddering bassline from the band's hit single 'Go!' blasts out of the sound system. A breakbeat thuds underneath, while New York rapper Q-Tip flows effortlessly over the track. An hour into the set there's a lull, until the band launch into 'Saturate', with its bleeping keyboard line and stabs of sub-bass, which brings the crowd back. All the elements of Bleep and Bass are here: rib-tickling bass, hip-hop's swagger and a beat that would work in a techno or house production.[38] It's polished and preened, the rougher edges of Nightmares on Wax's early productions removed and integrated into the most exciting live act in dance music.

Unsurprisingly, The Chemical Brothers – teenagers when Unique 3's 'The Theme' came out in 1988 – took inspiration from the Bleep and Bass artists. The scene itself was short lived – by the end of 1991 producers had moved on and the sound evolved – and many of the acts that defined it have slipped from the historical record. But the influence of Bleep and Bass on today's musical acts continues, and not just at Glastonbury. Look at any British musical movement of the last thirty years and you'll find elements of those stark records that emerged from Yorkshire in the late 1980s. When Winston Hazel ventured out beyond the Black ring of security, he couldn't have known he would play a part in reshaping British culture. His goal was more personal. 'It was a desire to find your own identity. That you can say is your own, that me and my mates related to. It was trying to form your own identity within your own tribe.'

Others were more aware of the impact they were having at the time. Evelyn tells a story of being at a warehouse party in Leeds and looking out across the floor at the dancers' frenzied reaction to 'Dextrous'. 'I'm looking at this party going off and there's a mishmash of people like nothing I've ever seen before,' he told me. There were skinheads, Leeds United football hooligans and his dreadlocked friend from home next to each other, dancing together.

'It was just like, shit – something's going on,' he said. 'I was scared of all that ecstasy thing. It wasn't part of my culture, but it had come into my culture. Now all of a sudden it was connected to my music.' After another rave, in a Blackburn abattoir, he was driving down a motorway, in convoy with his friends. Everyone was on a high after hearing their friend's music being blasted out into the Lancashire night; they'd gone from a few hundred people in Leeds dancing to their tunes to thousands every weekend. He stuck his head out of the window and let the cold air cool him down. This must have been what the 1960s counter-culture felt like, he told himself. Evelyn and the other Bleep and Bass producers were part of a revolution. This wasn't about flower power, LSD or student revolt, but through their music they helped lead the way for Black British culture to be accepted as British culture.

That same year at Glastonbury, the grime artist Stormzy headlined the Pyramid Stage – one of the most coveted slots in live music – becoming one of only a handful of Black Brits to receive top billing. I watched as he brought out gospel singers dressed all in white. He wore a stab-proof vest created by the street artist Banksy, and delivered his verses while staring into the barrel of the cameras as thousands watched at home.

Again, some of the Bleep and Bass elements were there: pulverising bass, grime's bleeping keyboard lines. There was a direct line from the work of Unique 3 in Bradford and this musician from South London, four decades later. This was a star, a man who'd taken the path forged by Martin Offiah and made it wider. Stormzy remixed it, combined it with the Black British culture that emerged in the Thatcher era and evolved it again. Even though few people would put The Chemical Brothers and Stormzy in the same musical conversation, here they were drawing from the same set of influences that had their roots in the former industrialised north, in cities like my hometown of Bradford.

As I stood in the crowd, I remembered something Stuart Hall had said in 1986 during a BBC interview. 'We are not prepared any longer to take a marginal role in institutions which like to, as it were acknowledge us just in a token way: when they want a flash of the exotic or the tropical to enliven a cold damp evening. We are here to stay,' he said. 'We are in the centre of the creative and cultural life of the society ... we want the path open, especially for the young people of this society. The young Black people in this society, who have created in their myriad art forms, from writing poetry, dance music, right through to rap, created a new culture. Culture which, in its variety and power, astonishes now the eyes of young white people in the society, which is a mark, a sign that they are the people of the future.'

We started with dancers moving slowly back under the spotlight at an old ballroom in Wigan. A decade later the Britain they knew had disappeared. Yes, Thatcher and her cabinet had driven much of the change, but so had Black Britons. Music, fashion, television, sport, politics had all evolved. The events of 1989 were further evidence of that: the brilliance of Ellery Hanley and Martin Offiah and the music of the Bleep and Bass artists, showed that, hundreds of miles from the cultural centre of London, in small mill towns, former mining communities, rural locations and cities built on the spoils of British Imperialism, Black British culture was evolving into an unignorable force. As Stuart Hall declared in 1986, Black British figures were 'the people of the future', and thirty years later, on the Pyramid Stage at Glastonbury, Hall's vision of a Black British future had arrived.

We Were There: Coda

In early June 2020, during the Covid-19 pandemic, I got on a hire bike and cycled from my home in east London to Parliament Square. I went with my wife and a couple of friends. We rode through Cable Street in Bethnal Green on to Embankment and then up into Whitehall. We joined thousands of others who had come. The murder of George Floyd by a police officer in Minneapolis, triggered mass protests all over the globe. I stood for around an hour – mostly in silence – holding a placard with the name 'David Oluwale' on it. I cannot remember why I chose the name of the Nigerian man who'd been hounded to his death by two West Yorkshire Police officers. Perhaps it was because of the way he'd died and its connection to Floyd. Maybe it was because he was a Yoruba man like my father. Very likely, it was both.

When I got home, I looked at social media and saw many of my friends had also been there. Meanwhile, the then Home Secretary Priti Patel had said the event was 'disgusting'. After posting a picture of me at the event, holding the placard, I started to get messages. The vast majority were supportive, while many wanted to know who this man was.

I was angry for days afterwards. The protest itself had been calm and respectful: small groups of people had walked around quietly handing out masks and hand sanitiser. That anger wasn't generated from the event, it was the immediate aftermath and the fact a name like Oluwale's *could* be unknown in Britain. Since the Black Lives Matter protests in the summer of 2020, there has been a surge of interest in Black British history, but the focus has been history that stretches back centuries, to the Tudors, the Regency and the Reformation. Those stories show the true depth of Black British presence on these islands. But in the history of the twentieth century, events such as the death of David Oluwale – that seem like they happened just yesterday – matter, and tell us about Britain and the country's relationship to its Black population.

Since 2022, there have been warnings from newspaper columnists and editorials that we're 'going back to the 1970s'. Seemingly endless strikes, spiking inflation and climbing unemployment – everywhere you look there's what newspapers like to call 'eerie echoes' of the decade. There is some truth to the caution. Throughout 2022 and 2023 there have been a large number of strikes, spanning rail unions to junior doctors, but they've caused nowhere near the disruption seen during the Winter of Discontent. Inflation did rise rapidly, but it was nothing compared to even the early 1990s, and it dropped almost as quickly as it increased. Unemployment sits at around 4.4 per cent now, and although that masks the true number – there are millions of Britons of working age who don't have a job – but the unemployment peak during the Thatcher era was far worse.

But one thing that does bear comparison is Britain's idea of itself and its place in the world. Just as when Thatcher came into office, the UK has once again suffered a loss of status. Its international standing has been harmed by Brexit, while its economy and self-esteem have hit lows not seen for decades – possibly since the late 1970s, where this book started. We've not 'been here before' but we have been somewhere similar, and that wasn't a good place for Black Britain. In the late 1970s the 'lack of prestige' that came after Britain lost its place as a major actor on the world stage upset the likes of Norman Tebbit, and saw Britain turn to Thatcher, who seemed to offer solutions.

The UK is once again at a turning point: there's a new Labour government after fourteen years of Conservative rule. But a hard-right party has also claimed 14 per cent of the vote and is running almost exclusively on an agenda of immigration, or, more specifically, ending it. The anti-immigrant sentiment of the 1970s never truly went away, and it's telling that the 'political hero' of Nigel Farage – the man who is leading the anti-immigration crusade – was Enoch Powell.[1]

At the time of writing, far-right groups have seized on the murder of three young girls in Southport to spread misinformation and incite riots across the country, once again attacking Black and brown British communities. Violent scenes from Manchester to Middlesbrough have left commentators wondering how this could happen. Of course, we've been here before – many times, from 1919 to 1981 and beyond. *We Were There* shows how Black Britain and its allies have fought back – and can continue to do so.

But the Britain we find ourselves in now has changed. Even as its status in the international arena slides, new forms of British identity are being birthed. The Black Caribbean influence on Black Britain has been overtaken by new waves of immigrants from West and East Africa. Black Britain's music, its food, its cultural ambassadors are more likely to have Igbo or Somali surnames than those from Jamaica or Trinidad. The demographic sands have also shifted around the country. London is no longer the place where the majority of Black British people live: more than 50 per cent of Black people live outside of the capital. A significant change – and one that should make those in power ask if they're doing enough to make sure Black voices are heard. This book shows the consequences of what happens when they don't. It also demonstrates what Peter Fryer dubbed 'staying power', that ability for Black Britons to persist in the face of what, at times, must have felt like an onslaught of hostility.[2] That tells us a new and profound truth about Black Britain in the Thatcher era: yes, there's courageousness and creativity, but there's also a love for this country – not necessarily as it is, but as it *could* be. It has already been forever changed because we were there.

End Notes

Introduction

1 'Unemployment Statistics', *Hansard*, HC Debate 24 February 1981, 999 cc317-8W1981: https://api.parliament.uk/historic-hansard/written-answers/1981/feb/24/unemployment-statistics [accessed 21 September 2024].
2 Tobi Thomas, 'Black youth unemployment rate of 40% similar to time of Brixton riots, data shows', the *Guardian*, 11 April 2021: https://www.theguardian.com/society/2021/apr/11/black-youth-unemployment-rate-brixton-riots-covid [accessed 21 September 2024].
3 William Keegan, 'It's just like the 1980s – except the riots have begun already', the *Guardian*, 14 November 2010: https://www.theguardian.com/business/2010/nov/14/william-keegan-just-like-the-1980s [accessed 21 September 2024].
4 Dalya Alberge, 'Half of Britons can't name a Black British historical figure, survey finds', the *Guardian*, 26 October 2023: https://www.theguardian.com/uk-news/2023/oct/26/half-of-britons-cant-name-a-black-british-historical-figure-survey-finds [accessed 21 September 2024].

1. Northern Souls – 1977

1 Although HMT *Windrush* is the ship considered by many to have started the wave of immigration from the Caribbean, it was preceded by two others in 1947: the SS *Ormonde* and the *Almanzora*.
2 Michael Hann, 'Leon Bridges and Curtis Harding: the new stars of classic soul', the *Guardian*, 18 June 2015: https://www.theguardian.

com/music/2015/jun/18/leon-bridges-curtis-harding-the-new-stars-of-classic-soul [accessed 5 September 2024].

3 Martin Horsfield, 'Wigan Casino voted greatest disco in the world', the *Guardian*, 15 June 2011: https://www.theguardian.com/music/2011/jun/15/wigan-greatest-disco [accessed 5 September 2024].

4 Commonwealth Immigrants Act 1962: https://www.legislation.gov.uk/ukpga/1962/21/enacted [accessed 5 September 2024].

5 Attlee and his Labour government accepted the migrants' Britishness but viewed them as opportunists who were taking advantage of a loophole. In truth, Attlee and his cabinet's vision of this new Britain was one re-energised by white Commonwealth migrants from Canada, Australia and New Zealand, not Black Britons.

6 Kathleen Paul, *Whitewashing Britain*, Cornell University Press, 1997.

7 Mr Andrew Turner MP, Immigration debate in the House of Commons, *Hansard*, 19 March 2003: https://api.parliament.uk/historic-hansard/westminster-hall/2003/mar/19/immigration [accessed 5 September 2024].

8 Richard A. Butler (Rab Butler), 'Commonwealth Migrants' internal memo, 6 October 1961: https://discovery.nationalarchives.gov.uk/details/r/D7659351 [accessed 5 September 2024].

9 Author and former Casino regular David Nowell described what made Wigan so special in his memoir, *Too Darn Soulful* (Robson Books, 2001, p. 133).

10 Daniel Trilling, *Bloody Nasty People: The Rise of Britain's Far Right*, Verso Books, 2012.

11 Michael Billig, 'Patterns of Racism: Interviews with National Front Members', *Race & Class*, 20(2), 161–79 (1978): https://doi.org/10.1177/030639687802000205 [accessed 5 September 2024].

12 Gavin Watson's photography book *Skins* (Music Press Books, 2015) follows the evolution of one racially diverse skinhead crew in Buckinghamshire in the 1970s and 80s.

13 The less explicitly racist Oi! movement, made up of skinhead punk bands, couldn't avoid the violence that accompanied the wider scene. In 1981, a group of Oi! bands played a gig in the South Asian area

of Southall in West London, which resulted in sixty-one police officers injured, seventy people arrested and the pub the groups played in being burned to the ground by anti-fascists from Southall Youth Movement.

14 Leroy Rosenior and Leo Moynihan, *It's only banter: The Autobiography of Leroy Rosenior*, Pitch Publishing, 2017.

15 The threat that the far right and skinheads posed was real and not only confined to the football terraces. A trades union report into racial violence in East London from 1976 to 1978 found one hundred incidents of people being attacked, usually by 'apolitical white youths' who'd been influenced by their 'unconscious absorption of the relentless propaganda'. Between 1976 and 1981, thirty-one Black and Asian people had been murdered by racists in Southall, Brick Lane, Swindon, Manchester and Leeds, according to Peter Fryer's *Staying Power*.

16 Twisted Wheel was the stomping ground of Roger Eagle, the Svengali-like, blues-obsessed DJ who had a huge influence in the city.

17 Music was deeply rooted in Rhonda's family. Her mother, Blanche Finlay, a jazz singer, won a scholarship to come to the UK to study psychiatric nursing. Her younger sister, DJ Paulette, would go on to become one of Manchester's most influential DJs in the 1990s, playing at the renowned LGBT night, Flesh.

18 One day, she came home from an excursion and found police at the door – her parents had reported her missing. Eventually, she struck a deal with her father: she'd always tell him where she was going, so there'd be no surprises. 'I mean, he still wasn't happy about it, but he accepted that I would be going,' she told me.

19 Les Back, 'White men can jump . . . but only when they're dancing to northern soul', the *Guardian* [archive], 1 December 1997.

20 Another part of the story is how white cultural figures, especially in the rock world, contributed to the problem of racism. In April 1976, David Bowie told reporters that the UK could 'benefit from a fascist leader' (https://www.theguardian.com/music/2023/aug/16/pop-stars-absurd-political-gaffes-nazi-bowie-nixon-brown-killers-brandon-flowers-georgia). The most infamous moment, however, came from

blues guitarist Eric Clapton, who had recently covered Bob Marley and the Wailers' 'I Shot the Sheriff'. While performing at the Birmingham Odeon in August 1976, Clapton drunkenly declared that Britain was becoming a 'Black colony' and that he wanted 'the foreigners out' (https://ultimateclassicrock.com/eric-clapton-rant-rock-against-racism/).

21 Margaret Thatcher, Granada *World in Action* interview, 27 January 1978: https://www.margaretthatcher.org/document/103485 [accessed 21 September 2024].

22 When asked by the BBC what part the 'swamped' debate had played in the victory, she replied: 'Not a tremendously significant part. I think what it has shown is that we are prepared to speak out and tackle difficult issues.'

23 Raymond Walter Apple Jr., 'Worried British Send 5,000 Police to Election Area', *The New York Times*, 26 February 1978: https://www.nytimes.com/1978/02/26/archives/worried-british-send-5000-police-to-election-area-all-marches-are.html [accessed 21 September 2024].

24 Margaret Thatcher, *Remarks on Ilford North By-election Victory*, 3 March 1978: https://www.margaretthatcher.org/document/103488 [accessed 21 September 2024].

25 Lindsay Mackie, 'Tackle race problems to avoid US-style violence, says Walker', the *Guardian* [archive], 3 March 1978.

26 *Ibid.*

27 'Five-fold plan to help integration of immigrants', the *Guardian* [archive], 1 February 1965.

28 Bernard Coard, *How the West Indian Child is Made Educationally Subnormal in the British School System*, McDermott Publishing, 1971.

29 There were exceptions: Obeng ran the Night Owl Soul Club in Stockport for twenty-five years and, along with record collector Tim Ashibende – who supplied many of the scene's DJs – was part of the underground network that powered Northern Soul.

30 'Minister of Sound', *The Observer* [archive], 23 June 2002.

31 After Norman Jay's trip to Wigan, he returned to London and started the Good Times sound system, playing soul music to majority-Black crowds at Notting Hill Carnival.

32 Letter titled 'Chuck Out The North!' by Grace Maynard from Birmingham, *Black Music*, March 1975.
33 Lloyd Bradley, *Bass Culture*, Viking, 2000.
34 An excellent account of the Huddersfield sound system scene can be found in the book *Sound System Culture*, One Love Books, 2013.
35 Carmichael's speech at the Roundhouse in 1967 was a catalyst for the British Black Power Movement, which took root as Northern Soul was coming of age. A year after Carmichael's address calling for Black unity in the face of imperialism, British-Nigerian activist Obi Egbuna and Trinidadian Darcus Howe, formed the British Black Panthers in London. The group had several offshoots, including the United Coloured People's Association whose branch members in Manchester stormed the city's cathedral in 1968, demanding better housing for Black people and, like Bernard Coard would argue a few years later, education free from racial bias. During the protest, they wore black leather berets and jackets like the Black Panthers. A silent, stunned crowd of parishioners looked on as they raised their clenched fists, shouting the Black Power slogan: 'Power to the people. Power to the Black People.'
36 Stokely Carmichael, *Speaking at the Dialectics of Liberation*, British Library, 1967: https://www.bl.uk/collection-items/stokely-carmichael-speaking-at-the-dialectics-of-liberation-1967 [accessed 5 September 2024].
37 Phil Harrel, 'Fight The Power: A Tale Of 2 Anthems (With The Same Name)', *NPR*, 7 December 2018: https://www.npr.org/2018/12/07/673845242/fight-the-power-american-anthem-public-enemy-isley-brothers [accessed 21 September 2024].
38 Obeng's hunch about his fellow dancers was probably accurate. In the aftermath of the Notting Hill race riots of 1958, a Gallup survey found that 71 per cent of people disapproved of mixed-race marriages.
39 Shirin Hirsch and Geoff Brown, 'Breaking the "colour bar": Len Johnson, Manchester and anti-racism', *Race & Class*, 64(3), 36–58 (2023): https://doi.org/10.1177/03063968221139993 [accessed 5 September 2024].

40 David Jesudason, 'What was the Colour Bar?', *CAMRA*: https://camra.org.uk/learn-discover/the-basics/what-was-the-colour-bar-2/ [accessed 21 September 2024].

41 'Notting Hill Carnival ends in riot', BBC, 30 August 1976: https://news.bbc.co.uk/onthisday/hi/dates/stories/august/30/newsid_2511000/2511059.stm [accessed 21 September 2024].

42 Based on an account in Lloyd Bradley's *Bass Culture*, Viking, 2000, p. 433.

43 The Clash's 1980 docudrama *Rude Boy* captures their Rock Against Racism performance and the racial tensions that existed within the punk scene.

44 Don Letts, Red Bull Music Academy lecture, 2010: https://www.redbullmusicacademy.com/lectures/don-letts-punk-politics [accessed 21 September 2024].

45 Bill Brewster and Frank Broughton, *Last Night a DJ Saved My Life*, Headline, 22 May 2006.

46 Francesco Mellina, *Last Night at Wigan Casino*, March Design, 2022: https://www.march-design.co.uk/portfolio_page/wigan-casino/ [accessed 21 September 2024].

2. Free George Lindo – Bradford, 1978

1 With a score by a then-unknown Peter Frampton.

2 Ashley Clark, 'Scenes from a hostile environment: a history of Black British protest film and television', BFI, *Sight & Sound*, 7 August 2020: https://www.bfi.org.uk/sight-and-sound/features/scenes-hostile-environment-history-black-british-protest-film-television [accessed 21 September 2024].

3 Hollie West, 'Britannica's Dark Side', the *Washington Post*, 2 June 1979: https://www.washingtonpost.com/archive/lifestyle/1979/06/02/britannicas-dark-side/a14a74fe-f883-4df1-abff-4f3e5d2e8055/ [accessed 14 September 2024].

4 David Koff and Msindo Mwinyipembe, 'The Black Scholar Interviews: David Koff & Msindo Mwinyipembe', *The Black Scholar*, 10(8/9), 68–80

(May 1979): https://www.jstor.org/stable/41066311 [accessed 20 September 2024].
5. Ted Cantle, *Community Cohesion: A Report of the Independent Review Team*, December 2001 (also known as the Cantle Report): https://tedcantle.co.uk/pdf/communitycohesion%20cantlereport.pdf [accessed 14 September 2024].
6. Simon Jenkins, 'Could Bradford be the Shoreditch of Yorkshire – or is it the next Detroit?', the *Guardian*, 3 May 2018: https://www.theguardian.com/cities/2018/may/03/could-bradford-be-the-shoreditch-of-yorkshire-or-is-it-the-next-detroit- [accessed 14 September 2024].
7. 'Channel 4 to Make Bradford British', Channel 4, 3 November 2011: https://www.channel4.com/press/news/channel-4-make-bradford-british [accessed 24 September 2024].
8. Anuskha Astana, 'Britain becoming more segregated than 15 years ago, says race expert', the *Guardian*, 23 May 2016: https://www.theguardian.com/world/2016/may/23/britain-more-segregated-15-years-race-expert-riots-ted-cantle [accessed 14 September 2024].
9. Adam Gabbatt, 'British winter was the coldest for 31 years', the *Guardian*, 2 March 2010: https://www.theguardian.com/uk/2010/mar/02/british-winter-coldest-30-years [accessed 14 September 2024].
10. David McKie, 'A keen nose for the winds of change', the *Guardian* [archive], 6 April 1976.
11. Mark Keighley, *Wool City*, G Whitaker and Company Ltd, 2007. The full report, 'The Atkins Report on the Strategic Future of the Wool Textile Industry' (University of Southampton, 1969) can be accessed at https://archive.org/details/op1268106-1001/page/n5/mode/2up.
12. Diane Coyle, 'When Britain Went Bust', *Financial Times*, 9 January 2017: https://www.ft.com/content/3b583050-d277-11e6-b06b-680c49b4b4c0 [accessed 24 September 2024].
13. The name *Blacks Britannica* was a play on *Pax Britannica* – the hundred-year period of relative peace in British-controlled colonies and protectorates that began in 1815.
14. *Thatcher: A Very British Revolution*, BBC: https://www.bbc.co.uk/programmes/m0005brf [accessed 24 September 2024].

15 The academic Paul Gilroy coined a term for the phenomenon: Postcolonial Melancholia. He argued that this romanticising of Britain's past Empire and its standing in the world had led to an 'insidious blockage in British culture', one that involved cherishing 'a resolutely air-brushed version of colonial history in which gunboat diplomacy was moral uplift, civilising missions were completed, the trains ran on time and the natives appreciated the value of stability.'
16 Charles Moore, *Margaret Thatcher: The Authorised Biography, Volume One: Not For Turning*, Allen Lane, 2013.
17 Margaret Thatcher, Speech to Conservative Party Conference, 12 October 1979: https://www.margaretthatcher.org/document/104147 [accessed 14 September 2024].
18 Margaret Thatcher, 'My Kind of Conservatism', *The Observer* [archive], 25 February 1979.
19 Michael Nally, 'National Front gains worry Bradford', *The Observer* [archive], 9 May 1976.
20 *Searchlight*, June 1975.
21 Mark Townsend, 'How the battle of Lewisham helped to halt the rise of Britain's far right', *The Observer*, 13 August 2017: https://www.theguardian.com/uk-news/2017/aug/13/battle-of-lewisham-national-front-1977-far-right-london-police [accessed 4 September 2024].
22 Shortly before the Lewisham march, a local council by-election in Deptford saw the far right secure 44.5 per cent of the vote, split between the National Front (NF) and the National Party. Although it wasn't enough to defeat Labour, it relegated the Conservatives to fourth place. The march led to a day of chaos, with bottles, bricks, and smoke bombs flying through the streets of the capital as the National Front was humbled. They turned up with 500 protestors, but despite their perceived local support, 4,000 counter-protestors took to the streets and prevented the NF from marching.
23 Kay Mellor's sex worker drama, *Band of Gold*, was set on Lumb Lane in the 1990s.
24 The concept of the frontline became so synonymous with Black Britain that Virgin Records created an imprint called 'Frontline', featuring

End Notes

a logo of a clenched fist grasping barbed wire and a tagline that read: 'the sounds of reality'.

25 Victor Wedderburn, 'Victor Wedderburn's photo archive captures Lumb Lane of the era', *Telegraph and Argus*: https://www.thetelegraphandargus.co.uk/news/23691578.victor-captures-camera-once-thriving-community/#gallery10 [accessed 24 September 2024].

26 Jim Greenhalf, 'A day of marching and mayhem', *Telegraph and Argus*, 24 April 2013: https://www.thetelegraphandargus.co.uk/tahistory/10375211.a-day-of-marching-and-mayhem/ [accessed 24 September 2024].

27 Details from the article, 'The Interrogators: How a policeman could make even YOU confess', *The Sunday Times* [archive], 10 August 1980.

28 Details from an interview with Lindo, 'George Lindo Speaks', *Bradford Black*, 2(4), 44–45 (March 1979).

29 Tony Geraghty, 'Bad day for a patrol officer in Rhodesian police', the *Guardian* [archive], 15 November 1965.

30 'Appeal Court frees four Blacks', the *Guardian* [archive], 31 July 1973.

31 Matt Foot, 'Corrupt Cops', *London Review of Books*, 8 February 2024, www.lrb.co.uk/the-paper/v46/n03/matt-foot/short-cuts.

32 His case is one of the most notorious in the history of British policing and led to two police officers being found guilty of assault, a landmark ruling that is still held up by campaigners as the last time an officer was successfully convicted after a death in police custody.

33 Chapeltown News Collective, 'Verdicts a Victory', *Chapeltown News*, No. 37, August 1976: https://harehills111.files.wordpress.com/2016/12/august-1976.pdf [accessed 5 September 2024].

34 'The Interrogators: How a policeman could make even YOU confess', *The Sunday Times* [archive], 10 August 1980.

35 Report of the West India Royal Commission (the Moyne Report), 1945: https://www.bl.uk/collection-items/the-moyne-report [accessed 31 August 2024].

36 Vicky Iglikowski-Broad and Rowena Hillel, 'Rights, resistance and racism: the story of the Mangrove Nine', *The National Archives*: https://blog.nationalarchives.gov.uk/rights-resistance-racism-story-mangrove-nine/ [accessed 5 September 2024].

37 A defence committee had been formed for Howe when he was imprisoned after an altercation with a barrister a few months before Lindo was sentenced. The committee created an international campaign on his behalf and peppered politicians with letters asking for support, which led to his release on appeal.

38 Darcus Howe, 'Enter Mrs Thatcher', *Race Today*, 10(3), (March 1978): https://catalogue.georgepadmoreinstitute.org/records/JOU/1/1/99 [accessed 20 September 2024].

39 Maya Jaggi, 'Poet on The Frontline', the *Guardian*, 4 May 2002: https://www.theguardian.com/books/2002/may/04/poetry.books [accessed 5 September 2024].

40 Philip Stevens and Carole F. Willis, 'Race, Crime and Arrests', *Research Studies*, Great Britain Home Office, 31 December 1979.

41 When that decision was made public it caused outrage. Robert Kilroy-Silk, then a young MP who would later become a daytime television host and co-found the UK Independence Party, asked the Attorney General why the facts of Mr George Lindo's innocence were withheld from his solicitors. He was informed that because Brierley was the 'junior member of the team' and hadn't taken the confession, the decision was made to withhold the information. The deputy chief constable of the West Yorkshire Metropolitan Police added that it 'should in no circumstances be disclosed to the defence'.

42 Duncan Campbell, 'It shattered me: Winston Trew on the decades-long fight to clear his name', the *Guardian*, 13 October 2019: https://www.theguardian.com/world/2019/oct/13/winston-trew-to-clear-his-name [accessed 21 September 2024].

43 He later told *Newsweek* that he 'was concerned with the film's endorsement of a Marxist viewpoint'; while after the July 1978 broadcast, WGBH president David Ives appeared on-screen to comment that 'the issue [was] not censorship but editorial control and integrity': https://www.artforum.com/columns/black-power-white-fear-204048/

44 J. Anthony Lukas, *Common Ground: A Turbulent Decade in the Lives of Three American Families*, Vintage, 1986.

45 'Sir Dudley Smith, Conservative MP – obituary', the *Daily Telegraph*, 19 December 2016: https://www.telegraph.co.uk/obituaries/2016/12/19/sir-dudley-smith-conservative-mp-obituary/ [accessed 5 September 2024].
46 Peter Biskind, 'Blacks Britannica: a clear case of censorship', *Jump Cut*, 21, 3–4 (November 1979): http://www.ejumpcut.org/archive/onlinessays/JC21folder/BlackUKBiskind.html [accessed 5 September 2024].
47 Philip French, 'The Pen and the Panther', *The Observer* [archive], 16 July 1978.
48 There was a bomb threat at the premiere of the film in San Francisco. 'Like the films in Africa, it was an effort to give a voice to those people who rarely, if ever, are presented on film,' said Koff (https://www.theguardian.com/film/2013/may/01/david-koff-documentary-occupied-palestine).
49 By 1989, Koff was working as a researcher and analyst for the hotel and restaurant employees' union in Los Angeles and Las Vegas, where he produced low-budget films about the labour movement and workers.
50 Martin Amis, 'A PM, a President, a First Lady', *Elle*, 1989.

3. Jah Warriors – Birmingham, 1979

1 Des Wilson, 'The police and the poor', *The Observer* [archive], 30 May 1971.
2 Martin Walker, 'City race row over housing policy', the *Guardian* [archive], 23 October 1975.
3 Maya Jaggi, 'Prophet at the margins', the *Guardian*, 8 July 2000: https://www.theguardian.com/books/2000/jul/08/society [accessed 24 September 2024].
4 Richard Vinen, *Second City: Birmingham and the Forging of Modern Britain*, Allen Lane, 2022.
5 The slogan made headlines around the globe and when the civil rights leader Malcolm X came to the UK he visited Smethwick. He toured the area, had a drink in one of the few pubs that would serve Black people and remarked he'd come to the West Midlands because 'I have heard [coloured people] are being treated as the Jews were under Hitler'. Malcolm X's presence in Birmingham inspired many to turn to

the nascent Black Power Movement that was growing in the US, which would take root in the UK during the late 1960s.

6 As the defeated Labour politician Patrick Gordon Walker, who was the shadow Home Secretary, left Smethwick town hall, Tory supporters yelled after him: 'Where are your niggers now, Walker?' and 'Take your niggers away!'

7 Publicly, Thatcher battered Callaghan's Labour as unemployment grew ever larger. But privately, Thatcher knew that the economic forecast meant things would be getting significantly worse. When she came to power in 1979, 1.5 million people were unemployed. By 1984 that number had more than doubled.

8 Vanley Burke, *By The Rivers of Birmingham*, Mac Birmingham, 2012.

9 Val Wilmer, 'Saxa obituary', the *Guardian*, 12 May 2017: https://www.theguardian.com/music/2017/may/12/lionel-martin-saxa-obituary [accessed 14 September 2024].

10 'Coronation of Ras Tafari – 1930', British Movietone, YouTube, (2018): https://www.youtube.com/watch?v=7CJsZjXsuHg&t=3s [accessed on 22 September 2024].

11 Evelyn Waugh, *The Coronation of Haile Selassie*, Penguin, 2005, p. 32.

12 Pogus is the second cousin of Northern Soul dancer Steve Caesar.

13 The reason for avoiding currency was because legal tenure had the Queen's head on it, 'and we didn't like the Queen'.

14 Benjamin Zephaniah, *The Life and Rhymes of Benjamin Zephaniah: The Autobiography*, Scribner UK, 2018, p. 107.

15 The group's 1973 record *Groundation* features the song 'Narration', which includes a passage about the enslaver John Hawkins getting a royal charter in 1565 from Queen Elizabeth I.

16 Howell and the early Rastas might have been seen as fringe lunatics in the 1930s but by the mid-1970s, Rastafarianism was so mainstream that *SkyWritings*, Air Jamaica's in-flight magazine, featured a portrait of Malachi the Prophet on its front cover to promote a feature on the movement and its importance to Jamaican culture.

17 Kieran Connell, *Black Handsworth: Race in 1980s Britain*, California University Press, 2019.

End Notes

18 Derek Bishton, *Talking Blues: The Black Community Speaks About Its Relationship with the Police*, Affor, 1978, p. 40.

19 Despite the confidence of some Rastas, most people were gleaning information on the best way to practise the religion, which was still in its infancy, from hearsay and rumour. 'To some extent, people just forged their own path,' says Riley, who remembers certain practices coming in and out of fashion. At one point, Rastas couldn't be with a white girlfriend, because they represented Babylon. At another point, they couldn't wear certain clothes because of who made them. 'For some, the statement made by just locksing up with your hair was what it was about – that was as militant as they got,' says Riley. 'For others, it became literally walking down the road with a Maccabee Bible in your hand.'

20 Norman Adams (Jah Blue), *A Historical Report: The Rastafarian Movement in England*, GWA Works, 2002, p. 105.

21 Ernest Cashmore, *Rastaman: The Rastafarian Movement in England*, Allen & Unwin, 1979.

22 Paul Gilroy argued that Rastafarians were the latest figures in a racist continuum that included muggers, undocumented migrants and Black Power activists. 'The Black folk-devil has acquired greater power with each subsequent mutation,' he wrote.

23 Brown spent time with community groups such as the housing collective Harambee, Handsworth Law Centre and the local police station during May and June, interviewing people and coming to conclusions about the Black community.

24 Brown would go on to make a TV documentary based on the report where he'd repeat his bleak, fatalistic claims about the Rastafarian – and by extension – the Black community of Birmingham.

25 Those who were committing the crimes were in Birmingham – on the whole – not new arrivals. In 1966, a study revealed that in Birmingham almost three-quarters of indictable offences were committed by white UK-born citizens, with half being Birmingham locals. The remaining crimes were split between Irish (20 per cent), West Indian (3 per cent) and Pakistani nationals (1 per cent).

End Notes

26 Malcolm Pithers, 'Police patrols stepped up to combat rising crime', the *Guardian* [archive], 5 December 1977.

27 George Brock, 'Police "dreadlock" report starts a row', *The Observer* [archive], 11 December 1977.

28 He kept extensive press clippings of the coverage Rastafarianism was receiving.

29 Ed Pilkington, 'Riots helped elect Nixon in 1968. Can Trump benefit from fear and loathing too?', the *Guardian*, 16 June 2020: https://www.theguardian.com/us-news/2020/jun/16/trump-nixon-1968-law-and-order-america [accessed 24 September 2024].

30 Margaret Thatcher, Speech to Conservative Party Conference, 13 October 1978: https://www.margaretthatcher.org/document/103764 [accessed 14 September 2024].

31 Philip Johnston, 'You mess with police pay at your peril', the *Daily Telegraph*, 31 December 2007: https://www.telegraph.co.uk/comment/columnists/philipjohnston/3645057/You-mess-with-police-pay-at-your-peril.html [accessed 22 September 2024].

32 'Note by director of programmes, television', BBC: https://downloads.bbc.co.uk/historyofthebbc/people-nation-empire/T66-15-1%252520 Community%252520Programmes.pdf

33 David Hendy, 'One of Us? Opening Doors', *History of the BBC*: https://www.bbc.co.uk/historyofthebbc/100-voices/people-nation-empire/opening-doors [accessed 20 September 2024].

34 Including Margaret Henry, who had worked as a researcher on *Blacks Britannica*.

35 The playwright and former journalist David Edgar – who had just staged his well-received play *Destiny* about the far right in the West Midlands – gave journalists tips on how to report on the NF.

36 David Hendy, 'The Black and White Minstrel Show', *History of the BBC*: https://www.bbc.com/historyofthebbc/100-voices/people-nation-empire/make-yourself-at-home/the-black-and-white-minstrel-show [accessed 20 September 2024].

37 David Hendy, 'Public Attitudes', *History of the BBC*: https://www.bbc.com/historyofthebbc/100-voices/people-nation-empire/public-attitudes/ [accessed 20 September 2024].

38 The prospect of a prime-time all-Black production on the BBC attracted a who's who of acting talent including Beaton, Joseph Marcell, Corinne Skinner-Carter, Thomas Baptiste and Rudolph Walker.
39 Ludovic Kennedy, *On My Way to the Club: An Autobiography*, William Collins, 1989, p. 405.
40 Steed had played a racist neighbour in the 1980 sound system drama, *Babylon*.
41 Day's nickname was the Grand Inquisitor.
42 Tim Adams, 'Jazz fan, hipster and a leftwing hero; the remarkable journey of Stuart Hall', *The Observer*, 18 August 2013: https://www.theguardian.com/society/2013/aug/18/professor-stuart-hall-multiculturalism-film [accessed 20 September 2024].
43 Clare Short remembers hearing about CCCS but it felt detached from the day-to-day of a Handsworth-based NGO. 'I mean, it's important, but it was a bit intellectual for us; we were out on the streets,' she told me.
44 The other issue was a more nuanced one, stemming from the Caribbean. Hall was a light-skinned, middle-class Jamaican whose parents had servants and hosted tennis parties. 'That was the very same class of people in Jamaica that had denigrated Rastafarianism, so there was a challenge there as to how to associate with this,' says Riley.
45 Vanley Burke, *Desert Island Discs*, BBC, 9 November 2018: https://www.bbc.co.uk/programmes/m0001opq [accessed 20 September 2024].
46 Significantly, Harambee was one Black-led organisation that survived. In 2023, it celebrated its fiftieth anniversary.
47 Tania Mason, 'Sector faced many similar challenges in Thatcher's 1980s Britain, shows report', *Civil Society*, 10 April 2013: https://www.civilsociety.co.uk/news/sector-faced-many-similar-challenges-in-thatcher-s-1980s-britain--shows-report.html [accessed 20 September 2024].
48 The Centre for Contemporary Cultural Studies never quite recovered from his departure; it eventually closed in 2002.
49 Stuart Hall, *Desert Island Discs*, BBC, 13 February 2000: https://www.bbc.co.uk/sounds/play/p0094b6r [accessed 20 September 2024].

End Notes

4. The Ghost of William Huskisson – Liverpool, 1981

1 The venue's names gave clues about the origins of the postcode's residents: alongside the Sierra Leone there was the Yoruba, Calabar and Igbo, the Freetown, the Somali Club, the Arab Club, the Ghana Club and the Caribbean Club.
2 A hot-wired car appearing wasn't that unusual in the 1980s. Joyriding was popular across the city and Cortinas were a favourite choice because of a design flaw that meant many could be opened using any car key.
3 The 1985 Swann Report into ethnic minority education: https://archive.org/details/educationforallr0000grea [accessed 20 September 2024].
4 Community Relations Council member Gideon Ben-Tovim told the *Liverpool Echo*: 'There were a lot of incidents of harassment, drug planting, people being criminalised for trivial reasons, heavy-handed policing and the final spark was the heavy-handed arrest of Cooper.'
5 Thatcher and her cabinet briefly debated bringing in the army.
6 In fact, the only person to die during the riots was David Moore, a disabled man who was hit by a speeding police vehicle.
7 'Merseyside Police officer recalls 1981 Toxteth Riots', BBC, 3 July 2011: https://www.bbc.co.uk/news/uk-england-merseyside-13956652 [accessed 25 September 2024].
8 When a fire at a club in Dublin resulted in the deaths of fifty people, Thatcher had quickly expressed her condolences, leading many to conclude that Black British lives didn't matter to this prime minister.
9 Alan Travis, 'Thatcher government toyed with evacuating Liverpool after 1981 riots', the *Guardian*, 30 December 2011: https://www.theguardian.com/uk/2011/dec/30/thatcher-government-liverpool-riots-1981 [accessed 20 September 2024].
10 Sanchia Berg, 'Thatcher "considered arming police" during 1981 riots', BBC, 30 December 2011: https://www.bbc.co.uk/news/uk-16313781 [accessed 20 September 2024].
11 'St Nicholas Church Gardens: Ranti Bam', Liverpool Biennial, 2023: https://www.biennial.com/venue/st-nicholas-church-gardens-ranti-bam/ [accessed 20 September 2024].

12 'Liverpool and the transatlantic slave trade', Archives Centre, Maritime Museum: https://www.liverpoolmuseums.org.uk/archivesheet3 [accessed 20 September 2024].
13 The Fletcher Report was supported by eugenicists such as Rachel Fleming, who advocated for the 'selective breeding' of humans. It was only in 1951, after the Second World War – when the Nazis' embrace of eugenics showed the ideology's true horrible potential, and when UNESCO said there were no disadvantages to 'race crossing' – that Fletcher's view began to be challenged. But the die was already cast in Liverpool: the Black population was a problem that needed to be solved.
14 Mark Christian, 'The Fletcher Report 1930: A Historical Case Study of Contested Black Mixed Heritage Britishness', *Journal of Historical Sociology*, 21(2/3), 213–41 (2008): https://doi.org/10.1111/j.1467-6443.2008.00337.x [accessed 20 September 2024].
15 There are estimates that there were up to 5,000 demobbed Black seamen in the city, and the three triggers of unemployment, racist attitudes towards mixed-race relationships and lack of housing resulted in an assault on Black Liverpool.
16 The situation was even more dire for Chinese seamen, some of whom were abducted and sent back to China by the police and immigration inspectorate in Liverpool after the government became concerned about the lack of housing for returning British navy personnel after the end of the Second World War. See: Dan Hancox, 'The secret deportations: how Britain betrayed the Chinese men who served the country in the war', the *Guardian*, 25 May 2021: https://www.theguardian.com/news/2021/may/25/secret-deportations-chinese-sailors-second-world-war-britain [accessed 20 September 2024].
17 'Liverpool Racial Disturbances: A Conviction Quashed', the *Guardian* [archive], 8 October 1948.
18 Christopher Fevre, 'Race and Resistance to Policing Before the Windrush Years: The Colonial Defence Committee and the Liverpool Race Riots of 1948', *Twentieth Century British History*, 32(1), 1–23 (2021): https://doi.org/10.1093/tcbh/hwaa022 [accessed 21 September 2024].

19 Lisa Rand, 'When they demolished them they demolished pages of history', *Liverpool Echo*, 6 October 2019: https://www.liverpoolecho.co.uk/news/liverpool-news/when-demolished-demolished-pages-history-16978106 [accessed 15 September 2024].

20 John Belchem, 'Race relations in the 1950s', in *Before the Windrush: Race Relations in 20th-Century Liverpool*, Liverpool, 2014: Liverpool Scholarship Online, 18 September 2014: https://doi.org/10.5949/liverpool/9781846319679.003.0006 [accessed 15 September 2024].

21 'City Demonstrates Racial Harmony', the *Guardian* [archive], 12 May 1961.

22 Anthony Hogan, *The Beat Makers: The Unsung Heroes of The Mersey Sound*, Amberley Publishing, 2017.

23 'Bobby Nyahoe performing a poem at the Black-E 1969 Liverpool': https://x.com/angiesliverpool/status/1321444259506040838?lang=en [accessed 25 September 2024].

24 Ray Costello, *Liverpool Black Pioneers*, The Bluecoat Press, 2007.

25 Stephen Small, 'Racialised relations in Liverpool: A contemporary anomaly', *Journal of Ethnic and Migration Studies*, 17(4), 511–537 (1991): https://doi.org/10.1080/1369183X.1991.9976265 [accessed 15 September 2024].

26 'In The Basement', Magnet TV Liverpool, YouTube (2012): https://www.youtube.com/watch?v=9vciXa_Bwdw [accessed on 22 September 2024].

27 The problem was so bad that a multiracial vigilante group known as The Green Jackets, who were inspired by the Black Panthers, emerged to patrol and protect L8.

28 Howard Gayle, *61 Minutes in Munich: The Story of Liverpool FC's First Black Footballer*, De Coubertin Books, 2016.

29 Lindsay Mackie, 'Race committee MPs reject Heseltine call for minister to handle city problems', the *Guardian* [archive], 7 August 1981.

30 Ernest Dewhurst, 'Race Prejudice "Entrenched" In Liverpool', the *Guardian* [archive], 29 September 1973.

31 This figure is disputed locally, and other estimates are much higher. For example, the 1989 'Loosen the Shackles' report lists the city's Black population (African, West Indian and Black British) in 1981 as between 11,400 and 18,000; while Nassy Brown cites the 1992 office of

population Censuses and Surveys estimate of 6,876 Black people in the city. Neither of these estimates is entirely accurate.
32 Bleasdale cut his teeth at *Pebble Mill* in Birmingham, the home of *Empire Road*, before creating *Boys From the Blackstuff* and later the political drama *GBH*, both of which would define Liverpool during the Thatcher era.
33 John Carvel, 'A dossier of inner city deprivation for Heseltine', the *Guardian* [archive], 19 August 1982.
34 Andy Beckett, *Promised You a Miracle*, Allen Lane, 2013, p. 49.
35 'Toxteth riots: Howe proposed "managed decline" for city', BBC, 30 December 2011: https://www.bbc.co.uk/news/uk-england-merseyside-16355281 [accessed 15 September 2024].
36 The main characters, Chrissie Todd and Yosser Hughes, became cult figures, with Hughes' line 'Gizza job' becoming a 1980s catchphrase. There was a Black character too: the crafty and sardonic Loggo, played by Manchester-born Alan Igbon.
37 Dawn Collinson, 'Boys From The Blackstuff: a look back at the Liverpool drama which captured the mood of a nation', *Liverpool Echo*, 8 October 2015: https://www.liverpoolecho.co.uk/news/nostalgia/boys-blackstuff-look-back-liverpool-10224085
38 Decca Aitkenhead, 'Michael Heseltine: "I would have liked to be prime minister"', the *Guardian*, 25 November 2012: https://www.theguardian.com/politics/2012/nov/25/michael-heseltine-would-have-liked-prime-minister [accessed 15 September 2024].
39 Heseltine has always denied this, saying in 2012: 'I just don't think it sounds like me. I'm too cautious.'
40 Labour ridiculed the move, with Roy Hattersley, the shadow Home Secretary, saying the opposition was all too familiar with the prime minister's view that the problems of inner cities could not be solved by throwing money at them. 'Mrs Thatcher was now going to throw ministers at Liverpool,' he quipped across the dispatch box.
41 Heseltine wasn't just there to deal with L8 but the title of the report he would eventually file to Thatcher and the rest of the cabinet – 'It Took A Riot' – made it clear why he'd been sent.

42 Although he was clear that there was 'no bag of money to dole out', he instead offered 'an open diary and plenty of time to listen'.
43 Tristram Hunt, 'Why cities can thank the Tories', the *Guardian*, 16 May 2004: https://www.theguardian.com/politics/2004/may/16/conservatives.interviews [accessed 25 September 2024].
44 'Toxteth riots: Timeline of key events and quotes from those involved', *Liverpool Echo*, 20 February 2011: https://www.liverpoolecho.co.uk/news/local-news/toxteth-riots-timeline-key-events-3384004
45 Colin Brown, 'Heseltine despatch to study Liverpool's problems', the *Guardian* [archive], 17 July 1981.
46 He had a long-running feud with Margaret Simey, whose husband, Lord Simey of Toxteth, was a life peer, while she worked in the same social sciences department as Muriel Fletcher at the University of Liverpool. Simey had become the first deputy chairperson of the Merseyside Police Committee in 1974. Oxford and Simey – a liberal who was fond of quoting William Beveridge, the economist and social reformer who designed the British welfare state – detested each other. The pair had clashed regularly since the case of Jimmy Kelly, a labourer who died in police custody in 1979. Oxford refused to explain himself or be held accountable for his force.
47 Ian MacDonald, 'Authority and Insurrection', *Liverpool City Police*: https://www.liverpoolcitypolice.co.uk/articles/authority-insurrection/ [accessed 22 September 2024].
48 Most L8 people I spoke to about Oxford have nothing but contempt, forty years on. Wally Brown dealt exclusively with his deputy, Peter Wright, even during the riots; others recalled the posters plastered around L8 that read 'Oxford Out' and were part of a sustained campaign to force his resignation.
49 Michael Heseltine, *Life in the Jungle*, Hodder & Stoughton, 2000, p. 220.
50 'TV documentary examining the Toxteth riots', Soul On Top, YouTube, (2017): https://www.youtube.com/watch?v=UkG-N7cReac&t=237s [accessed on 22 September 2024].
51 'Liverpool's Original Gangster: Michael Showers', True Crime Podcast 129, Shaun Attwood, YouTube: https://www.youtube.com/watch?v=s3foB4tLnnY

52 He would eventually be jailed for a plot to import heroin, something he always maintained was fabricated by the police who couldn't get him for his other crimes. In 2021, he appeared in the Sky TV show *Liverpool Narcos*, where he was billed as 'The Godfather of Merseyside Crime'.

53 Alan Travis, 'Thatcher government toyed with evacuating Liverpool after 1981 riots', the *Guardian*, 30 December 2011: https://www.theguardian.com/uk/2011/dec/30/thatcher-government-liverpool-riots-1981 [accessed 21 September 2024].

54 'A Legacy in Liverpool', the *Guardian* [archive], 13 April 1984.

55 The economic decline of the UK threatened many independent filmmakers. In 1982, Channel 4, the British Film Institute (BFI) and the Arts Council responded with the Workshop Declaration – a commitment to support independent collectives. The Liverpool Black Media Group would be one of the forty-four workshops Channel 4 supported by 1988: there was Amber in Newcastle-upon-Tyne, plus Black-led groups such as Black Audio Film Collective, Sankofa and Ceddo (of whom Steve Caesar's older brother Imruh was a member) in London.

56 On the face of it, Militant Tendency might seem like perfect allies for the radical elements of Liverpool's Black community, many of whom were influenced by far-left ideology. But Militant's strain of socialism was extremely narrow: class was king, everything else was a bourgeois distraction, including race. Initially, the Black community of L8 did support Militant who were engaged in a battle with Whitehall and refused to impose cuts to council services, but things ignited between L8 activists and Hatton when he installed Sampson Bond, a Black Militant member from north London, as the council's Principal Race Relations Advisor in October 1984. Members of the Black Caucus, a grouping of Black community initiatives in the city, were enraged and protests followed. Hundreds of people took to the streets and the decision to appoint him ultimately led to an occupation of the Liverpool City Council by protestors who forced Hatton to sign a statement denouncing the appointment.

57 Tellingly, his successor Patrick Jenkin came to Merseyside nine times but never to Liverpool.

58 https://www.nytimes.com/1985/10/03/world/riots-continue-in-british-cities.html

59 Geraldine Bedell, 'A colour the city can't forgive', *The Independent*, 13 August 1994: https://www.independent.co.uk/news/uk/home-news/a-colour-the-city-can-t-forgive-liverpool-split-after-future-first-citizen-s-crime-record-is-revealed-1376382.html [accessed 15 September 2024].

60 Aamna Mohdin, Pamela Duncan and Niels de Hoog, 'Manchester urged to act on "scandalous" lack of Black people in prominent roles', the *Guardian*, 3 April 2023: https://www.theguardian.com/news/ng-interactive/2023/apr/03/manchester-urged-act-scandalous-lack-black-people-prominent-roles [accessed 21 September 2024].

61 David Humphreys, 'Black community "gaslit" over police tactics as figures show disproportionate use of force', *Liverpool Echo*, 30 June 2024: https://www.liverpoolecho.co.uk/news/liverpool-news/Black-community-gaslit-over-police-29442172 [accessed 25 September 2024].

62 Wally Brown, *Wally Brown: A Life – Born and Raised in L8*, Writing on the Wall, 2023.

63 Stephen Kelly, 'Toxteth's toxic legacy: Liverpool is still feeling the impact of the Toxteth riots', *The Independent*, 1 July 2011: https://www.independent.co.uk/life-style/history/toxteth-s-toxic-legacy-liverpool-is-still-feeling-the-impact-of-the-toxteth-riots-2305044.html [accessed 25 September 2024].

64 The First Asian and Black Parliamentarians: https://heritagecollections.parliament.uk/exhibits/pioneers

65 Akyaaba Addai-Sebo, an officer of the Greater London Council (GLC), developed the first Black History Month in Britain before Linda Bellos launched it after the GLC was abolished.

5. Black Art an'done – Wolverhampton, 1982

1 Hugh Trevor-Roper, *The Rise of Christian Europe*, History Book Club, reprint, 1967.

2 Keith Piper, 'Keith Piper on the Legacies of the BLK Art Group', *Frieze*, 3 March 2023: https://www.frieze.com/article/keith-piper-legacies-blk-art-group [accessed 25 September 2024].

3 Powell's attitude to immigration and race was forged in the last days of the British Empire. He served in India with the British army, and while there had fallen in love with the country and cemented his belief in the power of the British Empire. He was so convinced of the importance of Britain's presence in India that he made an impassioned argument to then Conservative leader Winston Churchill for holding onto it beyond 1947, when the country would gain its independence. Afterwards, Churchill is reported to have asked 'Who was that young madman who has been telling me how many divisions I will need to reconquer India?'

4 The Commonwealth Immigrants Act 1968.

5 Mark Lattimer, 'When Labour Played the Racist Card', *The New Statesman*, 22 January 1999: https://www.newstatesman.com/long-reads/1999/01/when-labour-played-racist-card [accessed 21 September 2024].

6 Richard Norton-Taylor and Seumas Milne, 'Racism: Extremists led Powell marches', the *Guardian*, 1 January 1999: https://www.theguardian.com/uk/1999/jan/01/richardnortontaylor2 [accessed 21 September 2024].

7 Shirin Hirsch, *In The Shadow of Enoch*, Manchester University Press, 2018, p. 6.

8 This account comes from *In The Shadow of Enoch* as Vanessa Kirkpatrick recalls her feelings as an eleven-year-old in the wake of 'Rivers of Blood'. The book is, along with Paul Foot's *The Rise of Enoch Powell*, an essential summary of Powell, his speech and its connection to Wolverhampton.

9 The Blk Art Group's location in the Black Country put them at the centre of Britain's historic links to the slave trade; towns like Wolverhampton were an integral part of the trade, providing metalworked goods such as shackles for the slavers. (See: Matthew Stallard, 'The Black Country flag row shows Britain is still blind to its colonial past', the *Guardian*, 21 July 2017: https://www.theguardian.com/commentisfree/2017/jul/21/black-country-flag-britain-colonial-past-slavery.)

10 'Unemployment statistics from 1881 to the present day', The Government Statistical Service.

11 Margaret Thatcher (1925–2013), Ipsos: https://www.ipsos.com/en-uk/margaret-thatcher-1925-2013

12 Chris Horrie, 'Gotcha! How the Sun reaped spoils of war', *The Observer*, Sunday 7 April 2002: https://www.theguardian.com/business/2002/apr/07/pressandpublishing.media
13 The conflict saw the paper win the ratings war with its rival the *Daily Mirror*.
14 Joe Shute, 'The 72-hour battle that won the Falklands War', the *Telegraph*, 12 June 2022: https://www.telegraph.co.uk/news/2022/06/12/72-hour-battle-won-falklands-war/ [accessed 21 September 2024].
15 'Speech to Conservative Rally at Cheltenham', 3 July 1982: https://www.margaretthatcher.org/document/104989 [accessed 21 September 2024].
16 Andrew Graham-Yooll, 'The islands taken to save a government's face', the *Guardian*, 3 April 1982: https://www.theguardian.com/theguardian/2012/apr/03/falklands-war-reasons-for-invasion-1982
17 Simon Jenkins, 'Falklands war 30 years on and how it turned Thatcher into a world celebrity', the *Guardian*, 1 April 2012: https://www.theguardian.com/uk/2012/apr/01/falklands-war-30-years-thatcher [accessed 21 September 2024].
18 Alexis Petridis, 'Ska for the madding crowd', the *Guardian*, 8 May 2002: https://www.theguardian.com/culture/2002/mar/08/artsfeatures.popandrock [accessed 21 September 2024].
19 Wenda Leslie and Janet Vernon were also members, with Andrew Hazel, Dominic Dawes and Ian Palmer all taking part in the very first exhibition, *Black Art an'done* in 1981.
20 The Nazi connection followed Riefenstahl for the rest of her life. She was incredibly litigious and would end up in court, seeking damages from those who attempted to claim she was complicit in some of the Nazi's crimes.
21 Kate Connolly, 'Burying Leni Riefenstahl: one woman's lifelong crusade against Hitler's favourite film-maker', the *Guardian*, 9 December 2021: https://www.theguardian.com/news/2021/dec/09/burying-leni-riefenstahl-nina-gladitz-lifelong-crusade-hitler-film-maker [accessed 21 September 2024].

End Notes

22 There were those who embraced the new, such as Anthony Caro, who taught Tony Cragg and Anthony Gormley, the sculptors who made work out of found objects and detritus.
23 When he moved to New York, he lived at the Chelsea Hotel (where he met Jasper Johns) before moving into a Soho loft on Broadway; it was there he created his large-scale abstract paintings that were shown in the Whitney.
24 Frank Bowling, Tate Britain retrospective catalogue, p. 21.
25 'MPs appeal to President on bombing', the *Guardian* [archive], 16 December 1966.
26 'Bill Schwarz Ed.,' *West Indian Intellectuals in Britain*, p. 213.
27 Anne Walmsley, *The Caribbean Artists' Movement*, p. 70.
28 During one meeting Gordon Rohlehr spoke about the language of calypso, which was a turning point for Andrew Salkey who said: 'If the culture had been derided by alien commentators, been ignored by our teachers, had been vilified by officialdom, there was Gordon telling us, convincing us we mattered.'
29 Although it only lasted for six years, CAM's influence was crucial. At the first conference held at the University of Kent in 1969, James Currey of Heinemann publishers would attend and afterwards start the Caribbean Writers Series, which helped launch the career of the poet Derek Walcott. Visual artists Aubrey Williams and Frank Bowling were CAM members, while Stuart Hall addressed the group's second conference to argue Caribbean art was shaped by its slave past and the European colonisers, who he called the 'enemy within'.
30 The Blk Art Group made audio recordings of the day which are available online in their archive: https://www.blkartgroup.info/blkartarchive.html
31 Although the Blk Art Group were all Black British, in the Thatcher era the term 'politically Black' emerged from the trade union movement and included everyone who wasn't white. It meant someone who was of East Asian heritage could describe themselves as Black, which was useful practically – because it meant all immigrants or people of colour could act as one group – and it also produced solidarity between different groups. Today it's rarely used outside of union contexts and its usefulness is a source of fierce debate.

32 But not everyone. Ingrid Pollard was slightly older and didn't go to university until she was thirty. She recalled being in the audience and hearing people 'moaning about the university and not getting the correct response from their tutors, and I thought, gosh, I'm having to be out actually working.'
33 It was the only moment in the day when a speaker was challenged during their presentation.
34 In the catalogue for Johnson's 2019 exhibition, *I Came To Dance*, the academic Ella S. Mills said that the moment denied Black female creativity a space for critical consideration. 'We witness the moment when, symbolically, the women of the Black British Art Movement refuse a non-discussion and instead choose their own space to talk to one another and, crucially, to talk about their work.'
35 It featured Brenda Agard, Sutapa Biswas, Sonia Boyce, Chila Burman, Jennifer Comrie, Ingrid Pollard, Veronica Ryan, Maud Sulter, plus Johnson and Smith.
36 'Anger at Hind', the *Guardian* [archive], 27 November 1985.
37 'Collision Culture', the *Guardian* [archive], 20 December 1989.
38 The portrait was based on a photograph taken by Chris Steele-Perkins called 'Disco in Wolverhampton'.

6. *The Black Door – Manchester, 1986*

1 Helen Pidd, 'Digging the Reno: Moss Side's legendary club unearthed – 30 years on', the *Guardian*, 17 October 2017: https://www.theguardian.com/uk-news/2017/oct/27/digging-the-reno-moss-sides-legendary-club-unearthed-30-years-on [accessed 21 September 2024].
2 Tom Sharratt, 'Moss Side committee rebuffs riots report and sets up own inquiry', the *Guardian* [archive], 14 October 1981.
3 James Lewis, 'Anderton, unabashed and quite unchanged', the *Guardian* [archive], 21 January 1987.
4 Alan Dun, 'Manchester disbands "gay patrol"', the *Guardian* [archive], 28 June 1982.

5. Tom Sharratt, 'Preacher Anderton thunders against the gays', the *Guardian* [archive], 12 December 1986.
6. Stuart Cosgrove, *Young Soul Rebels*, Polygon, 2016, p. 17.
7. James Lewis, 'Mistrust deepens between police and inner-city Blacks', the *Guardian*, 8 June 1981.
8. Stuart Hall, 'The law's out of order', the *Guardian* [archive], 5 January 1980.
9. 'Margaret Thatcher saved career of police chief who made Aids remarks', the *Telegraph*, 4 January 2012.
10. List of Black businesses collated in Bill Williams' unpublished history of Black Manchester.
11. The Reno, The Edinburgh and later The Russell Club were part of a club network, not just in Manchester but around the country, run by Black people for Black people who were excluded from mainstream venues. There was the Mayflower in Bradford, Killymans in Oldham and The Timepiece in Liverpool, while it's been claimed that Chapeltown in Leeds had more illicit clubs and parties than the whole of London at one point (Matt Anniss, *Join The Future*, Velocity Press, 2019). The capital had its own network including – one of the very first – Club Noreik in Tottenham, Mr Bee's in Peckham and Dougie's Hideaway in Archway.
12. Kath Locke interview with Paul Okojie in 1992.
13. Makonnen, who had Ethiopian roots, was deeply invested in the Pan-Africanist movement, and along with the Trinidadian Marxist George Padmore, fellow Guyanese Peter Millard and Alfred Gaisie, he became a key organiser of the 1945 Pan-African Congress. He used his connections to help find accommodation for attendees and speakers, booking rooms at the Grosvenor and Midland hotels; while also securing airfares for those coming from overseas.
14. T Ras Makonnen, *Pan-Africanism from Within*, p. 136.
15. Marika Sherwood, '"Mak": Ras T Makonnen, the unrecognized hero of the Pan-African Movement', Ahmed Iqbal Ullah Race Relations Centre.
16. In a scene where Kitchener plays the club Joseph describes him as he watches the clientele – made up of West African students, white boys in denim and patent leather, young women with chiffon scarfs and

West Indian jazz men in zoot suits – while 'the scent of stewed chicken and beans weaves its way up from the kitchen downstairs'.
17 She was part of Colin Prescod's mother's 'powerful sisterhood'.
18 Hakim Adi and Marika Sherwood, *The 1945 Manchester Pan-African Congress Revisited* New Beacon Books.
19 Sven Beckert, *Empire of Cotton: A New History of Global Capitalism*, Penguin, 2015, p. 115.
20 Eric Williams, *Capitalism and Slavery*, Penguin.
21 Andy Burnham, 'Westminster has become a living nightmare', *GQ*, 28 August 2019.
22 The Manchester Plan (abridged): https://personalpages.manchester.ac.uk/staff/m.dodge/plans/1945-City_of_Manchester_Plan_Abridged.pdf
23 Paul Rotha's documentary *A City Speaks* starts with a sweeping aerial shot of Moss Side and Hulme before the clearances. Row upon row of houses flash up on screen, with the images captured a few years before they were razed.
24 Laurence Brown and Niall Cunningham, *The Inner Geographies of a Migrant Gateway: Mapping the Built Environment and the Dynamics of Caribbean Mobility in Manchester, 1951–2011*, Cambridge University Press, 25 January 2016.
25 'Minister's tribute to Manchester's slum clearance', the *Guardian*, 23 November 1965.
26 'Alleged Vice in Moss Side: City Council Not to Seek Home Office Inquiry', the *Manchester Guardian*, 2 March 1950.
27 'Still Seeing "Vice" in Moss Side: Commitee's Campaign', the *Manchester Guardian*, 4 February 1950.
28 Roots: Oral History, (pamphlet), published 1992, p. 8.
29 'Slum clearance project causes hardship', the *Guardian*, 22 July 1963.
30 Diana Watt and Adele Jones, *Catching Hell and Doing Well*, Trentham Books, 2015, p. 19.
31 Taken from an interview held as part of the Olive Morris Collection at Lambeth Archives.
32 'The Hulme Crescents, Manchester: a "British Bantustan"', Municipal Dreams, 11 March 2014.

33 John Harris, 'The great reinvention of Manchester: "It's far more pleasant than London"', the *Guardian*, 3 November 2015: https://www.theguardian.com/cities/2015/nov/03/the-great-reinvention-of-manchester-its-far-more-pleasant-than-london [accessed 21 September 2024].

34 https://personalpages.manchester.ac.uk/staff/m.dodge/Heliport_dreaming-WP.pdf

35 Persian stayed on the cutting edge of Black music's evolution via his close relationship with Lane – who would often let him shop by himself – and because of his regular visits to the Diskery in Birmingham, another Black music specialist record shop. He also had a special record-buying connection, a Jamaican friend called Kenny B who would travel to South America and the US before coming back to the UK as a seaman. 'I used to give him money and he used to go through Philadelphia and he would buy records for me,' Persian once said. 'So I started getting music direct from the States, stuff like Al Green and James Brown that nobody else knew here then.'

36 Manchester reggae act Harlem Spirit immortalised the police's tactics on their track SUS.

37 James Lewis, 'The force of law and order seen in a new light', the *Guardian* [archive], 24 July 1981.

38 Tom Sharratt, 'Moss Side committee rebuffs riots report and sets up own inquiry', the *Guardian* [archive], 14 October 1981.

39 Michael Morris, 'Attack on "bias" in Hytner report', the *Guardian*, 6 November 1981.

40 The description was apt: house innovator Marshall Jefferson said he was trying to emulate Led Zeppelin and Black Sabbath on his early tracks.

41 'Mastermind Roadshow with performance by Foot Patrol – Moss Side, Manchester 1986', Choyc3 YouTube, (2011): https://www.youtube.com/watch?v=46jB4yohiKA [accessed on 22 September 2024].

42 Tim Lawrence, 'Discotheque Hacienda', *FAC51 The Hacienda*, 16 July 2013: https://fac51-thehacienda.com/tim-lawrence-discotheque-hacienda/ [accessed 21 September 2024].

43 'New Heroin Outbreaks Amongst Young People in England and Wales', Crime Detection and Prevention Series Paper 92, Home Office Police Research Group, 1998.
44 Helen Carter, 'Farewell to Gunchester', the *Guardian*, 11 April 2011: https://www.theguardian.com/global/the-northerner/2011/apr/11/manchester-guns-gunchester-police [accessed 21 September 2024].
45 Neil Hodgson, 'Plans submitted to transform historic Whalley Range property', *The Business Desk*, 14 February 2023.
46 Damon Wilkinson, 'Iconic West Indian Community Centre at Carmoor Road spared from demolition as fresh plans for huge new student digs revealed', *Manchester Evening News*, 4 December 2022.
47 'Greater Manchester Police authorise third consecutive section 60 authority in Hulme and Old Trafford areas of Manchester', GMP, 3 June 2023.
48 Charles Hymas, 'Anti-woke chief constable turns failing force around with back-to-basics approach', the *Telegraph* [archive], 28 October 2022.
49 Rumeana Jahangir, 'Manchester IRA bomb: Terror blast remembered 20 years on', BBC, 16 June 2016.
50 Helen Pidd and Charlie Cocksedge, 'How Manchester developers dodge affordable housing', the *Guardian*, 6 March 2018: https://www.theguardian.com/cities/2018/mar/06/the-o-city-how-manchester-developers-dodge-affordable-housing [accessed 21 September 2024].
51 Daniel Timms, 'The billion pound Manchester question: Who has benefited from the city's breakneck growth?', *The Mill*, 29 July 2023: https://manchestermill.co.uk/p/the-billion-pound-manchester-question [accessed 21 September 2024].

7. The Last Fort – 1987

1 'What is Windrush and who are the Windrush generation?', BBC, 27 July 2023: https://www.bbc.co.uk/news/uk-43782241
2 'Willie Whitelaw dies aged 81', the *Guardian*, 1 July 1999: https://www.theguardian.com/politics/1999/jul/01/uk.politicalnews6 [accessed 21 September 2024].

End Notes

3 William Whitelaw, *The Whitelaw Memoirs*, Aurum, 1989.
4 'The Country and the City' (1979) by Raymond Williams and Mike Dibb, Raymond Williams Society, YouTube, (2011): https://www.youtube.com/watch?v=DV1krEyCgCM&t=1299s [accessed on 22 September 2024].
5 'Rural Heritage and Colonial Nostalgia in the Thatcher Years: V. S. Naipaul's The Enigma of Arrival', Lucienne Loh, in *Thatcher and After: Margaret Thatcher and He Afterlife in Contemporary Culture*, Elizabeth Ho and L. Hadley (eds), 2010.
6 The issue would really escalate in the 2000s, with the percentage of white Britons in the capital dropping dramatically from 59.8 per cent in 2001 to 44.9 per cent in 2011.
7 TCPA Journal No 12 December.
8 Julian McLauchlan, 'Black Shepherd'.
9 Paul Henderson, 'Isolation in the shires', the *Guardian* [archive], 14 July 1999.
10 Madeleine Bunting, 'In pursuit of the Suffolk maharajah', the *Guardian* [archive], 3 March 1993.
11 He'd been wrongly convicted of arson as part of the Wilmington Ten.
12 Graham Coster, 'Another Country', the *Guardian* [archive], 1 June 1991.
13 The nature writer Robert MacFarlane included 'Pastoral Interlude' in a book about the eeriness of rural settings.
14 '"Big Bang" Deregulation Bolsters London's Position as Global Finance Center', Goldman Sachs history.
15 Heather Stewart and Simon Goodley, 'Big Bang's shockwaves left us with today's big bust', the *Guardian*, 9 October 2011: https://www.theguardian.com/business/2011/oct/09/big-bang-1986-city-deregulation-boom-bust [accessed 21 September 2024].
16 'How the Big Bang changed the City of London for ever', BBC, 27 October 2016: https://www.bbc.co.uk/news/business-37751599 [accessed 21 September 2024].
17 Michael Durham, 'England's green unpleasant land: Bad housing, bad neighbours, bad services, bad pay', *The Observer* [archive], 20 March 1994.

18 After he left the church, he spent almost a decade as director of the Camden Commission for Community Relations before stepping down in 1981 and becoming a consultant with the Commission for Racial Equality.
19 Eric Jay, 'Keep Them in Birmingham', CRE, 1991.
20 He formed it along with Ingrid Pollard, Vijay Krishnarayan and Roland De la Mothe, while Judy Wong served as director.
21 Debbie Humphry interviews Julian Agyeman, 'Black Environmental Justice: From urban studies to radical rurals in England', 9 July 2022: https://www.peoplesplans.org/black-environmental-justice-from-urban-studies-to-radical-rurals-in-england/ [accessed 21 September 2024].
22 TCPA Journal, No 12, December 1989.
23 'Gifted, Black . . . and gone', the *Guardian*, 30 May 2000: https://www.theguardian.com/uk/2000/may/30/race.biography [accessed 21 September 2024].
24 'Black Environmental Justice: From urban studies to radical rurals in England', PeoplesPlan.org.
25 'Meet The London Birdwatching Collective Founded By And For People Of Colour', *Vogue*, 12 September 2020: https://www.vogue.co.uk/arts-and-lifestyle/article/flock-together-interview [accessed 21 September 2024].
26 Hannah Pool, 'Question Time', the *Guardian*, 21 May 2009: https://www.theguardian.com/lifeandstyle/2009/may/21/benjamin-zephaniah-interview [accessed 22 September 2024].

8. The Myth and The Bay, Cardiff – 1988

1 Howard Spring, *Heaven Lies About Us: A Fragment of Infancy*, Constable, 1939.
2 Dennis Barker, 'Wales white hope that became a white elephant', the *Guardian* [archive], 10 March 1979.
3 Jonathan Freedland, 'Eugenics and the master race of the left', the *Guardian*, 30 August 1997: https://www.theguardian.com/politics/from-the-archive-blog/2019/may/01/eugenics-founding-fathers-british-socialism-archive-1997 [accessed 22 September 2024].

4 Alan Llwyd, *Black Wales: A History of Black Welsh People*, Hughes & Son (Publishers) Ltd, 2005.
5 Jacqueline Jenkins, *Black 1919: Riots, Racism and Resistance in Imperial Britain*, Liverpool University Press, 2008.
6 The police narrowly stopping a man who owned a fish and chip shop with his wife from being attacked by the mob of fifty workmen.
7 Llwyd, 2005.
8 The leaders were ex-colonial soldiers from Australia and New Zealand.
9 The Chief Constable blamed the white seamen for the violence, but in his report to the Home Office advised that there should be immediate moves to repatriate all the unemployed coloured seamen. 'If no steps are taken in this direction these men are faced with destitution and they may become desperate,' he wrote.
10 Black people charged by the police received stiffer sentences than whites, while others, including a mob that allegedly stripped a woman naked and knocked her teeth out because she'd married a Black man, escaped justice entirely.
11 The act had a dramatic effect on the number of seamen. In 1919, there were 7,408 foreign seamen registered in Britain; five years later that number dropped to 4,846. The vast majority were Arabs; while Somalis, West Africans and nearly 800 seamen came from the Caribbean. The other factor was the worldwide recession after the First World War, which reduced demand for the produce coming in and out of British docks. The number of Black and minority ethnic seamen working on British ships peaked at 24,184 in 1917 at the height of the First World War but had halved by 1925.
12 'Tiger Bay is My Home', Channel 4, 1984: https://www.concordmedia.org.uk/products/tiger-bay-is-my-home-624/
13 Wilson wanted action. His idea was the implementation of an apartheid system to be introduced based on the 1927 Immorality Act in South Africa, which made it illegal for people of different races to marry.
14 Little's report and his move to the University of Edinburgh, where he ran the anthropology department, ushered in a new era. Students and

peers produced several landmark reports on Black British communities: Michael Banton's 'The Coloured Quarter', A.T. Carey's 'Colonial Students', Sydney Collins' 'Coloured Communities in Britain' and Sheila Patterson's 'Dark Strangers' all broke new ground. In fact, so much work was being produced that the department was jokingly referred to as the 'Negroes in Britain Industry' because of its prolific output, led by Little.

15 'Britain needs "Commonwealth consciousness": Links of the past not enough', the *Manchester Guardian* [archive], 6 January 1959.
16 Kenneth Little, *Negroes in Britain*, Routledge & Kegan Paul, 1972.
17 Kenneth Little, 'The BBC and Colour Problems', letter to the editor, the *Manchester Guardian* [archive], 10 October 1958.
18 Marcus Hughes, 'The extraordinary rarely seen images of working life in Cardiff 90 years ago', *Wales Online*, 19 January 2020: https://www.walesonline.co.uk/lifestyle/nostalgia/gallery/extraordinary-rarely-seen-images-working-17577692
19 *Tiger Bay and The Rainbow Club* – I, BFI Player, 1960: https://player.bfi.org.uk/free/film/watch-tiger-bay-and-the-rainbow-club-i-1960-online.
20 Two decades later, as Home Secretary, Callaghan introduced the 1968 Commonwealth Immigrants Act, which represented a turning point in Britain's attitude towards race. The legislation was hurried through parliament by a panicked Callaghan after Jomo Kenyatta launched his 'Africanisation' policy in Kenya – an attempt to ethnically cleanse the country of the South Asians installed by the British as a managerial class during the colonial period. The 1968 act has since been dubbed 'the most nakedly racist piece of legislation of the postwar years' (see: Kenan Malik, 'Racist rhetoric hasn't been consigned to Britain's past', *The Observer*, 4 March 2018: https://www.theguardian.com/commentisfree/2018/mar/04/commonwealth-immigrants-act-1968-racism). While Callaghan never stated that Little's study influenced his actions, the MP for Butetown did more to prevent citizens like those he represented from entering the country than any other politician in the twentieth century.
21 The Commonwealth Immigrants Act 1968.
22 'Student of Independence', the *Guardian* [archive], 2 July 1990.

23 Kelefa Sanneh, 'Is Gentrification Really a Problem?', *The New Yorker*, 4 July 2016: https://www.newyorker.com/magazine/2016/07/11/is-gentrification-really-a-problem [accessed 20 September 2024].

24 Letter from St Clair Drake to W. E. B. Du Bois.

25 While in Cardiff, he wrote to W. E. B. Du Bois about the concerns of Somalis he'd spoken to who were worried about Italian threats to put their country under 'trusteeship' of the European nation.

26 *The Crisis*, 56(6), June 1949, The Crisis Publishing Company: https://archive.org/details/sim_crisis_1949-06_56_6/page/188/mode/2up [accessed 20 September 2024].

27 Thomas Deacon, 'The genuinely bonkers plan for Cardiff', *Wales Online*, 27 January 2019: https://www.walesonline.co.uk/news/wales-news/genuinely-bonkers-plans-cardiff-drawn-15728080 [accessed 20 September 2024].

28 Leon Gooberman, 'The State and Post-Industrial Urban Regeneration: The Reinvention of South Cardiff', *Urban History*, 2018, 45(3), 504–23: https://doi.org/10.1017/S0963926817000384 [accessed 20 September 2024].

29 William Rees, *Cardiff: A History of the City*, 1969.

30 David Conn, 'The Scandal of Orgreave', the *Guardian*, 18 May 2017: https://www.theguardian.com/politics/2017/may/18/scandal-of-orgreave-miners-strike-hillsborough-theresa-may [accessed 25 September 2021].

31 Keith Harper, 'Pit strike ends in defiance and tears', the *Guardian*, 4 March 1985: https://www.theguardian.com/fromthearchive/story/0,,1429566,00.html [accessed 25 September 2024].

32 In reality, like in Moss Side, the older houses either needed to be torn down or retrofitted. Damp was rife in the properties, a fact that resulted in Butetown having a tuberculosis rate that was higher than anywhere else in Cardiff, while politicians and locals complained of slum landlords who hiked rents, crammed families into rooms and refused to carry out basic maintenance.

33 Accounts taken from interviews in the film *The Demolition Of Old Cardiff Housing*, Archif ITV Cymru/Wales @ LlGC | ITV Cymru/Wales Archive @ NLW, 1962: https://www.youtube.com/watch?v=TO_SLAICVyU [accessed 26 September 2024].

34 Joel Day, 'Neil Sinclair: The Welshman who put Tiger Bay in the history books', the *Daily Express*, 30 October 2021: https://www.express.co.uk/news/uk/1511222/black-history-month-neil-sinclair-welshman-tiger-bay-history-cardiff-docklands-spt [accessed 21 September 2024].
35 *Centreplan 70* documentary, British Pathé: https://www.britishpathe.com/asset/206965/ [accessed 21 September 2024].
36 In his memoirs, Heseltine boasted that the area had been changed from 'desolate open spaces and dreary council estates' to a 'vibrant community'.
37 Despite being a government-free zone, the LDDC sucked in £443 million in public money between 1981 and 1988.
38 Leon Gooberman, *The State and Post-industrial Urban Regeneration: The Reinvention of South Cardiff*, Cambridge University Press, 2017.
39 Abdullahi had a solid alibi. He'd been working on a ship called the *Coral Sea* in Barry, a claim he made 545 times during his interviews. John Actie was questioned nine times and knew he was being fitted up. 'It was the white guy on the telly, and now you're just picking up Black guys,' he told the officers, who sound offended that he's suggested there may be a race element at play. Tony Paris was subjected to bullying tactics by officers who banged tables and shouted in his face.
40 The interview tapes reveal the police's reliance on the classic good cop, bad cop technique. Miller was repeatedly told he'd killed his girlfriend, that he knew more than he was letting on – that he was a killer and a cold-blooded one. Then another officer would help him come up with a 'reason' for his 'memory lapse': he'd been smoking weed, he was 'off his box'. Once that seed was sown, the police kept working Miller until he started to admit, theoretically, he *could* have been at the scene of the crime.
41 The BBC's *A Killing in Tiger Bay* provides a full account of the Cardiff Three case: https://www.bbc.co.uk/iplayer/episodes/m000zhgf/a-killing-in-tiger-bay [accessed 25 September 2024].
42 Atlantic Wharf, Butetown, Cardiff: https://atlanticwharfcardiff.co.uk.
43 Aaron Morby, 'United Living bags landmark £55m Cardiff resi job', *Construction Enquirer*, 29 September 2021: https://www.constructionenquirer.com/2021/09/29/united-living-bags-landmark-55m-cardiff-build-to-rent-job/ [accessed 25 September 2024].

44 'Cardiff: The Embankment planned for Butetown', BBC, 30 March 2021: https://www.bbc.co.uk/news/uk-wales-56576951 [accessed 21 September 2024].
45 'Building work begins at 700-apartment scheme in the centre of Cardiff', *Wales Online*, 17 March 2023: https://www.walesonline.co.uk/news/wales-news/huge-waterfront-scheme-centre-cardiff-26493076 [accessed 21 September 2024].
46 'Work begins on new Butetown railway station', *Transport For Wales*, 11 January 2023: https://news.tfw.wales/news/work-begins-on-new-butetown-railway-station [accessed 21 September 2024].
47 'What people in Butetown think of the huge multi-million plans to redevelop Cardiff Bay', *Wales Online*, Reem Ahmed, 29 March 2022: https://www.walesonline.co.uk/news/wales-news/butetown-cardiff-bay-arena-regeneration-23485082 [accessed 22 September 2024].
48 'The grand promises of Cardiff Bay: Success and failure in the biggest regeneration in Welsh history', *Wales Online*, 9 January 2018: https://www.walesonline.co.uk/business/business-news/grand-promises-cardiff-bay-success-14070156 [accessed 22 September 2024].

9. The English Disease, Edinburgh – 1989

1 Like other parts of Britain, Scotland had many prominent enslavers. Large companies, such as J. T. and A. Douglas & Co., enslaved hundreds of people, while wealthy families like the Beckfords and the Lambies owned sugar plantations in Jamaica. After abolition, when the British government compensated enslavers – a move fiercely opposed by Scottish merchants – one of the youngest recipients was a six-year-old girl from Glasgow.
2 'Hugh MacDiarmid: Scots would have been better off under the Nazis', the *Scotsman*, 5 April 2010: https://www.scotsman.com/arts-and-culture/hugh-macdiarmid-scots-would-have-been-better-off-under-the-nazis-1726579 [accessed 22 September 2024].

End Notes

3 Arnold Kemp, 'Who asked Hitler to set up a Scots republic?', the *Guardian*, 3 June 2001: https://www.theguardian.com/uk/2001/jun/03/theobserver.uknews1 [accessed 22 September 2024].

4 It's unlikely he meant the Scots Guards. A more likely regiment would be the 51st Highland Division who were left in northern France, under French command, and cut off from the Dunkirk retreat in 1940; they were ordered to fight on and unable to retreat fast enough. They were killed or captured. However, a sizeable chunk of the division was made up of specialist army regiments with English and Welsh units.

5 John Hancox, 'The underdog bares its teeth: The Scots are too busy hating the English to abuse ethnic minorities', the *Guardian* [archive], 11 March 1992.

6 'Prison Ships', *Hansard*, HC Debate 21 October 1987, vol 120, cc781-3W: https://api.parliament.uk/historic-hansard/written-answers/1987/oct/21/prison-ships [accessed 14 September 2024].

7 The Anfal Campaign, *Human Rights Watch*, 1993: https://www.hrw.org/reports/1993/iraqanfal/ANFALINT.htm [accessed 21 September 2024].

8 A full account of the event can be found at: 'Fighting Denial: The Lothian Black Forum and Anti-Racist Protests in Edinburgh, 1989–1992'.

9 Brian Ferguson, 'Edinburgh's slave trade past highlighted in new guide to the city's historic buildings and landmarks', the *Scotsman*, 22 January 2021: https://www.scotsman.com/whats-on/arts-and-entertainment/edinburghs-slave-trade-past-highlighted-in-new-guide-to-the-citys-historic-buildings-and-landmarks-3109834 [accessed 21 September 2024].

10 Robin Ward, *Exploring Edinburgh*, Luath Press, 2021.

11 This took place just eight days before the famous Battle of George Square when the Clyde Workers Committee demonstrated to support the forty-hour week, a key moment in the Scottish trade union movement that is commemorated every year.

12 CRER BHM, 'Lessons from the Glasgow race riots', *Black History Month Scotland*: https://www.blackhistorymonthscotland.org/blog-4/lessons-from-the-glasgow-race-riots-1919–2019 [accessed 21 September 2024].

End Notes

13 'Colour Bar in Edinburgh', the *Manchester Guardian* [archive], 1 June 1927.
14 'The Colour Bar in Edinburgh', the *Manchester Guardian* [archive], 28 May 1931.
15 'Colour Bar at Universities', the *Manchester Guardian* [archive], 23 January 1931.
16 Maureen Blackwood, *A Family Called Abrew*, BFI: https://player.bfi.org.uk/free/film/watch-a-family-called-abrew-1992-online [accessed 21 September 2024].
17 Forestry and Land Scotland, British Honduran Forestry Unit: https://forestryandland.gov.scot/learn/heritage/world-war-two/british-honduran-forestry-unit
18 Vicky Allan, 'The Last Lumberjack', the *Herald*, 15 January 2006: https://www.heraldscotland.com/default_content/12443406.last-lumberjack-sam-martinez-left-homeland-british-honduras-1941-bound-new-life-woodcutter-scotland-now-96-shares-wisdom-vicky-allan-talks-changed-times-staying-positive-life-local-celebrity/ [accessed 21 September 2024].
19 Elizabeth Quigley, 'Scotland's debt to forgotten Belize lumberjacks', BBC, 2 February 2019: https://www.bbc.co.uk/news/uk-scotland-47049573 [accessed 21 September 2024].
20 Gaynor Legall's grandfather was one of the men who came to Britain and eventually settled in Butetown.
21 'Amos Ford, forester – obituary', the *Telegraph*, 18 May 2015: https://www.telegraph.co.uk/news/obituaries/11613375/Amos-Ford-forester-obituary.html&lang=en [accessed 21 September 2024].
22 Martinez eventually settled in Edinburgh, where he lived the remainder of his life, becoming an ardent Hibernian fan. It was a club he supported until his death in 2016 at 106 years old. Martinez would have sat in the same stadium as Sheekh's killers, and while we don't know if his path crossed with them or with the Abrews, it's a distinct possibility.
23 Gary Younge, 'Races apart on the Celtic fringe', the *Guardian* [archive], 6 January 1993.
24 Arshad had studied under Cecil Gutzmore – the editor of the *Black Liberator* newspaper and a contemporary of Colin Prescod, who was at Reading University, where he taught a youth and community work

course. Gutzmore organised his course around the themes of race, gender, sexual politics, class, and lesbian rights. His presence in Reading attracted many Black Londoners who travelled west to study under him, including Stafford Scott, a young community leader from Tottenham. 'I think that politicisation, that opening of eyes was occurring as part of my learning process,' Arshad recalls. Attending protests was the norm, as was carrying chilli in her pocket in case she ran into skinheads and needed to throw it in their eyes. 'I missed the radical politics that I was exposed to down south and found it quite tame and mild,' she says. '[People] were really into race relations, as opposed to challenging racism.'

25 They ultimately received some help from the disgraced press baron Robert Maxwell who eventually provided £250,000 (after promising £2 million), leaving the organisers £4.5 million in debt.
26 'Glasgow's estates of hate', the *Guardian* [archive], 13 April 1988.
27 'Region probes allegation that teacher taunted Asian pupil', *The Observer* [archive], 17 September 1989.
28 'Victims of the English Disease', the *Guardian* [archive], 6 August 1989.
29 She also hated the fact state spending was higher north of the border than it was in England, blaming Malcolm Rifkind and his time in the Scottish Office, which ran affairs in the country for the government.
30 Scotland had much more in common with the north of England, which had largely rejected Thatcherism due to the damage her policies inflicted on the industrialised economy the region depended on. It couldn't pivot to a service-based economy like the south-east and London during the 1980s; the Edinburgh shipbuilders had far more in common with striking miners than with the banking Yuppies of the City.
31 Those suspicions were confirmed after the 1987 election when the Conservative vote in Scotland collapsed, reducing the number of sitting MPs from twenty-one seats to ten – a result the party has never truly recovered from.
32 Colin Kidd, 'Brown v. Salmond: Colin Kidd on the State of the Union', *London Review of Books*, 29(8), 26 April 2007: https://www.lrb.co.uk/the-paper/v29/n08/colin-kidd/brown-v.-salmond [accessed 21 September 2024].

End Notes

33 The party's newfound confidence played well with voters: in the first of 1974's two elections the party gained seven seats, which went up to eleven in the second election that October.

34 Colin Kidd, 'New Unions for Old', *London Review of Books*, 43(5), 4 March 2021: https://www.lrb.co.uk/the-paper/v43/n05/colin-kidd/new-unions-for-old [accessed 21 September 2024].

35 Its approach was designed to do two things: involve as many people as possible in its nationalism, regardless of race – a vital consideration for a country with fewer than five million residents – and to dispel concerns among Black and Asian Scots, who observed the ethnic violence and bigotry associated with burgeoning nationalist movements in other parts of Europe and former Soviet countries.

36 It's important to note that Celtic fans could be just as racist as those who followed Rangers. When Mark Walters signed for Rangers in 1987 – the only Black top-flight player at the time – bananas and darts were thrown at him during the Old Firm derby.

37 'Anger at "racist" myths', *The Observer* [archive], 29 January 1989.

38 The head teacher was a woman called Margaret MacIntosh who was sympathetic to what Arshad and the group were trying to accomplish. Her son, Ken MacIntosh, eventually became the speaker for the Scottish Parliament.

39 Some of the Lothian Black Forum members were also part of the General Workers Union, which Bill Morris – the first Black union boss – was leading at the time.

40 Callum MacRae, 'Ethnic fear as death probe ends', the *Guardian* [archive], 13 August 1989.

41 Callum MacRae, 'Region probes allegation that teacher taunted Asian pupil', the *Guardian* [archive], 17 September 1989.

42 Callum MacRae, 'Lothian police chief defends delay in defining racial killing', the *Guardian* [archive], 7 January 1990.

43 Herman Ouseley, 'A Problem Shared', the *Guardian* [archive], 2 May 1999.

44 The members went on to hold prestigious academic posts, governmental positions and become groundbreaking journalists. Younge became a celebrated journalist largely working for the *Guardian*,

reporting for over a decade in America before moving into academia. Arshad and McCrum also became academics in Scotland, while Said Bakar returned to the Comoros, where he worked with the government on educational programmes. Gata-Aura became a human rights lawyer. Philomena De Lima stayed in the Highlands, where she still studies ethnic minority communities living in isolation.

45 Libby Brooks, ' "A special day": how a Glasgow community halted immigration raid', the *Guardian*, 14 May 2021: https://www.theguardian.com/uk-news/2021/may/14/a-special-day-how-glasgow-community-halted-immigration-raid [accessed 21 September 2024].

46 Sophie Law, 'Every street name in Scotland linked to the slave trade', the *Daily Record*, 10 June 2020: https://www.dailyrecord.co.uk/news/scottish-news/every-street-name-scotland-linked-22167876 [accessed 21 September 2024].

47 Libby Brooks, 'Police Scotland chief constable says force is institutionally racist', the *Guardian*, 25 May 2023: https://www.theguardian.com/uk-news/2023/may/25/police-scotland-chief-constable-says-force-is-institutionally-racist [accessed 21 September 2024].

48 *The Political Party*, Show 217 – Humza Yousaf, 26 April 2021: https://uk-podcasts.co.uk/podcast/the-political-party/show-217-humza-yousaf [accessed 21 September 2024].

49 When the surviving cast of *Porridge* were reunited in 2003 for a mockumentary about the former inmates, Tony Osoba's McLaren had become a politician: representing the SNP in Glasgow East at the European Parliament.

50 *Private Eye*, 5–12 June 2023, p. 11.

10. The People of the Future – 1990

1 Greg Wilson, 'Electrospective: Hewan Clarke' (interview).
2 Mike Pickering, Red Bull Music Academy, interview: https://daily.redbullmusicacademy.com/2017/04/mike-pickering-interview
3 Fergal Kinney, 'Pills, mills and bellyaches: how Blackburn outpartied Manchester', the *Guardian*, 28 May 2020: https://www.

theguardian.com/music/2020/may/28/pills-mills-and-bellyaches-how-blackburn-out-partied-manchester [accessed 21 September 2024].

4 Matt Anniss's book *Join The Future* (Velocity Press, 2021), is the definitive account of the Bleep and Bass scene.
5 *History of the BBC – Grandstand*: https://www.bbc.com/historyofthebbc/anniversaries/october/grandstand/ [accessed 21 September 2024].
6 Simon Barnes, 'Peerless leader who draws strength from the sound of silence', *The Times* [archive], 30 April 1994.
7 Paul Fitzpatrick, 'Northern waste Hanley heroics', the *Guardian* [archive], 28 March 1983.
8 The try is emblematic of Hanley's qualities: tenacity, talent and – like all truly great players – selfishness. Mike Ford, who was a teammate of Hanley's at Wigan and for Great Britain, remembers playing alongside him. Their teammate Steve Hampson broke through the opposition's line and had an easy pass to Ford, who could walk over the line to score. Suddenly, Hanley appeared over his shoulder and bumped him out of the way, taking the ball and scoring himself. 'He ran past me and just giggled afterwards,' says Ford.
9 Simon Kelner, 'Failing to cover Rugby League in glory', *The Observer* [archive], 28 April 1985.
10 'No happy Valley return for Northern as Wigan turn on the power', the *Guardian* [archive], 11 April 1988.
11 He'd been spotted by Ray French playing Rugby Union sevens, a quick, frantic version of the fifteen-man code. The commentator flagged him to Rugby League club St Helens who famously scouted him, returning with the verdict that he was an 'uncoordinated clown'.
12 Doug Laughton, *A Dream Come True*, London League Publications Ltd, p. 77.
13 Laughton travelled to London to sign Offiah, failing at the first attempt with the player deciding he would stick with his plan to play union. But when Laughton came back with a much-improved offer (a total package of £85,000, with £25,000 up front and a car) he decided to chance his arm and move to the north-west. 'I hadn't even seen Widnes, let alone lived there,' Offiah wrote in his biography. Incredibly, for someone who'd just been signed for such a fee, he'd never played Rugby League before.

End Notes

14 Jimi Famuwera, 'Farmed: why were so many Black children fostered by white families in the UK?', the *Guardian*, 15 September 2022: https://www.theguardian.com/society/2022/sep/15/farmed-black-children-fostered-white-families-uk [accessed 21 September 2024].
15 John Vercarre-Shaw, *Poor Man's Eton*, BBC documentary, 2012: https://www.youtube.com/watch?v=hvjC4ULnavM [accessed 20 September 2024].
16 Billy Boston statue in Wigan: http://www.offbeat.group.shef.ac.uk/statues/STUK_Boston_Billy.htm [accessed 20 September 2024].
17 Many of the sport's Black heroes were originally from Butetown and had left after facing exclusion from Welsh Rugby Union, which, like its English counterpart, operated a de facto colour bar for much of the twentieth century.
18 'Offiah hurtles to his record', *The Observer* [archive], 3 January 1988.
19 Film director Juliet Ellis, who was fifteen when she first went, explained the appeal. 'I'd left home, was living in a bedsit and had nothing,' she said. 'Jive Turkey became my world. I'm mixed race and there were a lot of Black people there. It felt like home and the music – damn. Like nothing else.'
20 Jon Savage, 'More Music' column, *The Observer* [archive], 13 November 1988.
21 BBC Music, 'My Generation goes back to the 1980s with Soul II Soul frontman Jazzie B', BBC, 2016: https://www.bbc.co.uk/mediacentre/latestnews/2016/bbc-music-my-generation-80s [accessed 20 September 2024].
22 Andrew Dickson, 'Everyone wanted to get one over on Thatcher' – the artists who raided the Enterprise Allowance Scheme', the *Guardian*, 23 July 2023: https://www.theguardian.com/culture/2023/jul/26/thatcher-enterprise-allowance-scheme-artists-rachel-whiteread-jarvis-cocker-britpop-ybas [accessed 22 September 2024].
23 Benji B interview with Steve Beckett, Red Bull Music Academy, 2007: https://www.redbullmusicacademy.com/lectures/steve-beckett-the-warp-factor [accessed 5 September 2024].
24 There should have been six Black players on the plane to Australia. The player who missed out was Jamaican-born Des Drummond,

following an incident while playing for Warrington against Widnes. After a particularly bad-tempered game where Offiah lined up against the winger, a Widnes fan confronted Drummond and racially abused him. Drummond – a judo black belt – allegedly hit the fan, causing a cut that required seven stitches. As a result, he was banned from the 1988 tour, and his international career was effectively over. The way the incident was handled by the authorities was typical of the period: Black players could not retaliate.

25 'Winning down there gave us credibility,' said Offiah. And they'd done it while being led by a Black captain. The team scored a total of eight tries against the Australians in the tests, but only one was scored by a white player. Henderson Gill's downtown boogie wasn't just a spontaneous celebration; it was a signal that the best players in the world were, once again, Black Britons.

26 Hanley was nicknamed the 'Black Pearl' by the Australian press.

27 After the touring party returned from Australia, Hanley and Offiah stayed close. They began going out together, and headed to the Haçienda, which in 1988 was at its peak of popularity. It's likely that when they walked into the club, bypassing the long line which included the future Oasis stars Noel and Liam Gallagher, they heard the sounds of A Guy Called Gerald's 'Voodoo Ray' echoing around the club.

28 Yvonne Roberts, 'Ringmaster who sells a good line', the *Guardian*, 31 March 1991: https://www.proquest.com/hnpguardianobserver/docview/477388130/8050B6E6EEC54111PQ/2?accountid=133107 [accessed 21 September 2024].

29 A rumour that he was gay began to circulate after he went to Flesh, the LGBT night in Manchester. He faced homophobic abuse while on the pitch.

30 Offiah's most iconic moment would come in the Challenge Cup Final in 1995. Playing against a Leeds team that Hanley captained, Offiah scored a try that was every bit as impressive as Hanley's against Featherstone that had stunned *Grandstand* watchers in 1983. Picking the ball up just in front of his own posts, Offiah weaved through the entire

Leeds team before touching down. As the enormity of what he'd done sunk in, he knelt with his head in his hands. It's arguably the most iconic Rugby League try ever scored at Wembley; in 2016, a statue of Offiah immortalising the moment was unveiled.

31 The campaign was designed by Mark Denton, one of the most influential ad men of the 1990s: https://davedye.com/2015/03/27/boss-no-5-mark-denton/ [accessed 21 September 2024].

32 Margaret Thatcher, Letter to Sir Geoffrey Howe MP (resignation), 1990: https://www.margaretthatcher.org/document/108236 [accessed 21 September 2024].

33 Margaret Thatcher, *The Downing Street Years*, William Collins, 1993.

34 Lauren Cochrane, 'Jazzie B: "Fashion was integral to what Soul II Soul did"', the *Guardian*, 11 April 2013: https://www.theguardian.com/fashion/fashion-blog/2013/apr/11/jazzie-b-fashion-soul-ii-soul [accessed 21 September 2024].

35 During the 1992 election, Major would knock on doors to drum up support for Taylor, who went on to lose a Tory safe seat to the Liberal Democrats.

36 Catherine Bennett, 'Why are political turncoats such hot property?', the *Guardian*, 3 May 2001: https://www.theguardian.com/g2/story/0,3604,482117,00.html [accessed 21 September 2024].

37 Dan Fisher, 'Split Between Britain, U.S. Seen as "Inevitable": Foreign policy: The Conservative Party chairman fears that a "less European" America will provide the wedge', *Los Angeles Times*, 19 April 1990: https://www.latimes.com/archives/la-xpm-1990-04-19-mn-2009-story.html [accessed 21 September 2024].

38 The Chemical Brothers – Live at Somerset 2019 (Full Set), arctiɪ Concerts, YouTube, 2021: https://www.youtube.com/watch?v=GikjhOEqX3Y [accessed on 22 September 2024].

We Were There: Coda

1 Farage described Powell as his political hero in a 2008 interview with *Total Politics* magazine. 'I would never say that Powell was racist in any

way at all. Had we listened to him, we would have much better race relations now than we have got,' Farage said.
2 Peter Fryer, *Staying Power: The History of Black People in Britain*, Pluto Press, 2010.

Acknowledgements

I completed dozens of interviews with people all over this country, and spent hours in archives stored in Bradford, Birmingham, Manchester and Lambeth. Those interviews and archival research are two key parts of this book, the other is academic work and previously published material.

There are a few books that were crucial as I began to work on *We Were There*. Clement Cooper's *Presence* acted as a portal to the world of 80s Manchester, Ferdinand Dennis' *Behind the Frontline* was a travelogue like no other, and Jacqueline Nassy Brown's *Dropping Anchor, Setting Sail* was a masterclass in research, nuance and compassion. I'm thankful for the films of Colin Prescod, Maureen Blackwood and Horace Ove; Steve McQueen's *Small Axe*, and Bea Freeman's work – all of which helped me grasp a world out of reach. The foundational text that is Peter Fryer's *Staying Power* was a constant source of information and inspiration, Sven Beckert's *Empire of Cotton* proved a crucial reference point, as did Mark Christian and Stephen Small's work on *Black Liverpool*. Hakim Adi and Marika Sherwood's writing was essential as I tried to understand the Pan-African Congress. The notes section lists the many books I drew from; my own work humbly stands on the shoulders of these giants.

I'm also thankful for early conversations with people who took the time to talk when this book was a nebulous idea. Andrew Lynch, Tony Collins, Francesca Sobande, Mother Tongue, Natalie Denny, Bolu Babalola, Dan Hancox, Arifa Akbar, Nesrine Malik, Douglas Franklin, Cairo Clarke, Daniel Trilliing, Dan Jones, Shirin Hirsch, Ashley Clark, Kevin Johnson, Clive Nwonka, Greg Wilson, Mark Sealy, Karl Oxford, Andy Beckett, Ekow Eshun and Matt Anniss – without your tips, support *We Were There* could not have taken shape.

Acknowledgements

Thank you to my agent Matthew Turner. Your encouragement forced this book into the world. Your sense of humour was a source of succour, especially when things were at their hardest. My editor Stuart Williams, you won a scrap for this book and then became its biggest defender and champion. Thank you, and all the team at Vintage and The Bodley Head, especially Laura Reeves, Amrit Bhullar and Joe Pickering.

Special thanks goes to Gary Younge whose walks around Victoria Park and coffees at Cafe Oto calmed my anxiety between drafts one and two; while your thoughts on Edinburgh and Scotland were vital in telling the Axmed Sheekh story.

I'll be forever indebted to the people who shared contacts and made connections, especially Philip 'Fred' Adedeji, DJ Paulette and Gemma Obeng without whom the Northern Soul chapter wouldn't have been possible. Alex Simmons opened a door for me to enter the world of 1980s rugby league, and Luke Bainbridge helped with Mancunian links. Joan Weir and Joyce Cochrane were crucial to the Edinburgh chapter, while Gaynor Legall and Trevor Godbold generously unlocked the Tiger Bay archive. Della George, answered a call from a stranger and made my connection with John Lindo. Clea and Kimera Koff, thank you for connecting me with your incredible mother Msindo – and for your memories of Blacks Britannica and your father, David. Courtney Hay, Lubaina Himid, Marlene Smith, Wally Brown, Maria O'Reilly, Claire Dove, Joanne Anderson, Julian Agyeman, Idell Kamili and Rhonda Finlayson all patiently put up with me as I tried to understand the various worlds I was writing about.

I'm incredibly grateful to everyone who took the time to speak with me for the book, but some people went far beyond anything I could ever have expected. Thanks to Claudette Johnson, not only for three interviews, but for allowing me to attend your honorary degree ceremony alongside family and friends – it was a beautiful day facilitated by Mags Winthrop at Wolverhampton University. Thanks to Henderson Gill for inviting me into his home and explaining the realities of rugby league life; Lord Heseltine for the interview at

Acknowledgements

Thenford House; Paul Gilroy for letting me delve into his incredible memory on a sunny afternoon in Finsbury Park, and Ingrid Pollard for her generosity. Thanks to Aniff Akinola and Hewan Clarke for an afternoon spent in a pub in Hulme, Linda Brogan for her tireless work unearthing the Reno, and to Bernard Leach for his Bill Williams connection – you gave me a road map with which to navigate Black Manchester, while Harold Offeh and Stephen Nze generously helped me understand their artwork about Liverpool. Appreciation goes to Larry Elliott for his economics expertise; Philip Inman for helping me grasp the wild days of Militant in Liverpool; and to Nasar Malik, who talked me through Scottish nationalism's history with race.

Second Home in Hackney provided me with a secure place to work on a first draft, while Humanities 2 at the British Library became a refuge as I completed edits. I'm forever grateful to Carol Gormer and the Gordon Burn Foundation who let me use Gordon's cottage in Duns (one of the places the Belizean foresters were sent) to produce a second draft during a cold week in October 2023. I'm also indebted to Ana Fletcher and Vimbai Shire, copy-editors who honed and pruned my work until it began to take the shape it is in today.

I owe a special debt to my editors at the Guardian: Alex Needham commissioned the Northern Soul feature that was a proof of concept, Fay Schlesinger gave me the time I needed and Kath Viner was a staunch supporter of the project. Thank you.

All the photographers who agreed to let me use your work: Derek Bishton, Vanley Burke, Ian Beesley and Nick Treharne. I'm especially grateful to Susan Sills for the image of Axmed Sheekh, Lisa Ayegun for sharing family pictures from The Reno's heyday and Keith Piper, for kindly allowing the use of the Blk Art Group's polaroids. To Leah Ellis and Warp, thanks for letting me use your images. I'm grateful to my friend and colleague Nick Pritchard who tracked down a beautiful picture of George Lindo.

Sadly, I didn't get the chance to speak to Leroy Cooper who passed as I was working on the Liverpool chapter. Researching his

Acknowledgements

art and activism was one of the most nourishing parts of working We Were There, he was a true artist and the fiercest defender of his community. Thanks to Bolaji Laurence for his memories of his mother Kathleen Locke and to the estate of Maud Sulter for their time and knowledge – both of them continue to be an inspiration to me. I'll be forever grateful to Duncan Campbell for connecting me to the Koff family, and Margaret Henry and Benjamin Zephaniah for their interviews, which came just a few months before they passed. This book and Black Britain is so much stronger because of their contributions.

Thanks also goes to Jonathan Shainin, Maya Wolfe-Robinson, Stephen Small, Joseph Harker, Severin Carrell, Libby Brooks, Gwilym Mumford and Oliver Laughland who all read early versions of chapters which were all improved and sharpened after their input. Of course, all errors and omissions are entirely my own. To Tom Lutz, thanks for searching the St Clair Drake archives in New York. Pete Kowalczyk, you put up with hours worth of whinging from me, thanks for your friendship and guidance. My fellow Bradfordian Alex Davids was a great advocate and my legal guide. Watching you operate was awe-inspiring, and reminded me about how far we'd come since running around boggy pitches with Bolton Woods u-15s and dancing to Sir Shina Peters in Palm Cove.

I'm immensely thankful to my family and the Nigerian community of Bradford. In the process of writing this book I came to understand just how important you've been to me and my writing in ways I still don't truly grasp. I'm especially thankful to have Grace and Ayo as my sisters, and for the guidance and counsel of my parents. The love and support you and the community gave to me growing up is a key part of the ballast which my sense of self rests on to this day. Sadly, right at the beginning of writing *We Were There*, we lost Gus Igbegbuna. He was, like many people in this book, someone who encouraged us as Black British kids to take our place in this country. Thank you now and always; your legacy is continued through your wonderful children: Kwame, Jade and Ruth.

Finally, I want to thank my wife Raquel who held it together

Acknowledgements

when I couldn't. This book took a lot of my energy, at a time when we had a two-month-old baby and a toddler to contend with. You are the centre of our home and our hearts. I want to thank my daughters: Temilola and Ayobami, your incredible ability to nap for three hours in the middle of the day while I was on paternity leave with both of you meant this book was possible. These stories are yours. I hope you use them to understand the country you're growing up in. I love you both more than any words could ever express.

Credits

Chapter One

Vernon Pryce and friend at the last night of Wigan Casino in 1981. Courtesy of Francisco Mellina.

The National Front and Communist Party holding a rally in Blackburn, Lancashire. 20th January 1973

Photo by Wallin/Mirrorpix via Getty Images.

Conservative Party leader Margaret Thatcher talking to constituents during a trip to High Wycombe to support Tory candidate Ray Whitney in the by-election. Photo by David Ashdown/Keystone/Getty Images.

Chapter Two

Rubbish piled up on streets of London, due to industrial action by refuse collectors, Soho, London. Photo by Alistar Macdonald/Daily Mirror/Mirrorpix via Getty Images.

Mill Chimneys, Bradford, 1970s. Courtesy of Ian Beesley.

Chapter Three

Professor Stuart Hall in his office by Vanley Burke. Courtesy of Vanley Burke/DACS.

Posed group portrait of Steel Pulse. Photo by Echoes/Redferns via Getty Images.

Participants in the Handsworth Self Portrait project conducted during 1979. Courtesy of Derek Bishton.

Chapter Four

Police officers in riot gear outside a burning looted shop in Park Road. Photo by John Davidson/Liverpool Echo/Mirrorpix via Getty Images.

Credits

Michael Heseltine Secretary of State for the Environment seen here touring Toxteth following the riots. 25th July 1981. Photo by Staff/Mirrorpix via Getty Images.

Chapter Five

A black man walks past graffiti in support of Enoch Powell. Photo by Hulton-Deutsch Collection/CORBIS/Corbis via Getty Images.
Claudette Johnson in her studio in London in 1986. Courtesy of Brian Shuel.
Polaroid of the Blk Art Group on the day of the convention in 1982. Courtesy of the Estate of Donald G. Rodney.

Chapter Six

The audience listening to speakers at the Fifth Pan-African Congress, 10 November 1945. Photo by John Deakin/Picture Post/Hulton Archive via Getty Images.
The Crescents in Hulme, 1987. Photo by Tom Stoddart via Getty Images.
Phil Magbotiwan and Lati at the bar in The Reno. Courtesy of Lisa Agyeun.

Chapter Seven

Farm labourers harvesting bracken on a hill overlooking Lake Windermere at Ambleside in Cumbria. Photo by Walmsley Brothers/Hulton Archive via Getty Images.
Portrait of Julian Agyeman taken by Ingrid Pollard in Essex in front of some oilseed rape fields. Courtesy of Ingrid Pollard.
The Cost of The Countryside by Ingrid Pollard. Courtesy of Ingrid Pollard.
Internal view of the London Stock Exchange. Photo by Eric Préau/Sygma via Getty Images.

Chapter Eight

Two friends playing outside in the dockland area of Cardiff. Photo by Bert Hardy/Picture Post/Hulton Archive via Getty Images.
The Queen, Prince Phillip and Prince Charles travel along Bute Street in May 1999 on their way to officially open the National Assembly for

Credits

Wales for the first time after Wales voted for Devolution in September 1997. Photo by Nick Treharne.

Chapter Nine

Axmed Abuukar Sheekh Maxamed of Somalia. Photo courtesy of Richard and Susan Sills.

Lines from 'Flag Up Scotland, Jamaica' in *May Day* by Jackie Kay (Picador, 2024). Reproduced with the kind permission of Jackie Kay.

West Indian Foresters In Britain: Cutting Wood In Scotland. Photo by Current Affairs/Imperial War Museums via Getty Images.

Chapter Ten

Nightmares on Wax pose outside Warp Records in Sheffield. Courtesy of Martyn Goodacre.

Winston Hazel and DJ Parrot. Courtesy of Warp Records.

English Rugby League tourists Roy Powell (left) and Henderson Gill have photos taken for their family albums at the new Sydney Football Stadium by teammate Carl Gibson this morning. Photo by Quentin Jones; Mark Douglas Baker/Fairfax Media via Getty Images.

Rugby League test at Sports Stadium Australia V England. July 9, 1988. Photo by Quentin Jones; Mark Douglas Baker/Fairfax Media via Getty Images.

Index

Abasindi Collective, 150, 166, 172
Abbensetts, Michael, 64, 79, 230
Abbott, Diane, 116, 257, 278
Abdi, Keith, 210
Abdullahi, Yusef, 225
Ability II, 260
Abyssinians, 70
acid house, 3, 32, 169, 258–62, 268–71, 278, 279–80, 281–3
'Acid Tracks' (Phuture), 258
Actie, John, 225
Actie, Ronald, 225
Adam, Robert, 161
Adamson, Barry, 159
Adell, 95, 113, 116
Adi, Hakim, 9
African Caribbean Self-Help Organisation, 67
Afro-bashment, 261
Agyeman, Julian, 175, 180–87, 191–6
AIDS, 147
Akomfrah, John, 2, 83, 86, 133, 137, 142
Albert Docks, Liverpool, 108, 110, 113
Aldershot, Hampshire, 94
Alexandra Park Estate, Moss Side, 170
Ali, Muhammad, 98, 165
Alien Acts, 208, 224
All Faiths For One Race (AFFOR), 74
Allen, Richard, 19
Ambassador, Bradford, 12
Ambleside, Cumbria, 180, 186
American Civil War (1861–5), 95, 157
Amis, Martin, 62

Anderson, Dean, 20
Anderson, Joanne, 99, 112, 113, 114
Anderson, Paul, 270
Anderson, Viv, 267
Anderton, James, 147–8, 150, 160, 166
Angelou, Maya, 124
anthropology, 212
Anti-Nazi League, 78
apartheid, 235, 240–41, 242, 243, 245, 248
Appiah, Joe, 153
Arab people, 202, 204, 207, 212, 213
Arab-Israeli War (1973), 243
Araeen, Rasheed, 137, 141
Aramaic, 235
Armley Prison, Leeds, 51, 55
Armstrong, Louis, 68
Arnolfini, Bristol, 130
Arshad, Rowena, 236, 239, 244–5, 250
Ashanti Roy, 70
Asian Youth Movement, 245
Attenborough, David, 77
Attlee, Clement, 15–16
authoritarian populism, 76
Awolowo, Obafemi, 152
Ayegun, Lisa, 148, 150
Azikiwe, Nmandi, 152

B-Rocket, 164
Babylon, 70, 72
Babylon (1980 film), 59, 93
Bacon, Francis, 134
Baldwin, James, 213

Index

Baldwin, Stanley, 52, 177, 189, 199
Balmain RFC, 274
Balmoral Castle, Aberdeenshire, 232
Balsall Heath, Birmingham, 67, 73, 87
Baltimore, Maryland, 222
Banda, Hastings, 152
Bank of England, 197
Banksy, 282
Baraka, Amiri, 124
Barclay, David, 156
Barker, Ronnie, 230
Barnes, Simon, 264, 267
Barratt, Richard, 269
Bass Culture, 25
Bassey, Solly, 107
Bassline, 261
Battle of Bradford (1976), 41–4, 48
Battle of Cable Street (1936), 41–2
Battle of Culloden (1746), 232
Battle of Lewisham (1977), 4, 42
Battle of Orgreave (1984), 219
Bayoh, Sheku, 253
Beat Boys, 12
Beat, The, 67, 124
Beatles, The, 98
Beaton, Norman, 79
Beaumont, Karis, 8
Beckert, Sven, 156
Beckett, Steve, 270, 271
Bedford, Bedfordshire, 94
Belfast, Northern Ireland, 9
Belize, 201, 238, 239
Bell, Laurence, 270
Benn, Nigel, 274
Berghaus, 199
Bernstein, Howard, 171–2
Betjeman, John, 178
Bevin, Ernest, 52
Bhangra, 36
Big Bang reforms (1986), 187–8

Billboard, 15
Birmingham, West Midlands, 2, 64–88, 210
  art scene, 123–4
  IRA pub bombings (1974), 226
  policing in, 73–7
  Ralph affair (1976), 66–7
  Rastafarianism in, 68–75
  toy industry, 65, 210
  unrest (1981), 6, 94
  unrest (1985), 86–7
Birmingham Six, 226
Bishton, Derek, 66, 67, 86
Biskind, Peter, 59
Black and White Minstrel Show, The, 78
Black Art an'Done, 123
Black Art Gallery, London, 141
Black Art Movement, 118–44
Black Arts Movement (1960s), 124
Black Audio Film Collective, 86, 133, 137, 142
Black Bag (TV series), 258
Black Environmental Network (BEN), 175, 189–96, 200, 233
Black Girls Hike, 198
Black History Month, 116
Black Lives Matter (BLM), 7, 117, 143, 196, 198, 284
Black Men Walking, 199
Black Metropolis (Drake), 214–17, 219, 227
Black Music, 24
Black Pack, 274
Black Panthers, 26
Black People's Day of Action, 93
Black Power Movement, 26, 31, 49, 50, 124
Black Sections movement, 191
Blackburn, Lancashire, 12, 18, 27, 81, 94
Blackpool, Lancashire, 12, 17, 26, 27, 31

Index

Blacks Britannica (1978 film), 34–7, 39, 43, 57–62, 93, 158
   broadcast of, 35–6, 57–62
   Lindo case and, 44–5, 48–9, 52–4, 61
Blackwood, Maureen, 237–9
Blakelock, Keith, 226
Bleasdale, Alan, 79, 100–102
Bleep and Bass, 260–62, 268–71, 278, 279–80, 281–3
Blk Art Group, 118–19, 123–5, 128–44, 183, 185
   First National Black Art Convention (1982), 133–40
Blue Beat, 164
Blue Story (2019 film), 7
Blues & Soul, 24, 165
blues music, 17
Boarders, 7
Boateng, Paul, 116, 257, 278
Bolan, Marc, 128
Bold, Jonas, 114
Bolsheviks, 208
Bolton, Manchester, 12, 17, 20, 29, 94
Booker Prize, 197, 232
Boston, Billy, 266
Botham, Ian, 94
Boucher, Constantine, 47
Boulton Road School, Birmingham, 67
Bourne, Stephen, 9
Bovell, Denis, 79
Bowie, David, 128
Bowling, Frank, 134, 135, 140, 142, 144
boxing, 46, 98, 152, 165, 215, 238, 274
Boyce, Sonia, 2, 134, 137, 138, 141, 144
Boyega, John, 2
Boys From The Blackstuff (1982 TV series), 100–102
Bradford Black, 44, 50, 55
Bradford, West Yorkshire, 3, 12, 17, 29, 36–62, 51, 77, 210

Blacks Britannica (1978), see *Blacks Britannica*
   Lindo case (1977–8), 45–57, 58, 61, 93, 97, 135–6, 167, 257
   unrest (1976), 41–4, 48
   unrest (1981), 6
   unrest (1995), 42
   unrest (2001), 36, 42
   wool trade, 38–9, 45, 210
Bradford Black, 44, 50, 55
Bradford Northern, 263–5
Bradley, Lloyd, 25
Braithwaite, Edward Kamau, 135
Bramble, Chris, 232
Brent, London, 7
Brewster, Bill, 30
Brexit, 285
Brierley, David, 46, 55, 56
Brighton hotel bombing (1984), 111
Bristol, England, 3
   art scene, 130, 142
   slave trade and, 117, 197
Bristol Steppin Sistas, 199
British Broadcasting Corporation (BBC), 77–83, 196–7
British Honduran Forestry Unit, 238
British Jazz, 261
British National Party (BNP), 27, 53, 241
British Nationality Act (1948), 15–16
British Union of Fascists, 232
Brixton riot (1981), 4, 93, 94, 116
Broadcast Over Britain (Reith), 80
Broadwater Farm riot (1985), 226
Brogan, Linda, 145, 146–7, 168, 170–73, 258
Bromley, London, 183
Bronzeville, Chicago, 215
Broughton, Frank, 30
Brown, Dennis, 70

347

Index

Brown, Ian, 163
Brown, James, 58
Brown, John, 73–4, 81–2
Brown, Manneh, 107
Brown, Otis, 12
Brown, Wally, 103–4, 109–10, 112, 115
Bruno, Frank, 275
BSA, 66
Bulldog, 19
Bumpkin Files, 8
Buppies, 274
Burke, Edmund, 65
Burke, Vanley, 63–5, 67, 83–4, 280
Burnham, Andy, 157
Burnham Beeches, Buckinghamshire, 176–7
Burning Spear, 70, 71, 86
Burroughs, William, 258
Butcher, Roland, 267
Bute House, Edinburgh, 236
Bute, John Crichton-Stuart, 2nd Marquess, 204, 220
Butetown, Cardiff, 3, 201–29
  gambling in, 215, 224
  interracial relationships in, 205, 209, 211, 213, 227
  sex work in, 204, 212, 223–6
  sports in, 215
  unrest (1919), 207–10
  urban renewal, 217–23, 224–5, 226, 227–8
  White murder case (1988), 223–6, 228–9
Butler, Richard Austen 'Rab', 16
Byrd, Gary, 27

Caesar, Pogus, 69, 132
Caesar, Steve, 11–13, 14, 21–4, 25, 26, 32, 33, 256

Callaghan, James 'Jim', 5, 37–8, 41, 76, 101, 121, 214
Campaign Against Racism in the Media (CARM), 78, 80
Campaign for Nuclear Disarmament, 111
Campbell, Naomi, 275
cannabis, 70, 107, 173
Cape Verde, 202
Capital City Service, 241, 246
Capitalism and Slavery (Williams), 156, 214
Carby, Hazel, 196
Cardiff, Wales, 3, 7, 94, 114, 201–29
  interracial relationships in, 205, 209, 211, 213, 227
  sex work in, 204, 212, 223–6
  unrest (1919), 207–10
  urban renewal, 217–23, 224–5, 226, 227–8, 256
  White murder case (1988), 223–6, 228–9
Cardiff Bay Development Corporation, 203, 222
Cardiff Five, 225–6, 228–9, 258
Caribbean Arts Movement (CAM), 135–6
Carlos, John, 31
Carmichael, Stokely, 26
Carr, Ronnie, 12
Carter, Angela, 257
Cassidy, David, 128
Casino Club, Wigan, 1, 9, 11–15, 17, 19–20, 21, 31, 32, 147, 256, 283
Catacombs, Wolverhampton, 12
Catholicism, 232, 241, 244
Cave, Nick, 159
Cayton, Horace, 215
Cecil Street, Manchester, 148
Celtic FC, 243

Index

Central St Martins, 130
Centre for Contemporary Cultural Studies (CCCS), 63, 82
Centreplan 70 proposal, 217–23
Certain Ratio, A, 162
Chambers, Eddie, 123–5, 132, 137, 141, 142, 185
Chants, The, 98
Chapeltown, Leeds, 8, 12, 21, 26
Charles III, King, 94, 181, 220
Charles Wootton House, Liverpool, 105, 114
Charles Wotton i-Tec, Liverpool, 112
Charles, Craig, 14
Charles, John, 161
Charles, Ray, 164
Charters, Michelle, 114
Chavis, Benjamin, 183, 192
Chemical Brothers, The, 281–2
Chester, Cheshire, 94
Chicago, Illinois, 215
Chicago house music, 168, 169–70, 258
China, 154
Chinese people, 202, 204, 206, 230, 239
Choice FM, 116
Christianity, 71, 147, 213
Christie, Linford, 274, 279
Christie, Sterling, 47
Church of England, 197
Church of the Morning Star, The, 71
Churchill, Winston, 40, 52
Cirencester, Gloucestershire, 94
City of London, 125–6, 187, 256
City Speaks, A (1947 film), 158
civic nationalism, 243, 254
civil rights movement (1954–68), 26, 31, 34, 78, 215
Clarke, Alan, 230
Clarke, Edward, 50

Clarke, Hewan, 146, 164, 165, 168, 170, 258
Clash, The, 4, 29
Clockwork Orange, A (1971 film), 76
coal industry, 110, 111, 204, 218–19, 228, 256, 259
Coard, Bernard, 22
Cochrane, Joyce, 236, 240
Cochrane, Kelso, 18, 98
Cockburn, Alexander, 60
Cocker, Jarvis, 270
Coit, James, 31
Coleman, David, 262
Collins, Tony, 265
Colonial Club, Manchester, 150–51
Colonial Defence Association, 216
colonialism, 34–5, 50, 119, 175, 184–5
    Pan-African Congress (1945), 44, 145, 151–5, 153, 159, 172, 214
    Scotland and, 231–3, 242
colour bars, 13, 28, 43, 66, 145, 149–50, 212, 237
Colston, Edward, 117
Commission for Racial Equality, 21, 189–90
Commonwealth, 15–16, 21, 41, 70, 174, 179, 213
Commonwealth Games, 240–41
Commonwealth Immigrants Act (1962), 15
Commonwealth Immigrants Act (1968), 121
communism, 18, 57, 58, 152, 154, 216
Comoros Islands, 234
compulsory purchase orders, 160, 220, 221
Congo Crisis (1960–65), 154
Conservative Party, 54, 242, 278–9
    see also Thatcher, Margaret
Constable, John, 177

Index

Conteh, John, 98
Coogan, Steve, 163
Coolie, 168
Cooper, Leroy, 91, 104, 110, 112
Cornwall, England, 181, 190
Cosmopolitan, 275
'Cost of the English Landscape, The' (Pollard), 185, 186
Cotton Club, Manchester, 149
cotton industry, 155–8, 197
Count Ossie, 70
Countryfile, 196–7, 198
countryside, 3, 8, 174–200
    Jay report (1991), 189–91
    slavery and, 185, 193–5, 197
Courtauld Gallery, London, 143
Coventry, West Midlands, 123, 124, 130, 132, 199
Covid-19 pandemic (2019–23), 115, 284
Cowgate, Edinburgh, 233, 235, 249
Cranfield Institute of Education, 74
Crawford, Cindy, 275
Creation Records, 270
Creech Jones, Arthur, 16
Creed, Martin, 140
Crescents, Hulme, 161–3, 162, 172
Crewe, Cheshire, 12, 17, 20
cricket, 215, 267
'cricket test', 279
crime
    drug trafficking, 107, 170, 203, 204
    false incriminations, 45–57, 58, 61, 93, 97, 224–6
    knife crime, 148, 204, 225, 235–6, 240
    muggings, 64, 73, 75, 81, 82, 93
    pornography, 147, 148
    sex work, 67, 87, 159–60, 204, 212, 223–6
    shebeens, 148

Sus laws, 53–4, 61, 64, 93, 115, 116, 166, 171, 257
    see also policing
Criminal Attempts Act (1981), 116
Criminal Justice and Public Order Act (1994), 171
Crisis, The, 217
Critchley, Julian, 102
Crompton Arms, Birmingham, 67
'Cubik' (808 State), 278
Curtis, Colin, 24, 31, 165

Da Costa, Paulinho, 164
Dadzie, Stella, 9
Daily Telegraph, 55, 193
Daley, Nicholas, 2
Dammers, Jerry, 128
'Dancing In The Street' (Gaye et al.), 31
Darling, Alistair, 248–50
Davies, Jonathan, 265
Dawes, Dominic, 123, 124
Day, Robin, 80, 82
De Lima, Philomena, 244
De Waal, Edmund, 270
Deedes, Bill, 193–5
deindustrialisation, 2, 111, 125, 218, 256
Deller, Jeremy, 270
Democratic Republic of Congo, 154
Denmark Road, Manchester, 148, 149
Dennis, Ferdinand, 9, 72, 192
Derby, Derbyshire, 94
Detroit, Michigan, 36, 179
devolution, 242–3
Devon, England, 190
'Dextrous' (Nightmares on Wax), 260, 269–70, 271, 281
Diana, Princess of Wales, 94
Dimmock, Peter, 262
Dixon, Colin, 266

350

Index

Do The Right Thing (1989 film), 275
Do You Remember Cable Street?, 41–2
Doctor D, 168
Domino, 270
Dorell, Dave, 270
Dorneywood, Buckinghamshire, 176
Dorset, England, 190
Douglass, Frederick, 156
Dove, Claire, 111–12
Drake, St Clair, 214–17, 219, 227, 228
Dread Beat An' Blood (Johnson), 50, 56
dreadlocks, 64, 69, 72, 73
Dream Weavers, The, 164
Dreaming Whilst Black (2021 TV series), 7
drugs, 107, 170, 203
    cannabis, 70, 107, 173
    ecstasy, 259, 261–2, 282
    heroin, 170
    opium, 204
Drum'n'Bass, 261
Drummond Community High School, Edinburgh, 245
Drysdale, Liz, 109, 112, 115
Du Bois, William Edward Burghardt, 152, 153, 154, 215
Duleep Singh, Sikh Maharajah, 182
Dundas, Henry, 236
Duns, Berwickshire, 238

Earl William, 233
Earth, Wind and Fire, 14
Ebony on the Road (TV series), 257–8
Ebrahim, Saeed, 228
Echoes, 24
ecstasy, 259, 261–2, 282
Edinburgh, Scotland, 4, 94, 197, 230–55
    Commonwealth Games (1986), 240–41
    knife crime in, 235–6, 240
    Sheekh murder (1989), 235–6, 244–55
    slavery and, 236
Edinburgh club, Manchester, 163
Edinburgh Workers Association, 248
education system, 6, 21–2, 42, 52, 67
Edwards, Beresford, 160–61
Edwards, Elouise, 160–61, 166, 172
Egypt, 201
808 State, 278
elections
    1965 general election, 66
    1976 local elections, 41
    1978 by-elections, 21, *23*
    1979 general election, 76–7, 241
    1987 general election, 188–9, 257, 278
Elfer, David, 225
Eliot, Thomas Stearns, 38
Elizabeth II, Queen, 70, 220
Elland Road, Leeds, 19, 26
Ellerker, Geoffrey, 48
Ellesmere Port, Cheshire, 94
Elveden, Suffolk, 182
Emin, Tracey, 140, 141, 270
Empire of Cotton (Beckert), 156
Empire Road (TV series), 64, 79, 86
Empire Windrush, 5, 13, 16, 28, 35, 90, 97, 118, 214
Energy Flash (Reynolds), 261
Engels, Friedrich, 154
England football team, 267
'English disease', 231–2, 249, 251
English Journey (Priestley), 96
Enterprise Allowance Scheme, 270
Environment Department, 189
environmental racism, 183
Epitome of Sound, The, 17
Erskine, Joey, 215
Estates (Hanley), 162–3
Ethiopia, 68–9, 152
eugenics, 90, 96, 103, 105, 205, 211, 227

351

Index

European Capital of Culture, 113
Evangelista, Linda, 275
Evans, Tony, 111
Evelyn, George, 262, 269–71, 281–2
Everton, Liverpool, 108
Everton FC, 98, 113

Factory Records, 162, 165, 258
Falklands War (1982), 6, 110, 111, 126–8, 189, 259
Falkner Place, Liverpool, 99
Family Called Abrew, A (1992 film), 237–9
Fanning, David, 57
far-right, 4, 6, 13, 17–19, 66–7, 199–200, 241–2, 285–6
   British National Party (BNP), 27, 53, 241
   British Union of Fascists, 232
   National Front (NF), *see* National Front
   policing and, 47, 73
   skinheads, 19, 20, 29, 99
   Union Movement, 17
Farage, Nigel, 285
Fashanu, John, 274
Fashanu, Justin, 279
fashion, 275
Fatinikun, Rhiane, 198, 199
Featherstone Rovers, 263–4
feminism, 112, 124, 132, 137, 139, 150, 152
Fields, Dwayne, 197
financial crash (2008), 187
Finlayson, Rhonda, 19–20, 24, 32, 33, 256
First National Black Art Convention (1982), 133–40
First World War (1914–18), 206–10, 237
Firth, Raymond, 212
Fisher, Mark, 219

Fitzpatrick, Paul, 264
Flack, Roberta, 167
Fletcher, Muriel, 96, 103, 105, 205, 213
Flock Together, 198–9
Floyd, George, 143, 196, 284
Focal Point, 250
Fon Records, Sheffield, 270
football, 16–17, 26, 98, 267
   far right and, 19, 28, 231, 235, 241–2, 251, 262
   Heysel disaster (1985), 111
Ford, 101
Ford, Amos, 239
Ford, Mike, 267–8
Ford, Phil, 272, 273
Forgemasters, 271
Fosters, The, 78, 79
Fourth Idea, Bradford, 42
Francis, Roy, 266
Frankfurt School, 63
Franklin, Aretha, 31
Fraser, Peter Lovat, 249, 250
Free Church of Scotland, 236
Freeman, Bea, 96, 109, 111
Freeman, Johnny, 266
French, Philip, 60
Friedman, Milton, 5, 6
Fryer, Peter, 286

Galbraith, Bill, 279
Galbraith, John Kenneth, 6
Gallagher, Liam, 275
gambling, 215, 224
gangs, 7, 76, 170
garage music, 261
Garvey, Amy Ashwood, 44, 152
Garvey, Marcus, 69
gaslighting, 249
Gata-Aura, Tarlochan, 245, 249
Gayle, Alan, 107

Index

Gayle, Howard, 98
General Belgrano, 127
general elections, *see* elections
George V, King, 68
George, Della, 48
Ghana, 15, 145, 152, 153, 154, 215
'Ghost Town' (The Specials), 91–2, 125
Gibson, Carl, 272, *273*
Gill, Henderson, 263, 266, 272, 273, *273*
Gilroy, Paul, 67–8, 72, 73, 86, 196
Gipton, Leeds, 22
Givanni, June, 9
Gladiators (TV series), 275
Glancy, Francis, 235, 241, 245–6
Glasgow, Scotland, 128, 197, 236–7, 251, 252
Glassford, John, 252
Glastonbury Festival, 280–83
'Go!' (The Chemical Brothers), 281
Godbold, Trevor, 201, 224, 228
Godin, David, 17
Goldman Sachs, 187
Goldsmiths University, 144
Golspie, Sutherland, 238
Gordon, Douglas, 140
Gordon, Rob, 260
Gramsci, Antonio, 63
Granby Street, Liverpool, 97, 110, 112, 115
Grandstand, 262, 263, 272, 275
Grangetown, Cardiff, 220
Grant, Bernie, 116, 257, 278
Grant, John, 165
Grassmarket, Edinburgh, 235, 248
Gray, Dobie, 12
Great Britain rugby team, 266, 272–4
Great Fire of London (1666), 206
'Great Moving Right Show, The' (Hall), 257
Greater London Council, 104, 116

Greek people, 202, 212
Green, Carlton, 75
Greengate, Salford, 148
Greg, Samuel, 156
Grieg, Tony, 267
Griffiths, George, 47
grime music, 261, 282
Guardian, 156, 197
gun violence, 170
Guscott, Jeremy, 267
Guy Called Gerald, A, 260
Guyana, 16

Haçienda, Manchester, 170, 258–60
Hackney, London, 7
Haile Selassie, Ethiopian Emperor, 68
Haiti, 152
Halifax, West Yorkshire, 94
Halifax Panthers, 266, 274
Hall, Stuart, 62–4, 65, 67, 75, 77, 79–83, 87–8, 122, 256–7, 282–3
Hamburg, Germany, 167
Hamilton, Anthea, 142
Hampton, Fred, 252
Handsworth, Birmingham, 64–88, 93
  policing in, 73–5
  Rastafarianism in, 68–75
  sex workers in, 67, 87
  unrest (1981), 6, 94
  unrest (1985), 86–7
Handsworth Revolution (Steel Pulse), 62, 64, 83
Handsworth Self-Portrait project, 83–6
Handsworth Songs (1986 film), 86, 133
Hanley, Ellery, 263–5, 266, 268, 271–7, 276, 279, 283
Hanley, Lynsey, 162–3
Happy Mondays, 162, 270
Harambee OBU, 67
Hardy, Ron, 169

Index

Harewood House, Leeds, 193, 198
Harlem Renaissance (1918 – c. 1935), 68–9, 71
Harper, Kevin, 270, 271
Harriott, Homer, 260
Harris, Naomie, 2
Harris, Richard, 263
Harris, Roxy, 50
Harrison, Charles, 143
Hathaway, Donnie, 167
Hatton, Derek, 110–11
Haughton, James, 105
Havelock Square, Sheffield, 268
Hay, Courtney, 48–9, 54
Hayward Gallery, London, 141
Hazel, Andrew, 123
Hazel, Winston, 268–70, 271, 281
Healey, Denis, 37
Heart of Midlothian FC, 241
Heath, Edward, 37, 122, 219
Hebden Bridge, West Yorkshire, 26
Hennessy, Peter, 94
Henry, Duke of Gloucester, 68
Henry, Lenny, 78, 275
Henry, Margaret, 58, 60
Herefordshire, England, 8
Heriot-Watt University, 240
heroin, 170
Heseltine, Michael, 102–3, 105–10, 106, 111–14, 221, 277
Heysel disaster (1985), 111
Hibbert, George, 156
Hibernian FC, 235, 240, 241
Higgins, Alex, 165
High Wycombe, Buckinghamshire, 23, 94
Highfields, Leicester, 94
Himid, Lubaina, 132–3, 137, 138, 139, 141, 142, 144
Hinds, David, 72

Hirst, Damien, 140
history, 116, 130
Hockney, David, 134
Holder, Ziggy, 181
Holloway, Nicky, 169
Holocaust (1941–5), 205
Homebeats, 251
Homer, Brian, 86
homosexuality, 147, 171, 279
hooks, bell, 124
house music, 144, 145–6, 168–71
    acid house, 3, 32, 169, 258–62, 268–71, 278, 279–80, 281–3
House of Dread, Birmingham, 70, 163
Housing Aid Centre, Liverpool, 112
Howe, Darcus, 50, 52, 54, 61, 257
Howe, Geoffrey, 94, 101, 108–9, 221, 277
Howe, Leila Hassan, 50
Howell, Leonard Percival, 68–9
Huddersfield, West Yorkshire, 94
Hughes, Langston, 68
Hull FC, 266
Hulme, Manchester, 53, 146, 148, 158, 159, 161–3, 171
Humphrey, Hubert, 76
Hurd, Douglas, 148
Huskisson, William, 89–90, 112, 117
Hussein, Ali, 49
Hytner, Benet, 167

I May Destroy You (2020 TV series), 7
Ibiza, 169
Ibrox Stadium, Glasgow, 241
Ikon Gallery, Birmingham, 123
Ince, Paul, 267, 274
Indian people, 230, 239, 241
inflation, 5, 37, 39, 92, 127, 285
Inner London Education Authority (ILEA), 116

Index

Institute of Contemporary Arts (ICA), 141
Institute of Race Relations, 192, 251
International Garden Festival, 109, 113
International Slavery Museum, Liverpool, 114
interracial relationships, 96–7, 105, 205, 209, 211, 213, 227
Iraq, 235
Irish Republican Army (IRA), 111, 171, 226
Ishiguro, Kazuo, 178–9, 189
Isley Brothers, 27
Israel, 153
It Ain't Half Hot Mum, 78, 80
'It's Almost Tomorrow' (The Dream Weavers), 164
Ital Rockers, 260
Italy, 202
Iyapo, Anum, 138

Jackson, Jesse, 34
Jacobite rebellion (1745–6), 232
Jah Shaka, 25
Jamaica, 19, 25, 49, 68, 69, 208
James IV, King of Scotland, 231
James Connolly Society, 248, 251
Jantjes, Gavin, 130, 141
Jay, Eric, 189–91
Jay, Norman, 24, 270
jazz music, 17, 261
Jazzie B, 270, 278, 280
Jenkins, Roy, 203
Jewish people, 38, 42, 205, 206
Jive Turkey, 269
John, Gus, 49, 167
Johnson, Claudette, 128–9, 131, 133, 137–40, 142, 144
Johnson, Kim, 115

Johnson, Len, 152, 157
Johnson, Linton Kwesi, 50, 56, 79, 86
Johnson, Lyndon, 135
Jones, Claudia, 54
Jones, Clem, 122
Jones, Gloria, 12
Jones, Tom, 12
Jordan, Glenn, 224, 226, 227
Jordan, Michael, 277
Joseph, Anthony, 151
Joseph, Paterson, 9
Joy Division, 162
Julien, Isaac, 196
Jungle music, 261
Junior Murvin, 29
Juno, 260

Kaluuya, Daniel, 2
Kamili, Idell, 25–6, 28
Kay, Jackie, 252
Keep Britain White, 17–18
Kelman, James, 232
Kenmure Street protest (2021), 251–2
Kennedy, Ludovic, 81, 82
Kennedy, Robert, 75–6
Kensit, Patsy, 275
Kent, William, 161
Kenya, 34–5, 121, 145, 152
Kenyatta, Jomo, 145, 152
Kerouac, Jack, 26
Kes (1969 film), 182
Keswick, Cumbria, 94
Kew Gardens, London, 197
Keynes, John Maynard, 205
Kidd, Colin, 243
King, Martin Luther, 26, 34, 58
King Edward VI School, Birmingham, 67
Kinlochewe, Ross and Cromarty, 238
Kinnock, Neil, 111, 188, 242

Index

Kirkby, Liverpool, 99
Kitch (Joseph), 151
Kitchen, Manchester, 162–3
Kitchen, The (2023 film), 7
Kitching, Kenneth, 48
knife crime, 148, 204, 225, 235–6, 240, 244–55
Knights, Philip, 74
Knowsley, Liverpool, 110
Knuckles, Frankie, 169
Koff, David, 34–7, 39, 44, 45, 57, 60
Koons, Jeff, 130
Kru Club, Manchester, 149
Ku Klux Klan, 241
Kubrick, Stanley, 76
Kurds, 235
Kurmask, SS, 208
Kuya, Dorothy, 98, 100

L8, *see* Toxteth
L8 Defence Committee, 105–10, 111–12, 114
L8 Law Centre, Liverpool, 112
La Rose, John, 50, 54, 135
Labour Party, 54, 110–11, 191, 242, 243
'Labour's Not Working' campaign (1978–9), 37
Ladbroke Grove, London, 7
Lake District, 180, 182–3, 184, 186
Lamont, Norman, 3
Lane, Gary, 165
Lascelles family, 193, 198
Lashley, Petrona, 114
Laughton, Doug, 265, 268
Laurance, Bolaji, 150, 165
Law and Order (1978 TV series), 230
law and order, *see* crime; policing
Lawrence, Stephen, 50, 195, 235, 250, 254
le Carré, John, 40

League of Coloured Peoples, 209
Leavis, Frank Raymond, 178
Lee, Spike, 275
Leeds, West Yorkshire, 8, 12, 21, 26, 276
    Oluwale, death of (1969), 48, 137, 284–5
    raves in, 262, 281
Leeds Service Crew, 262, 281
Leeds United FC, 19, 26, 261
Leese, Richard, 163, 171–2
Legall, Gaynor, 201, 210, 214, 222–3, 224, 226–8
Lehman Brothers, 187
Leicester, Leicestershire, 94
Leith, Edinburgh, 237–8
Leslie, Wenda, 124
Letts, Don, 29–30
Levine, Ian, 24, 26
LFO, 260, 271
LGBT community, 147, 171, 279
Liberia, 152
Lincoln, Abraham, 157
Lindo, George, 45–57, 58, 61, 93, 97, 135–6, 167, 257
Listener, The, 105
Little, Kenneth, 211–14, 217, 227
Little Alex pub, Manchester, 149
Little Richard, 98
Liver Building, Liverpool, 103, 114
Liverpool, Merseyside, 2, 3, 4, 7, 88, 89–117
    Huskisson statue toppling (1982), 89–90, 112
    International Garden Festival, 109, 113
    policing in, 104–7
    segregation in, 98–100
    slave trade and, 89–90, 95, 112, 114
    unemployment in, 100–104, 111–12
    unrest (1919), 97, 99

Index

unrest (1948), 97, 99
unrest (1972), 99
unrest (1981), 6, 89, 91–2, 99, 103–17
urban renewal in, 108, 110, 113–14, 256
Liverpool Black Organisation, 112
Liverpool FC, 98
Livingstone, Iain, 253
Livingstone, Ken, 103, 116
Lloyd's, 197
Loach, Ken, 79, 182
Locke, Kath, 54, 150, 154–5, 158–9, 163, 173
Lofgren, Nils, 131
London, England, 3–4, 7–8, 28–9, 36, 88
art scene, 134–5, 141, 142
Cochrane murder (1959), 18, 98
Docklands, 114, 221, 256
finance sector, 125–6, 187
Great Fire (1666), 206
Lawrence murder (1993), 50, 195, 235, 250, 254
policing in, 47–8, 50, 53
unrest (1958), 98
unrest (1976), 4, 28–9, 93, 118
unrest (1977), 4, 42
unrest (1981), 4, 93, 94, 116
unrest (1985), 226
London Caribbean Trekkers, 199
London Docklands Development Corporation (LDDC), 221
London Monarchs, 276
London Stock Exchange, 187
Longsight, Manchester, 128
Lord Woodbine, 98
Lorenzo, Donville, 69, 72
Lothian Black Forum, 245–51, 254
Lothian Campaign Against Racism, 251
Loudon Square, Cardiff, 219

Loudoun Square Coloured Mission, 216
Loughrigg Fell, Cumbria, 180, 182, 183, 186
Loy, Linda, 107
Lumb Lane, Bradford, 42–3, 48, 61
lumberjacks, 238–9
Lumumba, Patrice, 154
Luton, Bedfordshire, 8, 9, 94

MacDiarmid, Hugh, 232
MacDonald, Ian, 50, 53
MacDonald, Ramsay, 52
MacDonald, Trevor, 275
Macpherson Inquiry (1997–9), 50, 195, 250–51
MacRae, Callum, 247
Magazine, 159
Magbotiwan, Phil, 148–52, 160, 163, 165, 168–9, 169
Major, John, 113, 278
Make Bradford British, 36
Makonnen, T Ras, 151, 157, 160, 172
Malawi, 152
Malaysia 201, 239
Malcolm X, 26
Malta, 212
Manchester, England, 3, 29, 54, 144, 145–73, 174
club scene in, 145–51, 163–73, 258–60
cotton industry, 155–8, 197
gang violence in, 170
IRA bombing (1996), 171
Pan-African Congress (1945), 44, 145, 151–5, *153*, 159, 172, 214
representation in, 115
slave trade and, 156–8
unrest (1981), 6, 94, 166–8
urban renewal in, 145–6, 158–63, 171–3, 221

357

Index

Manchester Plan (1941), 145–6, 148–63
Manchester United FC, 16
Mandela, Nelson, 240–41, 242
Mangrove Nine, 50, 53, 97
Manningham, Bradford, 42
Mansfield, Michael, 226
Māori people, 212
Marley, Bob, 70, 71, 165
Martin, David, 211
Martin, Lionel, 67
Martinez, Sam, 238, 239
Marxism, 58, 60, 63, 131
Mathison, Trevor, 133
Matumbi, 29
Mau Mau rebellion (1952–60), 34–5
McCarthy, Joseph, 58
McCrum, Mukami, 244, 246, 251
McGee, Alan, 270
McLauchlan, Julian, 181
McNee, David, 94
McPherson, Ian, 250
McQueen, Steve, 2, 141
MDMA, 259, 261–2, 282
Mecca, Blackpool, 12, 26, 27, 31
media, 7, 77–83, 116
Mellina, Francesco, 32
Melville, Herman, 96
Melville Monument, Edinburgh, 236
Memphis, Tennessee, 17
Mendy, Ambrose, 274–5, 278
Merchant Navy Club, Manchester, 149
Mersey Beat poets, 98
Mexico City Olympics (1968), 31
'Midnight' (Charles), 164
Militant Tendency, 110–11, 188
Miller, Stephen, 224–6
miners' strike (1984–5), 110, 111, 218–19, 256, 259
mixed-race people, 96–7, 105, 205, 209, 211

Mobutu, Joseph-Désiré, 154
Molema, Silas Modiri, 237
Mona Lisa's, Sheffield, 269
monetarism, 92, 125
Morgan, Kenneth, 121
Morisca Club, Manchester, 149
Moses, 168
Mosley, Oswald, 17, 122, 209, 232
Moss Side, Manchester, 53, 94, 144, 145–73
    club scene in, 145–51, 163–73
    gang violence in, 170
    unrest (1981), 6, 94, 166–8
    urban renewal in, 145–6, 148–63, 221
Motown, 27
Mound, Edinburgh, 236, 248
Mount Stuart Square, Butetown, 202
Mufti, Rashid, 106, 107
Muggeridge, Malcolm, 80
muggings, 64, 73, 75, 81, 82, 93
Muirhouse Against Racism, 251
multiculturalism, 87, 192, 199, 200, 201, 203, 226
Murdoch, Rupert, 127
Murphy, Alex, 268
Music Box, Chicago, 258
Muslim Hikers, 199
MVP, 17
Mwinyipembe, Msindo, 34–7, 39, 43, 44, 57, 59, 60

NAACP, 217
Nash, John, 161
Nassy Brown, Jaqueline, 100, 113
National Front (NF), 4, 13, 18, 19, 21, 27, 209, 231, 241, 249
    Battle of Bradford (1976), 41–4, 48
    local elections (1976), 41
    North Ilford by-election (1978), 21
    Ralph affair (1976), 66–7

Index

National Health Service (NHS), 15
National Trust, 175, 180, 194, 195, 197, 198
Negroes in Britain (Little), 211–14, 217
Nello James Centre, Manchester, 165, 171
Nelson, Trevor, 270
Netherley, Liverpool, 99
New Cross fire (1981), 93
New Faces, 78
New Left, 63, 177
New Order, 162
New Orleans, Louisiana, 17
Newcastle, Tyne and Wear, 3, 94
Nigeria, 16, 97–8, 107, 148, 152, 168
Nightmares on Wax, 260, 261, 262, 269–71, 279–80, 281
Nike, 277
Nile, Manchester, 148, 150, 166, 173
Nixon, Richard, 27, 75–6
Nkrumah, Kwame, 145, 152, 154, 215
'No Way Back' (Adonis), 170
Noble, Maria, 161
North Ilford by-election (1978), 21
North Sea oil, 101, 243
Northern Ireland, 9, 91, 176, 232
Northern Soul, 1–2, 11–33, 147, 256
  all-nighters, 12–15, 19, 20, 24
  black fanbase, 1–2, 13
  black fist emblem, 31
  class and, 30
  dance, 11–13, 32
  DJs, 24, 165
  fashion, 22
  political songs, 31
  racism and, 13, 14, 18, 20, 27–8, 31, 147
  white fanbase, 1, 14, 25, 27
Notting Hill, London, 7
  Carnival, 4, 28–9, 54, 93
  unrest (1958), 98
  unrest (1976), 4, 28–9, 93, 118

Nottingham, Nottinghamshire, 9, 94, 98, 123
Nyahoe, Bobby, 98, 111
Nze, Stephen, 89–90, 112, 117

O'Reilly, Maria, 99, 107, 112
Oakenfold, Paul, 169
Obeng, Ian, 14–17, 24, 27, 32, 33, 256
Occupied Palestine (1981 film), 60
Offeh, Harold, 117
Offiah, Martin, 265–8, 271–7, 276, 278, 279, 282, 283
Ofili, Chris, 130–31, 141
Okundaye, Jason, 9
Olusoga, David, 9
Oluwale, David, 47–8, 137, 284–5
Olympic Games, 31
On The Road (Kerouac), 26
Open Door, 77–83
Open University, 87
Osoba, Tony, 230
Oti, Chris, 267
Oval Four, 47, 56
Ové, Horace, 59, 79
Oxford, Kenneth, 104–5, 211
Oyelowo, David, 2

P-Funk, 14
Paisley, Bob, 98
Pakistan, 36, 41, 230
Palestine, 153
Palmer, Ian, 123
Palmer, Tony, 1, 9, 13–15, 20, 24, 32
Pan-African Congress (1945), 44, 145, 151–5, 153, 159, 172, 214
Pan-African Publishing Company, 151
Pan-Africanism, 3, 69, 150–55, 159, 172, 213, 214, 215
Paris, Tony, 225
Parker, Paul, 19

Index

Parks, Rosa, 252
Parliament Street, Liverpool, 91, 97, 109
Parmar, Pratibha, 43, 50
Parrot, 269
'Pastoral Interlude' (Pollard), 184–7
Patel, Priti, 284
Peak District, 198
Peaks of Colour, 199
Peckham, London, 7
Pemberton, Eric, 132, 138
Pentecostalism, 71
People of Kau (Riefenstahl), 129
People of the Wind, 34–5
Perera, Nadeem, 199
Persian, 146, 163–8, 173
Peters, James, 266
Philip, Duke of Edinburgh, 220
Philips, George, 156
Phillips, Caryl, 52, 196
Phillips, Mike, 60
Phillips, Ron, 53, 54
Phuture, 258
Piccadilly Radio, 165
Pickering, Mike, 259
Pines, Jim, 9
Piper, Keith, 119, 123–5, 132, 137, 141, 142, 185
Plantation of Ulster (1609), 232
Play for Today, A, 79
Plymouth, Devon, 9
Poland, 41
Police and Criminal Evidence Act (1984), 116
'Police and Thieves' (Junior Murvin), 29
policing, 45–57, 59, 61–2, 73–7, 147–8, 150, 171, 211
    false incriminations, 45–57, 58, 61, 93, 97, 224–6
    institutional racism reviews, 250–51, 253
    Sus laws, 53–4, 61, 64, 93, 115, 116, 166, 171, 257
    unrest and, 91, 93, 104–7, 166
    urban renewal and, 159–60, 224–5, 226
Policing The Crisis (Hall), 75, 82
political representation, 115, 116, 257, 278–9
Pollard, Ingrid, 133, 138, 141, 142, 175, 183–7, 191, 196
Pollokshields protest (2021), 251–2
pornography, 147, 148
Porridge (TV series), 230
Portsmouth, Hampshire, 86, 94
post-punk music, 32
Powell, Enoch, 53, 81, 119–23, 125, 209, 285
Powell, Roy, 272, 273
Pratt, Glynn George, 98
Pre-Raphaelites, 184
Prescod, Colin, 39–40, 44–5, 58, 60, 93, 257
Pressure (1977 film), 59, 79
Preston, Lancashire, 94
Priestley, John Boynton, 96
Princes Boulevard, Liverpool, 89, 100, 117
Princess Road, Manchester, 148, 168
Private Eye, 253
prostitution, 67, 87, 159–60, 204, 212, 223–6
Proud Valley (1940 film), 215–16
Pryce, Vernon, 11, 32
Psaila, Angela, 225
Pulp, 270
punk music, 19, 27, 29, 30

Q-Tip, 281
Quarless, Ray, 96, 99, 108, 111

Index

Queenie (2024 TV series), 7
Question of Immigration, The, 81

Race Relations Act (1968), 121–2
Race Today Collective, 50–52
racism, 4, 13, 17–19, 98–100
   education system and, 6, 21–2, 42, 52, 67
   eugenics, 90, 96, 103, 105, 205, 211
   far-right politics, see far-right
   media and, 77–83
   Northern Soul and, 13, 14, 18, 20, 27–8, 93
   policing and, see under policing
   Scotland and, 231–3, 241, 243–4, 249, 251
   segregation and, see segregation
Rafters, Manchester, 165
Rainbow Club, Butetown, 213
Rainy City, Manchester, 149
Ralph, Robert, 66–7
Rampling, Danny, 169
Rance Allen Group, 27
Rangers FC, 241, 243
Ras Michael & the Sons of Negus, 70
Rastafarianism, 2, 43, 62, 64, 68–75, 78, 81, 112
raves, 259, 262, 281
Ray, Don, 17
Read, John Kingsley, 53, 81
Reading, Berkshire, 94
Real Thing, The, 98, 271
Reardon, John, 86
Red Scare (1947–57), 58
Redgrave, Vanessa, 165
Reeves, Martha, 17
Reform UK, 285
reggae, 17, 25, 29, 33, 43, 67, 70, 86, 98, 143, 166, 173
Reilly, Terence, 235, 241, 245–8

Reith, John, 80, 81, 158
Remains of the Day (Ishiguro), 178–9, 189
Remond, Sarah Parker, 156
Reno, Manchester, 145–51, 163–73, 258
'Respect' (Franklin), 31
retrospective regret, 178
Reynolds, Simon, 261
Rhodesia (1965–79), 47
Rhondda Heritage Park, 228
Richards, Viv, 267
Riches (2022 TV series), 7
Ridgewell, Derek, 47, 56
Riefenstahl, Leni, 129
Riley, Mykaell, 70, 83
riots, see unrest
Rise of Christian Europe, The (Trevor-Roper), 130
Rising Damp (TV series), 230
'Rivers of Blood' speech (Powell), 81, 119–23, 125, 209
Robeson, Paul, 215, 238
Robinson, Smokey, 20
Rochdale, Manchester, 141, 198
Rock Against Racism, 4, 29, 30
Rodney, Donald, 123, 132, 133
Roman Britain (43–410), 182–3
Rosenior, Leroy, 19
Rosso, Franco, 59
Rotha, Paul, 158
Rotherham, South Yorkshire, 219
Rothery, Anna, 116
Roundhouse, Camden, 26
Roxy Club, London, 29, 30
Royal College of Art, 132–3, 134
Royal Commonwealth Society, 213
Royal Palaces, 197
Royal Society for the Protection of Birds, 195
rudeboy culture, 19

Index

rugby, 182, 262–8, 271–7
Runnymede Trust, 64, 244
Rural Development Commission, 189
Rushdie, Salman, 257
Russell Club, Manchester, 162
Russian Revolution (1917), 208
Ryan, Veronica, 142
Ryder, Shaun, 270

S.O.U.L., 27
Saatchi, Charles, 140
Sade, 275
Said Bakar, Abdourahim, 234, 235, 236, 240, 245, 246, 247
Said Barre, Mohamed, 233
Sale, Manchester, 16
Salford, Manchester, 148, 154, 172
Salkley, Andrew, 135
Samantha's, Sheffield, 12, 20
Santille, SS, 208
Savage, Jon, 269
Saxa, 67
Scala cinema, King's Cross, 57–8
Scargill, Arthur, 218, 219
Scotland, 230–33
  devolution in, 242–3
  far right in, 241–2
  Kenmure Street protest (2021), 251–2
  knife crime in, 235–6, 240, 244–55
  lumberjacks in, 238–9
  nationalist movement, 242–3, 253, 254
  Sheekh murder (1989), 235–6, 244–55
  slavery and, 231, 236, 252
Scott, Jim, 249
Scott-Heron, Gil, 31
Scottish Black Women's Group, 244
Scottish Campaign Against Racism, 251

Scottish Council for Racial Equality, 241
Scottish National Party (SNP), 242–3, 253, 254
Scum (1979 film), 230
Searchlight, 42
Searle, Adrian, 130
Searling, Richard, 24
Second World War (1939–45), 39–40, 205, 210, 216, 238
Section 60 powers, 171
Seel, Thomas, 114
segregation, 36, 98–100, 204, 213, 215, 216, 261, 269
  colour bars, 13, 28, 43, 66, 145, 149–50, 212, 237
Selecter, The, 124
sex workers, 67, 87, 159–60, 204, 212, 223–6
'Shades of Grey' report (1977), 74, 81–2, 87
Shaft, Mike, 170
Sham 69, 29
Sharpton, Alfred, 226
Shaw, George Bernard, 205
shebeens, 148
Sheekh, Axmed, 233–6, 234, 239, 244–55
Sheffield, South Yorkshire, 3, 12, 17, 20, 94, 260, 268–71
Sherwood, Marika, 9
Short, Clare, 74–5
Showers, Michael, 107
Sierra Leone Club, Liverpool, 89
Sikhism, 182
Simone, Nina, 86
Simpson, Gerald, 260, 278
Sinclair, Neil, 220
Sink, Liverpool, 26
Sir Coxsone, 25
Sissay, Lemn, 163

Index

Sivanandan, Ambalavaner, 54
ska music, 67, 124, 164
skinhead culture, 17, 18–19, 20, 29, 99, 281
Skinhead series (Allen), 19
Skrewdriver, 19, 27
slavery, 7, 123, 125, 156–8
   Bristol and, 117, 197
   countryside and, 185, 193–5, 197
   Liverpool and, 89–90, 95, 112, 114
   Scotland and, 231, 236, 252
slum clearance, *see* urban renewal
Smethwick, West Midlands, 66, 123
Smith, Adonis, 170
Smith, Dudley, 58
Smith, Marlene, 123–4, 128, 132, 133–4
Smith, Tommie, 31
Smithdown Lane, Liverpool, 97
Somalia, 114, 202, 233
Somerset, England, 190
Sons of Africa, 212
Soul II Soul, 270, 280
sound systems, 25, 29, 59, 63, 70, 143, 164, 170, 261
South Africa, 235, 240–41, 242, 243, 245, 248
South Asian community, 35, 36, 41, 43, 81, 121, 230
South Liverpool Festival, 98
South-West England, 190–91
Southampton, Hampshire, 94
Southport stabbing (2024), 286
Soviet Union (1922–91), 40, 41, 154
Spanish flu (1918–20), 210
Spanish people, 212
Sparkbrook, Birmingham, 73
Specials, The, 91–2, 125, 128
Spectator, The, 197
Spin Inn Records, Manchester, 165
Spitting Image, 222

sports, 215, 274
   athletics, 215, 240–41, 274, 275, 279
   boxing, 46, 98, 152, 165, 215, 238, 274
   cricket, 215, 267, 279
   football, *see* football
   rugby, 182, 262–8, 271–7
Spring, Howard, 202, 204, 210
Sri Lanka, 233
St Andrew Square, Edinburgh, 236
St Kitts, 11, 21, 22, 69, 263
Stafford, Staffordshire, 17
Stanford University, 224
Steed, Maggie, 81
Steel Pulse, 4, 29, 62, 64, 70, 71, 72, 83, 86, 275
Steppas, 199
Steve Biko Housing Association, Liverpool, 108, 114
Stevenson College, Edinburgh, 236
Stockport, Manchester, 94
Stockwell Six, 48
Stoke-on-Trent, Staffordshire, 12, 17, 20, 31, 32
Stone Roses, The, 163
stop and search, 171
   see also Sus laws
Stopes, Marie, 205
Stormzy, 282
Strangeways Prison, Manchester, 55
Straw, Jack, 195
Stringer, Graham, 148
Stuart, Moira, 275
Sturgeon, Nicola, 253
Sturt, George, 178
Suez Crisis (1956), 40
Sullivan, Clive, 182, 266
Sunny's Blues, 269
Sus laws, 53–4, 61, 64, 93, 115, 116, 166, 171, 257

Index

Sutherland, William, 249
Sweet Sensation, 271

Tactical Action Group, 166
Tait, Alan, 265
'Talking Blues' report (1978), 74
Tamils, 233
Tate & Lyle, 101, 108
Tate galleries, 108, 110, 113, 123, 140
Taylor, John, 278–9
Tebbit, Norman, 40, 279, 285
television, 7, 77–83, 257–8
Thatcher, Denis, 241
Thatcher, Margaret, 1, 2, 5, 23, 37, 40–41, 52, 256–7, 277
  Big Bang reforms (1986), 187–8
  Commonwealth Games (1986), 241
  death (2013), 278, 280
  deindustrialisation, 2, 111, 125, 218, 256
  entrepreneurialism, support for, 270–71, 278
  Falklands War (1982), 6, 110, 111, 126–8, 189, 259
  immigration, views on, 6, 20–21, 33, 40–41, 52, 76–7, 118, 209
  leadership election (1990), 113, 277–8
  Liverpool, views on, 101, 103, 108–9, 113
  miners' strike (1984–5), 110, 111, 218–19, 256, 259
  monetarism, 92, 125
  policing, views on, 61–2, 76–7, 148
  public spending cuts, 87, 94, 125
  resignation (1990), 277–8
  Scotland, views on, 242
  small state ideology, 125, 221
  unrest (1981), 92, 103–4
  World in Action interview (1978), 20–21, 33, 41, 52, 76–7, 118, 209

'Theme, The' (Unique 3), 260, 261, 281
Thenford House, Northamptonshire, 102
They Haven't Done Nothing (1985 film), 110
Third World Club, Hamburg, 167
This Sporting Life (1963 film), 263
Thomas, Anita, 167
Thornhill Road Station, Handsworth, 73–5
Tiger Bay, Cardiff, *see* Butetown
Tiger Bay (Martin), 211
Tiger Bay and the World archive, 224
Tinker, Tailor, Soldier, Spy (le Carré), 40
Top Boy (TV series), 7
Top of the Pops, 15
Torch, Stoke-on-Trent, 12, 20, 31, 32
Tottenham Three, 226
Touchstone gallery, Rochdale, 141
Toxteth, Liverpool
  policing in, 104–7
  segregation, 98–100
  unemployment in, 100–104, 111–12, 115
  unrest (1981), 6, 89, 91–2, 99, 103–17
'Track With No Name' (Forgemasters), 271
trade unions, 2, 37, 40, 76, 92, 101, 157, 248, 251, 285
  miners' strike (1984–5), 110, 111, 218–19, 256, 259
Trainspotting (Welsh), 232
Tranent, East Lothian, 238
Trebilcock, Michael, 98
Trent Polytechnic, 123
Trevelyan, George Macaulay, 184
Trevor-Roper, Hugh, 130
Trew, Winston, 47, 56
Trinidad and Tobago, 16

Index

Trotskyites, 110–11, 188
tuberculosis, 214
Tufts University, 196
Turlington, Christy, 275
Turn-Ups, Sheffield, 269
Turner Prize, 140–41, 143
Twisted Wheel, Manchester, 19
Two Step Garage, 261
Two Tribes (Evans), 111
two-tone music, 67, 91–2, 124, 125, 128
Tyndall, John, 41
Tynecastle Park, Edinburgh, 241
Typhoo Tea, 66

Uganda, 121
Ukraine, 41
Ullapool, Ross and Cromarty, 238
unemployment, 5, 36, 37, 66, 90, 92, 259, 285
  in Liverpool, 100–104, 111–12, 115
Union Movement, 17
Unique 3, 260, 261, 280, 281
United States
  Black Power Movement, 26, 124
  Chicago house music, 168, 169–70, 258
  civil rights movement (1954–68), 26, 31, 34, 78, 215
  Civil War (1861–5), 95, 157
  Red Scare (1947–57), 58
  slavery in, 95
  unrest (1968), 75–6
  unrest (2020), 143, 196, 284
  Vietnam War (1955–75), 75–6, 135
  Watergate scandal (1972–4), 27
Universal Negro Improvement Association, 69
University of Birmingham, 63
University of Bradford, 43
University of Cambridge, 197–8, 212

University of Central Lancashire, 141
University of Chicago, 215
University of Glasgow, 197, 252
University of Liverpool, 96
University of the Arts London, 130
unrest
  1919 nationwide, 97, 99, 207–10, 236–7
  1948 Liverpool, 97, 99
  1958 Notting Hill and Nottingham, 98
  1972 Liverpool, 99
  1976 Bradford, 41–4, 48; Notting Hill, 4, 28–9, 93, 118
  1981 nationwide, 2, 4, 6, 89–117, 118–19, 133, 166–8, 175–6, 233, 257
  1985 Handsworth, 86–7; Tottenham, 226
  1995 Manningham, 42
  2001 Bradford, 36, 42
  2024 nationwide, 286
Up The Junction, Crewe, 12, 20
urban renewal, 53, 113, 146, 158, 160, 203, 217
  in Cardiff, 217–23, 224–5, 226, 227–8, 256
  in Liverpool, 108, 110, 113–14, 256
  in London, 114, 221–2, 256
  in Manchester, 145–6, 158–63, 171–3, 221

Va-Va's, Bolton, 12, 20
Vagrancy Act (1824), 53–4, 61, 64, 93
veganism, 70, 72
Vel-Vets, The, 17
Venice Biennale, 86, 119, 142
Vernon, Janet, 124
Victoria, Queen, 68, 182
Vietnam War (1955–75), 75–6, 135
Vilday, Leanne, 225

Index

Vinen, Richard, 88
Voice, The, 116, 192, 198, 276
'Voodoo Ray' (A Guy Called Gerald), 260

Wales Bonner, Grace, 2
Walker, Barbara, 142, 143
Walker, Johnny, 169
Walker, Peter, 21
Wanderlust Women, The, 199
Warp Records, 260, 270
Warrington Wolves, 274
Washington, Cecil, 28
'Waste Land, The' (Eliot), 38
Watergate scandal (1972–4), 27
Watkins, Olwen, 221
Watson, Stephen, 171
Watts, Los Angeles, 27, 179
Waugh, Evelyn, 68
Webb, Beatrice, 205
Webb, Sidney, 205
Webster, Martin, 19, 41, 42
'Weight of the Bass' (Unique 3), 261
Weir, Joan, 235–6, 245, 246, 254
welfare state, 87, 94
Welsh, Irvine, 232
West Indian Centre, Hulme, 171
'West Indians', 6
Wester Hailes Anti-Racism Project, 251
WGBH Boston, 34–5, 57–9
'white flight', 179
White, Lynette, 223–6
Whitelaw, William, 103, 105, 166, 176–7, 184
Whiteread, Rachel, 140, 270
Whitney, Ray, 23
Widnes, Cheshire, 12, 267
Widnes Vikings, 267–8, 274, 276

Wigan Casino, The (Palmer), 1, 9, 13–15, 17, 19, 20, 24, 32
Wigan, Manchester, 1, 9, 11–15, 17, 19–20, 21, 31, 32, 147, 256, 283
Wigan Warriors, 265, 266, 274
Wilkie, Derek, 98
Williams, Emmanuel, 97
Williams, Eric, 156, 193, 214
Williams, John, 223, 225
Williams, Martin, 260
Williams, Raymond, 177–8
Wilson, Frank, 28
Wilson, Harold, 121
Wilson, James Arthur, 211, 224
Wilson, Jonathan, 252
Wilson, Tony, 162, 165, 258
Windrush Generation, 5, 13, 16, 28, 35, 90, 94, 97, 118, 214
Windrush scandal (2018), 143
Winstanley, Russ, 24
Winter of Discontent (1978–9), 37–8, 76, 101, 256, 285
'woke', 130, 171
Wolverhampton Young Black Artists, 123
Wolverhampton, West Midlands, 12, 94, 118, 143–4
  First National Black Art Convention (1982), 133–40
women, 25–6, 131–2
  feminism, 112, 124, 132, 137, 139, 150, 152
Wonder, Stevie, 27
Wong, Ansel, 103
Woolverstone Hall, Suffolk, 266
Wordsworth, William, 180, 184, 186
World in Action, 20, 33, 41, 52, 76, 77, 118, 209
World League of American Football, 276

Index

Wotten, Charles, 97, 105
Wright, Ian, 3
Wright, Letitia, 2

X-Ray Spex, 4, 29

Yemen, 208
Yiadom-Boakye, Lynette, 142
Yom Kippur War (1973), 243
Yorkshire Ripper, 55, 223

Yoruba people, 97
Young British Artists, 140, 270
Young, Carl, 245
Younge, Gary, 240, 243, 244, 245
Yousaf, Humza, 253
Yuppies, 188, 274
Yusuf, Abdiriziak, 233, 235, 246

Zephaniah, Benjamin, 70, 72, 73, 75, 86, 132, 199

penguin.co.uk/vintage